The Bohemian South

EDITED BY
SHAWN CHANDLER BINGHAM
AND LINDSEY A. FREEMAN

The Bohemian South

Creating Countercultures,
from Poe to Punk

The University of North Carolina Press *Chapel Hill*

This book was published with the assistance of
the Fred W. Morrison Fund of the University of North Carolina Press.

The University of North Carolina Press has been a member of the
Green Press Initiative since 2003.

Library of Congress Cataloging-in-Publication Data
Names: Bingham, Shawn Chandler, 1976– editor. | Freeman, Lindsey A., editor.
Title: The bohemian South : creating countercultures, from Poe to punk / edited by Shawn
    Chandler Bingham and Lindsey A. Freeman.
Description: Chapel Hill : University of North Carolina Press, [2017] |
    Includes bibliographical references and index.
Identifiers: LCCN 2016046165| ISBN 9781469631660 (cloth : alk. paper) |
    ISBN 9781469631677 (pbk : alk. paper) | ISBN 9781469631684 (ebook)
Subjects: LCSH: Southern States—Civilization. | Bohemianism—Southern States. |
    Counterculture—Southern States.
Classification: LCC F209 .B64 2017 | DDC 975—dc23 LC record
    available at https://lccn.loc.gov/2016046165

Cover: Likeness of Black Mountain College's seal is used with the permission of the Black
Mountain College Museum and Arts Center.

To the jazz prince of Savannah, Dr. Boo Hornstein,
and to my bohemian queens, Angela, Eva Grace and Isla Maeve.
—Shawn

To the ghost of James Agee.
—Lindsey

Contents

Figures

Acknowledgments

Behind the success of many of the figures written about in this book—authors, musicians, and poets—were lesser-known agents, editors, and record producers. This project could not have come together without the patience, creative guidance, and humor of Joseph Parsons at the University of North Carolina Press. From our first pitch of this project in Denver (over mint juleps) to constructing a Spotify soundtrack for the book, Joe and the wonderful team at the Press embraced the challenge of working with a range of authors on an eclectic project.

We would also like to thank the reviewers for their insightful critique and support of this unique project. Finally, we thank the contributing authors, whose work does not map a new South but brings attention to a South that has long existed.

The Bohemian South

Bohemian Groves in Southern Soil

Shawn Chandler Bingham

Down there a poet is now almost as rare as an oboe-player, a dry-point etcher or a metaphysician . . . that stupendous region of worn-out farms, shoddy cities and paralyzed cerebrums . . . it is almost as sterile, artistically, intellectually, culturally, as the Sahara Desert.
—H. L. Mencken

Despite the more hackneyed perceptions of the South that pervade, the bohemian South is alive and well. Consider Savannah: Lurking amid the tourists wearing fanny packs and visors, piling off busses and into Paula Deen's restaurant and gift shop, and beyond the traditional architecture, is the city's creative underbelly. Savannah, once called "a pretty woman with a dirty face" by England's Lady Astor, has always had an artistic side. Today, wiry, aloof art students can be seen all over downtown carrying their oversize portfolios and tackle boxes filled with brushes, chalk, and pencils. Their sanctuary, the Savannah College of Art and Design, has helped create a revival in the historic area of the city, drawing the next generation of art students from every state in the Union and over twenty foreign countries.

North about five hours by car, Asheville, North Carolina, has drawn fresh attention as a Southern darling with a number of snappy monikers bandied about, especially in the travel sections of Northern newspapers: the Paris of the South, the San Francisco of the East, and the *New York Times*' bucolic-busting description as the "Appalachian Shangri La."[1] Meanwhile, *Rolling Stone* has christened the seat of Buncombe County "America's New Freak Capital." These nicknames are more than romantic forms of marketing to draw tourists from the North. The city has bona fides: it is home to a thriving arts scene, complete with a large fringe arts festival, a vibrant music community, and as much focus on food ethics as aesthetics. Asheville was the birthplace of bluegrass legend Bill Monroe, Moog synthesizers, and novelist Thomas Wolfe—a major literary influence on James Agee and Jack Kerouac, among countless others. And in the mid-twentieth century, the area was home to Black Mountain College, where R. Buckminster Fuller came up with his design for a geodesic dome, Merce

Cunningham began his dance company, and John Cage's first "happening" happened.

The resurgence of the American South in cities and small towns like Savannah and Asheville, as well as Athens, Louisville, Oxford, and many others, is a story that travel writers for national and international magazines and newspapers grind for print. And people are coming: Asheville, Austin, and other Southern cities are experiencing a housing crisis on par with other bohemian destinations like Portland, Oregon. Not only are Southern bohemias drawing creative people from both coasts and everywhere in between; cultural hubs around the rest of the country are looking to the south for cultural inspiration and authenticity. Pickling, banjo picking, bourbon sipping, and the sporting of gingham plaid covers Brooklyn, both Portlands, Chicago, San Francisco, and other destinations of cultural cool. The interest in these places goes beyond Southern aesthetics; it is one of studied appreciation. What is happening in American cities is not redneck chic or an attempt at irony in a trucker hat. Instead, mixologists are studying cocktails from famed Southern institutions and replicating them; chefs are composing simple and elegant dishes inspired from Southern cookbooks;[2] and musical historians are (re) introducing Southern music and musicians that might have fallen by the wayside to new generations of appreciators.

True enough, an outsider fixation now shines much brighter on Southernness, focusing on cities like Asheville, Austin, and Nashville, but a bohemian South has long existed in ways that contest views of a region lost in time, fossilized in traditionalism. The fruits of this creative South—its literature, music, art, and cuisine—have famously been celebrated, exported, and expropriated by the rest of the United States and lands beyond. Jazz and blues migrated quickly to large cities in both the United States and internationally, becoming quintessential American art forms; Southern literature made its way from bohemian haunts below the Mason-Dixon Line to New York and Los Angeles, landing on Broadway stages, movie screens, and eventually the reading lists of elite New England boarding schools and Ivy League universities; and restaurants serving Southern cuisines have become destination spots in cosmopolitan cities. Even the early king and queen of the bohemian movement in the United States—Edgar Allen Poe and Ada Clare—had roots in Southern soil.

Yet even as outsiders consumed the South's cultural handiwork, some have mocked the very region from which it emerged. The most haunting and notorious came from Baltimore satirist H. L. Mencken, whose 1917 essay "Sahara of the Bozart" in the New York *Evening Mail* hurled insult and injury on the South for its lack of "a single picture gallery worth going into, or a single opera-house, or a single theatre devoted to decent plays, or a single public monument worth looking at, or a single workshop devoted to the making of beautiful things."[3] To his credit, Mencken did give the South kudos for long ago besting a more dogmatic New England in its attention to the "art of living," its tolerance, and its willingness to "toy with ideas."[4] But after the Civil War, he argued, the South became a land that "gives one the creeps."[5] From the essay title—a mockery of the Southern pronunciation of Beaux Arts—to his reflection upon its impact years later, Mencken's satire skewered the South. In a reprinting of the essay, Mencken even credited himself, in part, for the reversal of "paralyzed cerebrums" that came with the Renaissance of Southern writers.[6]

Ironically, Mencken's ghost still haunts some of the very same publications responsible for attaching a tourist's gaze squarely on cities like Asheville, Austin, Chattanooga, and Savannah. In a recent article for the *New Yorker*, "Southern Discomfort," George Packer made the case that the "South is becoming isolated again." The Southern way of life, he argued, has been "embraced around the country" so much that "real America" is now represented by "country music and Lynyrd Skynyrd, barbecue, and NASCAR, political conservatism, God and guns, the code of masculinity, militarization, hostility to unions, and suspicion of government . . . a cultural draw for the rest of the country, with a hint of the theme park."[7] Author Gary Wills echoed these notions just a few weeks later in "Dumb America," a post on his *New York Review of Books* blog: "This is the thing that makes the South the distillation point for all the fugitive extremisms of our time, the heart of Say-No Republicanism, the home of lost causes and nostalgic lunacy. It is as if the whole continent were tipped upward, so that the scattered crazinesses might slide down to the bottom. The South has often been defeated. Now it is defeating itself."[8]

Sometimes it seems that Wills is half right. Between 2011 and 2012, states such as Georgia, South Carolina, and Texas made legislative moves that would reshape artistic structures in these states. Governor Nathan Deal of Georgia moved the Georgia Council of the Arts into the Department of Economic Development, while Governor Nikki Haley of South Carolina recommended eliminating funding for the South Carolina Arts Commission altogether. In Texas, the Senate, House, and governor approved a budget plan that reduced the Texas Commission of the Arts fund appropriations by more than 50 percent.

Meanwhile, many gatekeepers of the art world occupy themselves with making sure to keep the "good stuff" from sliding down south. Consider the recent uproar when Walmart heiress Alice Walton began buying up important pieces of art for the Crystal Bridges Museum in Bentonville, Arkansas; debates quickly ensued over whether or not the cream of the crop of American art belongs in rural Arkansas rather than a cosmopolitan city. Another debate has led to musical artists canceling tours through the state of North Carolina, whose governor, Pat McCrory, signed the nation's first "bathroom bill" in 2016, which prevents individuals from using state-managed restrooms that do not match the sex listed on their birth certificate. Mix in *Here Comes Honey Boo Boo* and *Duck Dynasty*, and a distinct, easily marketed, one-dimensional frame emerges. What's more, these contemporary slights on the South stand on a soapbox with much broader bandwidth than Mencken's journalistic stabs. But if you look beyond this crude frame you will find another South, a textured, creative, and contrarian South lurking beneath the tropes of tradition: rogue farming movements, trainhopping punks who play traditional mountain music, Athens' outburst onto the national art rock scene, Austin's struggle to stay weird, and William Shakespeare invading the land of Bear Bryant. Bother to poke at the easy, curbed assumptions about the American South and you stumble on these creative landscapes—both rural and urban—populated with folks engaged in practices that allow a bohemian South to thrive.

The authors in this collection travel the social landscapes and psychogeographies of the idiosyncratic, wonderful, and at times surreal South. Piling up the creative, quixotic, visionary and eclectic Souths, they offer novel understandings of how progressive forms of creativity bloom in a region that is, at best, known for its traditions, and at worst, suspected of racism, sexism, homophobia, and overall backwardness. The bohemian South is rich and varied, and for the sake of accuracy should be represented as such, especially considering the flat and cheap representations of the South that get doled out so easily and so often. The authors of *The Bohemian South* are part of a new generation of writers and scholars on the alert for new meanings in regional understanding and open to reshaping an identity—or, more accurately, multiple identities—that seeks to capture the folks who occupy the storied landscape of the American South.

Bohemia offers a novel lens for reconsidering the South as a staid, traditional, cultural backwater. There is no doubt that distilled images of bohemian life—urban, freethinking vagabond artists committed to novelty and change—starkly contrast with a rural, traditional, and provincial region so strongly tied to a sense of place, the cast iron South. But this contrast is what makes bohemianism in the region so intriguing. This blend not only challenges our contemporary understanding of the South; it gives us a look at bohemia's important cultural work, especially as it reacts to a larger regional culture. Indeed, bohemia not only exists in the South, but its cultural work is arguably greater here than other bohemian centers, in part because it is unexpected.

The Seeds of Bohemian Groves

Defining the term *bohemian* proves a tricky and elusive task, one that depends on historic and geographic context. Its origin in France was both a mistake and a slur used to describe the Romani, nomads whom the French called "les Bohémiens." (The French erroneously thought the Romani came from the Bohemia region of the Czech Republic.) Idealizing the independence of the Romani life, young counterculturists embraced the label.[9] The word later evolved to describe "penniless and carefree writers, poets, journalists, artists, actors, sculptors, and other members of that wide group" who would be regarded as the "intellectual proletariat."[10] Living on the margins, early bohemians valued creative expression and novelty; they experimented in all aspects of their lives, from their art to their dinner plates to their beds. City life allowed them eclectic experiences and access to diverse people and art. Living for the moment often meant geographic mobility and wandering in search of the unfamiliar.

While some bohemians were apolitical, others were central figures in the modernist reactions to broader social and cultural changes. For all their vagabonding, these young bohemian circles were disciples of dissent, loudly proclaiming what bohemia was *not*: the cold materialism and industrial strut of cultural rivals the bourgeoisie. And, for a short time during the French Revolution of 1848, it seemed that their vision of a new society might be realized: the working class rebelled against the aristocracy, women's rights were finally being debated, and a romantic poet (Alphonse de Lamartine) headed the liberal opposition's interim government. But when the dust settled after the revolution, a middle class of social climbers made a power grab. With the French monarchy out of the way, financial aristocrats began a new grand design under the aptly named Party of Order. By mid-1848, military forces squashed the working-class uprising, and in December Napoleon III won a four-way election. A Napoleon had returned to power in France, and in response Karl Marx famously wrote that such an occurrence came "the first time as tragedy, the second time as farce."[11]

Under the farcical regime, staring down a new social order ruled by bourgeoisie conformity and the routinized work of modernity, many found an alternative lifestyle in bohemia. Creative enclaves were not only filled with those from the revolutionary classes; many of the children of bourgeoisie families also awakened to the dull, philistine, and materialist life ahead of them and turned bohemian. Others were victims of the industrialization reshaping French society, as modern factories pushed crafts and petty trades to the margins. Many well-educated sons of craftsmen found little opportunity,[12] especially since the upper class often restricted job opportunities to its own circles.[13] Instead, they escaped bourgeoisie stuffiness and careerism in the Latin Quarter on the Left Bank of the Seine River. There, in the low light of the cafés, they mocked the bourgeoisie with their ideas and exploits.

As modernism took hold in Europe, bohemian circles crept into the cheap tenements of other European cities, too; strongholds developed in the Chelsea and Soho districts of London as well as in Berlin, Budapest, and Munich. These alternative lifestyle pockets ignited a creative explosion that led to shifts in modern literature and art. In the early twentieth century, for example, Paris's Left Bank served as a home base to Ernest Hemingway, Henri Matisse, Pablo Picasso, Arthur Rimbaud, and Gertrude Stein, while Francis Bacon and Dylan Thomas made a playground of London's Soho. And from novel to opera to magazine, other writers glorified and celebrated the bohemian lifestyle, sometimes captivating a bourgeoisie audience with its spectacle. Henri Murger's *Scenes of Bohemian Life* (1851), a semiautobiographical account, went from a literary magazine to the stage of Théâtre des Variétés to eventually end up a novel. William Thackeray's novel *Vanity Fair* (1848), a parody of Victorian conservatism and consumerism, popularized *bohemian* as a label for the lifestyle. George du Maurier's story of 1850s bohemian Paris, *Trilby* (1894), sold over 200,000 copies in its first year of publication in America and later became a popular play. Puccini's *La Boheme* (1896), based on Henri Murger's novel, remains one of the most widely performed operas worldwide. But the bohemian-bourgeoisie dichotomy is not so clean. As mockery of early bohemians gave way to fascination (and even envy), for example, the masses lapped up the exploits of bohemian life. The *Trilby* "craze" even led to the hawking of *Trilby*-inspired products, including ice cream, sausage, and even a Disneyesque town, Trilby, Florida, developed by railroad baron Henry B. Plant.[14] While many from the upper classes lived the lifestyle vicariously through books and plays, scores of American artists and writers traveled to Europe and tasted bohemianism firsthand.

A New York bohemian scene soon emerged in the mid-1800s, and its hub was Pfaff's beer cellar, a German bar in Greenwich Village. Led by writers Henry Clapp and transplant Southerner Ada Clare, the Pfaff's scene included Walt Whitman and a range of other artists seeking to replicate Paris's

Trilby

Latin Quarter.[15] Clapp, who is credited with importing bohemia after his own jaunt in Paris, held the nickname King of Bohemia; he founded the *Saturday Press*, a bohemian weekly featuring poetry and politics, helped to publicize Whitman, and was the first to publish Mark Twain in the eastern United States. The *Saturday Press* and the circle Clapp created helped to attract other artists to the city.[16] What began at Pfaff's was inherited by folks such as dancer Isadora Duncan, political activist Emma Goldman, and writers such as Eugene O'Neal and even William Faulkner, who all helped to turn Greenwich Village into an important artistic epicenter of literary, musical, political, and theatrical movements. (Faulkner's main bohemian nest remained New Orleans, however.)

Meanwhile, nearly three thousand miles away, bohemian San Francisco emerged on the heels of the gold rush. The city's population had doubled during the 1850s to just less than 56,000. Among these were opportunists, schemers, and other artful dodgers who looked to capitalize, and whose get-rich-quick stories of greed, corruption, and exploitation caught the eyes of the West Coast bohemian contingent led by columnist Bret Harte. A Brooklyn transplant, Harte wrote critically about bourgeoisie culture under the pen name The Bohemian, with a particular eye toward racism, the cruelty of the gold rush, and the influence of "civilization" on the American West. San Francisco served as a western hub for American bohemia, but the city also became home to the more bourgeoisie-infested Bohemian Club, which bypassed anticapitalism as a mere suggestion by waving entrepreneurs and financiers who supported the arts into the grove.

Chicago's bohemian scene arrived as early as 1866, but its real growth happened just in time for the World's Columbian Exposition of 1893. The 1890s brought a Bohemian Club, publications, and a breeding ground in the exposition's Fine Arts Building, which was designed to house writers, artists, and even political groups. Artists and intellectuals squatted in many of the empty buildings and stores left behind in the wake of the exposition, hatching a creative colony in the process. Certainly cities served as muse and holding space to some of the most well-known bohemian artists and writers. Whitman and the Beat poets eulogized New York City, and Hemingway and Stein captured the zeitgeist of the Parisian expat bohemian lifestyle of the 1920s and 1930s in *A Moveable Feast* and *The Autobiography of Alice B. Toklas*, respectively. Faulkner wrote his famous friends and literary cohort into his novels, along with yarns about rum-running and carousing that were soaked in the magic of New Orleans. City life offered a literal collage of faces, stories, and experiences that allowed for a life at the fringes in the center of it all. Scenes in other large cities would follow, often shaped as much by economics and politics as itinerant wandering. Bohemia, though, did not just wander west and north.

Bohemians in and of the South

Even before the Civil War, protobohemians Edgar Allen Poe and Ada Clare had already left the South for parts north. Their influence on the Northern scene had clear links to their Southern identities and their desire to escape the constrictive bourgeois values of their Dixie pasts. If bohemia offered a refuge from a struggle to belong in a world of traditional social hierarchies, Poe and Clare charted the course for the future wanderlust of American bohemians. Poe's bohemianism was a clear reaction to the South he knew, as the original historian of the American bohemian scene, Albert Parry, describes:

> When the Allans adopted him, the memory of his outcast ancestry was not allowed to fade but was persistently brought back, ostensibly to remind him of his everlasting debt of gratitude to his adopters but really to drive home the fact that he was among ladies and gentlemen on sufferance only, that he did not belong among them and never could. . . .
>
> The desire to escape from the painful reality of an uncertain social position has been, in all lands and times, one of the chief distinguishing reasons for Bohemianism. Poe was the first American refugee of this sort. He began to dream of fame easily in his life, because as a returning hero with laurels on his brow he could build a base for the doubtful respect shown to him by southern society, and so strengthen it beyond any taint of his real origin and any taunt of his enemy.[17]

But Poe's bohemianism is much more complicated than simply a reaction against the South. He has been credited as a forefather of Southern gothic literature and the Southern Renaissance. He wrote for and edited the *Southern Literary Messenger*. And as Edward Whitley explores in this volume, Poe's style of writing influenced the New York bohemian literature scene.

Rebelling from another corner of the Southern caste system, Ada Clare ditched her aristocratic roots in Charleston for Paris and later New York, where she became a central fixture of the scene at Pfaff's bar in Greenwich Village. As Whitley reveals, the tapestry of American bohemianism is woven through with many threads emerging and finishing in the South. A great number of bohemians of antebellum New York interpreted their own bohe-

mian identities through the examples of Poe's Southern-outsider pose and/
or Clare's distinctive Southern charm peppered with radical feminism and
artistic knowledge. Whitley describes Clare's disposition as a unique amalgamation of Southern hostess and bohemian queen, whose freedom to travel
and experiment was funded by plantation spoils. Poe had a slinky, dark, smart
sexiness that excited and inspired his peers. Both of these models of bohemianism held grand appeal for the emergent scene. And yet, the South would
help mold this Northern scene again. The Civil War effectively drained the
life from the scene at Pfaff's; William Swinton, Walt Whitman, and a "bohemian brigade" of other journalists and artists such as cartoonist Thomas
Nast, illustrator Alfred Waud, and even painter Winslow Homer, would all
"take the field" in the war to be part of "the greatest undertaking in the history
of journalism."[18]

While Northern bohemians made a patron saint of Poe, who sought refuge from the cotillion laughter of Southern high society, an early Southern
bohemia evolved in reaction to the blue-blooded, snobbish North.[19] Seen
collectively as a "booshie bah-hee-moth," Northern states boasted most of the
country's arts schools, publishing houses, orchestras, and museums. Crafting
their own flavor of bohemia gave Southerners a way to rebel against Northern
stuffiness and cultural snobbery—but not, of course, without creating their
own snobberies.[20] In this spirit, the South laid claim to the first American
publication titled *Bohemian*, a journal printed in Richmond in 1863. Additional publications would appear alongside other Southern bohemian circles,
where the early varieties suffered the same perverted bohemianism that had
crept into San Francisco's Bohemian Grove—the bourgeoisie did not just
sneak into the party, it owned it.

In Fort Worth, Texas, Henrie Clay Ligon Gorman, a society columnist for
the *Gazette* and relative of Kentucky senator Henry Clay, published the *Bohemian* magazine and founded a corresponding group, Our Literary Club in
Bohemia. The magazine had its own reading room and boasted a list of members firmly rooted in mainstream or even traditional culture and politics: the
mayor of the town, plus a collection of judges and pastors and, to top it all off,
the Women's Christian Temperance Union. Despite the *Bohemian*'s artistic
coverage, and its success, its mild-mannered and tempered bohemianism
"craftily managed to avoid any mention of their [bohemian artists] sins and
libation in the Paris attics."[21] The magazine featured photographs of the homes
of wealthy Texans and was even endorsed by the Fort Worth Board of Trade.
Parry concluded that Main Street made a go at bohemianism, and "had a
good time of it, within bounds strictly moral and bone-dry."[22]

The first major legitimate bohemian center to flourish in the South was New Orleans. As an international port city, a literal and metaphorical confluence of backgrounds, persons, and ideas formed in Louisiana's most famous town. New Orleans was a real bohemian hotbed, especially following the First World War. Although the success of the scene brought its own segment of pretenders and hangers-on, as might be expected, there was nonetheless a lively core of bohemians to be found. The literary scene was especially busy: the novelists Sherwood Anderson and William Faulkner, along with many other aspiring writers, could often be found at the Pelican Bookshop on Royal Street.[23] The musical scene was also famous, with jazz flowing as freely—even during Prohibition—as the abundant liquor bohemians drank to excess. In this volume, Joanna Levin covers New Orleans's first major bohemian publication, the *Double Dealer*.[24]

Later, more authentic bohemian scenes would develop elsewhere—in Houston and Austin, where Will Porter, also known as O. Henry, was attracted to the "boisterous awakening," emerging slums, and the industrial cities.[25] It was in Austin that O. Henry wrote "Chanson de Boheme," his nod to Texas in the 1890s, and it was the author's experience there that led his biographers to argue that, in all its wandering, the bohemian lifestyle knew no bounds: "Bohemia flowers in strange places. . . . It does not need a great city or a colorful setting . . . or climbing, winding streets of old Montmartre . . . or London's Bloomsbury or Chelsea; or the Washington Square neighborhood of yesterday; or the Greenwich Village of the present. Red Gap [Washington] had a Bohemia of its own; so, in the late 1890s, did Austin and Houston."[26]

Over a hundred years ago, Memphis began drawing blues musicians from all over Mississippi. John Lee Hooker, Howlin' Wolf, and Muddy Waters were just a few of the musicians who eventually found Beale Street to host a hospitable mix of venues. Like New Orleans's Storeyville, when Beale Street was shut down to move prostitution, illegal drug trades, and gambling out, musicians left for cities like Chicago and Detroit. But, as Zandria Robinson illustrates in this volume, bohemianism still lives in Memphis a century later. A number of smaller bohemian groups emerged in other places, too, including Black Mountain College (1933–57) started by faculty members from Rollins College (see Jon Horne Carter's chapter in this volume). Black Mountain went on to collect a concentration of John Dewey disciples and an impressive array of cutting-edge artists, including Ruth Asawa, John Cage, Robert Creeley, Merce Cunningham, Willem and Elaine de Kooning, and Walter Gropius, all in the midst of rural North Carolina. Bohemian circles like these shielded "radical ideas from interference,"[27] especially in the arts; they pioneered Southern spaces of acceptance and creativity, forming environments where artists and scholars could hatch ideas, learn from one another, and organize their activities. Today throngs of Southerners attached to their unique communities romance the counterculture campaign—via bumper stickers and billboards—to KEEP AUSTIN WEIRD or KEEP ASHEVILLE WEIRD. And it was bohemia that helped make the cities that way.

Nashville, a country music mecca that proudly flaunts its nickname, Music City, USA, also has bohemian ties. Michael Streissguth, author of *Outlaw County: Waylon, Willie, Kris, and the Renegades of Nashville*, has rightly pointed out that despite the city's stereotypes, "There was very much a Greenwich Village-like scene in the West End."[28] Nashville, of course, is where Bob Dylan recorded *Blonde on Blonde*, and as Streissguth argues, Dylan changed Nashville. But, before that, Nashville was already influencing Dylan, when he was Bobby Zimmerman in Hibbing, Minnesota, listening to the Grand Ole Opry live on the radio.[29] From Kitty Wells's reminder that "It Wasn't God Who Made Honky Tonk Angels" to the visual artist Red Grooms to Young Buck's "Straight Outta Cashville" to Jack White's headquartering of Third Man Records, Nashville has a long history of providing a space for creative life.

These scenes are no panacea, though. Southern bohemians long grappled with harsh traditionalism, poverty, and racism, particularly as they intersected with industrial shifts during the twentieth century. Intense oppression, along with significant economic changes in the labor market, lead Southern bohemians like Zora Neale Hurston, James Weldon Johnson, and Richard Wright, among others, to leave the South during the Great Migration. Just as their predecessors overseas had done more than a century before them, they left in search of new forms and places where they could find their own identity and means to access their self-expression. Wright's experimental style of writing drew on urban life, Marxism, and even surrealism, while his geographic path took him from Mississippi to Tennessee, then Chicago, New York City, and eventually, Paris. Zora Neal Hurston, another leading figure of the Harlem Renaissance, left Florida and would become both an anthropological researcher and an influential novelist; like Wright, she drew heavily on black vernacular language and wrote about groups at the margins of social life. With other Southerners, Hurston had a profound influence on the Harlem Renaissance. She helped found *Fire!!* along with Langston Hughes and other writers; the magazine with the double exclamation points had the goal "to burn up a lot of the old, dead conventional Negro-white ideas of the past," according to Hughes.[30] Ironically, the magazine's headquarters burned down after only one issue, and it was never published again. Still, it would take much more than a fire or the collapse of one literary magazine to end Hurston's effect on both the Northern and Southern bohemian scenes.

As part of their bohemian inquiry, these Southerners took on such issues as alienation and racism, and what came out were important forms of self-expression that brought a Southern influence to much broader artistic movements. Included among these are jazz, the quintessential example of modernist philosophies set to music, and the blues, a form born of alienation, racial inequality, loss, and even anomie. These musical forms were brought to larger urban cities like Chicago and New York via Memphis, New Orleans, and rural towns across Mississippi and the South. Through the diaspora of people seeking civil rights and the means of making a living, these musical genres—in both form and content—brought a uniquely Southern experience and experimentation to bear on the larger artistic and political scenes in America and the world.

One of the South's most beloved modernist writers, and the writer that many critics credit with reinventing the American novel, cut his teeth in the bohemian scene in New Orleans: William Faulkner. The Shakespeare of the South traveled to Europe after New Orleans, but then returned home to settle in Oxford, Mississippi. While other bohemians wrote about urban life, Faulkner derived a clear sense of place through his fictitious Yoknapatawpha County, a rural node in Mississippi of 25,611—of which 6,298 were white and 19,313 African American. Faulkner drew significantly on aspects of the Old South. He utilized traditions of storytelling and vernacular language, and he mobilized these cultural forms in his inquiries into the ways the past guides the present. Throughout Faulkner's work the South does not appear simply as a location where the action takes place; it becomes both a character itself and a medium through which to address history, memory, and social and psychological themes. Faulkner used modernism to explore the South, but he also brought a unique Southern influence to modernist writing beyond the United States, and for his efforts he won the Nobel Prize in Literature in 1950.

Mapping the Bohemian South

From Chapel Hill to Savannah to Fort Worth to New Orleans to Black Mountain, bohemia has served a variety of roles in the South: mixing the modern with the traditional and the local with the far-reaching, rebelling against Northern snobbery, complicating the overly simplistic notions of race and gender, and setting itself apart from other avant-gardes. As the bohemian

South has evolved, its most important work has been to nurture experimentation and free thought amid a more traditional social context while incorporating Southern places in its own unique ways. Exploring and celebrating these circles and scenes gives us a more complex and nuanced portrait of the South, expanding the concept of bohemia and the cultural work it does in the process. What better way to understand a region stereotyped for its provincialism, staunch connection to place, and parodied worship of rural life than by examining its avant-garde artists, writers, thinkers, and cultural producers who take creative approaches to food, culture, art, and living? The convenience of categories that cleave—*traditional* or *modern, city* or *country, bohemian* or *bourgeoisie, nomadic* or *rooted*—might make it easy for the mind, but the real world makes a mess of those filing systems. And there is no more fitting place to clutter these tidy classifications than the American South.

This collection does its own wandering, unraveling tropes by trolling through a range of topics and questions: How has the South uniquely influenced broader bohemianism in America? How has bohemia melded with a unique Southern identity? To use Whitman's poetic description, what sorts of bohemian "vaults" exist down south, and how have these nurtured and sustained bohemian scenes? What cultural work does bohemia do in the South, and how has the South profited from bohemian "cultural creatives"? Throwing light on a sampling of Southern bohemian communities we hope to draw a clearer map of the bohemian South. We begin with a couple of historical chapters in which Edward Whitley and Joanna Levin trace the Southern origins of America's bohemia, from Edgar Allen Poe to William Faulkner and his scene around New Orleans's Royal Street. Jon Horne Carter explores Black Mountain College, itself an experimental college of exiles—cultural, political, and social—who created a utopian Appalachian avant-garde art community that emerged in Asheville, North Carolina in 1933.

Of course, Southern literature is much more than Faulkner. We can see this in Lindsey Freeman's chapter on the Southern superreal and Knoxville-born James Agee, bohemian writer, cocklebur to the profession of journalism, cultural critic, and Southern dandy in reverse. Daniel Cross Turner also illustrates the wide and ever-widening world of Southern letters in his exploration of how contemporary Southern poetry and poets—including Kwame Dawes, Yusef Komunyakaa, Brenda Marie Osbey, and Derek Walcott—can move us from weary conceptions of Southernness into a new ethos that encompasses a more bohemian and complicated South that shares culture and ideas along and across the Gulf and Atlantic coastlines. Bringing us into what she terms "intersextionalities," Jaime Cantrell's chapter on lesbian poets and writers examines place, palate, and pleasure, demonstrating that second-wave feminism and modern lesbian politics have extensive Southern literary roots.

Chris Offutt plays with tensions and themes around trying to navigate the cool, cultured bohemian circles that sometimes touch the worlds of writing and academia along with the contemplation of "trash food" and second-hand shopping. Allen Shelton, writing in his own superreal style, ponders the unmistakable draw of the South for the bohemian prodigal son, who may move away in body but not in spirit. His Alabama is a dreamworld seen through time and memory from the once dreamy city of Buffalo, New York; it is a sociology of exile. Both of these essays depict the liminal space of a bohemian South, with all of its struggles, pull, ironies and negotiations.

Zachary Vernon digs into depictions of a rough and ragged South, a turn he notices in the emergent genre of "post-South" film. Vernon gives specific attention to appropriation and glorification of the down and out, a classic bohemian tenet that can be found in films such as *Beasts of the Southern Wild*.

Like film and literature, the diversity of Southern music goes way beyond the simplistic shiny, sugary country pop music that can dominate corporate radio stations. Central sounds of American twentieth- and twenty-first-century bohemianism, such as jazz, blues, bluegrass, rock 'n' roll, important scenes of indie rock, and many styles of hip-hop can trace their roots to a Southern heritage. Scott Barretta takes us into folk scenes of the Deep South in Atlanta, Houston, Memphis, and New Orleans with an eye toward the blues and racially integrated bohemian music scenes that defied the segregation of public spaces.

Moving east, Grace Elizabeth Hale examines the sonic landscape of Athens, Georgia, which was an epicenter for cutting-edge music from the late 1970s to the early 1990s, leading the way for the college rock and independent music scenes. Heading north to rural North Carolina and Virginia, Daniel Margolies takes on the resurgence of old-time music and its recent mixing with do-it-yourself punk lifestyles. Margolies explores trainhoppers, many of whom have relocated to the rural South in a quest for simpler living, both to mingle with existing communities and to create new spaces of radical politics, off-the-grid lifestyles, and bohemian experiences.

In her chapter, Zandria Robinson explores cultural and intellectual scenes in postsoul Memphis, showing how historical and contemporary patterns of cultural consumption and racial segregation have influenced the emergence and maintenance of black bohemian cultures.

Some bohemians have hidden their aristocratic ties and traded on the bourgeoisie as a foil; yet the pragmatics of paying the bills have come back to haunt many a bohemian. In the later chapters of the book, we explore the of-ten shared space of creative enclaves and creative economies. While these are not all the same, "creative class" economic development has more recently attempted to capitalize and profit from bohemian ingenuity and novelty, even bohemian lifestyle products.[31] These chapters follow in the footsteps of Richard Lloyd's examination of neobohemia, beginning with Alex Sayf Cumming's take on how developers in North Carolina's Research Triangle leveraged a kind of "bourgeois bohemianism" to attract a creative class to the area. This same type of bourgeois bohemian marketing has found its way into new kinds of Southern magazines. In a chapter that helped birth the idea for this collection, Shawn Bingham traverses the magazine merge lane, where an edgy bohemian aesthetic meets bourgeoisie advertising and lifestyle. And Joshua Long rounds out the collection with his examination of gentrification, the marketing of bohemianism, and the possibility of bohemianism's endur-ance in Austin.

We offer one conceptual caveat: in this collection we take an expansive view of the South, a view we know not all readers will share. We see the South stretching from Kentucky and West Virginia to the southern tip of Florida, and from Texas to the coasts of the Carolinas and Virginia. We see the Amer-ican South as a place of varied cultures, climates, and accents. The Mississippi Delta, the Smokey Mountains, and the low country of Georgia and South Carolina are all part of the South, but there is more: New Orleans, the Okefe-nokee Swamp, the Piedmont, the Blue Ridge Mountains—on and on it goes. The South can be hard to contain; its reach extends to these boundaries and beyond, showing up in other places. And outside influences, in turn, affect the South. Still, there is a set of cultural understandings that operate that help to define place, even though these, too, can become fuzzy at the borders. We chose to sit with the complexity, and to allow the chapters in this volume to help shape some versions of the South while not coming even close to claim-ing to contain it all.

The South has had its own ways of being bohemian—distinct from North-ern and Western scenes, even as scenes copy and borrow from each other—and this has become a tradition as well. Indeed, despite bohemia's addiction to movement, novelty, and change, certain ideals have endured, becoming tradition: the desire to live a life full of art and beauty, antibourgeois aesthet-ics and politics, sexual freedom, and gender, ethnic, and racial equality among them. Despite radical change to the region over the last thirty years, the South still holds on to its uniqueness as a contrary and paradoxical region full of conservatism, yes, but also full of avant-garde bohemianism. In 1983, W. L.

Taitte published a chapter on the state of the arts in the South in *Dixie Date-line* and made this argument:

> If the south continues to become more populous, more urban, and more like the rest of the country, arts institutions in the South will continue to become more prominent and less southern. Already most of the attempts to project a regional flavor in the arts result in either self-conscious kitsch (ceramic armadillos and cowboy boots) or in unconscious kitsch (the outdoor dramas of Paul Green that have proliferated in summertime evenings throughout the south). And the biggest cities will have the most visible and most internationalized arts institutions. . . .
>
> One may find it sad that homogenization between places and cultures seems to go along with modern improvements in the arts, as with so many other modern improvements, But when the Sahara sprouts oases and eventually turns into an Eden, perhaps we should not complain that one Edenic outpost looks pretty much the same as all of the others.[32]

With the present volume we challenge this notion. Edenic outposts in the South do not look "pretty much the same" as all of the others. Lurking in "outposts" like Asheville, Athens, Austin, Chapel Hill, Memphis, and New Orleans are the trainhoppers, the "Dirty South bohemians," the avant-garde poets, the banjo bohemians, the bluesmen and blueswomen, the radical dancers, the indie rockers, the jazz musicians, the genre-busting writers, those who inspire Southern sociologists in exile, and hordes of others who are complicating traditional notions of the South and Southernness. And it is that cultural work we unveil here.

Notes

1. Lyttle, "In Vanderbilt's Backyard"; Dixon, "36 Hours in Asheville."
2. See Fabricant, "Pile High the Chicken and Biscuits Florence Fabricant"; and Mischner, "The Southern Invasion of NYC."
3. Mencken, "The Sahara of the Bozart," 159.
4. Ibid., 158.
5. Ibid.
6. Mencken later added this paragraph for a reprint of the essay: "This essay produced a ferocious reaction in the South. The essay in its final form, as it is here reproduced, dates sadly, but I have let it stand as a sort of historical document. On the heels of the violent denunciations of the elder Southerners there soon came a favorable response from the more civilized youngsters, and there is reason to believe that my attack had something to do with that revival of Southern letters which followed in the middle 1920's." Mencken, "The Sahara of the Bozart," 157.

7. Packer, "Southern Discomfort."

8. Wills, "Dumb America."

9. Turman, "Bohemian Artists and 'Real Bohemians,'" 94.

10. Parry, *Garrets and Pretenders*, xxi.

11. Marx, *The Eighteenth Brumaire of Louis Bonaparte*, 15.

12. Parry, *Garrets and Pretenders*, xxii.

13. See Smith, "New York Bohemianism."

14. Levin, *Bohemia in America: 1858–1920*, 194–95.

15. Parry, *Garrets and Pretenders*, xxv.

16. Smith, "New York Bohemianism," 214.

17. Parry, *Garrets and Pretenders*, 5.

18. Starr, *Bohemian Brigade*, 9.

19. Joanna Levin has argued this previously in *Bohemians in America*, 257–75, and expands on these ideas in her chapter in the present volume.

20. Levin, *Bohemia in America*, 257.

21. Parry, *Garrets and Pretenders*, 172.

22. Ibid., 173.

23. See Reed, *Dixie Bohemia*; and Peters, "The Beat Generation."

24. On New Orleans' early bohemian scene, see Reed, *Dixie Bohemia*.

25. Parry, *Garrets and Pretenders*, 167.

26. Bob Davis and Arthur B. Maurice, quoted in Parry, *Garrets and Pretenders*, 169.

27. Grana and Grana, "Preface," xvii.

28. Michael Streissguth, quoted in Gross, "The Outlaws of Country."

29. Along with the Grand Ole Opry, Dylan even mentioned William Faulkner as an influence in his memoir *Chronicles*, 1:37.

30. Samuels, "From the Wild, Wild West to Harlem's Literary Salons," 14.

31. See Florida, *The Rise of the Creative Class*.

32. Taitte, "Springtime in the Desert," 95.

References

Brooks, David. *Bobos in Paradise: The New Upper Class and How They Got There*. New York: Simon and Schuster, 2000.

Dixon, Chris. "36 Hours in Asheville, NC," *New York Times*, September 30, 2007.

Du Maurier, George. *Trilby*. Boston: Digireads, 2011. Originally published 1894.

Dylan, Bob. *Chronicles*. Vol. 1. New York: Simon and Schuster, 2004.

Fabricant, Florence. "Pile High the Chicken and Biscuits." *New York Times*, September 9, 2015. http://www.nytimes.com/2015/09/09/dining/Southern-restaurant-openings-nyc.html?_r=0.

Florida, Richard. *The Rise of the Creative Class: And How It's Transforming Work, Leisure, Community and Everyday Life*. New York: Basic Books, 2002.

Grana, Cesar, and Marigay Grana. "Preface." In *On Bohemia: The Code of the Exiled*, edited by Cesar Grana and Marigay Grana, xv–xviii. New Brunswick, NJ: Transaction, 1990.

Gross, Joseph. "The Outlaws of Country," *Austin Statesman*, June 3, 2013.

Hemingway, Ernest. *A Moveable Feast*. New York: Scribner's, 1964.

Larson, Jonathan. *Rent*. New York: HarperCollins, 1997.

Levin, Joanna. *Bohemia in America: 1858–1920*. Stanford, CA: Stanford University Press, 2009.

Lloyd, Richard. *Neo-Bohemia: Art and Commerce in the Postindustrial City*. New York: Routledge, 2006.

Lyttle, Bethany. "In Vanderbilt's Backyard," *New York Times*, May 7, 2009.

Marx, Karl. *The Eighteenth Brumaire of Louis Bonaparte*. Translated. New York: International, 1994. Originally published 1854.

Mencken, H. L. "The Sahara of the Bozart." In Mencken, *The American Scene: A Reader*, edited by Huntington Cairns, 157–68. New York: Knopf, 1977.

Mischner, Jessica. "The Southern Invasion of NYC." *Garden and Gun*, April–May 2010. http://gardenandgun.com/article/Southern-invasion-nyc.

Murger, Henri. *Scenes of Bohemian Life*. Translated. Whitefish, MT: Kessinger, 2009. Originally published as *Scènes de la vie de Bohème*, 1851.

Packer, George. "Southern Discomfort." *New Yorker*, January 1, 2013, http://www.newyorker.com/magazine/2013/01/21/Southern-discomfort-4.

Parry, Albert. *Garrets and Pretenders: A History of Bohemianism*. Mineola, NY: Dover, 1960.

Peters, Nancy. "The Beat Generation and San Francisco's Culture of Dissent." In *Reclaiming San Francisco: History, Politics, Culture*, edited by James Brooks, Chris Carlsson, and Nancy Peters, 199–215. San Francisco: City Lights, 1998.

Puccini, Giacomo. *Puccini's La Bohème*. Coral Gables, FL: Opera Journeys, 2001. Originally published 1896.

Reed, John Shelton. *Dixie Bohemia: A French Quarter Circle in the 1920s*. Baton Rouge: Louisiana State University Press, 2012.

Samuels, Wilfred. "From the Wild, Wild West to Harlem's Literary Salons." *Black Issues Book Review* 2 (2000): 14.

Smith, Marc. "New York Bohemianism in the Second Half of the Nineteenth Century," *ARS: Journal of the Institute of Art History of the Slovak Academy* 45 (2012): 212–22.

Starr, Louis Morris. *Bohemian Brigade: Civil War Newsmen in Action*. New York: Knopf, 1954.

Stein, Gertrude. *The Autobiography of Alice B. Toklas*. New York: Modern Library, 1990. [1933].

Streissguth, Michael. *Outlaw Country: Waylon, Willie, Kris, and the Renegades of Nashville*. New York: It Books, 2014.

Taitte, William. "Springtime in the Desert: The Fine Arts and Their Patronage in the Modern South." In *Dixie Dateline: A Journalistic Portrait of the American South*, edited by John Bolles, 81–96. Houston: Rice University Studies, 1983.

Thackeray, William. *Vanity Fair*. New York: Penguin, 2003. Originally published 1848.

Turman, Karen. "Bohemian Artists and 'Real Bohemians': Life as Spectacle in Hugo's *Notre-Dame de Paris* and Gautier's *Les Jeunes-France*." *ARS: Journal of the Institute of Art History of the Slovak Academy* 45 (2012): 94–107.

Twain, Mark. *Roughing It*. New York: Signet, 2008. Originally published 1872.

Whitman, Walt. "Two Vaults." Unpublished poem. https://pfaffs.web.lehigh.edu /node/55710.

Wills, Garry. "Dumb America." *NYR Daily* (*New York Review of Books* blog), January 21, 2013. http://www.nybooks. com/blogs/nyrblog/2013/jan/21/dumb-america/.

Wilson, Elizabeth. *Bohemians, the Glamorous Outcasts*. New Brunswick, NJ: Rutgers University Press, 2002.

Zeitlin, Benh, dir. *Beasts of the Southern Wild*. New Orleans: Court 13 Films, 2012. DVD.

The Southern Origins of Bohemian New York
Edward Howland, Ada Clare, and Edgar Allan Poe

Edward Whitley

One of the most often recounted stories about the bohemians of antebellum New York City took place in the fall of 1861 at Charles Pfaff's Manhattan beer cellar. The story goes that Pfaff's regular, Walt Whitman, read aloud his pro-Union poem "Beat! Beat! Drums!" only to have fellow bohemian George Arnold raise his glass of wine to toast to the success of "the Southern rebellion." According to one account, "Walt warned George to be more guarded in his sentiments. George fired up more and more. Walt passed his 'mawler' toward George's ear. George passed a bottle of claret toward the topknot of the poet's head." Tensions escalated. Restaurant owner Pfaff, a German immigrant often mocked for his thick accent, "made a jump and gave a yell of 'Oh! mine gots, mens, what's you do for dis?'" while the "King of Bohemia," Henry Clapp Jr., "broke his black pipe while pulling at Arnold's coat-tail." Ned Wilkins, another of Whitman's friends, "lost the power of his lungs for five minutes after tugging at the brawny arm of Walt; and we all received a beautiful mixture of rum, claret, and coffee on the knees of our trousers."[1]

Biographers and critics have been drawn to this story (which Whitman claimed was the "silliest compound of nonsense, lies & rot"[2]) for obvious reasons: it provides a rare glimpse into Whitman's passionate, even visceral, commitment to defending the Union cause; it illustrates the anything-goes atmosphere of the bohemian beer cellar; and it demonstrates how the violence that plagued the United States in the first half of the 1860s had spread beyond the battlefields of the Civil War and penetrated into even the most remote and seemingly apolitical corners of the nation. The story also gives lie to the myth that New York's first bohemians were displaced Parisians living in a section of the Latin Quarter magically transplanted to the United States—a myth that, until relatively recently, literary historians have been content to rehearse. David Reynolds's assessment from the mid-1990s that the antebellum bohemians were "[u]nable to cope with the national crisis . . . [and] playing a desperate game of evasion"[3] has since been revised by Mark Lause's argument that radical political movements on the eve of the Civil War were

"inexorably intertwined with the personnel, practice, and persuasion of bohemian life."[4] Robert Scholnick and Amanda Gailey have also shown how the
periodicals that served as the voice of bohemian New York—*Vanity Fair* and
the *Saturday Press*—were bound up in the conflict between the North and the
South in ways that make a Southern presence integral to the history of the
United States' first bohemians.[5]

That Southern presence manifests itself in three of the key figures associated with the origins of bohemian New York: Edward Howland, Ada Clare,
and Edgar Allan Poe. Poe may have died almost a decade before the birth of
the New York bohemian scene, but his willingness to sacrifice wealth, status,
and personal well-being in the pursuit of art provided the habitués of Pfaff's
with the raw materials for what would become a homegrown legend of American bohemianism. In addition to Poe's reputation as a Southern writer
(Whitman described him as "Southern from top to toe"[6]), American bohemianism has roots in Charleston, South Carolina, the hometown of both Ada
Clare and Edward Howland. The cotton plantations of Charleston provided
Howland and Clare with the money to fund the institutions French sociologist Pierre Bourdieu claims are essential for bohemianism to flourish: the periodical and the salon.[7] Clare used her sizable inheritance to re-create the
bohemian salons she had witnessed firsthand in Paris, and Howland gave a
portion of his own fortune to fund the *Saturday Press*, the literary weekly that
served as the bohemians' house organ during the late 1850s and early 1860s.
For both Charlestonians the source of their money was the same: cotton harvested by African American slaves.

These Southerners help to complicate the received notion that American
bohemianism was, in William Dean Howells's words, "transplanted from the
mother asphalt of Paris" to the rapidly growing urban culture of antebellum
New York.[8] Instead, with Poe at the imaginative center of American bohemia
and Clare and Howland at its financial center, bohemianism in the United
States emerged as a complex network of people, money, and ideas circulating
between the North and the South as well as New York and Paris. As John T.
Matthews has argued, the South is a region "whose material and cultural
history prove, on closer inspection, to be more complex and more central
to national bearings than previously appreciated."[9] Bohemia's migration from
Paris to New York was dependent upon people, money, and ideas from the
South that have been overlooked, forgotten, or deliberately obscured—including
the African American slaves who populated Poe's Southern fiction and harvested the cotton that fed Howland's and Clare's bank accounts. For Howland, Clare, and Poe, a pattern emerges wherein a Southern presence is

rendered invisible in order to present New York and Paris as the bohemian capitals of the nineteenth century. That Southern presence, however, re-emerges in subtle, yet instructive, ways.

Edward Howland and Ada Clare

When Henry Clapp Jr., returned from Europe in the winter of 1853 with hopes of reproducing *la vie bohème* of Paris's Latin Quarter under the sidewalks of Manhattan, he found a welcome host in Charles Pfaff, whose German beer cellar was mere blocks from both the theater and publishing districts of mid-century New York.[10] When he wanted to start a literary weekly patterned after Parisian periodicals such as *Le Figaro*, he found his financial angel in Edward Howland, the son of a prominent cotton merchant from Charleston who had moved his family to New York City a decade earlier. After graduating from Harvard University and "representing his father in the cotton business for seven years," Howland turned his attention to a literary career.[11] By 1858, the twenty-six-year-old Howland "had spent many years and a fortune to collect" what A. L. Rawson called a "choice library" of rare books that were sold "so Clapp could have the money to launch the *Saturday Press*."[12] William Winter, who frequented Pfaff's beer cellar in his twenties, recalled that, in addition to providing the initial capital for the *Saturday Press*, Howland also wrote unpaid contributions in an effort to keep the paper financially solvent.[13] Howland also met his wife Marie through his associations at Pfaff's, and his lifelong involvement in the radical social politics that Clapp and other bohemians espoused suggests that his investments in the first bohemian movement were sincere.[14]

Nevertheless, at least one contemporary observer of bohemian New York characterized Howland as less of a collaborator with Clapp and more of a target. Thomas Butler Gunn, a British writer living in New York, wrote in his diary soon after the first issue of the *Saturday Press* appeared in the fall of 1858, "The paper will last just as long as the milch-cow Howland sinks money in it. And—God save the mark!—before the ineffable trash appeared, if they didn't talk of it's going to be equal in merit to the Atlantic Mag[azine], in point of literary production!"[15] Whether Howland was a trust fund baby exploited by Clapp or a radical activist who sacrificed his bourgeoisie status to bohemian ideals, what emerges from these accounts of the birth of the *Saturday Press* is a story about the antebellum literary marketplace that ignores the Southern origins of bohemian New York. The image of Howland liquidating his "choice library" of rare books to pay for an ephemeral weekly like the *Saturday Press* becomes a parable on the vagaries of the literary marketplace: while rare books carried the prestige of both their age and their content, a new periodical could just as easily become "ineffable trash" as it could a cultural tastemaker on the scale of the *Atlantic*.[16]

Both versions of this story—either the (negative) ephemerality of print in an overcrowded public sphere or the (positive) power of a single periodical to influence national taste—depend on the transfiguration of Howland's rare books into a mass-market periodical through the liquidating power of capital. Neither version, however, captures the reality that these books were purchased with money from cotton harvested by slaves. That the liberatory project of bohemianism was funded by chattel slavery casts a dark shadow on the freedom of expression that bohemian experimentation provided to its participants; but given that virtually *every* institution in the antebellum United States, both North and South, was implicated in the slave trade, this realization is less an indictment of bohemian New York than it is a reminder of what Houston A. Baker Jr. and Dana D. Nelson call "the nuanced inseparability of North and South."[17] Baker and Nelson critique the illusion of the South as a "territory that contains white racism" and characterize the persistent desire to seal off the slaveholding South from the industrial North as a fantasy of "white geographical innocence."[18] For the bohemians of antebellum New York, this became a fantasy of white transatlantic innocence that allowed them to believe that they had transplanted the freeing power of a European subculture to the United States without taking with it the national—and not merely Southern—legacy of slavery.

When we identify the origin of bohemian New York as Clapp bringing the radical spirit of Parisian literary weeklies from Paris to New York and not Howland donating the earnings from his family's cotton plantations, the South is effectively written out of the transatlantic circuit that connects the cultural capitals of the Old World and the New. By ignoring the Southern origins of bohemian New York, Howland's rare books—and not the labor of African American men and women—become the starting point of a narrative that defines bohemianism as a refuge for art against the injustices of the marketplace. One example to illustrate this point comes from the story that scholars tell about the *Saturday Press* reviving Whitman's anemic career in 1860: The first two editions of *Leaves of Grass* in 1855 and 1856 sold poorly, but with the constant support of the bohemians writing for the *Saturday Press* the third edition quickly sold out its first print run and put Whitman back on track to becoming America's "good, gray poet." In this version of the story, Howland's valuable collection of rare books directly contributed to the success of that most valuable of books—our quintessentially American poem, *Leaves of Grass.*

This image of books creating more books presents the world of literature as an autonomous and self-contained realm. It presents art and literature as laws unto themselves—as, in Pierre Bourdieu's terms, "foreign to the ordinary logic of the ordinary economy."[19] For Bourdieu, the bohemians of nineteenth-century France were instrumental in perpetuating a worldview that made art and literature function outside the demands of commerce and society. It is tempting to see in Bourdieu's French bohemians a model for those in the antebellum United States as well. (Indeed, Justin Martin has written, "The Pfaff's Bohemians were part of the transition from art as a genteel profession to art as a soul-deep calling."[20]) But when the birth of the *Saturday Press* and the fate of *Leaves of Grass* are intimately linked to the labor of slaves on cotton plantations in the American South, it becomes increasingly difficult to claim that art and literature exist in an autonomous realm sealed off from the world around them. In this sense, then, the Southern origins of bohemian New York provide an important critique of Bourdieu's foundational theory of bohemianism.

For Bourdieu, periodicals like the *Saturday Press* are a necessary feature of the bohemian experience; another necessity is the salon. The primary salon of the New York bohemians—Ada Clare's West Forty-Second Street brownstone—was also paid for with cotton money. Ada Clare was born Ada Agnes Jane McElhenney in Charleston in 1834. As the daughter and granddaughter of "the richest cotton planters in the Sea Islands," Clare was expected to marry well and continue her family's aristocratic traditions by becoming a plantation mistress in her own right.[21] Instead, in 1854 she stole the money that her grandfather had collected for a monument to John C. Calhoun and ran off to New York to pursue a career as an actress. Despite finding early success with prominent theater managers such as Laura Keene and Lester Wallack, she struggled to make ends meet and asked that she be given her inheritance on her twenty-first birthday.[22] While waiting for the inheritance to come through she adopted the name of a character from Charles Dickens's *Bleak House* (1852–53) whose future was similarly tied to a delayed family inheritance: Ada Clare. As an American incarnation of the British Ada Clare, she was a sympathetic, beautiful young woman whose future hung in the balance of an antiquated legal system and the legacies of past family conflicts. The pseudonym Ada Clare gave her a connection to British literary culture while hiding her Southern name. But Clare's Southern fortune echoed every time she said or wrote her pseudonym, and the struggle she faced to claim her inheritance—the struggle of Dickens's Ada Clare—silently conjured the slaves who worked to earn it.

Clare left New York as soon as she received her inheritance and went to Paris to experience French bohemianism firsthand. Unlike Henry Clapp, who lived with the writers and artists of the Latin Quarter, Clare lived a fashionable life in elegant neighborhoods. On one occasion she met a woman she would later describe in the column she wrote for the *Saturday Press* as "the highest type of a Bohémienne": "She had been left a widow with two children and a very large fortune. . . . She was extremely hospitable, and entertained much company, but selected them with utter disregard to the mandates of society. Any entertaining person . . . whether he were artist, poet, banker, statesman, or man of leisure, was equally welcome."[23] The virtues that Clare locates in this idealized *bohémienne*—an "utter disregard [for] the mandates of society" and a staunch determination to live "in her own way"—are consistent with those she espoused in columns that advocated for gender equality and railed against conventional social norms.[24] Clare's own project as a bohemian writer and salon host was modeled, in many ways, on a woman whose freedom was enabled by "a very large fortune," even though the source of that fortune (like Clare's own) was quickly overlooked.

In 1859 Clare moved into a five-hundred dollar-per-year, three-story brownstone at 86 West Forty-Second Street in Manhattan and began hosting a Sunday night salon that rivaled Pfaff's bar as the intellectual and cultural center of bohemian New York. If Pfaff's downtown bar played the part of the café from the Latin Quarter, Clare's Sunday night gatherings in her upscale brownstone filled the role of the aristocratic salon. As we know from Clare's family history and the generations of plantation mistresses that she descended from, it's clear that Paris was not the first place she had seen a wealthy woman preside over a social gathering with elegance, largess, and grace. Clare's biographer Gloria Goldblatt has written that when Clare was leading her brownstone salon "she was as much the hospitable gracious hostess as if she had stayed in Charleston, and was entertaining the planter aristocracy."[25] The echoes of that aristocratic upbringing could be heard whenever Clare was referred to as "Her majesty, the Queen of Bohemia."[26]

Clare's reign as the queen of bohemian New York began in the plantation culture of Charleston as much as it did in the salons of Paris. And despite her efforts to present herself as a displaced Parisian living in New York, one moment in particular from Clare's 1860 *Saturday Press* column about the *bohémienne* she met in Paris betrays the legacy of the plantation mistress whose angelic poise offsets the cruelty of the cotton fields: "And thou, loveliest image of womanly grace, if thou art not the type of the Bohemian, thou shalt be to me the type of all that is noble among women; for thou has taught me . . . one woman can spread forth the white wings of an angel, and rising above them all, draw up to her own ardent height those who assemble around her."[27] Given that the balance of the column is a manifesto-like defense of bohemian culture, it is more than a little startling to see Clare refer to this Parisian *bohémienne* as the "loveliest image of womanly grace," as a "type of all that is noble among women," and— most strikingly—as a beneficent figure with "the white wings of an angel." Joanna Levin reads this curious eruption of domestic discourse as Clare's attempt to create a "new metacultural figure" that included "feminism and sentimental convention, bohemianism and the genteel tradition."[28] We could add to that list the figure of the plantation mistress as the "angel in the house,"[29] and read this passage in light of John T. Matthews's argument that, in antebellum literature, "forms of fetishistic evasion" of the nation's slaveholding legacy "work by hiding Southern plantation economy in plain sight."[30] Just as Ada Clare's pseudonym from *Bleak House* hid her Southern heritage behind a British name that silently evoked her family inheritance, her manifesto on the ideal *bohémienne* similarly summoned a Charleston parlor within a Parisian salon.

As with the revelation that the *Saturday Press* was funded with cotton money, the point to be made here is not merely that the salon culture of bohemian New York was founded on the labor of slaves who toiled invisibly in South Carolina. Once we realize that bohemianism was not a neat transplant from the Paris to New York, we can appreciate the insight from Baker and Nelson that "as a nation, we are always already in 'The South,' that it is unequivocally and intricately lodged in us, a first principle of our being in the world."[31] Running parallel to Levin's notion of bohemia as an "expansive cultural geography" is Baker and Nelson's version of the South as more of a symbolic than an actual geography that defines both national and transatlantic culture.[32] For Baker and Nelson, the South is the entire nexus of relationships that, for centuries, connected Europe, Africa, and the Americas. Clare's salon, with its equal parts New York, Paris, and Charleston, condensed that long history to the space of a single Manhattan brownstone.

Edgar Allan Poe

Charles Baudelaire is the most famous nineteenth-century writer to claim Edgar Allan Poe as a bohemian, but he was not the first.[33] That honor goes to Fitz-James O'Brien, an Irish American writer who also has the distinction of writing the first literary representation of bohemianism in the United States. In the 1855 short story "The Bohemian," O'Brien has one of his characters lament the poverty-stricken career of "poor Poe . . . who was a Bohemian."[34] When Poe died in 1849, Parisian bohemianism was already more than a decade old, but Henri Murger's bohemian stories would not be published in book form until 1851, and English translations would not appear in an American publication until 1853.[35] During Poe's lifetime, bohemianism had not yet made its way to the United States, meaning that his poverty, alcoholism, conflicts with the marketplace, and commitment to literary art were not seen as part of a larger effort to bring Parisian counterculture across the Atlantic. For O'Brien and many of the other writers who gathered at Pfaff's beer cellar in downtown Manhattan, however, Poe was considered the original American bohemian.

New York bohemians such as George Arnold, Ada Clare, Charles Gardette, William North, and William Winter, among others, all paid homage to Poe, either by adopting his style, writing commemorative verses in his honor, or claiming that their works were actually his.[36] Eliza Richards has found that the Pfaff's bohemians published numerous parodies and homages of Poe's "The Raven" in the *Saturday Press*, "giving Poe's voice an afterlife that allowed it to intermingle and inform the works of this new generation of writers."[37] By the early 1880s, erstwhile bohemian Edmund Clarence Stedman claimed that Poe "was one of the first to lead a rebellion against formalism, commonplace, the spirit of the bourgeois" even if, ultimately, "Poe, with his sense of the fitness of things, could see that Bohemianism, the charm of youth, is a frame that poorly suits the portrait of a mature and able-handed man."[38]

None of the New York bohemians embraced Poe more fully than O'Brien, who patterned many of his own poems and tales after Poe's.[39] Early in his career, O'Brien wrote a poem in imitation of Poe's "Shadow: A Parable" that, in a playful hoax that would have made Poe proud, he claimed to have found in an unpublished magazine said to predate Poe's original, writing that the poem "recall[s] Poe's artifices so powerfully, that we cannot avoid the conclusion that he must have seen it some where . . . and we must in justice say that he has immeasurably surpassed his original."[40] O'Brien's fantastic claim that Poe had not only read but improved upon a poem written three years after his death makes essentially the same gesture as claiming Poe for bohemian New York: had Poe lived to see bohemianism take root in the United States he would have been the greatest bohemian of them all.

O'Brien's 1855 story begins with a character named Philip Bran introducing himself as a disciple of the Latin Quarter: "Have you read Henri Murger's

Scènes de la vie de Bohème? ... Well, then, you can comprehend my life. I am clever, learned, witty, and tolerably good looking. I can write brilliant magazine articles ... I can compose songs, make comedies, and captivate women."[41] Unlike the characters in Murger's stories, however, this bohemian does not sacrifice his personal well-being in the pursuit of his art. Instead he proposes a scheme that involves mesmerizing the narrator's fiancée in order to draw out from her the location of a hidden treasure. It is at this moment in the story that O'Brien invokes the legacy of the bohemian Poe: "This island and its vicinity abounds in concealed treasure. ... Captain Kyd [*sic*] and other buccaneers have made numberless caches containing their splendid spoils, which a violent death prevented their ever reclaiming. Poor Poe, you know, who was a Bohemian, like myself, made a story on the tradition, but, poor fellow! he only dug up his treasure on paper."[42]

The "story on the tradition" of Captain Kidd's buried treasure is Poe's 1843 tale "The Gold-Bug," which, like O'Brien's "The Bohemian," is told from the perspective of a naive and trusting narrator who is drafted into helping a more intelligent and dynamic man search for Kidd's hidden treasure.[43] The throwaway line in "The Bohemian," that the "poor fellow" Edgar Allan Poe "only dug up his treasure on paper"—an allusion to the meager fortune Poe made in his career as a writer—is central to O'Brien's rewriting of "The Gold-Bug." "The Bohemian" focuses on the risks posed to the artists and writers who worked in the expanding U.S. culture industry, where riches "on paper" (books, periodicals, works of art, etc.) were difficult to come by. For example, when Bran uses his mesmeric powers on the narrator's fiancée she produces a sketch of the location of the buried treasure that is not only a functional map but also an exquisite piece of art: "Its vividness, its desolation, its evident truth were so singularly given that I could scarcely believe my senses," says the narrator.[44] After the fiancée produces so exceptional a piece of art, she collapses from exhaustion and later dies.

Despite making the ultimate sacrifice to produce a remarkable work of art, the fiancée does not profit from her artistic labor; Bran ultimately takes all the treasure for himself. While Poe only hints at the possibility that the narrator of "The Gold-Bug" will die before he can enjoy the fruits of his labors, O'Brien makes it clear that regardless of the skill and the sacrifice that go into producing a work of art, someone other than the artist herself will ultimately profit from her efforts. Philip Bran's exploitation of the fiancée's artistic powers is at the center of O'Brien's story. At the edges of the story are two additional moments that illustrate how workers in the culture industry are insufficiently compensated for their labors. The fiancée's father is a struggling writer, and the narrator himself tries to supplement his income by writing historical fiction for *Harper's* magazine.[45] The conclusion we are to draw is obvious: if writing literature could really pay the bills, the narrator would have turned the bohemian away and gone back to making money as a writer. It is precisely because writing *doesn't* pay that he takes Bran up on his offer, only to watch his life fall apart as a result, leaving him just like "poor Poe."

"The Gold-Bug" is set on Sullivan's Island in South Carolina.[46] O'Brien, however, moves the location of Captain Kidd's treasure to Coney Island and has most of the action in "The Bohemian" take place in New York City, which allows him to emphasize the exploitative nature of the Manhattan culture industry. Nevertheless, traces of the South remain in O'Brien's story and in his efforts to claim Poe as the original U.S. bohemian, particularly in how "The Gold-Bug" traveled from South Carolina to New York by way of Paris in order to become O'Brien's "The Bohemian." And just as Howland and Clare ignored (or obscured) both slavery and the South in their transatlantic bohemian migrations, so too does O'Brien's use of "The Gold-Bug" as his bohemian source text overlook the Southern and slaveholding elements of Poe's story in order to focus on "poor Poe" and his struggles as a writer. For bohemians in Europe and America alike, the greatest tragedy was the unjust marketplace for cultural goods. Reorienting American bohemia to its Southern origins—and, specifically, to the cotton fields tended to by African American slaves—offered a useful corrective to that myopic view.

"THE GOLD-BUG" has one African American character: a minstrel figure named Jupiter whose presence in the story is played mostly for laughs. He assists the story's two white characters—the narrator and his friend, William Legrand—and then recedes into the background as Legrand provides a lengthy explanation of the process led to the location of the treasure. Jupiter's near invisibility in the final pages of the tale plays an important role in giving the conclusion its particularly unnerving effect. When Legrand suggests to the narrator that Captain Kidd would most likely have killed his accomplices in order to take their share of the treasure ("Perhaps a couple of blows with a mattock were sufficient, while his coadjutors were busy in the pit; perhaps it required a dozen—who shall tell?"[47]), readers hold their breath at the possibility that the narrator could meet a similar fate. Legrand's final, ominous words— "who shall tell?"—leave unspoken the implied threat that, once the narrator is dead, he'll never be able to tell how many blows it took to kill him. But for readers attentive enough to recall that Jupiter—who hasn't been heard from for a number of pages—is still close by, the threat resonates on a different frequency. We can imagine Legrand asking the narrator, "Who shall tell that I killed you? Certainly not Jupiter. No one would believe him. No one would value his testimony in a court of law."

With this cliff-hanger ending, "The Gold-Bug" stops short of being a morality tale. Poe famously wanted his conclusions to have a stunning, disorienting effect.[48] In order to achieve that effect, we are not allowed to see the outcome of the treasure hunters' actions. Ironically, though, the precise phrase that takes us to the threshold of the narrator's potential tragedy—"who shall tell?"—implicitly directs us toward a morality tale that the story only vaguely hints at: Jupiter's subhuman status. Jupiter will never be able to tell of the injustice done to the narrator, nor will he tell of the injustice done to him as a slave. Indeed, he cannot even comprehend the injustice he suffers. We learn from the outset of the story that Jupiter has long since been manumitted, but either through ignorance or desperation refuses to leave his master.[49]

While "The Gold-Bug" stops at the brink of tragedy, "The Bohemian" plays out the tragic events of the narrator's choices and delivers the moral that writers and artists should be paid fairly to prevent their being taken advantage of by con men and crooks. (O'Brien was not above such moralizing: he once famously stood in front of the *Harper's* offices with a sign around his neck that read, "One of Harper's authors, I am starving."[50]) When "The Gold-Bug" moves to New York and becomes "The Bohemian," the tragedy of a poverty-stricken writer supplants the exploitation of an African American slave. O'Brien, like Howland and Clare, hid the Southern origins of bohemian New York in plain sight with his reference to "poor Poe" and his "story on the tradition" of South Carolina treasure. But just as the cotton-funded treasures of Howland and Clare peek out from behind their rare books and stories of Parisian salons, so too did O'Brien leave traces of the South in a story that would otherwise make New York the origin point for U.S. bohemianism.

When we neglect both the South and the history of slavery in the stories that we tell about bohemia's migration from Paris to New York, we tend to follow European thinkers like Walter Benjamin in registering our concern for the tenuous economic status of bohemian writers and artists.[51] This is not to say that "poor Poe" and his bohemian descendants did not deserve to be treated fairly in the literary marketplace but rather to suggest how much richer the story of American bohemianism becomes when we follow its Southern routes to the deeper structures of injustice that connect underpaid writers and artists to African American slaves. A critical understanding of the relationship between bohemian New York and the history of American slavery speaks to the decades-old concern that Benjamin himself articulated when he said of the bohemians of early-nineteenth-century Paris, "To the uncertainty of their economic position corresponded the uncertainty of their political function."[52] Benjamin's concern, like Karl Marx's before him,[53] centers on whether or not the bohemians' critique of the capitalist market for cultural goods could contribute to a broader critique of unjust social and economic practices. O'Brien, Howland, and Clare did not themselves explicitly connect the rise of American bohemia to the history of American slavery, but in preserving the traces of bohemia's passage through the South in their lives and their works they allow us to retell the origins of bohemian New York within a context that redirects the hardships of struggling writers toward the exploitation of African American slaves.

Notes

1. Charlton, "Bohemians in America," 166–67.

2. Whitman, *The Collected Writings*, 40.

3. Reynolds, *Walt Whitman's America*, 378.

4. Lause, *The Antebellum Crisis*, viii.

5. Gailey, "Walt Whitman and the King of Bohemia." Scholnick, " 'An Unusually Active Market.' "

6. Traubel, *With Walt Whitman in Camden*, 23. Poe's relationship to the South is discussed in David Leverenz, "Poe and Gentry Virginia"; Goddu, *Gothic America*; Gray, *Southern Aberrations*; Kennedy and Weissberg, *Romancing the Shadow*; Peeples, *The Afterlife of Edgar Allan Poe*; Greeson, *Our South: Geographic Fantasy and the Rise of National Literature*; Kerkering, "Poe and Southern Poetry"; and Hutchison, *Apples and Ashes*. My thanks to Paula Bernatt Bennett, Jess Bowers, Hal Bush, David Faflik, Lydia Fash, Erin Forbes, and Scott Peeples for these recommendations. I am particularly grateful for Scott Peeples's insights about Poe's Southernness.

7. Bourdieu, *The Rules of Art*, 53.

8. Howells, "First Impressions of Literary New York," 63.

9. Matthews, "Southern Literary Studies," 295.

10. Blalock, "*Go to Pfaff's!*," 14–18.

11. "Obituary: Edward Howland," *New York Times*, 1891. "Obituary: Edward Howland," *New York Times*, January 22, 1891, 4; ProQuest Historical Newspapers.

12. Rawson, "A Bygone Bohemia," 106. See also G. J. M., "Bohemianism," 9; and "General Gossip of Authors and Writers."

13. Winter, *Old Friends; Being Literary Recollections of Other Days*, 137, 294–95.

14. "Obituary: Edward Howland."

15. Gunn, *Diaries*, 10:18, entry dated November 23, 1858. My thanks to Robert Weidman for finding this passage and helping me to understand its relevance.

16. My thanks to Anna Brickhouse for this observation.

17. Baker and Nelson, "Preface." 231.

18. Ibid., 234.

19. Bourdieu, *The Rules of Art*, 81.

20. Martin, *Rebel Souls*, 2.

21. Rawson, "A Bygone Bohemia," 100.

22. Goldblatt, "Ada Clare."

23. Clare, "Thoughts and Things," 2.

24. See Levin, " 'Freedom for Women,' " 75–97.

25. Goldblatt, "Ada Clare."

26. Gay, "The Royal Bohemian Supper," 2; see also "The Vault at Pfaff's: An Archive of Art and Literature by the Bohemians of Antebellum New York," https://pfaffs.web.lehigh.edu.

27. Clare, "Thoughts and Things."

28. Levin, " 'Freedom for Women,' " 93.

29. For the figure of the "angel in the house" within plantation discourse, see Weiner, *Mistresses and Slaves*, 53, 67, 108, 124.

30. Matthews, "Southern Literary Studies." 303–4.

31. Baker and Nelson, "Preface," 243.

32. Levin, *Bohemia in America*, 5.

33. Baudelaire, "Further Notes on Edgar Poe," 94.

34. O'Brien, "The Bohemian," 62.

35. See Murger, *Scènes de la Vie de Bohème*; and Bristed, "The Gypsies of Art," 217.

36. Charles D. Gardette published "The Fire-Fiend. A Nightmare" in the *New York Saturday Press* on November 19, 1859, and attributed the work to Poe. Similarly, the George Arnold poem "Drinking Wine" was attributed to Poe by Thomas Ollive Mabbott in 1939. Ada Clare's Poe-like story "What Sequel?" was published in the *New York Atlas* on March 15, 1857. Similarly Poe inspired was William North's "The Living Corpse," published initially in *Putnam's Monthly* on January 1, 1853, and reprinted in the *Saturday Press* on October 23, 1858. William Winter's "Edgar Poe," published in his *Wanderers*, 170–71, was written for the dedication of a Poe monument in Baltimore in November 1875.

37. Richards, "Poe's Lyrical Media," 216.

38. Stedman, *Edgar Allan Poe*, 86, 26.

39. Francis Wolle, in his biography *Fitz-James O'Brien: A Literary Bohemian of the Eighteen-Fifties*, identifies numerous parallels between works by O'Brien and Poe (39–40, 44–45, 58, 63, 81, 152, 162–63).

40. O'Brien, "Fragments from an Unpublished Magazine," 566.

41. O'Brien, "The Bohemian," 58.

42. Ibid., 62.

43. Poe, "The Gold-Bug," in *Selected Writings*, 348.

44. O'Brien, "The Bohemian," 66.

45. Ibid., 55.

46. Poe, "The Gold-Bug," 321.

47. Ibid., 348.

48. See Poe, "The Philosophy of Composition," 480, 490.

49. Poe, "The Gold-Bug," 322.

50. "Some Recollections of Two Publishers," 514.

51. Benjamin, "Paris: Capital of the Nineteenth Century," 170.

52. Ibid.

53. An overview of Marx's commentary on the bohemians can be found in Cottom, *International Bohemia*, 9, 85–86, 97, 109.

References

Baker, Houston A., Jr., and Dana D. Nelson. "Preface: Violence, the Body and 'The South.'" *American Literature* 73, no. 2 (2001): 231–44.

Baudelaire, Charles. *The Painter of Modern Life and Other Essays*. Edited and translated by Jonathan Mayne. New York: Da Capo, 1964.

Benjamin, Walter. "Paris: Capital of the Nineteenth Century." *Perspecta* 12 (1969): 163–72.

Blalock, Stephanie M. *"Go to Pfaff's!": The History of a Restaurant and Lager Beer Saloon*. Bethlehem, PA: Lehigh University Press, 2014. http://digital.lib.lehigh.edu /pfaffs/goto.pdf.

Bourdieu, Pierre. *The Rules of Art: Genesis and Structure of the Literary Field*. Translated by Susan Emanuel. Stanford, CA: Stanford University Press, 1996.

Bristed, Charles Astor. "The Gypsies of Art: Translated for *The Knickerbocker* from Henry Murger's 'Scenes de La Boheme.'" *Knickerbocker* 41, no. 3 (1853): 217.

Charlton, Jay. "Bohemians in America." In *Pen Pictures of Modern Authors*, edited by William Shepherd, 161–68. New York: Putnam, 1882.

Clare, Ada. "Thoughts and Things." *New-York Saturday Press*, February 11, 1860, 2.

———. "What Sequel?" *New York Atlas*, March 15, 1857.

Cottom, Daniel. *International Bohemia: Scenes of Nineteenth-Century Life*. Philadelphia: University of Pennsylvania Press, 2013.

G. J. M. "Bohemianism: The American Authors Who Met in a Cellar." *Brooklyn Eagle*, May 25, 1884, 9.

Gailey, Amanda. "Walt Whitman and the King of Bohemia: The Poet in the *Saturday Press*." *Walt Whitman Quarterly Review* 25, no. 4 (2008): 143–66.

Gardette, Charles D. "The Fire-Fiend. A Nightmare." *New York Saturday Press*, November 19, 1859, 2.

Gay, Getty. "The Royal Bohemian Supper." *New York Saturday Press*, December 31, 1859, 2.

"General Gossip of Authors and Writers." *Current Literature*, January 1, 1888, 476–80.

Goddu, Teresa A. *Gothic America: Narrative, History, and Nation*. New York: Columbia University Press, 1997.

Goldblatt, Gloria Rudman. *Ada Clare: Queen of Bohemia*. n.p.: Author, 2015. http:// digital.lib.lehigh.edu/pfaffs/clare.pdf.

Gray, Richard. *Southern Aberrations: Writers of the American South and the Problems of Regionalism*. Baton Rouge: Louisiana State University Press, 2000.

Greeson, Jennifer Rae. *Our South: Geographic Fantasy and the Rise of National Literature*. Cambridge, MA: Harvard University Press, 2010.

Gunn, Thomas Butler. *Diaries, 1849–1863*. Vol. 10. St. Louis: Missouri History Museum, n.d. http://pfaffs.web.lehigh.edu/node/60175.

Howells, William Dean. "First Impressions of Literary New York." *Harper's New Monthly Magazine*, June 1, 1895, 62–74.

Hutchison, Coleman. *Apples and Ashes: Literature, Nationalism, and the Confederate States of America*. Athens: University of Georgia Press, 2012.

Kennedy, J. Gerald, and Liliane Weissberg, eds., *Romancing the Shadow: Poe and Race*. New York: Oxford University Press, 2001.

Kerkering, John D. "Poe and Southern Poetry." In *The Cambridge Companion to Nineteenth-Century Poetry*, edited by Kerry Larson, 193–207. New York: Cambridge University Press, 2011.

Lause, Mark. *The Antebellum Crisis and America's First Bohemians*. Kent, OH: Kent State University Press, 2010.

Leverenz, David. "Poe and Gentry Virginia." In *The American Face of Edgar Allan Poe*, edited by Shawn Rosenheim and Stephen Rachman, 210–36. Baltimore: Johns Hopkins University Press, 1995.

Levin, Joanna. *Bohemia in America, 1858–1920*. Stanford, CA: Stanford University Press, 2010.

———. "'Freedom for Women from Conventional Lies': Ada Clare and the Feminist Feuilleton." In *Whitman among the Bohemians*, edited by Joanna Levin and Edward Whitley, 75–97. Iowa City: University of Iowa Press, 2014.

Mabbott, T. O. "Newly-Identified Verses by Poe." *Notes & Queries 177*, no. 5 (1939): 78–79.

Martin, Justin. *Rebel Souls: Walt Whitman and America's First Bohemians*. New York: Da Capo, 2014.

Matthews, John T. "Southern Literary Studies." In *A Companion to American Literary Studies*, edited by Caroline F. Levander and Robert S. Levine, 294–309. New York: Blackwell, 2011.

Murger, Henry. *Scènes de la Vie de Bohème*. Paris: Michel Lévy Frères, 1851.

North, William. "The Living Corpse." *Putnam's Monthly*, January 1, 1853, 32–39.

"Obituary: Edward Howland." *New York Times*, January 22, 1891.

O'Brien, Fitz-James. "The Bohemian." *Harper's New Monthly Magazine*, July 1, 1855. Reprinted in *Behind the Curtain: Selected Fiction of Fitz-James O'Brien, 1853–1860*, edited by Wayne R. Kime, 53–72. Newark: University of Delaware Press, 2011.

———. "Fragments from an Unpublished Magazine." *American Whig Review* 16 (1852): 566.

Peeples, Scott. *The Afterlife of Edgar Allan Poe*. Rochester, NY: Camden House, 2004.

Poe, Edgar Allan. *The Fall of the House of Usher and Other Writings*. Edited by David Galloway. New York: Penguin, 1986.

———. *The Selected Writings of Edgar Allan Poe*. Edited by G. R. Thompson. New York: Norton, 2004.

Rawson, A. L. "A Bygone Bohemia." *Frank Leslie's Popular Monthly*, January 1, 1896, 96–107.

Reynolds, David. *Walt Whitman's America: A Cultural Biography*. New York: Knopf, 1995.

Richards, Eliza. "Poe's Lyrical Media: The Raven's Returns." In *Poe and the Remapping of Antebellum Print Culture*, edited by J. Gerald Kennedy and Jerome McGann, 200–226. Baton Rouge: Louisiana State University Press, 2012.

Scholnick, Robert J. "'An Unusually Active Market for Calamus': Whitman, *Vanity Fair*, and the Fate of Humor in a Time of War, 1860–1863." *Walt Whitman Quarterly Review* 19, no. 3 (2002): 148–81.

"Some Recollections of Two Publishers." *Publisher's Weekly*, October 5, 1889, 514.

Stedman, Edmund Clarence. *Edgar Allan Poe*. Boston: Houghton, Mifflin, 1881.

Traubel, Horace. *With Walt Whitman in Camden*. Vol. 4. Edited by Sculley Bradley. Philadelphia: University of Pennsylvania Press, 1953.

Weiner, Marli F. *Mistresses and Slaves: Plantation Women in South Carolina, 1830–80*. Urbana: University of Illinois Press, 1998.

Whitman, Walt. *The Collected Writings of Walt Whitman*. Vol. 6, *The Correspondence*. Edited by Edwin Haviland Miller. New York: New York University Press, 1977.

Winter, William. *Old Friends; Being Literary Recollections of Other Days*. New York: Moffat, Yard, 1909.

———. *Wanderers: The Poems of William Winter*. New York, Macmillan, 1892.

Wolle, Francis. *Fitz-James O'Brien: A Literary Bohemian of the Eighteen-Fifties*. Boulder: University of Colorado Press, 1944.

The Double Dealers in Bohemian New Orleans

Joanna Levin

The first Southern city widely associated with bohemianism was New Orleans, where the Creole heritage and the French Quarter provided one of the likeliest stand-ins for the original homeland of bohemia—the Parisian Latin Quarter—in the nation. Though a favorable exchange rate led many American artists and writers to travel to Paris in the 1920s in search of *la vie bohème*, other self-declared bohemians cherished, in writer Hamilton Basso's words, their own "Creole version of the Left Bank." Basso later reflected, "If I never much hankered after Paris in the 1920s it was because, in the New Orleans of that era, I had Paris in my own backyard."[1]

In a drawing from 1926 captioned "Ham Basso and the Muse Do the Charleston," a dreamy Basso dances with a flapper, his gaze firmly fixed on the clouds overhead. This sketch is one of the forty-two included in William Faulkner and William Spratling's limited-edition book *Sherwood Anderson and Other Famous Creoles* (1926). Dedicated to the "Artful and Crafty Ones of the French Quarter," and published by the Pelican Bookshop in New Orleans, the book sought to represent and reinforce the local bohemian community that had developed throughout the 1920s. As John Shelton Reed has recently demonstrated, the "Famous Creoles" featured in the sketches, though often divided by age and social class, made up a "*social circle*, a loose network of relationships linked by friends in common (if nothing else, they all knew [the artist] Bill Spratling), by association with the same institutions, and by common interests." This network included the Arts and Crafts Club, the Newcomb College Art School, Le Petit Theatre du Vieux Carré, and Tulane University, as well as the *Times-Picayune* daily newspaper and the modernist literary journal the *Double Dealer*. Reed describes the "criss-crossing patterns of interaction" and shared interests in "art, literature, drama, and historical preservation" that held the bohemian circle together.[2]

This essay focuses on the *Double Dealer*, the literary journal that the *New York Times* called "the heart and backbone of the Quarter."[3] The offices and pages of the journal provided the stage for bohemian self-fashioning and community building. Edited by Julius Weis Friend, Albert Goldstein, John McClure, and Basil Thompson, the *Double Dealer* began publication early in 1921. Its offices were located on 204 Baronne Street in a building owned by Friend's uncle. There, *la vie bohème* flourished in a dirty, unused third-floor space, once home to a "struggling" artist named Molinaire. With a two-headed manikin's double skull adorning the wall of the main room, 204 Baronne became a principal center of the city's artistic and literary life during the bohemian 1920s.[4] In keeping with bohemian tradition, the journal routinely fulminated against heartless landlords, railed against "the bourgeois flavor" that had reduced American culture to "mediocrity," and sought to emancipate the artist "from the deadly dullness of group-standards and group-technique."[5] Friend retrospectively connected the magazine to a "wider cultural movement—a revolt against current American restrictions and stereotypes in favor of more freedom of expression."[6]

Yet the journal carefully navigated bohemian-bourgeois tension, the modern and the traditional, the conservative and the progressive. Jerrold Seigel argues, "Bohemia grew up where the borders of bourgeois life were murky and uncertain. It was a space where newly liberated energies were continually thrown up against the barriers that were erected to contain them, where social margins and frontiers were probed and tested."[7] The New Orleans bohemia that existed on and off the pages of the *Double Dealer* provided such a liminal territory, alternately challenging and reinforcing dominant ideologies and mediating a series of social and cultural divides. The lively, engaging, frustrating, and often offensive "talk, talk, talk" (in Faulkner's words) that circulated between *Double Dealer* publications and the extended dialogues of Faulkner's roman à clef, his apprentice novel *Mosquitoes* (1927), reveal the gendered, racial, socioeconomic, regional, national, and temporal fault lines at the base of this Southern bohemia.[8]

The *Double Dealer*, the Bohemian Renaissance, and New Orleans

As a "real-and-imagined" place (in geographer Edward Soja's terms), Bohemia always exists at the intersection between "the forms and patternings of 'real' material life" and the "mental and ideational worlds of abstract or 'imagined' spaces."[9] From Henri Murger's early sketches of bohemian life in the *Corsaire-Satan* to the definitions of bohemia that emerged in such U.S. periodicals as the *Saturday Press* and the *Masses*, this intersection between the romance of bohemia and specific locations has been forged through the medium of print. In a 1922 article in the *Double Dealer* titled "The Renaissance of the Vieux Carre," T. P. Thompson participates in this tradition, explicitly linking New Orleans's French Quarter and bohemia: "May I say that at last the new day seems dawning and New Orleans has gone up into its garret and is pulling down the best that it has in the way of sentimental worth. Today we can say the ante-bellum grandeur of the early fifties is likely to be reproduced by a post-bellum culture probably aroused by the world's latest conflict, and an eminent desire to enjoy that freedom of intercourse which the Bohemian atmosphere of the old Square seems to inspire." For Thompson, the romantic "atmosphere" of the French Quarter fosters *la vie bohème* by providing an ongoing imaginative stimulus, a bracing collision of past and present.[10] Thompson further cements the identification by referring to the "group of regulars—Bohemians who like the atmosphere sufficiently to pay it the tribute of residing in the shadow of the Cathedral" in St. Anthony's Place at a time when such a residence was of dubious respectability. "The real sportsmen in Bohemia," according to Thompson, were the artists, writers and dedicated historical preservationists who would "dig out their romances of ancient houses and sites, explore and chat with the habitants for traditions, etc."[11] Such historical preservation was part of the larger cultural restoration project that the *Double Dealer* championed as early as its fourth issue: "It is the concern of this magazine to assist in bringing about the restoration of a venerable city to its former standing as a cultural center second to none in America."[12]

To facilitate such restoration in New Orleans, the *Double Dealer* looked toward "some Southern Sherwood Anderson" to "emerge from the sodden marshes of Southern literature,"[13] but it was none other than Anderson himself who arrived on January 13, 1922, at the office on Baronne Street, outfitted in a Windsor tie, velour hat, and green corduroy shirt, announcing, "I am Sherwood Anderson, and I'm planning to stay in New Orleans for a while and thought I'd come up. I am greatly interested in what you fellows are doing here. It's a fine undertaking."[14] Anderson's presence and legendary hospitality enlivened the burgeoning bohemia and gave it instant credibility. Anderson had just been honored as the first recipient of the annual Dial Award, a prestigious two-thousand-dollar prize designed to recognize "service to letters."[15] He characterized the bohemians of the *Double Dealer* in a letter to the prominent critic H. L. Mencken as being "as pleasant a crowd of young blades as ever drunk bad whiskey."[16] In turn, Anderson's prestige and charm magnetized the crowd. As Friend remembered, "He met everyone on a personal level, never the official. No one felt that he was young or old, famous or unknown, while in contact with him. . . . One felt himself living more vividly."[17]

In his first essay written for the journal, Anderson attested to the mutually constitutive properties of "New Orleans, the *Double Dealer*, and the Modern Movement in America." He shared the editors' belief that the specific traditions of New Orleans needed to be retained and cultivated so that they might provide the cultural resources that would enable the modern artistic movement to combat modernity itself. For Anderson, the "speeding up and the standardization of life and thought" threatened individuality, and he defined "the Modern Movement" in the arts as "really no more than an effort to reopen the channels of individual expression." This bohemian imperative found its objective correlative in the Vieux Carré (French Quarter), which he pronounced "the most cultural city I have yet found in America." For Anderson, the division between the old and the new city spatialized bohemian-bourgeois tension. In the old city, "there is something left in this people here that makes them like one another, that leads to constant outbursts of the spirit of play," while outside the Vieux Carré in the "newer New Orleans . . . there is no doubt a good deal of the usual pushing and shoving so characteristic of American civilization."[18] This effort to preserve the inner (the old city) over and against the encroachments of the outer (the new city) implicitly paralleled Anderson's own fictional quest to recover "the spirit of the inner man."[19]

Yet, for the group at the center of the journal the bohemian spirit depended not only on the historical memory preserved by narrow streets and quaint architecture but also on the diversity of contemporary New Orleans. In particular, the self-declared bohemians of the *Double Dealer* valued the presence of the Italian and African American communities and their contributions to the local atmosphere—though representatives of these communities did not tend to become regular members of this bohemian social circle. Nearly 100,000 Italian immigrants settled in New Orleans (many in the French Quarter) between 1898 and 1930,[20] and the *Double Dealer* bohemians insisted, "The native Latin note, always so conspicuous in the South's metropolis, hereabouts fairly captivates you. A fine sort of old world flavor insinuates itself."[21] Connecting this bohemia to its continental counterparts (and to other American bohemias that grew up amid immigrant populations), this "native Latin note" allowed the self-declared bohemians of New Orleans to imagine themselves transported far away from contemporary bourgeois America and its restrictive "Puritanism."[22]

In his *Double Dealer* essay, for example, Sherwood Anderson asks, "Is there a quieter, more leisurely and altogether more charming way of life we might begin to live, here in America, instead of having to run off to Europe to find it?" Answering in the affirmative, he first describes viewing "an oyster shucking contest going on in Lafayette Square, in the heart of the city" and the "handsome Italian" who won the championship. He then describes walking on the Mississippi River front, "looking at negro laborers at work," and concludes, "They are the only laborers I have ever seen in America who know how to laugh, sing and play in the act of doing hard physical labor."[23]

As Chip Rhodes notes, during the 1920s "white artists and intellectuals spoke and wrote copiously about their envy of blacks' [supposedly] more immediate connection to nature and sexual liberation. Blacks became the now-notorious 'primitive.'... Particulars aside, this body of work almost uniformly portrays the basic conflict between culture and nature, between a repressive and arbitrary civilization and a variously coded but generally black subjectivity that is too unconventional to fit into such a rigid social order." Overlapping with constructions of the unconventional bohemian, the contemporary discourse on "the primitive" led many artists and writers searching for *la vie bohème* to look to African American culture for a healthy alternative to bourgeois repression. Anderson explicitly viewed blacks in these stereotypical primitivist terms, writing to his friend John Gould Fletcher of his time in New Orleans, "What we whites seem so to have lost, the power of doing—the power of feeling, sensing each other . . . the blacks seem to have."[24] However, despite many of these bohemians' stated interest in black culture, the "Famous Creole" circle remained, as Reed has argued, "a lily-white bohemia," a product of the Jim Crow South and its racial ideologies.[25]

For the *Double Dealer* historical richness and the presence of cultural diversity (in the larger culture, if not in the famous Creole circle itself) were thus two of the factors that made New Orleans especially ripe for bohemia. The journal made it increasingly clear that what most needed exposure and cultivation in New Orleans and the South at large was a new cultural territory. The stakes were high. In 1920, H. L. Mencken had laid down the gauntlet, writing in a scathing essay titled "The Sahara of the Bozart" that the South "is almost as sterile, artistically, intellectually, culturally, as the Sahara Desert."[26] The bohemian renaissance sought to counter this purposefully provocative claim.

Dealing Double: Region, Identity, and Literary Tradition

Proudly announcing in its first issue that it had "no policy whatever but that of printing the very best material it can procure, regardless of popular appeal, moral or immoral stigmata, conventional or unconventional technique, new theme or old," the *Double Dealer* held out the promise that "the very best material" could transcend contemporary aesthetic and moral and ideological controversies, resist the imperatives of the commercial marketplace, and retain an abiding commitment to honesty.[27] Naming itself after William Congreve's comedy *The Double Dealer*, the journal stated that it would "deal double, to show the other side. We expect to be called Radical by Tory and Reactionary by Red."[28] Unlike the Greenwich Village bohemians of the *Masses*, the Double Dealers were, in Friend's words, "nearly ignorant of politics and entirely scornful of it."[29] Conversely, much like the New Critics (who would emerge from the contemporary Southern Agrarians, several of whom also published in the *Double Dealer*), the editors valued a literary work—or a sum total of literary works—that would produce a balancing of opposites that would rise above the social and political fray. And yet, the pages of the *Double Dealer* registered the pressure of many of the conflicts that the journal had hoped to balance, resolve, or circumvent. In particular, issues of region, race, gender and aesthetic ideology complicated the process of "dealing double" and constructing a rarified bohemia with stable boundaries.

From his perch in Baltimore, Mencken remained a looming presence, a constant reminder of the need to counter claims that the South had become a cultural wasteland. The editors quote Mencken's "The Sahara of the Bozart" in the very first issue, concurring that "down there [in the South] a poet is almost as rare as an oboe player, a dry point etcher or a metaphysician." But they qualify their agreement, noting, "he is as rare, likewise, 'up there' and 'out there' and 'anywhere.'"[30] At times the editors continue in this vein, upholding a lofty realm of "the best" that would remain untethered to any geographic locale—one that would implicitly transcend the problem of regional marginality. At other times they embrace becoming a regional cause célèbre, the bohemian antidote to both Southern backwardness and the dominance of the bourgeois Northeast and its literary establishment, insisting, "*The Double Dealer*, with all due modesty, wishes to be known as the rebuilder, the driver, of the first pile into the mud of this artistic stagnation which has been our portion since the Civil War. The magazine is, beyond this, a movement, a protest, a rising up against the intellectual tyranny of New York, New England, and the Middle West. . . . *Aux armes, en garde, on les aura!*"[31]

Following this call to arms, however, the editors temporarily back off. They once again uphold their commitment to the rootless category of "the best," asserting, "Great literature is rarely national and rarely local in aroma. It is, in its nature, at once universal and individual."[32] And yet, the pendulum shifts rapidly yet again, and by the seventh issue the *Double Dealer* had fully rebranded itself, announcing, "From 'A Magazine for the Discriminating' we have now become 'A National Magazine from the South.' . . . Here beginning it is purposed to provide a national medium for Southern writers and readers." In this somewhat paradoxical formulation, this "National Magazine from the South" seeks to strengthen the national center by bolstering the regional margins and displacing, however partially, the cultural centrality of Northern literary centers. The journal connects such defiance to its larger bohemian imperative and opposition to "rigid Puritanism."[33] Still, its editors warn, "the imported matter will continue to go in, and in the same quantity, unless the quality of the Southern matter meets our standard."[34]

Thinly veiled versions of key Double Dealers appear in Faulkner's *Mosquitoes*, and much of their talk centers on precisely these issues: the tension between the regional, national and universal. For example, the character Julius, often known in the novel as "the Semitic man" (apparently modeled on *Double Dealer* editor Friend) levies a common critique of Anderson when he calls out Dawson Fairchild (Anderson's fictional counterpart) for "clinging spiritually to one little spot of the earth's surface" and lacking "a standard of literature that is international."[35]

As for Mencken, he continued to influence the *Double Dealer* through his correspondence with editor McClure, and he ultimately praised the journal when he became convinced that it was inciting Southerners "to revolt": "It has the right air. It struts a bit and doesn't give a damn for the old gods. I have read all of its issues diligently, and haven't found a single reference, direct or indirect, to the charm and virtue of Southern womanhood, or to the mad way in which the slaves used to love their masters."[36] This praise was not lost on the editors, and, in their first anniversary issue, the *Double Dealer* proudly echoed Mencken: "I stalk 'Bozartian Sahara' in jaunty unconcern."[37]

Mencken cheered the magazine for eschewing plantation romances and glorifications of the antebellum South. Yet, even though the *Double Dealer* avoided some racial stereotypes, its representation of race and race relations remained deeply problematic. An unsigned review of W. E. B. Du Bois's *Darkwater*, for example, seeks to deny the persistence of racial oppression in the South:

> "Darkwater" is an attempt to convey the impression that all negroes of the South lie under a monstrous shadow and are deeply depressed by a burning sense of inferiority that the white people will never for a moment permit them to forget. This is essentially false. The negro of the masses, certainly the agricultural negro of the South, is little concerned with the ever-present agitation carried on ostensibly in his behalf by mulattoes and white politicians. These negroes are busy emphasizing negro traits, and

the ever growing nucleus of negro land owners testifies to their thrift and industry, and are building for negroes a high place in the esteem of whites.[38]

The insistence upon "negro traits" echoes the troubling racial essentialism articulated by the likes of Anderson and many others. McClure's review of Jean Toomer's *Cane* also relies on the stereotypical discourse of black primitivism, extolling the book for its "injection into our polite letters of the emotional ecstasy of the black man." Nonetheless, the review insists that "this racial significance of Jean Toomer's work . . . is not all" and ultimately concludes that Toomer is "as indubitably a genius in prose as any man now writing in America." Comparing Toomer to the bohemians' own resident literary star, McClure even went so far as to note, "Jean Toomer accomplishes effects that Sherwood Anderson at his best might envy."[39] The journal published a number of Toomer's poems, thus expanding the racial boundaries of its bohemia, but the color line remained so intractable that Toomer didn't visit the offices of the *Double Dealer* when in New Orleans, afraid that he wouldn't have been received (though the editors retrospectively said they would have been delighted to host him).[40]

Discussions of race are strikingly absent from the extended conversations recorded in Faulkner's *Mosquitoes*, and, as John H. Duvall has argued, "African American characters in the novel's portrayal of New Orleans . . . are so minor as to be merely decorative." Still, Duvall notes, "other black figures (Caucasians tropologically linked to blackness)" inhabit the novel and become versions of "the primitive, . . . what in Freudian terms needs to be repressed in civilized society, most notably sexual license prior to cultural taboos."[41] It is this version of the primitive that Anderson and other white bohemian Double Dealers sought in local African American culture in their effort to counter bourgeois repression; and it is this version of the black primitive that also surfaces in *Mosquitoes*, though in the novel—as opposed to the journal—such blackness appears largely disconnected from African American bodies and essentialist notions of racial difference. Several of the white artist figures, for example, are described as being figuratively "black" or "dark," including the white sculptor Gordon (a composite of Faulkner and Spratling).[42]

As was noted above, Mencken praised the *Double Dealer* not only for moving beyond the representations of race found in plantation romances but also for avoiding clichés about Southern womanhood. And yet, even though the *Double Dealer* refused to idealize the plantation mistress of yore, many of its editorials betrayed blatantly sexist views and looked askance at the effects of women's rights. "What is prohibition but the female mind?" asked the editors in "The Dominant Petticoat": "Shades of Mary Wolstonecraft [*sic*], 'women's rights' forsooth! They have the vote. Subtly they run the country."[43] Like other male modernist contemporaries, the editors sought to combat the perceived feminization of American literature—especially the "treacly sentimentalities" that they ascribed to Southern "lady fictioneers." Not only did they insist that the time had now past "when the business of being musician, painter, and most especially poet, was considered quite unmanly, decidedly effeminate," but they engaged in aggressive overcompensation, arguing, "as a creative artist woman is a complete failure, a nonentity."[44] Some of this rhetoric might possibly be attributed to willful provocation or even intentional irony, though it can't be said that the journal undermined these assertions in any clear or systematic way. Still, despite the sexist rhetoric in many of the editorials, women were important contributors to the *Double Dealer*. It featured three to four women writers per issue,[45] and, according to Frances Bowen Durrett's history of the *Double Dealer*, Lillian Friend Marcus (sister of founding editor Friend) soon shared with her brother the "bulk of the financial problems involved, the task of organizing, and the actual work of publishing."[46]

Faulkner's *Mosquitoes* provides a glimpse into how Marcus may have responded to the sexism of the male Double Dealers. Faulkner himself had written in the journal, "Ah, women, with their hungry snatching little souls! With a man it is—quite often—art for art's sake; with a woman it is always art for the artist's sake."[47] Julius (based on Friend) echoes these words in the novel, telling his sister, Eva Wiseman (a version of Marcus), "You'd better let art alone and stick to artists, as is your nature." Dawson (i.e., Anderson) interjects, "But women have done some good things," yet Julius short-circuits the discussion: "they bear geniuses." Nonetheless, Eva ultimately puts them all in their place. When Dawson proclaims, "All artists are kind of insane," Eva responds, "Yes, . . . Almost as insane as the ones that sit around and talk about them."[48]

Though *Double Dealer* editorials frequently upheld traditional gender binaries, the journal nonetheless demonstrated a willingness to think outside the constraints of heteronormativity. At a time when the term *perversion* was frequently used to describe both decadent art and the sexual practices that took place outside of heterosexual, procreative marriage, the *Double Dealer* affirmed the artistic spirit as "the imp of the perverse" (with a nod to Poe, the original Southern bohemian): "What is art but a make-believe for neurotics? Why try to gull us into the belief that it has any utility in normal life? 'The business of the race,' says Remy de Gourmont, 'is reproduction.' The business of art is directly opposed to this. . . . And now, after all this tirade, let me say quite frankly that I am on the side of the devils."[49] Extending the spirit of play, the journal criticized those contemporary sexologists and writers who addressed their chosen subject too seriously or hesitantly: "Heavies like Freud, Krafft-Ebing and Edward Carpenter seem much too solemn to be regarded seriously. . . . If the dear people want sex, give the dear people sex. . . . Surely phallic worship and Lesbianism are preferable to prurient stench given out by polite panderers of sugarcoated pornographia."[50] Indeed, on and off the pages of the *Double Dealer*, the French Quarter provided a modern, cosmopolitan setting that enabled the expression of diverse sexualities. According to Reed, among the New Orleans bohemians, "roughly a third of the male artists, writers, and musicians . . . seem to have been homosexual or bisexual."[51]

As Minrose C. Gwinn has demonstrated, *Mosquitoes* also contains multiple "queer spaces" that "challenge and subvert the 'regulatory fiction' of heterosexuality" and its gender norms, especially in its original typescript (before four substantial passages had been cut by the publishers Boni and Liveright).[52] The typescript, for example, features explicit sexual contact between two female characters and this statement from Julius: "Art is against nature. Those who choose it are perverts."[53] Reminiscent of *Double Dealer* assertions, this cut passage connects with Dawson's musings in the published novel, where he claims that "in art, a man can create without any assistance at all: what he does is his. . . . A perversion, I grant you, but a perversion that builds Chartres and invents Lear is a pretty good thing."[54]

The *Double Dealer*'s mixture of the progressive and the conservative also extended to matters of literary aesthetics. With respect to contemporary artistic movements, the magazine saw itself as "a half-way house" between the traditional and the modern, the academic and the experimental.[55] "It may be quite true . . . that the trite and conventional stigmata are death to productions of art," the *Double Dealer* maintained, "But it is doubtless equally true that the production whose only distinction is that it is unconventional or that it is not trite is as dead as its opposite."[56] Faulkner agreed. In an essay for the journal, he recalled his brief stint among "the pack belling loudly after contemporary poets" before announcing his desire for a return to "formal rhymes and conventional forms again."[57] Nonetheless, many of his own literary publications in the *Double Dealer* were notably experimental—especially the series of vignettes titled "New Orleans" that fed into *Mosquitoes*.[58]

As was noted earlier, Anderson had hoped that the "modern movement" in the arts that would counter the incessant drive of an industrial society that standardized the self. But other *Double Dealer* editorials express concern that, taken too far, this modern bohemian quest could lead to self-absorption and pretension, less to the reclamation of "basic human attributes" that Anderson had envisioned than to a restless quest for novelty: "He or she—but let me call them 'they,' for they are increasing by leaps and bounds—they are to be found in Villages, or at 4 P.M. or 4 A.M. in tea-gardens with picturesque names like 'The Green Beetle.'... They represent, some of them, a wealthy group with only one expressed interest and that is what they believe to be the expression of their own individualities.... They are the camp-followers of all the 'neo-movements.'"[59] With such narcissistic "camp-followers," the *Double Dealer* suggests, the modernist "neo-movements" were themselves of dubious worth.

Coda: Bohemian versus Bourgeois

The aforementioned "they" were prevalent in "Villages" such as Greenwich Village, but the Double Dealers were well aware of the pivotal role of wealth and the local bourgeois establishment in bohemian New Orleans. The journal touted the "the various clubs and coteries whose apparent purpose it is to nourish the traditions of the old ground,"[60] and, as Reed has demonstrated, these institutions "sometimes bridged the divide between Bohemia and Society, between 'uptown' and 'downtown.'"[61] The *Double Dealer* understood both the potential benefits and the limitations of this bohemian-bourgeois alliance: "To be sure, we are not spellbound with the illusion that such things usually carry; we know well that part of the artistic audiences are but figures in the social world, and a great many of the dilletantes [sic] who grace the studio firesides are mere tea drinkers of a virulent type."[62] The journal affirms that "interdependence as ever prevails" and that the "quixotically constructive enterprises" of bohemia—from the Petit Theatre to the *Double Dealer* itself—must receive financial support or "sink into the Sisyphusean [sic] futility of finer things."[63]

Faulkner's *Mosquitoes* centers on such bohemian and bourgeois interdependence (while also calling into question regional, racial, and sexual boundaries). Its very title invokes the idea of parasites and hosts, and the novel begs certain questions: In the interactions between the bohemians and the bourgeoisie, who are the parasites? Who are the hosts? Who is more dependent upon whom? Most of the action of the novel takes place in the French Quarter and aboard the *Nausikaa*, a yacht—and proverbial ship of fools—owned by the wealthy dowager Mrs. Maurier. A woman with high Victorian taste, Mrs. Maurier represents several of the uptown women who were active in the

French Quarter preservationist movement, and she sees herself as a consummate hostess and patron of the arts. Faulkner describes the Vieux Carré as "an aging yet still beautiful courtesan in a smokefilled room, avid yet weary too of ardent ways."[64] Mrs. Maurier, with her "decayed coquetry," is an ironic extension of this trope: she lacks the dignity and seductiveness that Faulkner and other bohemians ascribed to the French Quarter.[65] Also decaying is the genteel rhetoric that she uses to discuss "the world of Art" and the ostensible "delicacy of soul" and "untrammeled spirit" of its creators.[66] The *Double Dealer* had insisted, "Enough of Beauty with a big B . . . Beauty, that marred, mishandled goddess,"[67] yet Mrs. Maurier still gushes over her "sensitiv[ity] to the beautiful in Art."[68] She insists that her "instincts are bohemian,"[69] but she acts as a voyeuristic tour guide when she swoops into Gordon's studio and invites him to the yachting party. Other bohemians encourage Gordon to accept the invitation ("You can't afford to ignore people that own food and automobiles, you know"[70]), while recognizing that her patronage has hidden costs, requiring the artist to "pay a fairly high price for his food" and embrace a degree of self-commodification.[71]

The most interesting moment of bohemian-bourgeois interdependence occurs during a heated interchange between Gordon and Mrs. Maurier on the yacht. She depends upon Gordon and the other artists for her sense that she has "given her mite to Art," the overarching transcendent force that calls forth their collective efforts. She positions herself as a relatively "humble laborer" in relation to the bohemians, telling him, "To live within yourself, to be sufficient unto yourself. . . . Ah, Mr. Gordon, how lucky you who create are." Yet in the next breath she reiterates the importance of her own role as hostess, patron, and would-be-muse, and in a passive-aggressive twist repositions the bohemians on her yacht as *her* dependents: "As for we others, the best we can hope is that sometime, somewhere, somehow we may be fortunate enough to furnish that inspiration, or the setting for it, at least."[72] Gordon responds by "fac[ing] the old woman again, putting his hand on her and turning her face upward into the moonlight . . . learning the bones of her forehead and eyesockets and nose through her flesh."[73] At this moment of contact her face does in fact inspire his art, ultimately providing the basis for a clay mask that penetrates her surface "silliness." Yet ironically enough, instead of inspiring a work of ideal beauty in line with her neo-Victorian aesthetics, Mrs. Maurier gives rise to a modern art of "savage verisimilitude" that shatters her own sense of self-mastery and control over her social world.[74]

This moment acknowledges the complicated interaction between bohemian and bourgeois in the New Orleans of the 1920s. Though the bohemian

Gordon may have asserted a measure of control over the bourgeois Mrs. Maurier in the novel, on the streets of the French Quarter, this bohemia remained vulnerable to bourgeois dominance and the demands of the marketplace. As Reed argues, "the common effort to preserve the Quarter papered over a cultural fault line" between the bohemian artists and uptown society figures.[75] Preservation efforts, as well as the commodification of bohemia, led to the gentrification that eventually priced out many of the artists and writers. Always in debt, the *Double Dealer* was itself the prototypical, insolvent bohemian trying to eke out a living from the market (from print advertisements and yearly subscription sales) and from the support of wealthy patrons, those local citizens whom Lillian Friend Marcus described as "guarantors" who defrayed costs by contributing at least ten dollars a month.

And yet, during its five-year run, the *Double Dealer* had the notable distinction of publishing the work of a host of emerging writers, including Djuna Barnes, Malcolm Cowley, Hart Crane, Ernest Hemingway, William Faulkner, Jean Toomer, and Thornton Wilder.[76] Its bohemian intention to "knock the bourgeois really silly" was noted by as far-flung a publication as England's *Manchester Guardian*.[77] It also had the fabled joy, camaraderie, and youthful spirit of *la vie bohème.* For participants like Hamilton Basso, "Those days of *The Double Dealer* were the real, genuine, 100% article. . . . We had the fact of being in our early twenties, we had a similarity of interest that made us enduring friends, we had the privilege of companionship with men like Sherwood Anderson, we had the whole page of our ambition to write upon as best we could, and we had fun. That many things don't often happen to come together all at once in one place and in one time."[78]

The experimental epilogue of *Mosquitoes* attempts to represent such a fortuitous confluence of location, ideas, and personalities. After the four-day yachting excursion, Dawson, Gordon, and Julius—finally free of Mrs. Maurier—return to the French Quarter and stay up all night imbibing spirits. As they drunkenly wander through the Quarter, the three characters become partially fused as they articulate aesthetic philosophies and principles. Their words mix and mingle, often with no clear point of origin. Prompted by their collective musings, and physically supported by Julius as he drunkenly stumbles, Dawson has a final epiphany: "Genius . . . is that Passion Week of the heart, that instant of timeless beatitude . . . in which all the hackneyed accidents which make up this world—love and life and death and sex and sorrow—brought together by chance in perfect proportions, take on a kind of splendid and timeless beauty."[79] This moment seems a triumphant endorsement of *la vie bohème*, of a shared commitment to nurturing such instances of "beatitude," but the epiphany is at least partially undercut by the fact that Dawson summarily vomits in its immediate aftermath.

As a record of a communal experience, the epilogue—indeed, the novel as a whole—becomes all the more strikingly polyvocal and collaborative when read alongside the *Double Dealer*, whose words it recycles and recontextualizes. Yet the question of whether *Mosquitoes* ultimately does more to endorse or critique the endless "talk, talk, talk" of the bohemians continues to divide critics. Is the point of the novel to demonstrate the pointlessness of the chatter, or do the parasites and hosts of *Mosquitoes* enable artistic vision and creation?[80] If Faulkner's final perspective on "our New Orleans bohemian life" is so difficult to gauge, it is perhaps because the novel so fully honors the journal that fostered it by "dealing double" with bohemia itself. At once a satirical and affirmative, uneven yet brilliant, frustrating and inspiring, *Mosquitoes* encapsulates the bohemian New Orleans of the *Double Dealer* and the many social and cultural divisions it sought to navigate while staking its claim to national and international relevance.

Notes

1. Lake, "Paris in My Own Backyard," 40.

2. Reed, *Dixie Bohemia*, 5–6.

3. Bent, "Greenwich Village on Royal Street," 45.

4. Durrett, "The New Orleans *Double Dealer*," 227.

5. "Diogenes on Landlords"; "Wherein We Yawn"; "Anniversary!"; De Casseres, "Decadence and Mediocrity," 150.

6. Julius Weis Friend, quoted in Reed, *Dixie Bohemia*, 40.

7. Seigel, *Bohemian Paris*, 11.

8. Faulkner, *Mosquitoes*, 186.

9. Soja, *Thirdspace*, 6.

10. The decaying French Quarter offered another necessary precondition for bohemia: rent was relatively cheap. See Reed, *Dixie Bohemia*, 87.

11. Bent, "Greenwich Village on Royal Street"; Thompson, "The Renaissance of the Vieux Carre," 89

12. "New Orleans and The Double Dealer," 126.

13. "Southern Letters," 214.

14. Durrett, "The New Orleans *Double Dealer*," 222; Rideout, "The Most Civilized Spot in America," 4.

15. Rideout, "The Most Civilized Spot in America," 2.

16. Sherwood Anderson to H. L. Mencken, January 25, 1922, quoted in Rideout, "The Most Civilized Spot in America," 4–5.

17. Julius Weis Friend, quoted in Rideout, "The Most Civilized Spot in America," 4.

18. Anderson, "New Orleans, The Double Dealer and the Modern Movement in America," 119–26.

19. Fagin, "Sherwood Anderson and Our Anthropological Age," *Double Dealer* 7 (January–February 1925): 96, 98.

20. Reed, *Dixie Bohemia*, 73.

21. Editorials, *DD* 11 (November 1921): 178.

22. The critique of American Puritanism was a staple of the cultural criticism that had been popularized by the likes of Van Wyck Brooks and Waldo Frank. On Anderson and the "Young Americans," see Whalen, *Race, Manhood, and Modernism*, 86–99.

23. Anderson, "New Orleans, The Double Dealer and the Modern Movement in America," 123–24.

24. Sherwood Anderson to John Gould Fletcher, June 30, 1924, quoted in Rideout, *Sherwood Anderson*, 541.

25. See Reed, *Dixie Bohemia*, 59–67.

26. Mencken, "The Sahara of the Bozart," 229.

27. "The Magazine in America," 83.

28. "Honesty and the Double Dealer," 3.

29. "Politics and the Artist," 126; Julius Weis Friend, quoted in Reed, *Dixie Bohemia*, 67.

30. "Mr. Bodenheim from the Sahara of the Bozart," 35.

31. "New Orleans and the Double Dealer," 126.

32. "American Literature," 171.

33. Jones, "Sabotaging American Literature," 128.

34. "A National Magazine from the South," 2.

35. Faulkner, *Mosquitoes*, 184, 242.

36. Hobson, *Serpent in Eden*, 51; Mencken, "The South Begins to Mutter," 141. Still, Hobson notes that during the last year of the *Double Dealer*'s publication, "no more than one-third of its contributors were Southern; and in these cases their subjects were rarely endemic to the South" (53).

37. "Anniversary!," 2.

38. McClure, "Jean Toomer," 26; "Darkwater," 256.

39. McClure, "Jean Toomer," 26.

40. Reed, *Dixie Bohemia*, 60.

41. Duvall, "Why Are You So Black?" 149, 152.

42. Faulkner, *Mosquitoes*, 25, 145.

43. "The Dominant Petticoat." 218.

44. "The Ephemeral Sex," 84.

45. Bonner, "The *Double Dealer* and the Little-Magazine Tradition," 29.

46. Durrett, "The New Orleans *Double Dealer*," 228.

47. Faulkner, "Verse Old and Nascent" 129.

48. Faulkner, *Mosquitoes*, 247–48.

49. "Art," 3. On the nexus between sexology, modernism, and notions of the perverse, see Schaffner, *Modernism and Perversion*.

50. "Sex Stuff," 230–31.

51. Reed, *Dixie Bohemia*, 69.

52. Gwinn, "Did Ernest Like Gordon?," 123.

53. Faulkner, *Mosquitoes* typescript, quoted in Gwinn, "Did Ernest Like Gordon?," 133.

54. Faulkner, *Mosquitoes*, 320.

55. Jones, "Sabotaging American Literature," 228, 231.

56. "The Awkward Rebel," 231.

57. Faulkner, "Verse Old and Nascent," 130.

58. Watson, "New Orleans, *The Double Dealer*, and 'New Orleans,'" 215.

59. "Catch-Words of the Sophisticated," 7.

60. "Axes on Edge," 4.

61. Reed, *Dixie Bohemia*, 77.

62. "Axes on Edge," 4.

63. "Editorials," 179.

64. Faulkner, *Mosquitoes*, 10.

65. Ibid., 31.

66. Ibid., 16, 18.

67. Wright, "The Dance of the Impotent," 67–68.

68. Faulkner, *Mosquitoes*, 23.

69. Ibid., 20.

70. Ibid., 50.

71. Ibid., 43.

72. Ibid., 153.

73. Ibid., 154.

74. Ibid., 322.

75. Reed, *Dixie Bohemia*, 86.

76. As Durrett, "The New Orleans *Double Dealer*," 212–13, notes, "during its existence, the *Double Dealer* had two hundred ninety-three contributors. Thirty years later, fifty-five of these were among the writers listed in Who's Who in America."

77. *Manchester Guardian*, quoted in Durrett, "The New Orleans *Double Dealer*," 233.

78. Hamilton Basso to Frances Bowen Durrett, August 3, 1952, quoted in Durrett, "The New Orleans *Double Dealer*," 230.

79. Faulkner, *Mosquitoes*, 339.

80. Millgate has argued in *The Achievement of William Faulkner*, 68, that the novel "constitutes in its overall effect a repudiation of New Orleans and of all such literary milieu." Others see a more ambivalent portrait of the bohemian scene; see, for example, Atkinson, "Aesthetic Ideology in Faulkner's *Mosquitoes*."

References

"American Literature." Editorial. *Double Dealer* 1 (May 1921): 171.

Anderson, Sherwood. "New Orleans, the Double Dealer and the Modern Movement in America." *Double Dealer* 3 (March 1922): 119–26.

"Anniversary!" Editorial. *Double Dealer* 3 (January 1922): 2.

"Art." Editorial. *Double Dealer* 4 (July 1922): 3.

Atkinson, Ted. "Aesthetic Ideology in Faulkner's *Mosquitoes*: A Cultural History." *Faulkner Journal* 17 (2001): 3–18.

"The Awkward Rebel." Editorial. *Double Dealer* 3 (May 1922): 231.

"Axes on Edge." Editorial. *Double Dealer* 1 (January 1921): 4.

Bent, Silas. "Greenwich Village on Royal Street." *New York Times Book Review and Magazine*, July 23, 1922, 45.

Bonner, Thomas, Jr. "The *Double Dealer* and the Little-Magazine Tradition." In *Literary New Orleans in the Modern World*, edited by Richard S. Kennedy, 23–35. Baton Rouge: Louisiana State University Press, 1998.

"Catch-Words of the Sophisticated." Editorial. *Double Dealer* 3 (January 1922): 7.

"Darkwater." *Double Dealer* 1 (June 1921): 256.

De Casseres, Benjamin. "Decadence and Mediocrity." *Double Dealer* 1 (April 1921): 150.

"Diogenes on Landlords." *Double Dealer* 1 (February 1921): 63.

"The Dominant Petticoat." Editorial. *Double Dealer* 1 (June 1921): 217–18.

Durrett, Frances Bowen. "The New Orleans *Double Dealer*." In *Reality and Myth: Essays in American Literature*. Edited by William E. Walker and Robert L. Welker, 227. Nashville: Vanderbilt University Press, 1964.

Duvall, John N. "'Why Are You So Black?' Faulkner's Whiteface Minstrels, Primitivism, and Perversion." In *A Companion to William Faulkner*. Edited by Richard C. Moreland, 148–64. Oxford: Blackwell, 2007.

"Editorials." *Double Dealer* 2 (November 1921): 178–79.

"The Ephemeral Sex." Editorial. *Double Dealer* 1 (March 1921): 84–85.

Faulkner, William. *Mosquitoes*. New York: Boni and Liveright, 1927.

———. "Verse Old and Nascent: A Pilgrimage," *Double Dealer* 7 (April 1925): 129–31.

Gwinn, Minrose C. "Did Ernest Like Gordon?: Faulkner's *Mosquitoes* and the Bite of 'Gender Trouble.'" In *Faulkner and Gender*. Edited by Donald M. Kartiganer and Ann J. Abadie, 120–44. Jackson: University Press of Mississippi, 1994.

Hobson, Fred. C., Jr. *Serpent in Eden: H. L. Mencken and the South*. Chapel Hill: University of North Carolina Press, 1974.

"Honesty and the Double Dealer." Editorial. *Double Dealer* 1 (January 1921): 3.

Jones, Llewellyn. "Sabotaging American Literature." *Double Dealer* 1 (June 1921): 228.

Lake, Inez Hollander. "Paris in My Own Backyard: Hamilton Basso." In *Literary New Orleans in the Modern World*. Edited by Richard S. Kennedy, 36–53. Baton Rouge: Louisiana State University Press, 1998.

"The Magazine in America." Editorial. *Double Dealer* 1 (March 1921): 83.

McClure, John. "Jean Toomer." *Double Dealer* 6 (January 1924): 26.

Mencken, H. L. "The Sahara of the Bozart." In *Prejudices: The First, Second and Third Series*, 229–40. New York: Library of America, 2010.

———. "The South Begins to Mutter." *Smart Set*, August 1921, 138–44.

Millgate, Michael. *The Achievement of William Faulkner*. Lincoln: University of Nebraska Press, 1966.

"Mr. Bodenheim from the Sahara of the Bozart." Review. *Double Dealer* 1 (January 1921): 35.

"A National Magazine from the South." Editorial. *Double Dealer* 2 (July 1921): 2.

"New Orleans and The Double Dealer." Editorial. *Double Dealer* 1 (April 1921): 126.

"Politics and the Artist." Editorial. *Double Dealer* 2 (October 1921): 126.

Reed, John Shelton. *Dixie Bohemia: A French Quarter Circle in the 1920s*. Baton Rouge: Louisiana State University Press, 2012.

Rideout, Walter B. "The Most Civilized Spot in America: Sherwood Anderson in New Orleans." In *Literary New Orleans in the Modern World*. Edited by Richard S. Kennedy, 1–22. Baton Rouge: Louisiana State University Press, 1998.

———. *Sherwood Anderson: A Writer in America*. Vol. 1. Madison: University of Wisconsin Press, 2006.

Schaffner, Anna Katharina. *Modernism and Perversion: Sexual Deviance in Sexology and Literature, 1850–1930*. New York: Palgrave Macmillan, 2012.

Seigel, Jerrold. *Bohemian Paris: Culture, Politics, and the Boundaries of Bourgeois Life, 1830–1930*. New York: Penguin, 1986.

"Sex Stuff." Editorial. *Double Dealer* 3 (May 1922): 230–31.

Soja, Edward W. *Thirdspace: Journeys to Los Angeles and Other Real-and-Imagined Places*. Oxford: Blackwell, 1996.

"Southern Letters." Editorial. *Double Dealer* 1 (June 1921): 214.

Thompson, T. P. "The Renaissance of the Vieux Carre." *Double Dealer* 3 (February 1922): 86, 88, 89.

Watson, James G. "New Orleans, *The Double Dealer*, and 'New Orleans.'" *American Literature* 56 (1984): 214–26.

Whalen, Mark. *Race, Manhood, and Modernism in America: The Short Story Cycles of Sherwood Anderson and Jean Toomer*. Knoxville: University of Tennessee Press, 2007.

"Wherein We Yawn." *Double Dealer* 2 (October 1921): 127.

A Community Far Afield

Black Mountain College and the Southern Estrangement of the Avant-Garde

Jon Horne Carter

Black Mountain is heretical . . .

—Black Mountain College prospectus, 1952

When John Andrew Rice was fired from his position at Rollins College in Florida in 1933, he dreamed of leaving the world of institutions and founding a nomadic school. In it, students and teachers would travel and study together, starting in England and reading the works of William Shakespeare. The school would have no physical institution, no higher administration, and no board of trustees to weigh it down. Rice had been fired due to a variety of allegations at Rollins, some against his pedagogy, others against his comportment, even his gait. The American Association of University Professors (AAUP) overturned his firing, but Rice and other professors were already moving on. They wanted their own college, a place where teaching and learning would be in the hands of its most passionate practitioners. Robert Wunsch, a drama teacher at Rollins, suggested that Rice and his supporters check out a complex of buildings near the remote town of Black Mountain, not far from Asheville in his native North Carolina. The buildings formed a kind of campus. The complex, built by the Blue Ridge Assembly of the Protestant Church, was fully furnished, outfitted with central heating, and used only during the summers for Christian retreats. It promised isolation. Liking what they saw, the Rollins College defectors rented the campus, breaking away from the growing power and influence of bureaucracy in higher education in the United States.

The list of celebrated intellectuals who were affiliated, visited, or resided at Black Mountain College (BMC) in its twenty-four years of operation is well known. Here I will focus on the narratives and memories of many other individuals who, in the day-to-day operation of the college, shaped a new home from scratch, and did so in a traditional and conservative region of the United States. The creation of BMC became far more than an iconoclastic outpost in the rural South. Just as its campus was etched into the local setting, this "virulently Yankee" community became saturated with the natural and cultural elements of Appalachia. It was out of this process of inhabitation—what the anthropologist Kathleen Stewart calls the "practices and practical knowledges . . . that pick up density and texture as they move through bodies, dreams, dramas and social worldings"—that BMC and the Appalachia of its time became extricated, each marking and transforming the other.[1]

College

I don't belong in institutions.

—John Andrew Rice

Lee Hall was a two-story building with stately columns and a sweeping view across the valley. Prior to the arrival of the Rollins cohort, it had been the center of the Christian retreat, and until Black Mountain College built its own campus a few miles away, it was the educational and residential locus of the college. Classes were conducted on the scenic front porch, and continued by the grand fireplace at night. The fact that Lee Hall had been named after Confederate General Robert E. Lee affirmed the college's sense of itself as a community in exile, haunted by antiheroes and vanquished political projects.

Philosopher of education John Dewey had been part of the AAUP committee reviewing Rice's dismissal at Rollins, and as Rice designed the college around the appealing spaces of Lee Hall, he drew on Dewey's "experience-based" education, premised on equal parts work and study. Students and faculty at BMC would live together, eat together, participate mutually in maintenance and upkeep, and jointly determine the everyday administration of the college. Dewey had urged that students not simply study the principles and conditions that create one's historical present but work *with* them, learning the world in order to refashion it. At BMC, learning and democratic governance would be mutually reinforcing.[2]

Sarah Lawrence College had been recently founded and, along with Swarthmore and Wellesley, offered innovative educational models. Rice set BMC apart from these institutions of progressive education by shifting art to the center of the curriculum.[3] Yet in so doing he openly ridiculed art when it was practiced purely as a means of self-discovery or an expression for personal struggles. At BMC art would be the means to producing well-rounded intellectuals by refining judgment, sense, and taste. The furniture, tapestries, and decor of the early BMC were produced in its material workshops. Rice's work-study model created feedback loops between classroom and workshop such that practical steps of building chairs and weaving curtains also produced foundational concepts within the college curriculum.

As Rice raised funds for BMC among well-known patrons of the arts, a curator at the Museum of Modern Art in New York City recommended Josef Albers as a fit for the college. Albers and his wife Anni arrived at the train depot in Asheville from the fascist purges in Europe. A photograph of the couple from the local newspaper shows them in formal attire, appearing weary and perhaps suffering culture shock.[4] The Alberses were the college's first link to an international avant-garde; at the Bauhaus they had been focused on emergent industrial forms and how artists might intervene in modern life through design innovation in industrial production processes. Once in Appalachia, however, the Alberses immersed themselves in the new surroundings and pioneered new ideas from local materials. Josef seeming to start anew, attempting "to dispel the idealization of the European tradition both in his teaching and in his own art."[5] Pedagogical aims at BMC were not directed at shaping industrial production but toward sculpting individuals, and Albers' courses bypassed the canon of Western art and began with what he called "thinking in situations." Through structured exercises, students sharpened the connection between mind, eye, and hand, developing basic dexterity and skills to allow them to move and think as artists.[6]

At the Bauhaus Albers had worked with glass and urban materials. At BMC he turned his attention to color, theorizing it as a dynamic and unfixed substance dependent upon context.[7] Across the seasons, color was abundant on the surrounding hillsides: "In the fall the leaves turned not just red and yellow, but pink, apricot, burgundy, ochre, and a hundred other heady colors. In spring the undergrowth bloomed canopies of dogwood, mountain laurel (pink geometric blossoms sticky to the touch), and a surprise of wild rhododendron."[8] While BMC struggled for funding, its studios were short of basic supplies, and Albers encouraged students to work with natural materials from the landscape. The Appalachian landscape appears in Albers' own works from this period not as representation but material, and many of the works incorporated local foliage. With the natural world as their source material, the Alberses developed a theory of "found" materials that they named *matière* studies. Tire tracks and foliage, even dung submitted to Albers as a prank, were tested in combination and arrangement as fragments of the natural and human worlds assembled together.[9]

When Anni Albers was at the Bauhaus she worked with industrial fabrics; after arriving at BMC, she initiated a weaving program at the college as the core of a curriculum she called "manual education." In weaving classes Albers began by asking students to imagine themselves in a Peruvian plateau, from a "zero point" of production, where they had to create the artifacts of life from nothing. Students linked the ideas and principles of design, with practices dependent on skill and technique. Trial and error in her workshops provided BMC with tablecloths, curtains, wooden furniture, and other necessities that added life to the Shaker plainness of Lee Hall.[10] During her Bauhaus years, Albers and her peers celebrated an ideal notion of the "designer-craftsman," but one that was savvy about the pitfalls of nostalgic overvaluation of handmade objects against the products of machines. She was similarly critical in her BMC workshops on weaving, woodworking, and vocational arts, and while she mined the local artisanship scene, involving carpenters from the nearby town, she invited them not to demonstrate artisanal tradition per se but to teach what she called "thinking in wood."[11] For Anni Albers, weaving and woodworking were an invitation to sensuous investigation of the simplest materials. Through this investigation students developed the principles of craft and, in so doing, allowed the surrounding material world to shape the college, itself an evolving manifestation of local craft and skill.

Locality

Rice had grown up on farms, and he did not romanticize manual labor. But in the early years of BMC, many faculty and students had read Ralph Barsodi's *Flight from the City* and arrived at the college excited about the chance for personal transformation through rustic independence.[12] Whether the practical tasks of operating the college were personally transformative or not, they began to connect the Black Mountaineers with the surrounding mountain community.[13] Students and faculty hauled coal to power the physical plant from the Western North Carolina Railroad; they felled trees and made wood planks with local farmers.[14] After a day's labor they drove into town to drink beers at Roy's Bar near the train depot. During their time off, students integrated into the cultural setting of Asheville; they saw films at the regional cinema, performing protosituationist pranks (such as firing off cap guns during Westerns),[15] and broke segregation lines by singing with choirs of black churches. Émigrés such as Albers wandered through Asheville department stores and boutiques to practice their English.[16] BMC permeated into the local setting, and the depot of the Asheville–Salisbury train line became an intersection of internationals and visitors to the college, where locals could easily pick out visitors and offer directions to the college grounds.

As students and faculty integrated with their cultural environs, the natural landscape seduced them into the hillsides. They went on long walks in nearby forests and spent time at hidden swimming holes.[17] "At eighteen I nearly fainted with wonder at the ferns and moss thick on the paths outside the buildings that led up the mountain to Blue Ridge," writes Jane Marquis. "My 'first love' and I would climb this trail late at night. I have forgotten him but not the pungency of the fragrant woods or the moonlight on them."[18] Nearby Craggy Dome offered mystical encounters. Some hiked for days, stumbling onto bootleg whiskey operations and knocking on remote shacks surrounded by dogs to ask for directions home.[19] Ruth Sussler describes a gothic Appalachia that beckoned from beyond the college grounds. "Most eerie of my glimpses of a different world in the South were those of chain gangs," she relates, "in striped uniforms and bound together with ankle irons or attached to iron balls that dragged along the dusty road."[20]

The Mountaineers reveled in this out-of-joint South. The urgency of racial integration forced the college to position itself within the political moment, however. When Yale University professor Charles Loram stopped by the college during his survey of "Negro education" in the South, debate over where his graduate assistant, an African American, would sleep exposed the college's fear of confronting segregation directly (he was eventually lodged at the home of a black family nearby). Debates over integration at BMC were recurrent. No student or faculty member ever argued for segregation, and Rice himself favored integration, but he was concerned that BMC would be co-opted by activists whose social and political agendas were not the transformation of higher education most broadly. Zora Neale Hurston, who visited in 1944, echoed that cautious stance. Hurston had been at Rollins during Rice's firing and, familiar with the BMC project from its outset, advised that moving too quickly could undermine the small space for equality that the school had already established, if slowly.

BMC was still in its early and vulnerable stages as an institution, and could not afford to have the town turn against it. If the Ku Klux Klan were to set fire to the school, irrecoverable financial loss would have ended the BMC project completely. European émigrés were shocked by the day-to-day realities of Jim Crow, especially when they ventured from the campus grounds into town. Zoya Slive recalls accidentally drinking from the wrong water fountain in a local department store. "I felt dozens of eyes piercing my back," she notes. "I turned around and saw people staring at me. What did I do wrong? A sign above the water fountain said 'For Colored.'"[21] Slive was among many who reacted against the insularity of BMC. She left the college for the University of Chicago, where she studied sociology and later became a civil rights activist.

In 1936 Louis Adamic, a Yugoslavian journalist, visited the college to write a short column but was so taken that he ended up staying a month. His glowing praise in *Harper's* magazine brought a stream of visiting scholars and artists to BMC and the Asheville area, and their enthusiasm and influence energized the school with cultural currents from bohemian scenes around the country. Thornton Wilder's visit in 1933 involved the public, and his well-attended lectures wowed students and members of the regional community. But after the publication of Adamic's article, BMC was sought out not only by established scholars and artists; lesser-known innovators in countercultural veins arrived searching for community. Henry Miller showed up unannounced and, enchanted by the atmosphere of the college, he later wrote that taking in the view from the front porch of Lee Hall made him "dream of Asia," a telos in his quest for spiritual transcendence.[22] The radical potential of the BMC project was broadened further in 1937 when Aldous Huxley introduced students to Eastern mysticism, including yoga, as a means to break cultural constraints that limit imagination and human potential. As such, new ideas shaped the college and its Mountaineers; they were packaged into radio shows by BMC students and broadcast on local stations, including public and guest lectures, radio dramas, and even the reading of scholarly papers. Later the Asheville radio station thanked BMC for bringing it its highest listenership on record.[23]

Refuge

In 1937 the college purchased nearly 674 acres a few miles away and invited Walter Gropius, the head of the Bauhaus, to design its first campus. The new campus would mean freedom from paying rent, but also a place of their own for the Mountaineers. Gropius's elaborate design proved too expensive, and the final plan by Lawrence Kocher, a retired professor of architecture from the University of Virginia, was initiated in 1940. BMC faculty accepted a 60 percent reduction in pay, and construction was integrated into the curriculum. The Mountaineers worked with a local carpenter and contractor to drive the pilings, dig the foundations, and build twelve structures clustered around a small lake.[24]

As World War II approached, other émigrés followed in the Alberses' footsteps. The idea of BMC as an isolated outpost was no longer accurate, as the community was deeply connected to international conflict and global transformation.[25] Other crafts schools in the region, such as the Penland School of Handicrafts (founded 1923) and the Highlander Folk School (founded 1932), had opened with the goal of both educating mountain communities and preserving their artisanal craftways. A handful of BMC alumni joined the potter and weaving programs at Penland, though BMC differed from these institutions. The college was not preserving community traditions; it was assembling an entirely new community, built of political refugees and cultural exiles—creating a world rather than preserving one. Among them were both pacifists and supporters of U.S. involvement in the war, and they debated vigorously—some arguing that they should submit a letter to the U.S. government declaring the college's position, if they could agree on one.[26]

Students sometimes arrived at campus directly from combat. Ike Nakata arrived at BMC from the Italian front, and brought with him the complete works of Le Corbusier for BMC's struggling library.[27] Ruth Asawa, one of the most highly regarded sculptors to train at BMC, arrived after spending four months in a U.S. internment camp built on a horse-racing track in California, where she and her mother had slept in the horse stalls. Asawa discovered her passion for art from Disney animators who, also interned at the camp, gave sketch classes to fellow prisoners in the racetrack's stands.[28]

During wartime the FBI investigated the BMC campus, interrogating international faculty suspected of espionage or others suspected of Nazi or communist sympathies.[29] Among the international faculty arriving during the war was Heinrich Jalowetz, who fled his position as first conductor in Prague and Cologne. At BMC he re-created the music curriculum in the Germanic tradition through the works of Johann Sebastian Bach, Ludwig van Beethoven, and Johannes Brahms.[30] Jalo, as he was affectionately nicknamed, became one of the most beloved figures in the college's history; his pedagogical and personal style contrasted with that of other émigrés, such as Erwin Straus, whose formal, nearly authoritarian manner typified a conservative Europeanism that ultimately would grate on the sensibilities of the postwar generation of Mountaineers.

With the world's attention turned toward the war, donor contributions to BMC slowed. Austrian chemist Fritz Hansgirg was hired at the college directly out of an internment camp. As a condition of his release to BMC, he could not leave campus without being chaperoned by a U.S. citizen. Walking the property, he discovered large shards of muscovite at the ruins of an old gold mine. Muscovite was essential in the production of certain war instruments, and offered a way to subsidize the college. The Mountaineers rallied to exploit the vein, excited also to contribute to the war effort. In a much remembered chapter of BMC history, the Mountaineers and local miners worked together, the local miners' harmonicas echoing deep inside the tunnels.[31] Though the vein was quickly exhausted, BMC was continually intertwined with faraway global events. Enrollment under the GI Bill increased to over one hundred students, and the student body came from a greater diversity of life experience than ever before. With record enrollment and limited space, the college obtained disassembled military barracks from the Federal Housing Authority, reassembling them on campus.[32] Other donations from the federal government were scattered across BMC's otherwise artisanal setting, including a printing press, meat grinder, dishwasher, office furniture, two typewriters, and one hundred swivel chairs.[33]

Ecosystem

> After ten minutes on the moonlit road, none of the lights from the school were visible to interfere with the vast, heavy, velvety blackness of the sky, nor did sounds of laughter and music penetrate the almost terrifying hush. We stood still, enveloped by the awesome multiplicity of the stars. "Let's get back to the party," said Bill. "The universe gives me the creeps."
>
> —Elaine de Kooning

At the time the college moved to the Lake Eden property, John Rice resigned over an affair with a female student, and BMC struggled to define itself in his absence. Josef Albers had seniority and dedicated much time and energy into mediating conflicts among a rotating cast of vibrant but often conflicting personalities. He canvassed for funding as the school stretched its inconsistent budget. Intergenerational feuding among the original faculty of the 1940s, which at times became quite theatrical, overwhelms many firsthand accounts of the period. In the background, however, faculty spouses and students remained outside the fray and cultivated the communal vitality of BMC. The college was over a decade old, and in that time children had come of age there, faculty and students had left and then returned, and the collective practices of living together had inscribed the site with monuments, narratives, and a powerful sense of itself.

Though BMC was organized around male leadership and did not escape the patriarchal conventions of its time, it is remembered as a setting in which many women felt for the first time that they were equal participants in the making of a community. Women shared duties on the farm, in the dining hall,

Studies Building / Camp Rockmont; 2016. Photo by Jon Horne Carter.

or at the physical plant, and had a voice in meetings regarding strategic is-sues.[34] Francine du Plessix Gray, who would go on to become a highly re-garded feminist essayist, experienced her individual awakening at the college as "symbolic parricide, a purging of the 'ancestral folderol' of childhood."[35] A community of faculty spouses also came together in the background of the college's more widely recited narratives. Though Frank Rice had resigned, his daughter Ann returned to BMC to teach German, and later described a unity among mothers who improvised playpens between the rows of donated mili-tary barracks. They nurtured a generation of toddlers who grew up as natives of the social experiment at BMC.[36]

Once students had spent time at Lake Eden, the Appalachia ecology seemed to permeate them. Students took on a "natural look" and sported lon-ger hair, sandals, and bare feet. They expanded the farm project, raising live-stock for the first time; built several cattle sheds, milking structures, a hog barn, and brooder and laying houses for poultry; and gathered daily suste-nance from the wild bounty of the campus itself.[37] They foraged wild per-simmons, butternuts, walnuts, cress, garlic, dandelions, blackberries, and strawberries, and tea was served in the dining hall made from local sassafras root and spicewood. Student memoirs from this period are awash in bloom-ing mountain laurels, orange azaleas, fields of daffodils, and a dozen strains of orchids that grew across the campus grounds.[38] With the arrival of spring, faculty and students planted trees on the hillside, creating enchanted groves of their own.[39] The memoirs teem with animals: cinnamon brown newts cov-ered walkways after summer rains, and hummingbirds hovered over honeysuckle vines;[40] mice, frogs, and snakes lay hidden in cabinets and closets, and there is even one account of a rattlesnake killed and skinned by a young woman, who converted it into a belt.[41] These tactile practices transformed Rice and Dewey's work-study pedagogy into an inspired communion with the Appalachian material world. When dancer and choreographer Merce Cunningham arrived in 1948, students fetched cattle hides from the barn and built instruments from animal skins for experimental projects taken beyond the traditional piano accompaniment. The extra hides lay stinking in the sun but were later repurposed as theater props.[42] By the time of Cunningham's arrival, the melding of the rural and the avant-garde at BMC culminated in a Dada party, the first of its kind at the college, whose centerpiece was a hanging mobile made entirely of hog bones that had been procured from the kitchen over a period of weeks.[43]

Bohemianism at BMC, emerging across the 1940s, was a powerfully modernist project. That sensibility was all the more excited as it was haunted by the gothic temporality of Southern life. Intimacy with the Lake Eden landscape began to make legible the traces of its premodern inhabitants; David Corkran, who taught English and history at BMC during the late 1940s, recalls taking walks into the hills and immersing himself in wildflowers to escape faculty squabbles, and there he developed a skill for identifying Native American projectile points; he also learned about the previous settlements in the swampy basin around Lake Eden from a barber in the town of Black Mountain who sold these projectile points. When Corkran left BMC he trained in Native American history, and his scholarly research examined that very site, which he determined to have been occupied for centuries by the Cherokee as either a trading post or a manufacturing site for stone tools.[44]

At the same time that the BMC community grew attuned to the resonances of the past that layered the landscape, the passing of some of the college's own members bound it to the land in new ways. Memorials and graves marked the campus with spiritual sites. Best known among these is the Quiet House, built by student Alex Reed after Ted Drier's son was killed in a car accident on nearby mountain roads. The Quiet House was a space of reflection, which Reed built singlehandedly, cutting the beams, setting the stones, and even weaving the curtains.[45] The beloved Jalowetz would pass away as he stepped out of a performance rehearsal in 1946, to be buried in the grove of dogwoods he had admired so much rather than in his native Germany.[46] Chemist Fritz Hansgirg would pass in 1949, from exposure to magnesium in his lab.[47] He was followed by Max Dehn in 1952, who was buried on the shore of Lake Eden.[48] Their deaths layered the campus with the spectrality of loss,

but at the same time muralist Jean Charlot revitalized the college's epistemological horizon, painting large frescoes—titled *Inspiration* and *Knowledge*—on
the pylons supporting the Studies Building. These mythologizing contributions to BMC's landscape were influenced by Charlot's years in Mexico working with muralist Diego Rivera. Lake Eden was becoming a sociocultural
laboratory, where infrastructure and landscape were an artistic medium
through which ideas materialized.[49] "Rarely has either an architect or a student had the opportunity to combine theory and practice of architecture so
closely," writes Paul Bielder, who studied architecture at BMC.[50] This density
of living and experimentation reached its saturation point during the construction of the Minimum House. The house was designed to test affordable
and functional design, and in gathering local stones for its walls students had
accidentally incorporated Jalo's gravestone from the dogwood grove (though
it was returned to the burial site).[51] The affection and attachment to this layered and meaningful campus-home was most visibly expressed during the
forest fires of 1949 when students and teachers dropped their books and fled
to the hills with pails of water as flames encircled the college. Later the Asheville fire chief instructed the BMC community in operating standard fire-
fighting equipment, so that they could defend the place in the future without
so much personal risk.[52]

Limits

> Isn't it interesting that the muddle of one's personal search turns into the
> history of others?
>
> —Mary Caroline Richards

The period of time between Rice's departure and Charles Olson's acceptance
of the title of rector in 1951 brought young faculty to the college who considered themselves emissaries of critical and cultural transformation. Eric Bentley was chief among the provocateurs of this period—an Oxford University
graduate who delighted in prodding the middle-class pretensions of the older
faculty, hardly concealing romantic affairs with female students, and staging
recently translated works of Bertolt Brecht, for which he would become a
well-known expert in the United States. John Foreman taught writing, but
also considered himself a crusader in the desegregation struggle, and he agi-
tated for BMC to clarify its stance. Frances de Graaf was hired as a literary
scholar but became renowned on campus for her refusal to police the boundaries of nude sunbathing, barefootedness, and cut-off jeans. After Bentley left

BMC he published "Report to the Academy" in the Partisan Review, claiming that although the experimental project at BMC had far surpassed the "educational primitivism" that dominated its early goals, it was incapable of producing the well-roundedness in students to which Rice and its founders had aspired. The campus was too prone to crisis.[53] Every few years the community descended into personal and ideological battles that it survived only by cutting out a part of itself;[54] by the late 1940s the school had produced defectors and splinter groups, even entirely new communities whose members packed up and left. Some went to the West Coast, others to Stony Point commune in upstate New York, but all were determined to practice ideals they felt were constrained by the insistence that BMC remain first and foremost a college institution.

To combat the cliquishness and formation of adversarial factions on campus, Josef Albers proposed thematic summer institutes. The intensity and brevity of these sessions attracted BMC's most celebrated luminaries, and by the late 1940s the summer institutes had become a home for the postwar avant-garde. The campus, meanwhile, was abuzz with creative intensity and invention as greater numbers of students enrolled under the GI Bill, bringing with them a greater diversity of class backgrounds and life experience than had been the case before. Merce Cunningham was reported to have been delighted when a patient escaped from a nearby mental hospital and wandered onto campus, meshing seamlessly into the lively conversations among students, fitting into the campus energy, until an orderly arrived at return him to the hospital.[55]

Playful and energized, the summer institutes shifted BMC to an entirely American, rather than European, postwar vision of literature and the arts. The arrival of R. Buckminster Fuller and John Cage in 1948 reorganized pedagogy and experimentation around their complementary yet opposite styles; Fuller was drawn to the utopian potential of engineering, and Cage to role of chance and play in disrupting the classical forms of the past.[56] Fuller's presence at the summer institutes attracted a number of students from Chicago's Institute of Design, whose urban style juxtaposed against the earthy bohemianism cultivated by the Mountaineers at Lake Eden. Fuller embodied the creative cross-pollination that BMC had nurtured for years, and while his famed geodesic dome is iconic within the history of BMC, Fuller was also training with Cunningham in dance while producing his theory of the dome; at the end of that summer session Fuller was the dramatic lead in Cage's production of Eric Satie's play *The Ruse of Medusa*. The college's combination of intellectual intensity and limited workspace was visible in Cage's new theory of method produced at BMC, particularly in which different formal techniques "brushed" against one another in an immanent field of inventiveness and production.[57] This mode of chaotic collaboration was materialized in Cage's first "happening," staged during the summer of 1947, in a scripted evening of "purposeful purposelessness." The overlapping and disjointed performances at the heart of the happening were staged in the dining hall, at the literal intersection of the college.[58] Charles Olson and M. C. Richards read their poetry, Robert Rauschenberg showed his paintings and playing a gramophone, David Tudor played piano compositions, Merce Cunningham danced, and Cage read and lectured with long silences from atop a ladder while a dog milled about and a baby cried. The happenings staged by Alan Kaprow during the 1960s configure prominently into the history of countercultural production of that later period, but Cage's innovation in mixed media at BMC emerged much earlier as an expression of a particular community forging space in arts and literature in the interests of antidisciplinarity.

By the end of the 1940s BMC no longer offered an education organized around art but had itself become a community of artists. Debates about pedagogy were supplanted by a fascination with the alchemy of creative practice. In an effort to add stability to the kinetic and heterodox scene, Josef Albers invited a contingent of Quakers to join the college. Meanwhile, the school also received defectors from Olivet College who were protesting the takeover of their college by conservative administrators;[59] BMC was known by then as a safe zone for dissident faculty. Joel Oppenheimer, who would become one of the celebrated poets of BMC, dropped out of sciences and engineering at Cornell University and arrived at Black Mountain as Quakers piloted World War I weapons carriers to collect campus garbage. In the summer of 1948, what became known as BMC's Homosexual Summer, writing instructor Paul Goodman's impact on the campus was made when his open and adventurous sexuality inspired many students to experiment themselves. Just a few years earlier, the topic of homosexuality at BMC had been something to be avoided; after Bob Wunsch, a founding member of the college, was caught by police in his car with a local marine and charged with "crimes against nature," he left BMC in the middle of the night and refused all contact from the school thereafter. Following Goodman's arrival, however, sexual experimentation was notable to the degree that many faculty resigned. By the spring of 1949, all remaining European faculty had moved on except Josef Albers.[60] But when Albers took a position at Yale University in 1950, the pedagogical horizon shifted to an entirely American view of the arts.[61]

Civilization

> Supercool pose of silence or monosyllabic utterances, bare feet, men's dark
> glasses and long hair, easygoing nudism and bisexuality—fads of the just
> nascent Beat Generation, precursors of the 1960's Movement style. (I hadn't
> skimped on Black Mountain's brand of unisex macho, chopping off my hair as
> short and jagged as a contemporary punk's.)
>
> —Francine du Plessix Gray

Charles Olson visited BMC for the summer institute of 1949 and, following
Albers's departure, returned. Faculty and students regarded him as a visionary, and believed he was the person to reignite the energy of the college. Olson was just back from the Yucatan Peninsula in Mexico, where he had been
studying Mayan glyphs. He regarded them as a pre-Homeric writing system,
from which one could imagine recasting Western social worlds by digging into
other linguistic foundations. The glyphs study fueled Olson's major break-
through at BMC, his notion of "composition by field," which shifted form and
voice in American poetry. At BMC Olson was dynamic and energetic, and in a
short time Lake Eden was saturated with his thinking and style. The pursuit of
refinement and beauty that had the defined the Alberses' influence on BMC
gave way to the quest for artistic immediacy that propelled the postwar U.S.
avant-garde. Olson's daunting standards for writerly authenticity required
more from students than what he called the "trivial recitals."[62] He demanded
historically transformative writing—which, in the case of the postwar generation, meant writing that overcame the alienation from experience that was
driving suburbanization and consumer capitalism.

Enrollment under the GI Bill waned and the college was left with fifteen
students. Faculty shrunk to nine. Still, the course catalog of 1953 was the largest ever, an expression of the renewed ambition and enthusiasm driving those
who remained. Olson moved to establish what he called a "Chinese system"
of year-round institute, in which faculty would come and go as suited them to
best utilize their creative energies.[63] Poet Robert Creeley arrived in 1954 after
years of correspondence with Olson, and they fashioned an artists' colony
with what remained of BMC. The residents of the final years invented a new
voice of American literature projected through a new journal created to both
publicize the college and disseminate its vision. Following his interest in
"primitivity," Olson initially titled it *Origin*, but then renamed it *Black Mountain Review*. Students who apprenticed in bookbinding with Anaïs Nin during her 1954 visit printed the first edition. The *Black Mountain Review* was the

instrument by which the creative vitality of the college left Appalachia, and was woven into countercultural scenes around the United States.

Ruins

When Creeley arrived in 1954, he found what he later described as a "highly volatile and articulate people in a rather extraordinary circumstance of isolation."[64] The physical campus was deteriorating, and longtime donors questioned whether any institution remained. Despite a decline in funding, the creative spirit of the college thrived. Innovative work was produced in the new ceramics institute, and workshops were opened for photography, woodworking, and bookbinding. Money was increasingly scarce, and Olson sold the beef cattle, then portions of the property, to carry the college through one semester at a time.[65] By 1954 there were no more than ten BMC participants left, and the climate was becoming increasingly ascetic. There was a suicide attempt.[66] The kitchen had been closed for several years, and when they were desperate, the Mountaineers shoplifted from the local grocery. There were weeks of nothing but okra and a mystery concoction the Mountaineers called "wheat bubbles."[67]

In his monumental history of BMC, Martin Duberman suggests that it was the drunken wrecking of a Buick Roadmaster on the way back from a bar in Asheville that marked the final chapter for the college; Creeley and others purposefully crashed it into a campus building as a repudiation of the "phoniness" of the 1950s. In the final years, poisonous snakes abounded across the campus, and kudzu vines crept over buildings and footpaths. When the college shuttered in 1957, the Mountaineers scattered to different bohemian scenes across the country: Stony Point colony in upstate New York, New York City, and San Francisco, where BMC alumni were creating new communities. One of the only alums to remain in the area was Jonathan Williams, who for a few years maintained a retreat for former Mountaineers to psychologically decompress from the intensity of the college in its final days.

Before he relocated back to New England, Olson sold the remainder of the college property to a Christian summer camp called Rockmont. The unusual and transgressive singularity of Black Mountain College's experiment is all the more stark as it is bookended by traditional Christian congregationalism and worship, from the Blue Ridge Assembly to Camp Rockmont. Rockmont continues to manage the site today. The college's iconic Studies Building, constructed in 1941 still perches at the edge of Lake Eden as an unmarked and

Deep in the rhododendrons. Photo by Jon Horne Carter.

silent monument, alive with summer campers and dormant during the winter. The Black Mountain Museum and Arts Center was founded in downtown Asheville in 1993 as a gallery and research center, and it organizes annual conferences on the college as well as an artists' gathering on Lake Eden that seeks the spark of Cage's now mythical happening.[68] Many of the liberal arts colleges influenced by BMC and flourishing in the space created by its impact on higher education, such as Evergreen State College, Marlboro College, and the New College of Florida, among others—still offer alternative models to standardized pedagogy. Today at the Lake Eden site, Jean Charlot's frescoes on the pillars of the Studies Building are but faint traces in the concrete. The Quiet House has been demolished. The Minimum House has been renovated to a contemporary style. Jalo's and Dehn's gravesites are enclosed within re-zoned, residential lots. The legacy of the college, however, grows. Perhaps it is best captured by Olson's phrase, uttered at the time of BMC's shuttering in 1957: "Her flag flies."[69]

Notes

1. Stewart, *Ordinary Affects*, 1–3.
2. Dewey, *Experience and Education*.
3. Reynolds, "Progressive Ideals," 1–2.
4. Harris, *The Arts at Black Mountain College*, 10.
5. Duberman, *Black Mountain*, 61.
6. Horowitz and Danilowitz, *Josef Albers*, 73.
7. Ellert, "The Bauhaus and Black Mountain College," 148.
8. Lane, *Black Mountain College*, 90.

9. Horowitz and Danilowitz, *Josef Albers*, 127; Troy, *Anni Albers and Ancient American Textiles*, 130.

10. Duberman, *Black Mountain*, 20, 76.

11. Lane, *Black Mountain College*, 38.

12. Ibid., 42.

13. Duberman, *Black Mountain*, 42.

14. Lane, *Black Mountain College*, 85.

15. Duberman, *Black Mountain*, 102.

16. Lane, *Black Mountain College*, 45.

17. Ibid., 67.

18. Jane Marquis, quoted in Lane, *Black Mountain College*, 90.

19. Ibid., 46.

20. Ruth Sussler, quoted in Lane, *Black Mountain College*, 147.

21. Zoya Slive, quoted in Lane, *Black Mountain College*, 97.

22. Benfey, *Red Brick, Black Mountain, White Clay*, 146.

23. Duberman, *Black Mountain*, 105; Smith and South, *Black Mountain College*, 107.

24. Duberman, *Black Mountain*, 163; Smith and South, *Black Mountain College*, 49.

25. Harris, *The Arts at Black Mountain College*, 53.

26. Lane, *Black Mountain College*, 77.

27. Ibid., 149.

28. Lanier and Weverka, "Internment."

29. Harris, *The Arts at Black Mountain College*, 168.

30. Ibid., 35.

31. Duberman, *Black Mountain*, 166; Harris, *The Arts at Black Mountain College*, 67.

32. Rice, *I Came Out of the Eighteenth Century*, 229.

33. Duberman, *Black Mountain*, 272.

34. Lane, *Black Mountain College*, 241.

35. Ibid., 301.

36. Ibid., 230–31.

37. Ibid., 134.

38. Ibid., 138–39.

39. Ibid., 208.

40. Ibid., 137.

41. Ibid., 208.

42. Ibid., 261.

43. Duberman, *Black Mountain*, 217.

44. Lane, *Black Mountain College*, 142.

45. Smith and South, *Black Mountain College*, 59.

46. Lane, *Black Mountain College*, 102.

47. Smith and South, *Black Mountain College*, 81.

48. Ibid., 80.

49. Brody Creeley, and Power, *Black Mountain College*, 77.

50. Smith and South, *Black Mountain College*, 63.

51. Duberman, *Black Mountain*, 273.

52. Smith and South, *Black Mountain College*, 72.

53. Lane, *Black Mountain College*, 110–18.

54. Ibid., 228.

55. Harris, *The Arts at Black Mountain College*, 108; Duberman, *Black Mountain*, 279.

56. Diaz, *The Experimenters*, 6–8.

57. Lane, *Black Mountain College*, 250.

58. Voyce, *Poetic Community*, 58–59.

59. Duberman, *Black Mountain*, 320.

60. Ibid., 225.

61. Ibid., 330.

62. Duberman, *Black Mountain*, 324; Harris, *The Arts at Black Mountain College*, 175, 182.

63. Duberman, *Black Mountain*, 340.

64. Ibid., 394; Harris, *The Arts at Black Mountain College*, 182.

65. Duberman, *Black Mountain*, 407.

66. Ibid., 401.

67. Lane, *Black Mountain College*, 167.

68. Black Mountain College Museum and Arts Center, http://www.blackmountaincollege.org/home.

69. Duberman, *Black Mountain*, 412.

References

Adamic, Louis. "Education on a Mountain." *Harper's*, April 1936, 516–29.

Benfey, Christopher. *Red Brick, Black Mountain, White Clay: Reflections on Art, Family, and Survival*. New York: Penguin, 2012.

Brody, Martin, Robert Creeley, and Kevin Power. *Black Mountain College: Experiment in Art*, edited by Vincent Katz. Cambridge, MA: MIT Press, 2013.

Dewey, John. *Democracy and Education*. New York: Macmillan, 1916.

———. *Experience and Education: The Kappa Delta Pi Lecture Series*. New York: Touchstone, 1997. Originally published 1938.

Diaz, Eva. *The Experimenters: Chance and Design at Black Mountain College*. Chicago: University of Chicago Press, 2015.

Duberman, Martin. *Black Mountain: An Exploration in Community*. Evanston, IL: Northwestern University Press, 2009.

Ellert, JoAnn C. "The Bauhaus and Black Mountain College." *Journal of General Education* 24 (1972): 144–52.

Gray, Francine du Plessix. "Black Mountain: The Breaking (and Making) of a Writer." In *Adam & Eve and the City: Selected Nonfiction*, 20. New York: Simon and Schuster, 1987.

Harris, Mary Emma. *The Arts at Black Mountain College*. Reprint ed. Cambridge, MA: MIT Press, 2002.

Horowitz, Frederick A., and Brenda Danilowitz. *Josef Albers: To Open Eyes*. London: Phaidon, 2009.

Katz, Vincent, ed. *Black Mountain College: Experiment in Art*. Cambridge, MA: MIT Press, 2013.

Lane, Melvin, ed. *Black Mountain College: Sprouted Seeds: An Anthology of Personal Accounts*. 1st ed. Knoxville: University of Tennessee Press, 2001.

Lanier, Addie, and Peter Weverka. "Internment." http://www.ruthasawa.com /internment/.

Reynolds, Katherine. "Progressive Ideals and Experimental Higher Education: The Example of John Dewey and Black Mountain College." *Education and Culture* 14 (1997): 1–9.

Rice, John. *I Came Out of the Eighteenth Century*. Columbia: University of South Carolina Press, 2014.

Smith, Anne Chesky, and Heather South. *Black Mountain College: Images of America*. Charleston, SC: Arcadia, 2014.

Stewart, Kathleen. *Ordinary Affects*. Durham, NC: Duke University Press, 2007.

Troy, Virginia. *Anni Albers and Ancient American Textiles: From Bauhaus to Black Mountain*. Burlington, VT: Ashgate, 2002.

Voyce, Stephen. *Poetic Community: Avant-Garde Activism and Cold War Culture*. Toronto: University of Toronto Press, 2013.

James Agee and the Southern Superreal

Lindsey A. Freeman

... to the local hipsters; a handful of hyper-literate hillbillies who spoke in reading lists, all of which began and ended with James Agee.

—Steve Earle

November 8, 1995, Thompson-Boling Arena, Knoxville, Tennessee. It is a Wednesday night, and I am seventeen. Michael Stipe, the bald, charismatic lead vocalist for the band R.E.M. takes the microphone, settles the crowd, and asks for quiet. With his long, thin arm he holds up James Agee's *A Death in the Family* and reads from "Knoxville: Summer 1915":

> On the rough wet grass of the backyard my father and mother have spread quilts. We all lie there, my mother, my father, my uncle, my aunt, and I too am lying there . . . They are not talking much, and the talk is quiet, of nothing in particular, of nothing at all in particular, of nothing at all. The stars are wide and alive, they seem each like a smile of great sweetness and they are very near. All my people are larger bodies than mine, quiet with voices gentle and meaningless like the voices of sleeping birds. One is an artist, he is living at home. One is a musician, she is living at home. One is my mother who is good to me. One is my father who is good to me. By some chance, here they are, all on this earth; and who shall ever tell the sorrow of being on this earth, lying, on quilts, on the grass, in a summer evening, among the sounds of the night. May God bless my people, my uncle, my aunt, my mother, my good father, oh, remember them kindly in their time of trouble; and in the hour of their taking away.
> After a little I am taken in and put to bed. Sleep, soft smiling, draws me unto her: and those receive me, who quietly treat me, as one familiar and well-beloved in that home: but will not, oh, will not, not now, not ever; but will not ever tell me who I am.[1]

From the stage, Stipe, my first Michel Foucault, called it one of the most beautiful passages in American letters and urged the audience to feel proud of this city, a place capable of producing such a writer. That was my introduction to Agee: "Knoxville: Summer 1915," another hit delivered along with the R.E.M.

songs "What's the Frequency Kenneth," "Losing My Religion," "Strange Currencies," "Country Feedback," and "Star 69."[2]

The weekend after the R.E.M. show I went to McKay's used bookstore and bought *A Death in the Family*. It had the ugliest cover of any book I had ever seen: a weird old princess phone and a cheap bouquet of sickly pale, almost translucent flowers floating on a Stilton blue background. There is no way I would have picked up that book at random; Stipe had pushed me in its direction. Purchase made, I drove to the Fort Sanders area of North Knoxville where Agee had lived, near the University of Tennessee and not far from my high school. I parked my 1966 Volkswagen Beetle on a hill littered with the exoskeletons of expired beer cans and the remains of cigarettes, wormy from a recent rain. I looked out across the city. From where I sat, I could see the Sunsphere—Knoxville's twenty-four-karat answer to the Eiffel Tower and the major relic left over from the 1982 World's Fair. The gold glass of the dome gleamed garishly as I began to read: "We are talking now of summer evenings in Knoxville, Tennessee in the time that I lived there so successfully disguised to myself as a child." Immediately I felt known by this author, who had died decades before I was born.

I continued reading for an hour or more without shifting my position, the book poised stiffly on the steering wheel, until I became overwhelmed with this novelistic version of Knoxville, more symphonic than the one I knew. I had never before read a piece of literature set near the place I lived. Moreover, I had never before thought of Knoxville as the subject or incubator of literature and poetics. I hadn't yet encountered the poet Nikki Giovanni, or read any early Cormac McCarthy novels, and although I remembered the thick spine on the bookshelf and knew the TV miniseries *Roots* had been a huge cultural event in 1977, I didn't know Alex Haley was from Knoxville. Back then I was guilty of thinking of the city as only a "scruffy little town."[3] I even participated in the local tradition of referring to the place disparagingly as "Knox Vegas." It took the combination of Agee and Stipe, and a teenage afternoon spent reading in my car, to open me up to another way of seeing the city I thought familiar.

The experience of reading *A Death in the Family* in the actual setting of the novel was vertiginous: time and space were sent whirling as I sat in my midcentury car in the mid-1990s with words written in the 1930s about Knoxville in 1915 echoing in my head in the voice of a contemporary rock 'n' roller from Decatur, Georgia. Stipe's voice and Agee's sentences suffused gritty Knoxville with an elegant excess, "articulating a second, poetic geography on top of the geography of the literal," and I was pulled up by my lapels into an experience of the southern superreal.[4]

Superrealism

Surrealism began in France around 1919 with a small grouplet of committed artists, including Louis Aragon, André Breton, Robert Desnos, Paul Éluard, and Philippe Soupault. When surrealism first appeared in the United States it was mistranslated—or perhaps, more accurately, it was reinterpreted and embellished through the American tendency to aggrandize and called *superrealism*. The first major exhibition of European surrealist art in the United States was held in 1931 at the Wadsworth Atheneum in Hartford, Connecticut, an unlikely place for a show of this magnitude. The exhibition, titled *Newer Super-Realism*, included works by Salvador Dali, Marcel Duchamp, Max Ernst, Man Ray, Joan Miró, Pablo Picasso, and others.

A year later the show moved to the Julien Levy Gallery in Manhattan and was slightly renamed as *The Super-Realists*. Although Levy knew Breton personally, he was relieved the French artist did not have a hand in curating the show. He knew Breton's version of the exhibition would have been "manifesto-heavy" and that "it might have collapsed of its own rigidity." Instead, as Levy wrote in his memoir, he "wished to present a paraphrase which would offer Surrealism in the language of the new world rather than a translation in the rhetoric of the old."[5] He was hoping to create an American surrealism with its own vernacular, distinct from its European counterpart.

Superrealism remained in the descriptive arsenal for this kind of art until the late 1930s, when it fizzled out and surrealism became the dominant way to talk about it. This linguistic practice linked surrealism more closely to Breton, his group, his enemies, and their political concerns—particularly the battles over communism and the revolutionary potential of art. A side effect of the narrowing vocabulary was that Americans were typically not thought of as practitioners of surrealist arts. Those who were often denied the connection, either out of fear of rejection by American audiences or due to an inability or unwillingness to align themselves with particular surrealist or similar factions.[6]

The surrealists and their similars practiced a radical reexamination of the everyday and turned it into art: they took ordinary objects and removed them from their contexts to produce strange effects; they were inspired by Sigmund Freud, and looked to the unconscious, dreams, nightmares, odd juxtapositions, and chance to reevaluate modern life; and they used techniques in the arts of assemblage such as collecting, bricolage, cut-up, and montage to shift perceptions. This is what Agee did in his most superreal moments of writing, and these were perhaps his best moments.

Agee moved in and around surrealist circles. He was a regular contributor to *transition*, a literary magazine for modernist and experimental writing, which was known as the "American surrealist review."[7] The journal grabbed attention in 1929 when its editor Eugène Jolas issued a manifesto for new kinds of writing that began, "Tired of the spectacle of short stories, novels, poems, and plays still under the hegemony of the banal word, monotonous syntax, static psychology, descriptive naturalism, and desirous of crystallizing a viewpoint. . . . Narrative is not mere anecdote, but the projection of a metamorphosis of reality. . . . The literary creator has the right to disintegrate the primal matter of words imposed on him by textbooks and dictionaries." Agee was not among those who explicitly signed, but it is safe to say that he followed the spirit of the proclamation.[8]

It is unknown whether Agee made it to the *Newer Super-Realism* show at Levy's gallery, but he did check out the 1937 exhibition *Fantastic Art, Dada, Surrealism* curated by Alfred Barr at the Museum of Modern Art. The show deeply moved him, and he wrote about it in his journal and in letters.[9] In January 1938, a year and a half after a research trip with the photographer Walker Evans to Alabama to collect material for what would become *Let Us Now Praise Famous Men*, Agee wrote in his journal, "It is funny if I am a surrealist."[10] This reflection comes after he was asked to submit some poems to the Danish journal *Konkretion*, which had a surrealist bent. Agee found the idea entertaining; he was amused that his work could be classified in this way. But the bracketing was not off the mark; his work was getting weirder, and he was thinking about the surrealist arts as he was writing new projects and as he was reworking his notes from his time in Alabama.

Agee's bundles of text fit nicely in *Konkretion* and *transition*, saddled next to a poem by Ernst or resting behind a Duchamp cover image of a silver comb on a cool gray background. His sentences could also have been aimed and shot like an arrow, hitting a bull's-eye placed at the back of the little bookstore in Paris where the College of Sociology held its meetings in the years 1937–39. Although Agee never attended the meetings, and it is unlikely that any members read his work during the two-year period in which the group was active, his efforts rhymed with the college's attempts to approach sociology at a slant; to reenchant everyday life; to break away from Breton's surrealism; to infuse sociological inquiry with a "moral meaning"; and to create a kind of "diagonal science," a poetic approach to the study of social life that combined "the web of dreams with the chain of knowledge."[11]

Southern Superrealism

Although the term *superrealism* faded from regular usage by the mid-twentieth century, it remained suspended in history, in a kind of coma, available for resuscitation. In 1997 Jonathan Veitch attempted to revive it with his book *American Superrealism*, an examination of the writings of Nathaniel West and the politics of representation in the 1930s. Veitch argues that in the context of the United States, *superrealism* has some real advantages over *surrealism*: "While both *sur* and *super* can be used almost interchangeably to mean 'on,' 'upon,' 'over,' the latter has assumed a special place in the American lexicon that speaks to the country's preoccupation with size, speed, and quantity—as in the supermarket, superhighway, superpower, Superman. In short, it is embedded in American life. . . . In addition, superrealism is a compound word, the first part of which acts as an intensifier . . . upon which more traditional forms of realism rely."[12]

Veitch's *American Superrealism* is a study of an author and his body of work, twentieth-century avant-garde movements, and the representation of politics and art. A similar book could be written about Agee, but instead of West's Manhattan or California (though Agee dipped his toes in those places too), the regional focus would point south; tenant farmers and Knoxvillians would replace Miss Lonelyhearts and the cast of characters found on Hollywood Boulevard. And instead of existential commentaries on the entertainment business and the loss of the American dream, it would be full of sociology at a slant and experimental writing—it could be called *Southern Superrealism*.

Southern superrealism is not yet a canonized art movement, nor is it a social science. It has no self-appointed leaders or manifestos, no museum retrospectives, no scholarly journals, and it has not been established as a field of literature—at least not yet. Like the line in the R.E.M. song, it is "a mean idea to call my own."[13] Southern superrealism can be thought of as a flavor of American superrealism, though one with a regional focus that folds in the geography, flora, fauna, machines, characters, and cultural contradictions of the South. Texts of Southern superrealism complicate ideas about American superrealism by bringing in a region of the country far removed from Levy's New York art gallery scene and West's warped Los Angeles. In examples from *Let Us Now Praise Famous Men* and *A Death in the Family*, we see some of the regional peculiarities commingling with and rubbing up against the rest of American culture: Agee piles on scraps of cotton, a broken watch, broken hearts, the red clay of Alabama, the gay and gritty streets of urban-Appalachian Knoxville, the Smoky Mountains, a Charlie Chaplin film, screeds of extreme empathy, poems, memories, dreams, nightmares, not enough whiskey, too much whiskey, car wrecks, and sexual fantasies. In these works the unconscious and the conscious commix, the poetic crosses the prosaic, the modern scrapes against the traditional, and the city and the country do the Tennessee Waltz.

Journalism and the Avant-Garde

Throughout the 1930s and 1940s, James Agee and Walker Evans were living bohemian lifestyles, consuming avant-garde ideas, hanging out with surrealists and their similars, and experimenting with form. Agee was not a self-identifying surrealist or superrealist, but he was spending time with artists deeply involved in those aesthetics and methods. He used some of those methods, combining them with his own highly lyrical style, to create something altogether new. The pair's contact with surrealists occurred mostly in New York, but Evans spent some time in Paris as well, where he studied French, read the poems of Charles Baudelaire and Arthur Rimbaud, and experienced the European avant-garde firsthand. Agee remained stateside, writing and rewriting, his style evolving with every paragraph.

While in New York, Agee worked for a series of magazines published by Henry Luce: *Fortune, The Nation, Time, Life*—not exactly bohemian outlets, although he was writing for those too. Writing for *Fortune*, Agee's first job out of college, seemed an especially odd fit, the pairing of a magazine reporting on wealth, economics, and the concerns of modern capitalists with a writer of lyrical poetry who had an interest in the proletariat and flirtations with Marxism and anarchism. Luce believed that talented writers could be trained to write about anything, and he was unconcerned with the rest (at least at the beginning of the relationship). As if to test the theory, Agee's assignments ran the gamut—the orchid trade, vacation cruises, industrial smoke; but he was also given a lot of Southern assignments because of his Tennessee roots and interest in the region.[14] Ensconced in an office on the fifty-second floor of the Chrysler building, the most gorgeous tower in all of Manhattan, with Benzedrine on one side of his desk, whiskey on the other, and the record player turned up to its highest volume, Agee wrote about the Tennessee Valley Authority, cockfighting and, most famously, tenant farmers in Alabama.

The Alabama project began in the summer of 1936; on *Fortune's* dime, Agee and Evans road-tripped, bohemian style, to Mills Hill, Alabama, about thirty miles south of Tuscaloosa. There they interviewed, observed, fantasized, photographed, and wrote about three tenant farming families.[15] The article was to appear in the magazine's Life and Circumstances department, but it never did; *Fortune* refused to run the piece. The historical record bares no clear indication of why, but it is likely that it was just too weird. Agee had produced something that was too subversive, too avant-garde, too out of step with contemporary documentary reporting, and much too long. The first finished draft stretched to thirty thousand words.[16] When the work finally appeared in 1941 as the book *Let Us Now Praise Famous Men*, it was a very different text from the one that was originally submitted to *Fortune*; its four-hundred-plus pages were far stranger, richer, and more sprawling and superreal than Luce—or, frankly, anyone—might have imagined.

Let Us Now Praise Famous Men

At this point in his career Agee wanted to push the limits of his writing—to push even beyond writing. At the start of *Let Us Now Praise Famous Men* he makes this wish explicit: "If I could do it, I'd do no writing at all here. It would be photographs; the rest would be fragments of cloth, bits of cotton, lumps of earth, records of speech, pieces of wood and iron, phials of odors, plates of food and excrement. . . . A piece of the body torn out by the roots might be more to the point."[17] In front of this vivid disclaimer, Evans's photographs begin the book without commentary. After the black-and-white images, the text is wild; Agee attempts to think and to represent everyday life in the dehumanizing vortex of 1930s tenant farming Alabama through its own twisted logic. He stacks up nearly every sensation, every smell, every stitch on threadbare clothes, and every inch of the knotty pine, bleached bone-white, that composes the ramshackle houses of the farmers' families. He really works at disturbing the surface of things. Like a game of Jenga, he pokes at this reality, removes a piece, and places it on top of the others, drawing our attention to the presence of absences and the precariousness of a life lived on the edge of collapse.

Agee's dazzling sentences animate a life deadened and dulled by exploitation through detailed descriptions that defy the actual. He tries every method he can borrow or invent. In his efforts, he delves into the seemingly insignificant, the tedious, and the inglorious and then shows us the terrible significance of such things. The cupboard of one of the families is described as "comic or even surrealist in this setting, as a frigidaire might" because of its middle-classness and its connection to contemporary advertising campaigns, so far removed from the tenant farmer's everyday experience. Four full pages are dedicated to overalls, where the simple garment is subjected to a sartorial examination, and ultimately a celebration:

> overalls are a garment native to this country . . . of the southern rural American working man: they are his uniform, the badge and proclamation of his peasantry . . . the cloven halls for the legs, the strong-seamed, structured opening for the genitals, the broad horizontal at the waist, the slant thigh pockets, the buttons at the point of each hip on the breast, the geometric structures of the usages of the simpler trades—the complexed seams of utilitarian pockets which are so brightly picked out against darkness when the seam-threadings, double and triple stitched, are still white, so that a new suit of overalls has among its beauties those of a blueprint: and they are a map of a working man.

The cupboard and the overalls are just a couple of the profane illuminations that pop out of the text. In their descriptions Agee brings "the immense forces of 'atmosphere' concealed in these things to the point of explosion," as Walter Benjamin writes in his essay on surrealism.[18]

With this approach Agee creates a strange ethnography of Southern super-realism, made all the more exotic because of the proximity of this depressed pocket of rural Alabama to the readers of *Fortune*, the citizens of the modern cities of the South and the greater United States, and even to Agee and Evans themselves.[19] Roy Stryker, the director of the Resettlement Administration that Evans was working for, described one aim of his agency as "introducing America to Americans."[20] Like the past, poverty sometimes seems to belong to another country. The geographical closeness and yet cultural remove mark the world of the tenant farmers as a place of fascination, not unlike ethnographies of tribes deep in the Amazon or of Aboriginal communities in the sparsest corners of Australia.

In superreal Hale County, Alabama, it is not only the experience of spatial distance that is warped; time works differently too. Agee writes by lamplight about the death of his watch battery and his greater temporal disorientation. He has no idea the time of night, the day of the week, or the calendar date: "The dollar watch bought a few days ago . . . ran out seventeen minutes past ten the day before yesterday morning, and time by machine measure was over for me at that hour; and is a monument."[21] For his stay in Alabama, Agee abandoned the clock-obsessed, deadline-driven New York magazine world for the circadian rhythm of the farming cycle measured by the rough and blistered hour and minute hands of exhaustion. He tried to labor like the tenant farmers, to work each day until he simply couldn't work anymore, or as they said: "from *can* to *can't*." As Evans wrote in his introductory essay to *Let Us Now Praise Famous Men*, Agee "worked in what looked like a rush and a rage. In Alabama he was possessed with the business, jamming it all into the days and nights. He must not have slept. He was driven to see all he could of the families' day, starting of course at dawn."[22]

In *Let Us Now Praise Famous Men* clocks, like watches, are rare. When they make an appearance, they are typically dead or severely incorrect. If a clock ticks, each harsh tone becomes a monument to another lick of life stolen. Utilizing the surrealist technique of bricolage, Agee shows how the monstrous Frankensteined family house magnifies the effect: "their home, as it is, in whose hollow heart resounds the loud zinc flickering heartbeat of the cheap alarm two hours advanced upon false time; a human shelter, a strangely lined nest, a creature of killed pine, stitched together with nails into about a rude a garment against the hostilities of heaven as a human family may wear."[23] The family home is an inadequate overcoat roughly crafted out of what was handy. Inside, their telltale hearts beat troublesome arrhythmias, out of time, out of step with the times, warning that time is short.

Agee attempted to scribble it all down: their lives, the injustice, his reactions. Every emotion and every object was subject to his intense scrutiny. In the years that it took for the book to be published, he kept working it, jostling the order of things, stretching the limits of the form. In the end Agee created what the French historian Michel de Certeau alludes to in his ruminations on the writing of history: a "literature of ellipsis, an art of expounding on scraps and remnants, or the feeling of a question."[24] Agee's sentences announce the fact that language is always already in the process of failing and that that process itself is a form of creation.

A Death in the Family

Agee's best work is about the South; it is also about himself. *Let Us Now Praise Famous Men* can be thought of as a lead-up to his most autobiographical and arguably ethnographic work, *A Death in the Family*. Throughout *Let Us Now Praise Famous Men* he identifies with the tenant farmers, at one point writing, "I certainly felt that they were my own people, and wanted them to be, more than any other kind of people in the world."[25] Agee felt that by being in the South, and not the genteel part, he was pulling on the Ariadne's thread of his Appalachian heritage, leading him through the labyrinth of his past.

Although he never moved back to Tennessee, Agee's past was working on him consciously and unconsciously, and up until his death he was trying to write his lost Knoxville—trying to conjure the memories of the industrial city on the Tennessee River, to catch them as they drifted into his thoughts. This process began with "Knoxville: Summer 1915." Agee claimed that he dashed the piece off in about an hour and a half in a process not unlike automatic writing:

> I was sketching around, vaguely, on a possible autobiographical novel (about 1937), and was so much involved and interested in early child-hood memories. I was greatly interested in improvisatory writing, as against carefully composed, multiple-draft writing: i.e., with a kind of parallel to improvisation in jazz, to a certain kind of "genuine" lyric which I thought should be purely improvised. This text turned up more out of both states of mind than anything else: specifically, remembrance of the way water from the garden hoses looked and sounded at twilight. This brought nostalgia for much that I remembered very accurately; all I had to do was write it; so the writing was easier than most I have managed.[26]

Future texts about his childhood would not flow as easily. In fact, no other Knoxville-focused piece would emerge until after Agee's death, with the post-humously published Pulitzer Prize–winning novel *A Death in the Family*, his most celebrated book. *A Death in the Family* is a Southern superreal Proustian vision of a Knoxville childhood. Autobiographical elements and ethno-graphic details of mountain-bred Southerners and transplanted Northerners come together like "the chance meeting on a dissecting-table of a sewing-machine and an umbrella."[27] This is the story of Agee's paternal and maternal lines crossing.

In some of the most superreal parts of the novel, modern and old-timey elements jostle for attention, as in a collage. This can be seen in a scene from a Knoxville night: "All the air vibrated like a fading bell and with the latest exhausted screaming of locusts. Couplings clashed and conjoined; a switch engine breathed heavily. An auto engine bore behind the edge of audibility the furious expletives of its incompetence. Hooves broached, along the hollow street, the lackadaisical rhythms of the weariest clog dancers, and endless in circles, narrow iron tires grinced continuously after. Along the sidewalks, with incisive heels and leathery shuffle, young men and women advanced, re-treated."[28] With these lines all the cloggers I have ever known danced them-selves across the streets of my youth, which are also the streets of Agee's youth.

In *A Death in the Family*, Knoxville is exposed as an exquisite corpse—a place of miscellaneous oddments sewn together—as in the surrealist game. This compositional needlework can be seen in the beginning when Rufus (the name James Agee went by as a child) and his father walk home after seeing a Chaplin film (and a quick trip to the bar):

> The deaf and dumb asylum was death and dumb, his father observed quietly, as if he were careful not to wake it as he always did on these evenings; its windows showed black in its pale brick, as the nursing woman's eyes, and it stood deep and silent among the light shadows of its trees. Ahead, Asylum Avenue lay bleak beneath its lamps. Latticed in pawnshop iron, an old saber caught the glint of a street lamp, a mandolin's belly glowed. In a closed drug store stood Venus de Milo, her golden body laced in elastic straps. The stained glass of the L&N Depot smoldered like an exhausted butterfly.[29]

Agee writes father and son on a somnambulant journey through a Knoxville vacillating between animation and nonanimation, sleep and waking.

In a newer version of the novel edited by Michael Lofaro, the gentle essay "Knoxville: Summer 1915," the one read by Michael Stipe, is replaced with a terrifying dream sequence. The switch creates a nonlinear narrative; it comes from the middle of the twentieth century; it is the adult Rufus's—that is, James Agee's—nightmare. In this scene the narrator is disoriented at first, unsure whether he is in Chattanooga or Knoxville. He feels home and not at home—a common feeling for Agee. Like a bird who makes its home in other birds' nests, Agee often felt himself an invasive species wherever he went—at Phillips Exeter Academy or Harvard University, in New York, rural Alabama, Hollywood, or Knoxville, sometimes reveling in these places and his place in them and sometimes wholly rejecting them by beak and claw.

This unease is apparent in the opening to the new version of *A Death in the Family*. As a dreaming, adult Agee begins to feel the violence of the city, he feels more at home, sickened by the changes and then nostalgic for all that has been lost: his father, his youth and, as he sees it, the possibility of a deeper connection and understanding of the place he comes from. He moves through Knoxville more confidently as he remembers it; the streets become more familiar as his memory plays navigator: "God how it all came back."[30] He walks quickly after all those years living in Manhattan with "the loose stride inherited from the mountains, but a little more briskly than Southerners walked."[31] It was this gait, this particular way of walking that garnered him the nickname "Springheeled Jim."

In the dream, he comes upon a man beaten to death, "a hero, not a neutral."[32] The man is John the Baptist; he is also his father. As he drags the body through the street he is watched and anticipates injury from the crowd. No violence comes from the onlookers; only indifference. He feels this sting as he moves with his burden. The dragged body further disintegrates in the journey, the head eventually wrenches loose from the body and folds up like a catcher's mitt. The ball of the brain is nowhere to be found.

This nightmare was first spilled out in Agee's psychoanalyst Frances Wickes's office. It became a germ for the book, which itself was the result of the fever Agee had for a set of books, a much larger project of which *A Death in the Family* was to be merely one part.[33] Each planned volume was intended as a step closer to his lost past. He was reading Marcel Proust's *In Search of Lost Time* and consuming large amounts of Freud, as well as the writings of Wickes—especially *The Inner World of Childhood*. In reading, writing, and talking through his work, Agee thought about his family: his father's side, with its mountain roots, and his mother's side, which—according to family lore—connected him to Walt Whitman, the quintessential American protobohemian. In homage to the bearded poet, Agee adopted the lilac as his favorite flower and good luck charm;[34] in homage to his father, he kept searching for where he came from, and kept writing toward Tennessee.

Tailpiece: The James Agee Loop

I used to live in Brooklyn, not too far from Agee's old apartment, located, quite appropriately, on St. James Place in the Clinton Hill neighborhood. When he was still living, someone had scrawled in the sidewalk outside his front door when the cement was still wet, "The man who lives here is a loony."[35] I used to run there pretty regularly on what I thought of as my James Agee loop, a six-mile jaunt that had me jogging up to the house where he had lived, occasionally listening to R.E.M. if I was feeling nostalgic, and running in place for a moment in an attempt to erase with my feet the cement text that called him loony. In its place, I wrote a new invisible message with my Saucony sneakers and my sweat, a message dedicated to James Agee, Michael Stipe, Southern bohemians, experimental ethnographers, Walt Whitman, and all the folks from superreal Knoxville: *Let Us Now.*

Notes

1. When Agee died in Manhattan in 1955, his heart giving out in the backseat of a taxi, his novel was unfinished. When it was published two years later, his friend David

McDowell edited it, trying to stick to what he felt Agee's vision for the book was, or perhaps to his own vision for the book. Agee never intended to use "Knoxville: Summer 1915" as the introduction to *A Death in the Family*; McDowell added the piece upon the book's 1957 publication. In 2007 a new version of the novel edited by Michael Lofaro was published with the subtitle *A Restoration of the Author's Text*. This version contained many changes, but the most drastic was the removal of "Knoxville: Summer 1915" and its replacement with a nightmarish scene of the death of the protagonist's father as John the Baptist. Lofaro maintains this is the way Agee intended to organize his novel based on documents that had recently been made available by the Agee Trust. Many Agee fans still prefer the "Knoxville" arrangement, and this is the version the publisher Penguin has maintained. It is impossible to know what would have happened to the book if Agee had continued to revise it. But we are richer for the two versions: the sweet summer sequence and the retelling of the gruesome nightmare. Or, as Steve Earle puts it in the introduction to the 2009 Penguin classics edition, "every passage [is] yet another testament to what a genuine literary badass Agee was." Earle, "Introduction," xii.

2. Agee's essay was later set to music by Samuel Barber as "Knoxville: Summer of 1915," which premiered in 1948 with the Boston Symphony Orchestra.

3. The insult "scruffy little town" comes from an article by Susan Harrigan that ran in the *Wall Street Journal* predicting that the 1982 World's Fair in Knoxville would be a flop. The fair ended up being successful, and local boosters created buttons in response that said, "The scruffy little city did it!" See Harrigan, "What If You Gave a World's Fair and Nobody Came?"; and Wheeler, *Knoxville, Tennessee*, 162.

4. De Certeau, *The Practice of Everyday Life*, 104.

5. Julien Levy, quoted in Davis, *The Making of James Agee*, 75; see also Levy, *Memoir of an Art Gallery*, 79–80.

6. Here I'm thinking of surrealism broadly as a set of avant-garde sensibilities and aesthetic practices from the mid-twentieth century that extends beyond the intimate circle of Breton's group to include its predecessors, such as the Comte de Lautréamont; fellow travelers and even their rivals, like the pataphysician René Daumal; and Georges Bataille, Roger Caillois, and other members of the College of Sociology. See, for example, Comte de Lautréamont, *Maldoror*; Breton, *Manifestoes of Surrealism* and *Conversation*; Bataille, *The Absence of Myth*; Caillois, *The Edge of Surrealism*; and Daumal, *Pataphysical Essays*.

7. Jolas and his wife Maria started *transition* in Paris in 1927. It was initially distributed through Shakespeare and Company, the famous bookstore run by Sylvia Beach. It later moved to New York, where Jolas teamed up with Robert Sage.

8. Jolas and Sage, eds., "The Revolution of the Word Proclamation." Among the authors and artists published in *transition* were James Agee, Jean Arp, André Breton, Alexander Calder, Marcel Duchamp, André Gide, Franz Kafka, Man Ray, Joan Miró, Piet Mondrian and Raymond Queneau. Perhaps most famously, *transition* 26, published in November 1937, contained a "work in progress" by James Joyce; the text was later published as *Finnegan's Wake*. Agee's work appeared in both the first and the last issue of the journal printed in the United States, bookending the whole experiment.

9. Davis, *The Making of James Agee*, 76.

10. Ibid., 72.

11. Bataille, "The Moral Meaning of Sociology," 103–12; Caillois, "The Natural Fantastic," 349.

12. Veitch, *American Superrealism*, 15.

13. While not yet established as a defined focus of study, examples of Southern superrealism abound. In addition to Agee's Southern texts there are moments in Cormac McCarthy's *Suttree* and Scott McClanahan's *Crapalachia* that hit this register, as well as the work by the anthropologist Kathleen Stewart in *A Space on the Side of the Road* and sociologist Allen Shelton in *Dreamworlds of Alabama* and *Where the North Sea Touches Alabama*, just to name a few examples. Regarding the "mean idea," see R.E.M., "King of Birds," on the album *Document*.

14. See Agee, *Selected Journalism*.

15. In *Let Us Now Praise Famous Men*, Mills Hill was changed to Hobe's Hill in order to provide some anonymity to the families and community.

16. The original typescript, titled "Cotton Tenants," was rediscovered in 2003 among several papers when Agee's daughter inherited his Greenwich Village apartment. After she donated the collection to the University of Tennessee Special Collections Library, the James Agee Trust made the papers available to scholars. Through the efforts of John Summers, an excerpt of "Cotton Tenants" first appeared in the *Baffler* in 2012. Another excerpt, titled "Landowners," appeared in the magazine in 2013. A year later the *Baffler* and Melville House published the original report in book form as *Cotton Tenants: Three Families*.

17. Agee and Evans, *Let Us Now Praise Famous Men*, 10.

18. Ibid., 234–38; Benjamin, "Surrealism," 210.

19. For the connection between ethnography and surrealism, see Clifford, "Ethnographic Surrealism," 539—64. For more on Agee's ethnographic surrealism, see Davis, *The Making of James Agee*, 105—98.

20. Roy Stryker, quoted in Haslett, "A Poet's Brief," 20.

21. Agee and Evans, *Let Us Now Praise Famous Men*, 46.

22. Evans, "James Agee in 1936," vi–vii.

23. Agee and Evans, *Let Us Now Praise Famous Men*, 121.

24. Certeau, *The Writing of History*, 288–89.

25. Agee and Evans, *Let Us Now Praise Famous Men*, 58.

26. James Agee, quoted in the program notes of the Boston Symphony Orchestra, April 9, 1948.

27. This is the Comte de Lautréamont's surreal definition of beauty in *Maldoror*, 193.

28. Agee, *A Death in the Family* (2009), 75.

29. Ibid., 16.

30. Agee, *A Death in the Family* (2007), 8.

31. Ibid., 4.

32. Ibid., 5.

33. See Agee, *A Death in the Family* (2007), app. 8, "Outline and Possible Introduction to Agee's Massive Autobiographical Project and the Place of 'This Book' in It," 579–80.

34. Susan Sontag named Agee's friend Evans as the inheritor of Whitman's "euphoric humanism" and heir in the grand American project of "leveling the discriminations between the beautiful and the ugly, the important and the trivial." The same could be applied to Agee. Sontag, *On Photography*, 29–31. For the poem, penned after the death of Abraham Lincoln, see Whitman, "When Lilacs Last in the Dooryard Bloom'd."

35. Agee lived at 179 St. James Place in Clinton Hill from 1938 to 1939 with his wife and a goat.

References

Agee, James. *A Death in the Family*. St. Albans, England: Panther, 1973.

———. *A Death in the Family*. Centennial ed. New York: Penguin, 2009.

———. *A Death in the Family: A Restoration of the Author's Text*, edited by Michael Lofaro. Knoxville: University of Tennessee Press, 2007.

———. "Plans for Work: October 1937." In *The Collected Prose of James Agee*. Edited by Robert Fitzgerald, 50. Boston: Houghton Mifflin, 1968.

———. *Selected Journalism*, edited by Paul Ashdown. Knoxville: University of Tennessee Press, 2005.

Agee, James, and Walker Evans. "Cotton Tenants: Three Families." *Baffler* 19 (2012). http://www.thebaffler.com/ancestors/cotton-tenants.

———. *Cotton Tenants: Three Families*, edited by John Summers. Brooklyn: Melville House, 2013.

———. "Landowners." *Baffler* 23 (2013). http://www.thebaffler.com/ancestors /landowners.

———. *Let Us Now Praise Famous Men*. New York: Mariner, 2001.

Bataille, Georges. "The Moral Meaning of Sociology." In *The Absence of Myth: Writings on Surrealism*. Translated by Michael Richardson, 103–12. New York: Verso, 2006.

Benjamin, Walter. "Surrealism: The Last Snapshot of the European Intelligentsia." In *Selected Writings 1927–1930*, vol. 2, pt. 1. Edited by Michael W. Jennings, Howard Eiland, and Gary Smith, 207–24. Cambridge, MA: Belknap, 1999.

Bergreen, Laurence. *James Agee: A Life*. New York: Dutton, 1984.

Breton, André. *Conversations: The Autobiography of Surrealism*. Translated by Mark Polizzotti. Cambridge, MA: Marlowe, 1995.

———. *Manifestoes of Surrealism*. Translated by Richard Seaver and Helen R. Lane. Ann Arbor: University of Michigan Press, 1972.

Caillois, Roger. *The Edge of Surrealism*, edited by Claudine Frank. Translated by Claudine Frank and Camille Naish. Durham, NC: Duke University Press, 2003.

Certeau, Michel de. *The Practice of Everyday Life*. Translated by Steven F. Rendall. Berkeley: University of California Press, 1994.

————. *The Writing of History.* Translated by Tom Conley. New York: Columbia University Press, 1988.

Clifford, James. "Ethnographic Surrealism." *Comparative Studies in Society and History* 23, no. 4 (1981): 539–64.

Comte de Lautréamont. *Maldoror and the Complete Works of the Comte de Lautréamont.* Translated by Alexis Lykiard. Cambridge, MA: Exact Change, 1994.

Daumal, René. *Pataphysical Essays.* Translated by Thomas Vosteen. Cambridge, MA: Wakefield, 2012.

Davis, Hugh. *The Making of James Agee.* Knoxville: University of Tennessee Press, 2008.

Earle, Steve. "Introduction." In James Agee, *A Death in the Family,* centennial ed., vii–xii. New York: Penguin, 2009.

Evans, Walker. "James Agee in 1936." In James Agee and Walker Evans, *Let Us Now Praise Famous Men,* v–vii. New York: Mariner, 2001.

Harrigan, Susan. "What If You Gave a World's Fair and Nobody Came?" *Wall Street Journal,* December 29, 1980.

Haslett, Adam. "A Poet's Brief." In James Agee and Walker Evans, *Cotton Tenants: Three Families.* Edited by John Summers, 13–30. Brooklyn: Melville House, 2013.

Jolas, Eugène, and Robert Sage, "The Revolution of the Word Proclamation," *transition* 16–17 (1929): n.p.

Levy, Julien. *Memoir of an Art Gallery.* New York: Putnam, 1977.

McCarthy, Cormac. *Suttree.* New York: Vintage, 1992.

McClelland, Scott. *Crapalachia: A Biography of Place.* Columbus, OH: Two Dollar Radio Press, 2013.

R.E.M. *Document.* Nashville: I.R.S. Records, 1998. CD. Originally released 1987.

Shelton, Allen. *Dreamworlds of Alabama.* Minneapolis: University of Minnesota Press, 2007.

————. *Where the North Sea Touches Alabama.* Chicago: University of Chicago Press, 2014.

Sontag, Susan. *On Photography.* New York: Picador, 2001.

Stewart, Kathleen. *A Space on the Side of the Road: Cultural Poetics in an "Other" America.* Princeton, NJ: Princeton University Press, 1996.

Veitch, Jonathan. *American Superrealism: Nathaniel West and the Politics of Representation in the 1930s.* Madison: University of Wisconsin Press, 1997.

Wheeler, William Bruce. *Knoxville, Tennessee: A Mountain City in the New South,* 2nd ed. Knoxville: University of Tennessee Press, 2005.

Whitman, Walt. "When Lilacs Last in the Dooryard Bloom'd." In *Leaves of Grass,* comprehensive reader's ed. Edited by Harold W. Blodgett and Sculley Bradley, 328–37. New York: New York University Press, 1965.

Wickes, Frances. *The Inner World of Childhood: A Study in Analytical Psychology.* New York: Appleton, 1929.

Countercultural Structures of Contemporary Global South Poetry

Daniel Cross Turner

To myriad fans worldwide, reggae artist Bob Marley embodied a bohemian ethos par excellence, attracting an almost cultish following that saw him less as an entertainer than a natural mystic. Raised Catholic, but bold in professing Rastafarianism, Marley appeared the ideal of laid back, yet politically if not prophetically intense, a confirmed outlier who nevertheless was the center of international attention from the late 1960s until the early 1980s. The mixed-race son of a white, English-born father and a black, Jamaican mother, Marley exemplified a particular bohemianism cultivated offshore in the Caribbean, but one that resonates with the American South when conceived beyond narrow bounds of regional or national exceptionalism: Marley was a transfixing figure of the Creole bohemian. Édouard Glissant notes that creolization reflects "unstoppable conjunction . . . like a tumultuous and boundless Mississippi."[1]

Integrating Jamaican English variants, Marley's reggae interleaves doo-wop and early rock 'n' roll; gospel and soul (driving organ and call-and-response vocals); and jazz (syncopated piano and horns) and folk forms (mento, ska, and rocksteady) through offbeat guitar riffs, rumbling bass lines, and clattering steel drums. His music lingers between worlds, aurally traversing national and ethnic histories. Likewise, both the bohemian and the Creole share a mixing of cultural strains, an impulse to push beyond set thresholds, and a capacity to create and explore new varieties.

But what makes Bob Marley's bohemian-Creole life and art "Southern"? The emphasis on ethnic hybridity connects with one thrust of the new Southern studies:[2] the desire to move offshore into the global or Hemispheric South to account for connections between the American South and the Circum-Caribbean, especially in the regions' shared histories of European colonial removal or suppression of indigenous peoples, the importation of African chattel slaves to support plantation economies, and the aftereffects of violent racial apartheid. Marley's work connects with the Creole poetics of other Hemispheric South artists, including Brenda Marie Osbey, Yusef

Komunyakaa, Derek Walcott, and Kwame Dawes, as one manifestation of Southern bohemianness.[3] Like these contemporary Southern/Caribbean writers, Marley's lyrics engage the poet's work of making memorable what otherwise may be lost to collective memory, performing the Orphic task of calling back the dead, of becoming—to cite one of his songs—a "duppy conqueror."

This conversation with the (un)dead is precisely what Keith Cartwright prescribes when considering the Hemispheric South as a deeply creolized space, urging us to consider "powerful southern countercultures of performance (and rememory, reemplacement, restoration of community)."[4] We should nurture "a *hippikat* (Wolof 'open-eyed') poetics" to salvage creolized countercultural structures, for "a truly open-eyed hipness calls us back to contact zones" where we "pour spirits at place-settings for the dead."[5] A *hippikat* poetics re-reckons both time and place, opening "an expansion of scale beyond the space of national sovereignty and beyond the periodicities of history, literary or otherwise."[6] Such poetries have us "turning gazes southward—and thankfully southward still, over the waters—to reconsider an aqueous set of relations with the postplantation Caribbean, the other Americas, the Atlantic rim, and the planet at large."[7] *Hippikat* poems open our eyes—and *ears*, for they bound with rhythmic undercurrents—to a bohemian-Creole ethos that shifts across cartographic borders of the U.S. South into the geopolitical and intellectual space of the Global South. Poetry by Osbey, Komunyakaa, Walcott, and Dawes uncovers disparate, resistant strains of remembrance, personal and collective, that counter official historiography: moments of countermemory.[8] The Gulf of Mexico and Atlantic Ocean rims engender transnational, cross-ethnic flows through black diasporic histories streamed along permeable coastlines,[9] "where disparate cultures meet, clash, and grapple with each other, often as highly asymmetrical relations of domination and subordination."[10]

In relocating countermemory from the margins toward the center and, by extension, amending and unabridging what counts as "Southern," these poets present a *trans-Southern* bohemia that "offers a site from which to replot ... territories" presented as a fait accompli by established regional and national definitions.[11] Their "complicating and defamiliarizing traditional categories of US space and place" is consonant with bohemian attitudes.[12] Their poetry also expands this legacy in unique ways by broadening the notion of bohemia as a place for whites only and as urban centered; by contrast, their bohemian South is ethnically diverse as well as Caribbean and coastal. Contra the civilizing (read: colonizing) power of Western technological and sociopolitical progress (read: racial and cultural superiority), these poets remediate the memory of blacks violently dispersed across the Atlantic through slavery and imperialism, which infused the American South through the plantation economy and its post-Emancipation aftermaths. These poets evoke visions of otherness, cultural and ecological, that varies from white, Western cultural norming and raise the etymological sense of verse in *versus* (meaning: "turning over"). Their poems are musical, yet muscular: their lines—even when written in open form—are filled with heavily inflected grounding rhythms. In addressing countercultural creolized histories, their work often makes recourse to wildly imaginative, if not surreal imagery and to the workings of the natural realm. These poets all have attained considerable notice in other contexts: Komunyakaa is famous for his poetry about the Vietnam War, Walcott for his revisions of classical forms, Osbey as an African American writer, and Dawes as an editor and activist. More recently, these poets have gained increasing critical and popular traction as Southern writers, viewed globally.[13]

Crossing the Gulf: Brenda Marie Osbey

Brenda Marie Osbey was born in 1957 in New Orleans, one of the South's urbohemian spaces. Her poems often take her home terrain as their setting, and typically figure the Louisiana coast as particularly open to diverse ethnic and ecological fluidities, to bohemian-Creole countercurrents against dominant culture. Osbey's poetry reflects her arch awareness of the deep-set, lasting throes of creolization that have shaped and reshaped, (re)rooted and (re)routed the histories of the region and continue to do so. She sees something redemptive amid the historicocultural transferences of the old city; her poetry is intricately calibrated to the Gulf Coast environs, maintaining "an unfading sense of the sacred in New Orleans's deep time," as the city acts "as a living totemic creature that—when fed—rides and feeds its *serviteurs*, generating a charged fossil energy."[14] If the gulf is a continuously churning contact zone, Osbey's poems reveal how transculturation changes the "conqueror" as well as the "conquered," how countercultural impulses can rise and disrupt dominant hierarchies.[15]

The mutually constitutive flows of transculturation are apparent in Osbey's surreal tour-de-force "The Head of Luís Congo Speaks" (1995). The sequential poem provides a revisionary account of an eighteenth-century freed African slave in Louisiana, who was named public executioner and given legal authority over enslaved blacks, overseeing severe whippings, maimings, and executions. In her accompanying glossary, Osbey describes Congo as "a free Kongo man who in 1726 was employed in New Orleans as keeper of the High or Bayou Road, where he established a plantation estate; the official executioner of slaves escaping New Orleans via Bayou St. John, he is said to have died mysteriously at the hands of slaves."[16] The poem imagines the voice of his severed head speaking to his fellow transplanted Africans. The undead head invokes a spectrum of dialects, regions, and tribal affiliations that have synthesized into the catchall "Creole," which amalgamates subcultures and linguistic patterns to enable understanding between enslaved Africans and their white slaveholders: "congo, tiamca, colango, matinga / bambara, nago / senegal, creole."[17] The aural reiterations, freighted with alliteration and assonance, with exact and slant rhymes, uncover forged links between diverse linguistic and social systems and show both the necessity and the insufficiency of "Creole" as a category of identity. The sound effects point to the materiality of language itself. Osbey merely catalogs the names with no connecting terms to establish context. Consequently, we must tie together separate utterances in a microcosmic exercise approximating the very process of linguistic and cultural creolization the poem describes. Creolization is further allegorized in the doubleness of Luís Congo's naming—his Congo roots set alongside his Francophone name.

His mutilated body "burnt and rotting in some farmer's field" and his detached head recall practices of bodily disaggregation endemic to chattel slavery. Congo's head grotesquely undercuts the colonialist ideology of a privileged white personhood. The head speaks less for the dead man than for the disciplinary structure made manifest through his limited agency: he is "free" (manumitted from enslavement), yet remains enthralled to the system of imperial violence. The "i" is disconnected from the "you," except insofar as the "i" is an implement to discipline and punish; to follow Osbey's double entendre, the head indeed delivers a "lying" speech:

> i am the head of luís congo
> and i speak for him
> lying
> burnt and rotting in some farmer's field.
> and you
> you may chant and shout
> and dance about your bonfires on the levees.[18]

If Luís Congo apologizes for past brutalities as keeper of the high road, it is an apology in the etymological sense as a means of defending his actions, not asking forgiveness. But ultimately the anonymous "you" masses and exacts retribution; Congo, in turn, is finally captured, tortured, and killed, and his severed head bids fair warning to any who would follow his lead. At poem's end, what remains of the "i" requests a last vain comfort:

> in the name of the fear and hatred you once knew of me
> give me please
> i beg of you
> a bit of your cool
> > fair
> > water.[19]

There is a jagged symmetry in this final request, as Congo's dark spirit is being exorcised to press away fear and hatred and to usher in a new structure in future, one of greater fairness and reciprocity, of *not* doing unto others the evil they would willingly do unto you. Despite the gritty subject, Osbey's poem offers hope for catharsis and remaking ethical codes, a cultural purification by water to come.

Cultural Mismatching: Yusef Komunyakaa

Born James William Brown Jr., the son of a carpenter, in Bogalusa, Louisiana, in 1947, Yusef Komunyakaa is the author of fifteen poetry collections. He changed his birth name to honor his grandfather, a stowaway from Trinidad, who made the voyage over to the United States wearing one boy's shoe and one girl's shoe. "Mismatched Shoes" (1992) describes this journey, where the conceit of mismatching takes on exponential meanings, striating personal, familial, biogeographic, national, and cultural lines. Mismatching becomes a figure for Creole mixing of heritage across the Hemispheric South, where differing cultural traditions do not neatly align—nor, in true bohemian fashion, should they. Shifting across porous geopolitical borders, Komunyakaa's grandfather is "Smuggled in like a sack of papaya / On a banana boat."[20] The poem is flooded with sensory images, commixing sound with taste and touch, from "gumbo to jambalaya to jazz " to the way

> a poor man might touch
> A lovers' satin glove.

Although the grandfather died young, his American grandson

> slipped into his skin. Komunyakaa.
> His blues, African fruit on my tongue.[21]

The poet thus takes up the African American practice of renaming as a means of remaking identity, casting aside a slave name (the ill-fitting, troubled Brown, which had "A plantation owner's breath / Clouding each filigreed letter") to reclaim genealogical and spiritual roots in Komunyakaa, which carries the whispered "deep song of Shango" and opens transit back to "another life."[22] This rememory of coextensive matching and mismatching symbolizes the process of transculturation from Trinidad to Louisiana, mango to gumbo, papaya to jambalaya, slavery to mill town, Christianity to Lukumi, Jesus to Shango, Komunyakaa to Brown, and back again. The litany of aural connectors across syllables, words, and lines ("papaya," "banana," "gumbo," "jambalaya," "jazz," "mango," "song," "Shango") stresses, literally, the fluid transferences between South and Caribbean.

Komunyakaa's *Taboo* (2004) thoroughly explores such transcultural contacts and clashes. Each poem in the volume is written in tercets and focuses on a particular event from the African, Afro-Caribbean, or African American past, and the volume covers an immense palette of black historical figures from around the Global South, from ancient warrior Masinissa, who founded the Kingdom of Numidia, to American colonial poet—and freed slave— Phillis Wheatly, to nineteenth-century violin virtuoso Claudio Brindis de Salas, to Dixieland jazz great Louis Armstrong. The three-line stanzas of the *Taboo* poems create an insistent, yet fluid form that gathers energy through repetition; as Komunyakaa noted during our interview, "I came to the three-line stanza, the tercet, and I felt like there was liberation because I could include various bits of information—names, places, dates—and still maintain a certain musicality and also give visual shape to the poems."[23]

Several poems jump-cut between mythic and religious structures, which, in proper bohemian-Creole mode, skew mainstream Christianity and instead espouse mixed or alternative spiritual practices that would be viewed as backward or primitive by dominant Western culture. In "Lucumi," the speaker crosses paths in Havana with Cuban poet/political activist Nicolás Guillén and African American writer Langston Hughes, a walking ideal of the modern bohemian-Creole: he was of mixed race (with black, native, and white bloodlines), probably gay, a leading figure of the Harlem Renaissance in the 1920s and 1930s, a celebrant of black folk forms (especially blues and jazz) at a time when these were dismissed by many prominent white cultural figures, and a committed socialist. This bilingual, transnational encounter is echoed by images drawn from the syncretic Caribbean religion of the title, as "Chango's thunderbolts" and "The Venus / Ochun swims the River / Oshun." The interspersing of religious and natural forms in Afro-Caribbean cultures, human faith intertwining with a heightened awareness of the nonhuman environment, fosters a multicultural primal unity. Under the transformed, transforming light of Japanese lanterns, beneath the clear stars, sundry rhythms, including the lines' own metrical pulsings, merge the scene into a thick aural "forest of gourds, guitars, / rattles, trumpets."[24] Just as national boundaries and customs thin to nearly nothing, Komunyakaa's poem deconstructs racial taxonomies as the foundation for socioeconomic divisions between haves and have-nots across the Atlantic basin.

"Séance & Shadowplay" intertwines the figure of Sierva María de Todos los Angeles, "red-haired Igbo,"[25] from Gabriel Garcia Marquez's *Of Love and Other Demons* (1994) with Bartolomé de Las Casas, a Spanish colonist and priest who opposed the genocide of native populations in the West Indies.[26] Through lines that are compressed, we are struck by the beauty of this contact zone scene, as the priest catches sight of the bright earrings worn by the Arawaks swimming out to receive the Spanish galleon; the effect is one of mesmerizing synthesis, as vision and sound transpose, the sunlight converting the gold adornments to resonant death tolls: "the sun / struck their little / gold death notes."[27]

In this moment of colonialist contact, the power lines surge, and beauty begets death: the bright earrings of the Arawaks metastasize by the strike of the sun's rays into the hollow echoes of "góld déath nótes," the gravity of the transformation resounded in the heavy spondaic beats that stress each word in the closing line, warning signs of dark matter to come in the Spanish imperialist mission.

For even as Las Casas wrote against the exploitation of the Amerindians, he encouraged the importation of African slaves into the region because they were deemed more constitutionally fit for enslaved labor, biologically destined to be beasts of burden. Komunyakaa therefore pictures the so-called Apostle of the Indies as a stand-in for "Satan's / timekeeper," who would pontificate about how Africans "worship sun-gods / & can endure the cat-o'- / nine-tails with less / blood on the grass."[28] Africans are dismissed as primitive sun worshippers, an image that rhymes grimly with the sun illuminating and initiating the death song for the Arawaks: both cultures are deemed primitive on the cultural evolution scale vis-à-vis "enlightened" Spanish civilization, and therefore made subject to colonial control, from chattel enslavement to sexual exploitation. In response, the native female victims of colonial trauma and sexual violence summon an animistic faith in their native environment. After being raped by Spanish colonialists, indigenous women "begged sacred trees / & stones to kill / curses hidden inside."[29] Their desired connection with living things of the nonhuman, natural world forms a countercultural striking back against the hegemonic dogma espoused by their new world Christian conquerors. The native women have lost power over their lives, but still hold a grim power over the lives hidden within them.

"Sunset in Surinam" continues Komunyakaa's countermemorial response to colonization and slavery across the black Atlantic, recounting details of the life and writing of Scots-Dutch solider and author John Gabriel Stedman in eighteenth-century Suriname. Like his friend, the English poet and artist William Blake, whose romantic works and unbounded life inspired later bohemian thinkers and artists, Stedman, too, can be seen as protobohemian in his countercultural writing against slavery in the Dutch colonies, his scandalous marriage to a mixed-race slave named Joanna, and his ultimate decision to return to Europe, which speaks to the bohemian paradox of the willed exile or expatriate who nevertheless feels nostalgic desire for home. Blake and Stedman collaborated on illustrations of punishments inflicted by Dutch soldiers onto captured "Maroons" (English) or "Bosnegers" (Dutch)—African slaves who escaped into the rainforest with the aid of indigenous South Americans and established new communities there. Stedman's *Narrative of a Five Years Expedition* (1796) was seen as a foundational work by early abolitionists. Komunyakaa's poetic revision, however, questions the depth of Stedman's commitment, imagining the soldier-author languishing "between one lonely idea / & another."[30] Where Stedman is lost in abstract thought, the enslaved Neptune is in the process of being physically disembodied, psychically disaggregated. Broken upon the rack, Neptune took hours to die and even joked with his Dutch executioners during the ordeal about whether they would like to cannibalize his dead body parts, calling out the purported sensibilities of his "civilized" tormentors. For Stedman, such a horrifying image becomes "less / than a wisp of smoke" as he turns from his earlier bohemian lifestyle,[31] returning to Europe while leaving his wife and son behind in Surinam. Although he eventually brought over the son to live with his new family in England, the poem ends with a reminder of Joanna's bleakly hybrid state, figuring her as a "mermaid / he courted in daydreams" who was, in reality, "the same Joanna / sold to a Mrs. Godefoy."[32] Stedman's vision of Joanna as mythic mermaid suggests her unredeemed multiplicity as woman and property, human and thing, situated between master and subjugated races, left unredeemed.

Natural Mystic: Derek Walcott

Derek Walcott's poetry covers similar geographic and conceptual territory, probing how animistic, nature-based spiritual traditions can assemble subcultural formations of resistance. A native of the former British colony of St. Lucia and the mixed-race descendent of slaves, Walcott draws on various mythic and religious traditions to delineate further hybridizations of Southern/Caribbean bohemian-Creole cultures. His version of black diasporic history is infused with images drawn from countercultural spiritual practices diverge from Christian dogma. Walcott's poetry vacillates between totemic kinship and animistic transformations, often crossing over into "a kind of ecumenical poetics of animism" that merges his "own dual legacies of African pantheism and Methodism."[33] Shifting between and beyond narrow sectarian claims, Walcott's syncretic spiritualism aims to rectify historical horrors under plantation economics aided and abetted by efforts to Christianize African and indigenous populations. The Circum-Caribbean ecology provides "an ambiguous repository and memorial site of the past as well as the starting point for bringing the New World's plurality of cultures together."[34] Walcott evokes metamorphoses to record "the inescapability and legitimate value of mutation, hybridity, and intermixture" that marks diasporic transformations of the black Atlantic.[35] These transfigurations are almost always situated in the natural world, drawing connections between "cross-cultural contact and contact with nature,"[36] especially vis-à-vis the animistic presences of animals (such as the iguana, St. Lucia's totem animal), stones, trees, and the sea. Such connections with the environment suggest the *parahuman*, according to which humans, nonhuman animals, and the environs coalesce into a "more than human collectivity,"[37] where humans are no longer seen as masters of nature. The parahuman acutely accords with the Southern-Caribbean black diaspora, for "the brutal colonial circumstance of dismemberment and bodily disaggregation" created in enslaved people "a deep skepticism about the desirability of the category of the human."[38]

Omeros (1990) resets Homer's *Odyssey* in Walcott's native Antilles. The epic poem provides a wealth of parahuman mergings that seek "fluidity, metamorphosis, the imperceptible shading of one thing into another,"[39] turning these against dominant Western narratives of the pre-Columbian Caribbean as a primitive, historyless place whose blank pages were waiting to be filled with the colonizers' words and deeds. *Omeros* commingles the processes of wounding and healing, both human (individual and collective) and ecological, in recurrent images of metamorphoses.[40] Walcott interweaves human and botanical histories of transplantation, where uprooted and resettled plant life symbolizes transplantations of diasporic blacks, and vice versa. The things of nature are recognized as sentient beings, as in the poem's opening scene, where we witness the sacrificial rite of chopping down cedars by artisanal fishermen who skillfully covert the trunks into canoes, interlacing wood and water. By the same token, enslaved humans are reduced to the state of natural things, particularly fragmented trees, becoming mere "coals, firewood, dismembered / branches, not men";[41] the Antillean people and landscape are immersed into the textures of the parahuman. These continuous metamorphoses—half literal, half figural, between the human and the nonhuman—also recall the animistic practices carried over from Africa to the Caribbean, and from there to syncretic variations in the Deep South. This impulse is evident in the description of root gathering by Ma Killman, who "glimpsed gods in the leaves."[42] As a consequence of serial uprootings and reroutings, the old gods are transmuted into the rites and figures of Christianity, for the African gods' features are "obscured / by the restless shade and light," and "unlike the logwood thorns of her Lord, / or that golden host named for her mother, Mary," they "had lost their names / and, therefore, considerable presence" in the new world and its changed ecology.[43]

Nevertheless, their buried power thrums through the natural surround, summoning the old spirits of Yoruba origin—Erzulie, Shango, Ogun—still echoing in Ma Killman's blood memory. The old African deities "swarmed in the thicket" of the grove and though their names escape conscious articulation, Ma Killman encounters their undead presence: "their sounds were within her, / subdued in the rivers of her blood."[44] She undergoes a parahuman metamorphosis, instantiating the divine through her body, which takes on the forms of natural *materia* encompassing her, reanimating through her physical frame "All the unburied gods, for three deep centuries dead"; her veins transmogrify to roots, her vocalizations knotted like a vine, her arms uplifted as branches that provide hints of regeneration, like "a tree carried across the Atlantic that shoots / fresh leaves as its dead trunk wallows on our beaches."[45] Ma Killman's transformation into a human-vegetable amalgam is particularly apt for the African Atlantic, since many of the tree species "have suffered the same history of transplantation and adaptation as the human populations of the Caribbean."[46] Walcott's poetry touts a residual animism, which insists "all natural resources, animal, vegetable, or mineral, have sentience" and "all human labor therefore potentially acts as a weapon on the so-perceived passive or nonexistent sentience of the physical world."[47]

This totemic impetus and sought-for intimacy with nature, threatened by the uprooted experience of the African diaspora, are carried forward through Walcott's description of the parallel removal of Native Americans by seventeenth-century English colonists, "the smoke-prayer of the tepees / pushed back by the Pilgrim's pitchfork." Even as he suggests that "Men take their colours / as the trees do from the native soil of their birth,"[48] Walcott does not hold to immanence in nature, to an essentialist anchorage of a culture in its original land. Rather, he understands the profound *affect* of the ecology on cultural beliefs and formations, on imminence and powerful adjacencies that accrue between our physical being in the world and constructions of identity in a given culture. Once "they are moved elsewhere, entire cultures / lose the art of mimicry." This conflict echoes traditional Southern understandings of "the land" as a factor of identity. And Walcott aligns forced transplantation with imperialism: compelling a native population to desert a place means "a desert place widens in the heart" where once "the trees were," and violently changing the ground under the "bare soles of a race" means laying bare the souls of a race, outstripping their collective memory.[49] Yet residual countermemories of African spirituality and ecology in *Omeros* espouse not assimilation, but creolization—where fluidity and interchange occurs between formerly distinct cultures, evolving a new, hybrid culture.

Redemption Song Redux: Kwame Dawes

Bob Marley's "Redemption Song" (1980) reflects an element of creolized tradition described by Charles Joyner in *Down by the Riverside* (1984), his landmark history of Gullah culture, which powerfully manifests creolization in the South Carolina low country. Joyner argues that Gullah trickster tales, many of which derive from West African sources filtered through Caribbean contexts, construe "situational ethics" according to which "theft from a fellow slave was wrong; but theft from the master was not really theft" because the enslaved believed "the relationship between master and slave to be one of 'thief' and 'stolen property.'"[50] This belief was expressed in the Gullah proverb, "Ef bukra [white man] neber tief, how come neggar yer?"[51] The opening lines of "Redemption Song" ("Old pirates, yes they rob I, sold I to the merchant ships / Minutes after they took I from the bottomless pit") invoke Jamaican-English idioms in the slippage between present and past tenses ("rob" instead of "robbed," suggesting the ongoing nature of slavery's injustice) and in the use of "I" as direct object, as the doubleness of "I" as both subject and object linguistically signals how chattel enslavement changed human subject into subhuman object. Yet Marley's song is one of redemption, a call to go "forward in this generation triumphantly." The theft of human property has been restructured in the postplantation Hemispheric South, transfigured into abstract machinations of what Marley calls "mental slavery": "Emancipate yourselves from mental slavery / None but ourselves can free our minds."[52] Emancipation, in true bohemian manner, is ideological, a matter of keeping alive—through verse, through song—the presence of the dead as resistant voices of the peripheral past, even or especially if these dead are unruly, dark spirits: *duppies.*

In our beginning is our end. Let's close with a poet who links directly with Marley's legacy of Creole bohemianism: Kwame Dawes. Born in Ghana in 1962, Dawes moved to Jamaica in 1971—precisely when Marley's music was rising to international prominence—and spent most of his childhood and early adult life in Marley's native land. A worthy heir to Marley's bohemian-Creole impetus, Dawes authored the critical study *Bob Marley: Lyrical Genius* (2002), and titled his 2013 poetry volume *Duppy Conqueror.* Dawes's work, like his life, has been filled with crossings and recrossings, and his poems mirror this nomadic imagination, teeming with Afro-Caribbean-Southern interchanges.

"Thieving" picks up the long tradition of enslaved Africans viewing chattel slavery as theft and weaves this into a new reckoning of the old account. Dawes's poem questions—quite rightly, since it runs in a series of rhetorical questions—the endgame of imperialism: "How long must pass / to make up for your hundred years of taking / from people everything they have?"[53] How can we balance the historical ledger? Can there be forgiveness of debts? Through retribution, reparation? The repetition of present participles ("taking," "giving," "thieving," "killing," "taking") indicates the past's continuing emergence in the present, showing us that these processes are not over and done, but ongoing. The *depth* of violent trauma transfers into the sheer *duration* of suffering, the necessity of quotidian endurance, prolonged waiting in vain. The transnational reach of these conditions is implied in that the poem is set nowhere in particular, just as contemporary notions of bohemia have little to nothing to do with the historical Bohemia being anchored in the Czech Republic. The nomadic setting of Dawes's poem suggests instances in the U.S. South, including allusions to bales of cotton picked for someone else's profit and "the bones in the backwoods" that are relics of lynched "blackened bloated bodies." The poem also moves offshore, expanding into the African Atlantic by recalling "the erasure / of the language of the ancestors" and "the valley of bones, / covered by the weight of the Atlantic," which entombs remnants of human cargo lost along the Middle Passage. Dawes's poem concludes without closure, with a final unanswerable question that exposes the cycle of violence at back of colonialism, asking how much must be stolen back before "we are even" and then each time "I take from them from now on, / you can call it thieving?"[54] In the end, there is no end, no lasting purpose to the historical terrors, the grand theft of black bodies and souls across the continents, across the centuries. Dawes writes to fill cultural memory gaps that would permit us to continue in a collective fugue. Working against unmindful, disembodied historiography, "Thieving" makes us feel the weight of the African Atlantic, recalls the language of the ancestors, fleshes out dead forms.

NEEDLESS TO SAY, the poets covered in this chapter are representative, not exhaustive. There is a spectrum of other writers whose work adds richness and nuance to countercultural poetics of the African Atlantic. Keith Cartwright, for instance, interprets work by Marion Bethel, Kamau Brathwaite, Adrian Castro, Aimé Césaire, Jerome Cartwright (the author's Bahamian kin), and Mona Lisa Saloy. Moreover, Virgil Suárez, Natasha Trethewey, and Jay Wright could also be fruitfully discussed in this context. Yet the black diasporic poetry of Osbey, Komunyakaa, Walcott, and Dawes reveals a glimpse of the array of contemporary countercultural poetries in form and content. Their work resoundingly resists the notion that poetry is somehow unworldly, transcendentally subsisting in some ethereal-ephemeral nether world. Such thinking, still prevalent in too many academic venues, is out of alignment with the sheer spectrum of poetries associated with the Global South and the diversity not only of the many volumes themselves but also of their audiences, critical and popular. This is particularly, pointedly clear in such poetries produced in, through, within, without, between, and beyond the American South, working across that permeable, unbounded, power-filled space of the African Atlantic.

Consider that Brenda Marie Osbey served as the keynote speaker for the March 2016 biennial conference of the Society for the Study of Southern Literature in Boston. This speaks to the increasing recognition of Southern poetry as a major arena in the overall field of Southern literature and reflects the spread of Global South approaches associated with new Southern studies. One of the conference's three main subtopics was "Continental, Caribbean, Hemispheric, Transatlantic, and Global Norths and Souths." It is no surprise, then, that Osbey's poetry has been recognized as current and central by the primary national organization for scholars of Southern literary studies.

Indeed, the *hippikat* poetics presented in the work of Osbey—as well as her fellow travelers in Global South verse, Komunyakaa, Walcott, and Dawes—outlines avenues for shifting past well-worn metaphoric correspondences between Southern studies *old* and *new*, between *what was* and *what is*, flatly divided. Their Global South poetry crafts *pataphoric divergences*, a crisscrossing unfolding scaffolding of expanding forms that remediate previous codes while occulting pat origins, thus skewing the zero-sum game of *before* versus *now*. Their countercultural work forms a pataphoric model for reviewing the American South, one that revels in undeadness, repurposing fragments of the old in building out further future connections. The diasporic scatterings and creolized convergences recorded in their *verses* generate new life, even if it is the uncanny afterlife of the undead—ancestral memories irrupting in the present. Through their poetic visions of Creole bohemianism, other possibilities are instituted, and countercultures evolve, thrive outward into the uncreated future.

Notes

1. Glissant, *Faulkner, Mississippi*, 30. Generally based in New World encounters in the Caribbean involving indigenous, African, and European peoples, creolization represents the process when established cultures come into contact, then conflict and converge into hybrid forms of social, cultural, religious, political, and linguistic practices.

2. New Southern studies, which emerged in the early years of the twenty-first century, critiques traditional Southernism, which held sway for approximately thirty-five years, from Rubin's *The Faraway Country* (1963), seen as initiating traditional Southern studies, to Kreyling's *Inventing Southern Literature* (1998), viewed as criticizing the institution of traditional Southernism.

3. Recent theories of the Hemispheric or Global South include foundational texts such as Jones and Monteith, eds., *South to a New Place*; Cohn and Smith, eds., *Look Away!*; Matthews, Peacock, and Watson, eds., *The American South in a Global World*; Handley, *New World Poetics*; Peacock, *Grounded Globalism*; Greeson, *Our South*; Cartwright, *Sacral Grooves*, the special issue of *American Literature* ("Global Contexts, Local Literatures: The New Southern Studies") edited by McKee and Trefzer; and the special issue of the *Mississippi Quarterly* ("Southern Roots and Routes") edited by Anderson, Donaldson, and Jones.

4. Cartwright, *Sacral Grooves*, 3.

5. Ibid.

6. Ibid., 5.

7. Ibid.

8. For a full analysis of countermemory, see Turner, *Southern Crossings*, chap. 6.

9. For detailed accounts of the history of the African Atlantic, see Brown, *African-American Cultures and the South Carolina Lowcountry*; and Gilroy's foundational study, *The Black Atlantic*.

10. Pratt, *Imperial Eyes*, 4.

11. Levin, *Bohemia in America*, 8.

12. Ibid.

13. Recent scholarly treatments of these poets as Southern writers include Cartwright, *Sacral Grooves*; Cartwright, "Weave a Circle Round Him Thrice"; Davis, *Southscapes*; Lowe, "An Interview with Brenda Marie Osbey"; Turner, "Modern Metamorphoses"; Turner, "Remaking Myth"; and Turner, *Southern Crossings*. Komunyakaa and Dawes are featured in Turner and Wright, eds., *Hard Lines*.

14. Cartwright, *Sacral Grooves*, 142.

15. As Pratt, *Imperial Eyes*, 6, notes, the imperial metropolis "habitually blinds itself to the ways in which the periphery determines the metropolis—beginning, perhaps, with the latter's obsessive need to present and re-present its peripheries and its others continually to itself."

16. Osbey, "Glossary and Notes," in *All Saints*, 124.

17. Osbey, "The Head of Luís Congo Speaks," in *All Saints*, 98.

18. Ibid.

19. Ibid., 103.

20. Komunyakaa, "Mismatched Shoes," in *Pleasure Dome*, 292.

21. Ibid., 292.

22. Ibid., 292.

23. Turner, "Remaking Myth," 345.

24. Komunyakaa, "Lucumi," in *Taboo*, 100.

25. Komunyakaa, "Séance & Shadowplay," in *Taboo*, 94.

26. Las Casas (1484–1566), a Dominican priest and first resident bishop of Chiapas, was called Protector of the Indians. His *Short Account of the Destruction of the Indies* (1552) chronicles atrocities by Spanish colonizers against indigenous peoples and was sent to Prince Philip II, leading to the abolition of native slavery in Spanish-held colonies. While Las Casas believed natives had souls worthy of salvation, he recommended importing enslaved Africans to the colonies, since he viewed them as subhuman. Although he later retracted this stance, Las Casas's initial view helped foster the transatlantic slave trade.

27. Komunyakaa, "Séance & Shadowplay," 95–96.

28. Ibid., 95, 94.

29. Ibid., 95.

30. Komunyakaa, "Sunset in Surinam," in *Taboo*, 25.

31. Ibid.

32. Ibid., 26.

33. Handley, *New World Poetics*, 316.

34. Ibid., 359.

35. Gilroy, *The Black Atlantic*, 223.

36. Handley, *New World Poetics*, 398.

37. Allewaert, *Ariel's Ecology*, 113.

38. Ibid., 86.

39. Breslin, *Nobody's Nation*, 265.

40. As Ramazani, *The Hybrid Muse*, 50, notes, Walcott transforms the wound into "a resonant site of interethnic connection within *Omeros*, vivifying the black Caribbean inheritance of colonial injury and at the same time deconstructing the uniqueness of suffering."

41. Walcott, *Omeros*, 150.

42. Ibid., 142.

43. Ibid., 292.

44. Ibid., 242–43.

45. Ibid., 243.

46. Handley, *New World Poetics*, 291.

47. Ibid., 392.

48. Walcott, *Omeros*, 207.

49. Ibid., 207, 208.

50. Joyner, *Down by the Riverside*, 134.

51. Ibid.

52. Bob Marley and the Wailers, "Redemption Song," on *Uprising*.

53. Dawes, "Thieving," in *Duppy Conqueror*, 273.

54. Ibid., 273–74.

References

Allewaert, Monique. *Ariel's Ecology: Plantations, Personhood, and Colonialism in the American Tropics.* Minneapolis: University of Minnesota Press, 2013.

Anderson, Eric Gary, Susan V. Donaldson, and Suzanne W. Jones, eds. "Southern Roots and Routes: Mobility and Migration." Special issue, *Mississippi Quarterly: The Journal of Southern Cultures* 65, no. 1 (2012).

Breslin, Paul. *Nobody's Nation: Reading Derek Walcott.* Chicago: University of Chicago Press, 2001.

Brown, Ras Michael. *African-Atlantic Cultures and the South Carolina Lowcountry.* Cambridge: Cambridge University Press, 2012.

Cartwright, Keith. *Sacral Grooves, Limbo Gateways: Travels in Deep Southern Time, Circum-Caribbean Space, Afro-Creole Authority.* Athens: University of Georgia Press, 2013.

———. "Weave a Circle Round Him Thrice: Komunyakaa's Hoodoo Balancing Act." *Callaloo* 28, no. 3 (2005): 851–63.

Cohn, Deborah, and Jon Smith, eds. *Look Away! The U.S. South in the New World Studies.* Durham, NC: Duke University Press, 2004.

Davis, Thadious M. *Southscapes: Geographies of Race, Region, and Literature.* Chapel Hill: University of North Carolina Press, 2011.

Dawes, Kwame. *Bob Marley: Lyrical Genius.* London: Sanctuary, 2002.

———. *Duppy Conqueror: New and Selected Poems.* Edited by Matthew Shenoda. Port Townsend, WA: Copper Canyon, 2013.

Gilroy, Paul. *The Black Atlantic: Modernity and Double Consciousness*. Cambridge, MA: Harvard University Press, 1993.

Glissant, Édouard. *Faulkner, Mississippi*. Translated by Barbara Lewis and Thomas C. Spear. New York: Farrar, Straus and Giroux, 1999.

Greeson, Jennifer Rae. *Our South: Geographic Fantasy and the Rise of National Literature*. Cambridge, MA: Harvard University Press, 2010.

Handley, George B. *New World Poetics: Nature and the Adamic Imagination of Whitman, Neruda, and Walcott*. Athens: University of Georgia Press, 2007.

Jones, Suzanne W., and Sharon Monteith, eds. *South to a New Place: Region, Literature, Culture*. Baton Rouge: Louisiana State University Press, 2002.

Joyner, Charles. *Down by the Riverside: A South Carolina Slave Community*. Urbana: University of Illinois Press, 1984.

Komunyakaa, Yusef. *Pleasure Dome: New and Collected Poems*. Middletown, CT: Wesleyan University Press, 2001.

———. *Taboo: The Wishbone Trilogy, Part One*. New York: Farrar, Straus and Giroux, 2004.

Kreyling, Michael. *Inventing Southern Literature*. Jackson: University Press of Mississippi, 1998.

Levin, Joanna. *Bohemia in America: 1858–1920*. Stanford, CA: Stanford University Press, 2009.

Lowe, John. "An Interview with Brenda Marie Osbey." In *The Future of Southern Letters*, edited by Jefferson Humphries and John W. Lowe, 93–118. New York: Oxford University Press, 1996.

Marley, Bob, and the Wailers. *Uprising*. Kingston, Jamaica: Tuff Gong, 1980.

Matthews, Carrie R., James L. Peacock, and Harry L. Watson, eds. *The American South in a Global World*. Chapel Hill: University of North Carolina Press, 2005.

McKee, Kathryn, and Annette Trefzer, eds. "Global Contexts, Local Literatures: The New Southern Studies." Special issue, *American Literature* 78, no. 4 (2006).

Osbey, Brenda Marie. *All Saints: New and Selected Poems*. Baton Rouge: Louisiana State University Press, 1997.

Peacock, James L. *Grounded Globalism: How the U.S. South Embraces the World*. Athens: University of Georgia Press, 2007.

Pratt, Mary Louise. *Imperial Eyes: Travel Writing and Transculturation*. New York: Routledge, 1992.

Ramazani, Jahan. *The Hybrid Muse: Postcolonial Poetry in English*. Chicago: University of Chicago Press, 2001.

Rubin, Louis D, Jr. *The Faraway Country: Writers of the Modern South*. Seattle: University of Washington Press, 1963.

Turner, Daniel Cross. "Modern Metamorphoses and the Primal Sublime: The Southern/Caribbean Poetry of Yusef Komunyakaa and Derek Walcott." *Southern Quarterly: A Journal of the Arts in the South*. 48, no. 3 (2011): 52–69.

————. "Remaking Myth in Yusef Komunyakaa's *Talking Dirty to the Gods, Taboo, and Gilgamesh*: An Interview." *Mississippi Quarterly* 62, no. 4 (2009): 335–50.

————. *Southern Crossings: Poetry, Memory, and the Transcultural South*. Knoxville: University of Tennessee Press, 2012.

Turner, Daniel Cross, and William Wright, eds. *Hard Lines: Rough South Poetry*. Columbia: University of South Carolina Press, 2016.

Walcott, Derek. *Omeros*. New York: Farrar, Straus and Giroux, 1990.

Down Home and Out
Southern Lesbian Writers and the Sex Life of Food

Jaime Cantrell

Food is more than sustenance: it is a history. I remember women by what we ate together, what they dug out of the freezer after we made love for hours.
—Dorothy Allison

A bohemian woman could be a Grisette or Mistress; Muse; Model; Wife; Mother; Salon Hostess; Independent Woman; Worker; 'Free Spirit'; Lesbian; or Artist.
—Elizabeth Wilson

In *The Real South* (2008), Scott Romine explores cultural consumerism through Mama Dip's Kitchen in Chapel Hill, North Carolina, where, with a spoonful of erotic innuendo, "diners are invited to 'put a taste of the South in your mouth.'"[1] In "Edible Labor," Patricia Yaeger evokes childhood kitchen memories blurring lines between the body and biscuit batter: "Even the biscuits—fluffy as popcorn—reeked of my grandmother's body. Her puffy arms swung too and fro as she kneaded the dough, and I grew dizzy watching her. Which was arm, and which was batter? How to tell flesh from dough or rough skin from biscuit crust?"[2] Romine and Yaeger narrow in on a concept that powerfully resonates with literary representations of lesbian hypervisibility I explore: food is memory, and both a key marker and component of identity and community. For "as long as there has been a South, and people who think of themselves as Southerners, food has been central to the region's image, its personality, and its character."[3]

Elizabeth Engelhardt, in the introduction to the field-forging book *The Larder: Food Studies Methods from the American South* (2014), explicitly links Southern foodways taxonomies with cultural processes and the production of communal relations: "The study of why we eat, what we eat, and what it means" directly reinscribes "social interactions and cultural exchanges."[4] Engelhardt notes that "for academic audiences focused on examining and criticizing dietary habits and patterns of exclusion," Southern food studies "offer approaches to race, class, gender, and ethnicity."[5] Despite all the attention

paid to the pleasure of food and food's usefulness as a critical node for analyzing Southern sociality, sexuality is elided—even as "the connection between
'lifestyle politics' and an earlier bohemianism was never made" by feminists
in the 1970s and 1980s.[6]

But such connections are far from missing in fiction and poetry by post-
Stonewall-era Southern lesbian writers. These quotations from Romine and
Yaeger suggest two concurrent strains of thought that pertain to the surface
and close readings of poems and fiction in my own analysis, works that illustrate what we get by putting the South in our mouths: Yaeger evokes a "foodways" approach where food is immensely salient to memory/history, while
Romine evokes expectations (imagery/stereotype/association) and rhetorical manipulation (particularly marketing) of those expectations. Both approaches are important for understanding why *Southern* food is so significant
in the poetry and fiction of Southern lesbian writers—works that celebrate a
bohemian South. We cannot understand these works of lesbian literature as
expressions of bohemia "as a recognized concept—a way of life encompassing
certain forms of behavior and a particular set of attitudes towards the practice
of art" that "came into existence only when writers began to describe it" without sustained attention to the ways in which food, art, and identity politics
intersect on the page and across the regional and national imaginary.[7]

Representations of food in literary productions are an especially appropriate lens for examining lesbian sex and assertions of sociality. Focusing on how
community, sex, and region intersect and produce ways of being and belonging in late twentieth-century writing by Southern lesbians, fiction and poems
can intricately illuminate how "[e]ating, writing, and loving can and must be
brought together," to quote Elspeth Probyn,[8] in order to place sex at the center of these intersectionalities—or what I call intersextionalities. Such an
analysis engages with Elizabeth Grosz's reconfiguration of lesbian desire, or the
drawing together of bodies, pleasures, surfaces, and intensities: formulated
contiguously as "a part of other relations . . . the bedroom is no more the privileged site of sexuality than any other space; sexuality and desire are a part of
the intensity and passion of life itself."[9] Explicitness is crucial; it involves developing a line of thinking that interweaves the lesbian body, eating, and food
with affective resonances that value tactile sensations, the sense of timing (or
ripening) that is so important in loving and eating, and the deliberate open-
ness with which these writers celebrate down-home Southern food and satisfying sex.

Such works posit lesbian sexuality (and the lesbian body) as a site of
production—energies and pulses that produce and generate, containing

history and memory—within a specific space. Significantly, Grosz's formulation of lesbian desire opens up multitudinous sites for bohemian sexualities—including the South as a region. Eating functions simultaneously as a cultural process of sexual and regional identification and a biological one: the body maps desire, appetite, and erotic / alimentary pleasure alongside the production of Southern lesbian sociality formation, affirmation, and delineation. Looking at and with lesbian hypervisibility represented through the vehicle of food in these works,[10] with the region functioning as a tenor concept, we see writers exploring the tangible connections and affective possibilities that thinking sex through Southern food reveals.

Beyond the body, in thinking sex and region through food, it is perhaps most useful to examine how eating offers a way to consider sexual difference in the social realm, for "examining the political and cultural meaning of eating culture . . . opens up a multitude of questions central to critical reflection about the production of asymmetrical social relations, both historical and contemporary."[11] These concerns are tied to the production of social relations in nuanced ways, requiring precision and an articulation of intersectionalities—for example, how specific foods suggest class, how food is made, who prepares it, and who gets to eat it along the axes of gender, race, and ethnicity, and how food and eating have been used to produce sites of belonging, relationships, reflection, and orientation. They reveal, too, the multiple identity axes that have long begged for conceptual reinvigoration: gender relations, economic status and class, geopolitical location, ethnicity, and race, effectively, "rooting actual bodies within these relations."[12] Food orients us to our personal, individualized selves while gesturing toward and resisting cohesive definitional meanings at local, regional, and national levels across time.[13] If we "stand detached" from sexuality and "bracket its familiarity" within the multiple identity forming sites and fracturing spaces that a model of thinking food reveals, we begin to develop a politics of sexuality rooted in connection and disconnection, where bodies live in food and sex knowledge and through structures of intense sociality.[14] An examination of the social function of food is by no means a simple task, although deeply thinking about food is a heuristic endeavor. Whether it suggests experimentation or the commonplace, eating signifies a pleasure of practice.

During the 1980s, at the height of the polarizing feminist sex wars, burgeoning Southern lesbian feminist communities bravely writing explicit, "outer limits" sex acts challenged the marginal status of lesbians in literature and academia as well as the marginalized positioning of certain sex acts both within and beyond the bedroom. These efforts solidified in the creation of a more honest body of lesbian literature that told the truth about outer limits, queer, and sadomasochistic sex acts that took place in the Southern geography of American bohemia.[15] They did so by explicitly representing specific sex acts, which had to that point not only been considered nonfeminist, but also within the realm of a male, heterosexual sex repertoire. "Going down" and being "out" about it was a radically activist and identity-constitutive act. In *Skin: Talking about Sex, Class, and Literature* (1994), Dorothy Allison laments a lack of truth and explicitness in the "brave new world of lesbian fiction," noting, "Love stories, grief and memory stories, sensual memory stories, one that played on the words *eating her*, featuring the body of the beloved, newly dead, cooked up as stew and savored—nonexplicit to the point of obscurity."[16] By honing in on what they knew best—region and Southern food—and drawing on the expectations of region and Southern foodways through allusion, imagery, and commonplace euphemisms, these lesbian writers truly bring flesh and texture to the act of eating.

Eros and Eating, Or You Eat What You Are

The communities that shape identity are not always welcome or welcoming ones. Feminist factions, family, and heterosexist patriarchy are sources of affective anger in Allison's collection *The Women Who Hate Me* (1991). These poems are seductively engaging for their emotional, linguistic precision, yet violent, explicit imagery shocks the reader out of that word spell. Written between 1981 and the summer of 1983 following her participation in the landmark and controversial feminist gathering, the Scholar and the Feminist Conference IX, held at Barnard College in New York, Allison's collection primarily evokes the pleasures and dangers in lesbian relationships. The majority of these poems focus tightly on demystifying lesbian romanticism: "I do not believe anymore in the natural superiority / of the lesbian," she writes in the title poem, "the women who hate me."[17] Other poems in the collection analogously trigger a sense of poignant resentment, including topics on childhood sexual abuse, class struggle, and volatile female relationships to divisive politics within the feminist movement and mendacity. Of the twenty-seven collected poems, four prominently feature food in their titles: "Dumpling Child," "Appetite," "Tomato Song," and "Butter My Tongue." Other poems incorporate food imagery, including "I Chose This Ground," where Allison laments living "a lifetime away from the cornbread / warm milk hunger of my childhood."[18] Southern foodstuffs are repeatedly and explicitly used to signal the poetics of sex acts throughout the collection: "Will you sit at my table, / eat my gravy . . . will you slide your cabbage hands over my belly / your dirty mouth up my thigh?"[19] Relieved of searching for the *what* of sexuality, we are freed to focus on the *how*—that is, how the intersections of region, sexuality, and sociality are conveyed and, inevitably, are in tension.

Examining "Dumpling Child" for its literal meaning is an exercise in savoring descriptive carnal desires. Born in Greenville, South Carolina, and raised in Florida, Allison echoes her Southern heritage vis-à-vis comfort food in the poem. Her use of food imagery overwhelmingly gestures toward regional cuisine, bringing lesbian experiences viscerally to life in an assertion of shared gustatory heritage and implied community. The first five lines of the poem describe down-home Southern cooking as a primary constituent of identity:

A southern dumpling child
biscuit eater, tea sipper
okra slicer, gravy dipper,
I fry my potatoes with onions
stew my greens with pork.[20]

The use of "child" suggests a nostalgic orientation toward Southern food, while the words "eater," "sipper," "slicer," and "dipper" indicate a doer behind the action, a regional subject. Pork-laced greens are particularly relevant to understanding Allison's roots as a "white-trash, no-account" Southerner. Turnip greens, simmered in poverty and leftover ham bones, "belong to the South, as firmly rooted as a peanut vine" whereas southern Louisiana recipes for greens, such as Spinach Madeleine, made famous in *The River Road Recipes*, suggest a certain cultural cachet.[21] Indeed, signaling fortune and class, or aspirations thereof, collard greens are traditionally eaten on New Year's Day to ensure good luck in the coming year. Allison concretely embraces regional food specialties like okra and tea, biscuits and milk gravy, to indicate their centrality to both her individual tastes and her Southern subjectivity.

The relationship between food and sex in this poem is even more explicit when considerations of affective sensory pleasures, tastes, and textures come into play. The assonance of "biscuit," "sipper," and "dipper" evokes euphemistic ways of reading. Repetitive sucking sounds link the food, the eater, and the reader, just as the poem weds culinary imagery with two female lovers.[22] Considering the poem at face value and analyzing its types of food for their literal meaning, it is clear that Allison blends salty flavors with savory ones— the flake of a briny biscuit, the thick consistency of flavorful gravy.

Taste is intrinsic to food and sex, both inside and outside of the kitchen. The longer second stanza of "dumpling child" melds food memories with erotic lesbian passion. Allison's lover tastes sweet, like watermelon; sprinkling red watermelon with sea salt expands the palate in a time-honored Southern tradition:

> And ride my lover high up
> on the butterfat shine of her thighs
> where her belly arches and sweetly tastes
> of rock salt on watermelon
> sunshine sharp teeth bite light
> and lick slow like mama's
> favorite dumpling child.[23]

The lover's thighs are polished like butter fat, the highest concentration of fatty cream in whole milk and velvety yellow butter; both lovers are white. Allison imparts a lush and indulgent female landscape where sex becomes a way to appreciate food and vice versa. She tastes her lover—slowly, she dines. The "sunshine sharp teeth bite light" as one's mouth does into a succulent dish. A child eats with abandon, savoring favorite foods carelessly and messily, never thinking to count calories or refrain from consuming what tastes good. Children are often picky about what they eat, wanting to maximize the delight of consumption; adults, meanwhile, are often partial to foods not because of a direct sensory pleasure but because they nostalgically remind them of home and family.[24] Likewise, Allison's inclusion of foodstuffs in this poem symbolizes relief and region (Southern food as comfort food) while connoting decadence. She makes visible the dual desires of food and sex as integral to her core self—not collapsing the two, but coupling each embodied, tactile experience to maximize their joint concupiscence.

Allison's memories of food are inescapably Southern. Lovemaking in the poem is affixed to and articulated through the vehicle of Southern food, making Allison's identity visible through this inextricable surface pairing. She asserts lesbian identity as a part of the Southern social realm, integrating sexual importance and validity while embodying a sexual identity she could be proud of and honest about—an identity that belongs to the broader feminist community and, by extension, the nation. Her work tells the story of Southern lesbian desire and sex made palatable and celebrated through Southern food—and affirmed through regional traditions.

Allison continues to explore intersecting relationships between regional affiliation and lesbian identity in her poem "Tomato Song," as setting and sense of place establish a fraught divide between urban New York and the rural South. Caught in the fray, Allison muses that she "Might as well live up to my reputation" as a lesbian, as a Southerner, and as an outsider on both scores.[25] She imagines herself wreaking havoc on the residents of New York, a hyperbolized figure wrecking bridges, ringing in the unwanted reign of a displaced, angry lesbian. It is important to emphasize that Allison, as an explicitly Southern lesbian, is not playing a catch-up game in the progressive city, but rather is at the forefront of challenging 1980s feminist and lesbian identity politics. Her reputation, and her experiences as a "White trash / no count / bastard" Southerner with deviant lesbian sadomasochistic proclivities were actively invalidated and spurned by the lesbian feminist movement at the time—one caught in a notorious scholar-activist debate surrounding sex-negative and sex-positive feminist politics.[26] Like "kind of a great red fruit" Allison envisions that she will

> . . . grow a rage like a tomato,
> . . . .
> . . . bring down sauce
> on half the city
> tell low-down jokes
> proposition old ladies
> lick their cheeks, offer to
> climb up under their skirts
> for free.[27]

Allison's choice of a vine-ripened, juicy tomato is a strategic one—tomatoes would not typically thrive in New York as well as they would in the South. While she presents readers with the portrait of a single garden tomato, Southerners might imagine fields filled with rows and rows of tomatoes ripe for the picking. Sun Belt crops sewn in New York City are as adventitious as the image of Allison's great, enraged tomato rolling up Broadway. Looking with the poem, Allison juxtaposes this ripe, hardy fruit alongside the hard streets of New York, suggesting the difficulty of nonnormative desires in even the most progressive of cities, as well as the regional and affective displacements she registers not only as Southerner living in New York but as a woman explicitly writing about sexuality in the national-level lesbian feminist political moment. Sex was important, serious, a battleground; writing was an act of self-discovery, self-revelation.[28]

This round, succulent, and crimson-colored fruit is not only symbolic of Allison's Southern roots—"last but not least in the pantheon of Southern vegetables"—but of her sexual identity and physiology as well.[29] Her tomato song is the lyrical melody of an angry vagina. Her rage is both literal and satirical, and above all, very public: she appropriates the stereotype that Southerners, women, and—in particular—lesbians are irrational and emotionally dysfunctional.[30]

Expanding her fantasy self to grotesque proportions, Allison gives a satirical embrace to the social disorder one might expect from a Southern lesbian's presence, body, and sexuality—although ostensibly, she's writing to other feminist lesbians more broadly. In *Rabelais and His World* (1984), Mikhail Bakhtin writes "the grotesque is always satire. Where there is no satirical orientation there is no grotesque."[31] Addressing a regional sexual context, Mab Segrest argues that the figure of the grotesque in Southern literature only serves to further marginalize the already marginal: "I knew in my guts that my strongest feelings, for women and girls, put me somehow on the outside, set me apart. Although I did not know what *lesbian* was, I felt myself a closet freak."[32] The grotesque body carries with it considerable potential for transgression by aligning the abject with the figural, the closeted with the exaggerated, and the normal with the freakish.[33] In sarcastic and humorous tones, Allison's epic adventures in the poem satirize the chaos she imagines her very presence as a Southern, sex-positive, sadomasochistic, kink-loving lesbian might cause.

Color choice is a prominent element in "Tomato Song," as red is a hue that prodigiously symbolizes passion and sensuality and, at times, violence. Like the watermelon in "dumpling child," Allison's red, pulsing desire for women parallels the tomato as a source of vitality and nourishment—and in some senses, sexual and regional orientation. Much as the tomato literally sustains life, so too does her vagina enliven the pleasures of her body—her anger and her desire both stem from that place where blood pumps and pulses. She melds sources of strength, thoroughly infusing red, red arousal, anger, fruit, and Southernness with oxygen and life. The poem concludes with Allison proclaiming that she will make no apologies about her sexual identity, that there will be "nothing but me, my tomato, my rages, / my name, / my name."[34] She accepts and claims her lesbian and Southern identities regardless of how she might be perceived or (mis)understood. Reading with the grain, her pride is evident, if not—like a tomato—somewhat vulnerable to bruising.

Class privilege, entitlement, and denial separated Allison from a wider, national feminist movement that increasingly became reactionary and exclusionary—not surprisingly, on the topic of sex. Drawing together the intensities and passions of life itself, Allison illustrates how she embodies rage and carnality irrespective of what society imagines those experiences to feel like, while powerfully defying her enemies within a feminist movement intent on speaking out against politically incorrect sex. In the 1980s, sex-negative feminists overwhelmingly viewed oral sex between women as a deviant practice; lesbian oral sex was invariably enmeshed in a heated national conversation surrounding the political meanings of sex acts and the radical nature of expressing and speaking them openly.[35] Such hypervisible representations of lesbian sex might have resonated strongly with prosex lesbian feminists, women who discussed and organized around "deviant" sexual desires—fetish specific and/or incorporating bondage and sadomasochism—in the public sphere, building lesbian sociality through intersextionality and positing "radical sex itself as a sign of radical politics."[36] Allison's anger reflects her desire for a new social order. As a Southern lesbian writing radically activist, avant-garde, identity-constitutive poetry, she embodies bohemian "dissidence, opposition, criticism of the status quo . . . expressed politically, aesthetically or in the artists behavior and lifestyle."[37]

Oranges Are Not the Only Fruit

Minnie Bruce Pratt's five-line poem "Peach," from her collection *We Say We Love Each Other* (1985) offers a metaphorical comparison between a uniquely state-specific Southern food—Georgia peaches, anyone?—and lesbian oral-anal sex (anilingus).[38] According to Virginia Willis, cookbook author of *Bon Appétit, Y'all* (2008) and frequent contributor to the Southern Foodways Alliance blog, "I'm certainly biased toward Georgia peaches, but it seems to me that the red clay soil and hot sun here create a taste like no other. . . . In keeping with the region's legendary sweet tooth, many Southern recipes can quickly turn the healthful peach into something terribly unvirtuous—though delicious." This observation recalls the injunction about "putting the South in your mouth," and Pratt's poem works with and against these associations while stressing the link between food and normative/virtuous and nonnormative/nonvirtuous sexual taboos:

> My tongue, your ass:
> the center of a peach,
> ripe, soft, pitted, red-fibred flesh
> dissolving toward earth, lust
> *Eat you?* I ask.[39]

The unvirtuous conflation of peach imagery and ass imagery in Pratt's "Peach" illustrates the ways in which one's tongue and ass are similar to a peach. Both are red, soft, and laden with small surface indentions. The center of the peach in this poem is pitted, characterized by absence, whereas the tongue fills the mouth. Indeed, looking at the very center of this poem, one notices absence: the pitted fruit, one's pitted ass. The word "pitted" falls within the center of a five-line poem: third line, third word. As an evocative focus for both the ass and peach, any lack or absence evidenced by the central placement of "pitted" in fact only illuminates a need to fill, penetrate. And yet while the reader sub-consciously sexualizes the peach—perhaps as a central, intended image—it is germane to consider how the tongue is ripe for hypersexualization: like "your ass," "my tongue" is lustful, juicy, and rutted.

Also notable here is a matter of sequence, and questions of forbidden eat-ing and the salacious. The final line of the poem is proleptic, evidenced by the interrogative, "*Eat you?* I ask." This act of oral-anal sex has not yet been acted upon; it is a future act that has not yet been consummated. Unlike our speak-er's romantic attachment to peaches—her sultry tactile descriptions of sight and feel—there is a curious absence of taste sensations with regard to the ass. This speaks to the lack established and performed by "pitted" as the center of the poem. As an interrogative, "*Eat you?*" is not merely an acknowledged invitation—a polite seeking of consent; it is an incredulous one. Perhaps our speaker has never tasted ass, and the interrogative suggests that eating ass might taste as good as a peach would. Sexual taboo is evocatively surfaced—in our face as well as the speaker's.

We might consider "Peach" at face value in terms of the sexual taboos it evokes, but the poem is also shockingly representative of a sexual conviction bravely steeped in validating the protagonist's unvirtuous desire for kink. Consider how the adage "tossed salad" serves as a colloquial referent to oral-anal sex. Here again we see the rhetoric of food used to discuss the sexed body, or the sex act of licking and eating around or in the ass. In "Thinking Sex: Notes for a Radical Theory of the Politics of Sexuality," Gayle Rubin theorizes sex negativity endemic to Western culture, diagramming a hierar-chical sexual value system oppressive to erotic misconduct and divergent sexual tastes. This hierarchy of sexual value—where sex is determined to be a sinfully destructive force—operates in much of the same ways as other ideo-logical systems do. Determined by a complex model, socially acceptable sex practices are dependent upon sex object choice (including sex, gender, race, ethnicity, and age), location, degree of familiarity, number of participants, and kind of experience.

Rubin posits a diametrically oppositional frame: good, normal sex or "the charmed circle" as relationally superior to bad, abnormal sex or "the outer limits."[40] Her work calls into question where oral-anal sex between lesbians would fall on a hierarchical table or circle. As a queer sex act, anal sex—at least in the popular imaginary—is frequently attributed to sex between men. The act itself is gendered, and in "Peach" we see a reversal of that attributive gender: much in the same way that peach imagery in the poem is overthrown, subverted—dare I say *tossed*—from its usual conflation with cunt to instead highlight a woman's ass.

These intersecting taboos bring into focus how occupying the outer limit—lesbian oral-anal sex—is a position of critical periphery. Sexual behaviors classified outside of the "charmed circle" dispute the normative position of such problematically structured systems of desire. Their positions in fact constitute one another even as the "outer limits" call into question how they are both mutually constructed by society's mores. This discussion is equally applicable to my readings of Allison's poetry. In "Sex Writing, the Importance and the Difficulty," Allison writes, "What was taboo? In what context? Sex had always been so risky. It had seemed enough just to pronounce myself a lesbian. Did I have to say what it was I truly desired, what I did and did not do, and why?"[41] Albeit from different perspectives, both Pratt and Allison are addressing what have been the "outer limits" of socially acceptable sexuality—foregrounding the intersection of not only nonnormative sexual identities, but also nonnormative sexual acts in what would have been a highly disputed emergent world of lesbian fiction—ultimately centering them, or at the very least, declaring them legitimate and therefore visible.

Pratt's poem "Plums," strategically placed on the page opposite "Peach," comprises two sentences:

I love the way you
give me cold plums. I love the
way you give me tongues.[42]

Here again, relieved of searching for sexuality, we see an exuberant celebration of lesbian sex acts metaphorically juxtaposed against commonplace table fruit. Reading with the grain of the poem, and of curve of the plum itself, we see Pratt gesturing toward oral sex between women as forbidden fruit: frisky, challenging, ironic, and wide open to sensations including hot and cold. Comparing tongue temperature play to a chilled plum, Pratt intimately shares with readers an expansive sexual repertoire laced with flairs of sexual kink.

Focusing on the sensual details of life, Pratt's "Peach" and "Plums" exhibit an assemblage of fruits swept up in the intensity of lesbian desire—common table fruits are libidinous. The sheer force of lesbian eroticism in these works speak to Grosz's reconfiguration of lesbian desire as she asks, "the question is not am I . . . a lesbian, but rather, what kinds of lesbian connections, what kinds of lesbian-machine, we invest our time, energy, and bodies in, what kinds of sexuality we invest ourselves in, with what other kinds of bodies, and to what effects? What it is that together, in parts and bits, and interconnections, we can make that is new, exploratory, opens up further spaces, induces further intensities, speeds up, enervates, and proliferates production . . . ?"[43]

The power of these poems lies in their multitude of sensory associations: drawing together surfaces through intersextionality, the skin of a woman's body similar to the skin of a fruit's peel, the flesh of both, the tactile sensations of eating warm or cool, and so too the literary production itself in turn producing lesbian sociality and community.

Continuing to explore the carnal appetites proliferating in Southern food, lesbian sexual identity, and ardent, pleasurable acts ripe in literary productions—invigorated specifically within a lens of succulent fruits—centralizes doris davenport's three-stanza poem, "Blackberry Time." According to *The Companion to Southern Literature*, davenport is a "lesser-known but important southern lesbian poet" who was born in Gainesville, Georgia.[44] While her six collections of poetry, in particular her self-published works *It's Like This* (1980), *Eat Thunder and Drink Rain* (1982), and *Voodoo Chile—Slight Return* (1991), have been neglected in contemporary literary criticism on the women's liberation movement and in the African American arts movement, as well as within a wider body of Southern literature, her work is ripe for examining the intersectionalities/intersextualities in Southern lesbian sociality and race.[45] Her contribution to the internationally groundbreaking anthology *This Bridge Called My Back* (1981), titled "The Pathology of Racism: A Conversation with Third World Wimmin," linked late 1970s and early 1980s feminisms with the lived experiences of women negotiating institutional and personal racism within a regional framework. Writing from her subjective perspective, davenport addressed the disparate struggles white women and women of color felt within a changing feminist movement, ultimately dismantling what Allison has called "the same old, slightly distant, and carefully respectable aura of feminist theory."[46] That defiant voice—declaring and reveling in explicitness, expanding and shifting early 1970s and 1980s mainstream feminisms—encompasses davenport's erotic poetry.

The wide availability of fruits and berries in the South extends to table accompaniments including jams, jellies, and preserves. Indeed, the processes of drying, salting, stewing, boiling, pickling, potting, freezing, and canning are historically enmeshed Southern traditions dating from the early 1800s until the post–World War II era as food was "put up" for later consumption.[47] One of the preserves that is closely identified with the South is blackberry jam. Blackberries were found "growing in Virginia 380 years ago by the first English settlers," and the very ripest of blackberries are naturally sweet.[48] Davenport exuberantly and playfully trades on the expectation of blackberry sweetness in her poem "Blackberry Time," paralleling Southern sun-ripened imagery associations with a woman's sexual readiness:

> at a certain time in summer
> they grow wild
> & lush everywhere each tiny
> grain filled with black
> juice / each little bubble a
> huge berry
>
> blackberries wild and loose—
> mixed with honeysuckles & weeds &
> all you have to do
> is fight off a few bugs, pick off
> a few stuck in the juice to get
> a mouthstained purple-black
> smiling over that
> juice / hot &
> sensuous to the tongue & throat
> & bare brown feet
>
> at *that* time in summer
> when black berries will
> again
> grow wild, free, unfenced
> & unpolluted i
> can find you
> in honeysuckles & weeds &
> know again your
> hot sweetness.[49]

The alimentary and sexual jouissance is unmistakable. In "One Child of One's Own" Alice Walker connects "the color of raspberries and blackberries" to a black woman's vagina and clitoris.[50] Soft, erotic tones of delighted discovery work us (the readers) over with honest, lesbian delectation and emergent meaning. The notion of "eating out" takes on a new layer as the affinity between berries and sugar—the clit or "huge berry"—and corporeal juices crystallize in sharp relief. The poetic persona in "Blackberry Time" must search for the berries she seeks, picking through obstacles and natural landscape to locate the hot sweetness she desires. And yet, these berries are in abundance as they in fact "grow wild & lush everywhere," ripe for the plucking and spreading. "Brown feet" walk barefoot over hot, overripened blackberries, mirroring her "mouthstained" purple-black grin. Each tactile, sumptuous-laden physical experience is commemorated in this poem, where black/berries are not only wild, but also free.

La Vie Bohème: A Place at the Table

It is important to note that in these poems, sex, food, and eating aren't conflated concepts or acts. Each is represented in its composite dimensions, yet connected through angry, playful, or suggestive connotations. Allison's delightful short story "A Lesbian Appetite" perhaps engages with these intersexualities more explicitly than any other text considered here, as she interweaves descriptions of poverty with food meanings, all the while paying homage to Southern appetites and lesbian sexuality. Southern identity and food thematics take precedence in the story, and are crucial to understanding her penurious childhood. As a young girl, Allison worries that she and her cousins aren't getting enough vitamin D; a teacher offhandedly remarks that "the children of the poor have a lack of brain tissue simply because they don't get the necessary vitamins at the proper age."[51] Allison's poor diet seems inextricably linked to her poor upbringing, and she interweaves her understandings of class and the painfulness of dieting in ways that limit, control, and shame her. Allison attributes her dietary habits, yearnings for Southern comfort foods that nourish both her body and soul, to a catalog of physical ailments including rotten teeth, bad skin, and rickets. These inescapable physical markers seem to brand her with a poverty that she can neither fully escape nor completely forget.

The salience of Southern food memory is articulated through Allison's personal sexual history—as she loves women, so too does she love eating: both are sources of pleasure and comfort. Whether achieved through food or sex, both of her drives for pleasure and comfort flirt with the realities of indulging:

"Swallow it," Jay said. . . . Her . . . hand worked between us, pinching me but forcing the thick cream out of my cunt. She brought it up and pushed it into my mouth, took the hand I'd cleaned and smeared it again with her own musky gravy.[52]

Sex for Allison is messy. It is textured, smelly, sweaty, and consuming. It is not mannerly or refined, but instead, it is thick and hearty, gravy and cream.

Allison's evocative eroticism mirrors her gastronomic desire for "southern beans, pork fat, buttermilk, barbeque, and hush puppies" as affective resonances stem from a pleasure in remembering: "I've only had one lover who didn't want to eat at all. We didn't last long. The sex was good, but I couldn't think what to do with her when the sex finished. We drank spring water together and fought a lot."[53] Food is seamlessly linked to sexuality in this story, and the space of the kitchen and home itself—the South—is inscribed with a reconceptualized, distinctive lesbian domesticity. Challenging implicit heteronormative narratives of cooking and kinship in the region, including her own family's kitchen back in South Carolina, presided over by her mother, Allison queers the home and, by extension, the region and nation through the impact of a lesbian new normativity. Indeed, she dreams of throwing a dinner party at the end of the story, where she invites all of the women from her life—lesbian lovers and girlfriends—to enter the now safe space of her mother's house and partake in the feast: "My mama is in the kitchen salting a vat of greens. Two of my aunts are arguing over whether to make little baking powder biscuits or big buttermilk logsheads."[54] Suddenly Allison, a woman whose childhood was characterized by hunger, no longer hungers. In the moment at which her lovers enter her home—the space where Southern food is prepared and the regional place in which she was raised—she finds a unifying fullness.

Allison's relief is apparent on the surface, too, after such a long separation from home and the food she is unable and unwilling to disassociate from it. Living in New York City, Allison nostalgically reflects on the fried, crisp, buttered, slathered, and marinated food of her Southern youth and the comforting feeling of home it evokes. One girlfriend from the North, Lee, is a health food nut. In preparing the food for the great Southeastern Feminist Conference, Lee tries to convince Allison that healthy, vegetarian food is the way to go.[55] She plies Allison with "poppyseed cake made with gluten flour," seven-grain bread, whole wheat pasta, granola, salad, and fruits—eventually enlisting Allison to peel, slice, and chop loads and loads of fresh vegetables, including "carrots, potatoes, onions, green and red peppers, leeks, tomatoes, and squash."[56] But Allison believes that the two hundred Southern women would rather have "donuts and coffee."[57]

At play in this story are multiple, traditionally diachronically opposed binaries: the North-South divide, healthy food versus junk food, and a highbrow versus lowbrow class-based hierarchy of food preferences. But these binaries extend beyond Southern regional identity, food, and class to engage with sex and nation: for Allison, what is considered "bad" junk food is good and tasty, no matter how it affects her body and health.

Nostalgia reverberates throughout this passage, too, as food is associated with comfort, comforting food is associated with Southern food, and Southern food is associated with home. For Allison, the relationship between what food is comforting and good directly parallels with what sex is comforting and good. In moments where food is not obviously linked to Southernness or region, she is able to transform the alimentary experience into a comforting sexual encounter, thus indirectly joining narratives of home by way of non-normative, messy, subversive lesbian sex:

> I took the wedge of eggplant and rubbed it on the back of her neck.
> "What are you doing?"
> "Salting the eggplant." I followed the eggplant with my tongue, pulled up her T-shirt, and slowly ran the tough purple rind up to her small bare breasts. Lee started giggling, wiggling her ass, but not taking her hands out of the flour to stop me. I pulled down her shorts, picked up another dry slice and planted it against her navel, pressed with my fingers and slipped it down toward her pubic mound . . . .
> "You are just running salt, girl," I teased, and pushed slices up between her legs, while I licked one of her nipples and pinched the other between a folded slice of eggplant. She was laughing, her belly bouncing under me.
> "I'm going to make you eat all this," she yelled.[58]

If we understand the home to be a microlevel representation of the nation, then both the home and nation are overwhelmingly fashioned within dominant ideologies of compulsory heterosexuality and normative sexual desires. Allison's short story "A Lesbian Appetite" subverts these dualistic frames, illustrating how lesbian hypervisibility works to accommodate other forms of sexuality and enable new conceptions of national subjects through the regional. Creating a "mythical terrain within" her "own regional culture," Allison's imagined *vie bohème* occupies a liminal space "between the national and the regional, refusing the centrality of the one and the limits of the other."[59] The South functions as tenor concept; Southern food is the vehicle for progressive social change or, at least, room for more nonnormativity at a national table. This story utilizes the most commonplace, messy, and low-quality Southern foods (red beans and rice, chicken necks and dumplings, pan-fried pork chops and red-eye gravy, barbeque and cole slaw) to translate large-scale, complex metaphors surrounding home, class, rurality, nostalgia, comfort, nation, and sexual (non)normativity—ultimately foregrounding importance of what we get from critically thinking about sex through food, and putting a taste of the South in our mouths.

And to what end? Intersextionality in these works enables Allison, Pratt, and davenport to transform the obvious, making lesbian eroticism and desire manifest through the vehicle of Southern food. This gesture asserts lesbian sexual identity as a politically viable subject position in the region, making their voices and writings important and valuable to an increasingly polarized national feminism centrally concerned with the meanings and implications of sex acts. Southern lesbian writers were at the center of those debates, causing more than their sexuality to surface on the textual page; their autochthonous regional roots are emphatic as well.

Moving from marginalization to unification, these women celebrate lesbianism through a love of food and a love for region, creating a sense of unity and sociality over the most mundane and routine of Southern foods: cabbage, tomatoes, peaches, plums, blackberries, and biscuits. The ordinary, commonplace quality of these foods, and their availability in the region, suggests something powerful and profound: that lesbians and their literary productions were, and still are, extant, plentiful, and thriving in the South.

Notes

An earlier version of this chapter appeared as "Put a Taste of the South in Your Mouth: Carnal Appetites and Intersextionality," *Study the South*, September 10, 2015, http://southernstudies.olemiss.edu/study-the-south/put-a-taste-of-the-south-in-your-mouth/.

1. Romine, *The Real South*, 108.

2. Yaeger, "Edible Labor," 150.

3. Egerton, *Southern Food*, 2. For a fracturing discussion on what constitutes Southern food across states in the region and among regional cultural identities, see Engelhardt's introduction to *A Mess of Greens*.

4. Engelhardt, "Introduction," 1–2. For a thoughtful and searing commentary on gender bias in Southern food writing, see Purvis, "The Testosterone Takeover."

5. Ibid., 4.

6. Wilson, *Bohemians*, 4. See also Levin, *Bohemia in America*, 215, which notes, "The very term *Bohemian* might thus have operated . . . as a homoerotic word."

7. Gluck, *Popular Bohemia*, 15.

8. Probyn, *Carnal Appetites*, 5.

9. Grosz, "Refiguring Lesbian Desire," in *Space, Time, and Perversion*, 181.

10. When I use the term *lesbian hypervisibility*, I mean a supersaturation or blatant celebration/recognition of lesbian topics and themes in selected texts—*understood relationally* in comparison to midcentury Southern literary works in which an absence/

presence of sexual otherness is a matter of willful denial or careful detection. Indeed, a close reading suggests a taboo; hypervisibilty represents an end of taboo, thus calling into question the necessity of close readings. A shift to hypervisibility opens up the complexity of literary space for critical analysis. If saturation already exists on the textual surface, we as readers must resist looking deeper into the narrative frame and instead favor new reading methods that examine how we might look *across* the surface of literary representations. For more on surface readings, see Marcus and Best, "Surface Reading: An Introduction."

11. Tompkins, *Racial Indigestion*, 185.

12. Probyn, *Carnal Appetites*, 9.

13. Engelhardt, *A Mess of Greens*, 15.

14. Foucault, *The History of Sexuality*, 3.

15. For a lengthier discussion of the feminist lesbian sex wars, see Lisa Duggan, *Sex Wars: Sexual Dissent and Political Culture* (New York: Routledge Press, 2006); Carol S. Vance, *Pleasure and Danger: Exploring Female Sexuality* (London: Pandora Press, 1992); and Jane Gerhard, *Desiring Revolution: Second-wave Feminism and the Rewriting of American Sexual Thought, 1920 to 1982* (New York: Columbia University Press, 2001).

16. Allison, *Skin*, 89.

17. Allison, "The Women," in *The Women Who Hate Me*, 21.

18. Allison, "I Chose This Ground," in *The Women Who Hate Me*, 63.

19. Allison, "Liar," in *The Women Who Hate Me*, 34.

20. Allison, "Dumpling Child," in *The Women Who Hate Me*, 9. I have made every effort in this essay to accurately represent the textual placement of these poems and fiction as they physically appear on the original page, keeping in mind the author's intentions with regard to form.

21. Allison, "The Women," 21; Crumpacker, *The Sex Life of Food*, 8, 109.

22. For more on the subtleties of rural Southern sound, see Southern Culture on the Skids' unapologetic rockabilly song, "Biscuit Eater" (1992).

23. Allison, "Dumpling Child," 9.

24. Crumpacker, *The Sex Life of Food*, 18.

25. Allison, "Tomato Song," in *The Women Who Hate Me*, 36.

26. Allison, "The Women," 21.

27. Allison, "Tomato Song," 36.

28. Allison, *Skin*, 39–40.

29. Egerton, *Southern Food*, 310. In a August 2014 Southern Foodways Alliance blog entry, Virginia Willis writes "Fresh tomatoes are only ever good in summer." http://www.southernfoodways.org/one-tomato-two-tomato/). There is also the unique festival nature of the South—its insistence on food as an occasion for social celebration—and, in particular, the decade-spanning French Market Creole Tomato Festival: "The French Market Creole Tomato Festival is a celebration of Louisiana's produce, farmers and the Pelican State's unique cultural and cuisine offerings, of which the Creole tomato is emblematic. Originally imported from the West Indies, the Creole tomato thrives in the rich alluvial soil and subtropical climate of south Louisiana,

especially in St. Bernard and Plaquemines parishes." City of New Orleans, "French Market Creole Tomato Festival."

30. Regarding Southerners' irrationality and violence, this is particularly true of white men (see, for example, Bertram Wyatt-Brown, *Honor and Violence in the Old South* (Oxford: Oxford University Press, 1986) but also white women, as representations of white women in the 2013 film *12 Years a Slave*, among others, show.

31. Bakhtin, *Rabelais*, 306.

32. Segrest "Southern Women Writing: Toward a Literature of Wholeness" in *My Mama's Dead Squirrel*, 20.

33. Ibid., 24–25.

34. Allison, "Tomato Song," 37.

35. Allison's 1981 consciousness-raising group, Lesbian Sex Mafia, and Pat Califia's book *Sapphistry: The Book of Lesbian Sexuality* (Tallahassee: Naiad Press, 1988) were groundbreaking in this regard.

36. Kahan, *Celibacies*, 152.

37. Wilson, *Bohemians*, 3.

38. Peaches not only suggest a rather state-specific association in the regional sense and sexually specific association in the corporeal sense but the fruit itself is frequently embodied as female and feminine. Consider Lynyrd Skynyrd's lyrics from "Georgia Peaches": "Well them Georgia peaches sure do got style/ They'll steal your heart with a Southern smile/ Well they talk a little funny but they look so fine."

39. Pratt, "Peach," in *We Say We Love Each Other*, 68.

40. Rubin, "Thinking Sex," 280.

41. Allison, *Skin*, 89.

42. Pratt, "Plums," in *We Say We Love Each Other*, 69.

43. Grosz, "Refiguring Lesbian Desire," 184.

44. Mark, "Lesbian Literature," 429.

45. In the preface to doris davenport's *Voodoo Chile*, vii–viii, AfraShe Asungi writes, "And to get finally to the CENTER of my point; given doris' 'gift of insight' and skill at her 'craft,' there is no SANE reason that I can find for doris' having to 'self-publish' THIS manuscript, and fortunately, she hasn't let THIS slight be a deterrent either, but doris says it better than I in her poem, 'about my manuscript rejected for the sixth time by seven *alternative* feminist-black-lesbian-small-press-publishers,' when she says 'I hear in silence / continue, as always, to sing / so i can not be stopped. nothing can stop my words.'"

46. Allison, *Skin*, 115.

47. Egerton, *Southern Food*, 179.

48. Ibid., 181.

49. davenport, "Blackberry Time," in *Voodoo Chile*, 17.

50. Walker, *In Search of Our Mothers' Gardens*, 374.

51. Allison, *Trash*, 156.

52. Ibid., 157.

53. Ibid., 151.

54. Ibid., 165.

55. Ibid., 159.
56. Ibid.
57. Ibid., 158.
58. Ibid., 155.
59. Levin, *Bohemia in America*, 243–44.

References

Allison, Dorothy. *Skin: Talking About Sex, Class, and Literature*. Ithaca, NY: Firebrand, 1994.
———. *Trash*. Ithaca, NY: Firebrand, 1988.
———. *The Women Who Hate Me: Poetry 1980–1990*. Ithaca, NY: Firebrand, 1991.
Bakhtin, Mikhail. *Rabelais and His World*. Translated by Helene Iswolsky. Bloomington: University of Indiana Press, 1984.
City of New Orleans. "French Market Creole Tomato Festival." http://www.neworleansonline.com/neworleans/festivals/culinaryfestivals/creoletomatofestival.html.
Crumpacker, Bunny. *The Sex Life of Food: When Body and Soul Meet to Eat*. New York: Dunne, 2006.
davenport, doris. *Voodoo Chile—Slight Return: Poems*. Charlotte, NC: Soque Street, 1991.
Egerton, John. *Southern Food*. New York: Knopf, 1987.
Engelhardt, Elizabeth. "Introduction: Redrawing the Grocery: Practices and Methods for Studying Southern Food." In *The Larder: Food Studies Methods from the American South*, edited by Elizabeth Engelhardt, John T. Edge, and Ted Ownby, 1–6. Athens: University of Georgia Press, 2014.
———. *A Mess of Greens: Southern Gender and Southern Food*. Athens: University of Georgia Press, 2011.
Foucault, Michel. *The History of Sexuality*. Vol. 2, *The Use of Pleasure*. Reissue ed. Translated by Robert Hurley. New York: Vintage, 1990.
Gluck, Mary. *Popular Bohemia: Modernism and Urban Culture in Nineteenth-Century Paris*. Cambridge: Harvard University Press, 2005.
Grosz, Elizabeth. *Space, Time, and Perversion: Essays on the Politics of Bodies*. New York: Routledge, 1995.
Kahan, Benjamin. *Celibacies: American Modernism and Sexual Life*. Durham, NC: Duke University Press, 2013.
Levin, Joanna. *Bohemia in America, 1858–1920*. Stanford, CA: Stanford University Press, 2010.
Marcus, Sharon, and Stephen Best. "Surface Reading: An Introduction." *Representations* 108 (2009): 1–21.
Mark, Rebecca. "Lesbian Literature." In *The Companion to Southern Literature: Themes, Genres, Places, People, Movements and Motifs*, edited by Flora, Joseph M., Lucinda Hardwick MacKethan, and Todd W. Taylor. Baton Rouge: Louisiana State University Press, 2001.

Purvis, Kathleen. "The Testosterone Takeover of Southern Food Writing." *Bitter Southerner: Stories about the South* (blog). http://bittersoutherner.com/the -testosterone-takeover-of-southern-food-writing/#.V3WMrPkrJpg.

Pratt, Minnie Bruce. *We Say We Love Each Other*. San Francisco: Spinsters/Aunt Lute, 1985.

Probyn, Elspeth. *Carnal Appetites: FoodSexIdentities*. New York: Routledge, 2000.

Romine, Scott. *The Real South: Southern Narrative in the Age of Cultural Reproduction*. Baton Rouge: Louisiana State University Press, 2008.

Rubin, Gayle. "Thinking Sex: Notes for a Radical Theory of the Politics of Sexuality." In *Pleasure and Danger: Exploring Female Sexuality*, edited by Carole S. Vance, 267–321. Boston: Routledge and Kegan Paul, 1984.

Segrest, Mab. *My Mama's Dead Squirrel: Lesbian Essays on Southern Culture*. Ithaca, NY: Firebrand, 1985.

Tompkins, Kyla Wazana. *Racial Indigestion: Eating Bodies in the 19th Century*. New York: New York University Press, 2012.

Walker, Alice. *In Search of Our Mothers' Gardens*. San Diego: Harcourt, 1983.

Wilson, Elizabeth. *Bohemians: The Glamorous Outcasts*. New Brunswick, NJ: Rutgers University Press, 2000.

Yaeger, Patricia. "Edible Labor." *Southern Quarterly* 30, nos. 2–3 (1992): 150–59.

Trash Food

Chris Offutt

Over the years I've known many people with nicknames, including Lucky, Big O, Haywire, Turtle Eggs, Hercules, two guys named Hollywood, and three guys called Booger. I've had my own nicknames as well. In college people called me Arf because of a T-shirt I wore that had a dog on it; back home a few of my best buddies still call me Shit-for-Brains because our teachers thought I was smart.

Three years ago, shortly after moving to Oxford, Mississippi, someone introduced me to John T. Edge. He goes by his first name and middle initial, but I understood it as a nickname—Jaunty. The word *jaunty* means lively and cheerful, merry and bright, so the name seemed to suit him perfectly. Each time I called him Jaunty he gave me a quick, sharp look of suspicion. He wondered if I was making fun of his name—and of him. The matter was resolved when I suggested he call me Chrissie O.

Last spring John T. asked me to join him at an Oxford restaurant. My wife dropped me off and drove to a nearby secondhand store; our plan was for me to meet her later and find a couple of cheap lamps. During lunch John T. asked me to give a presentation at the Southern Foodways Alliance symposium, over which he presided every fall.

I reminded him that I lacked the necessary qualifications. At the time I'd only published a few humorous essays that dealt with food. Other writers were more knowledgeable and wrote with a historical context, from a scholarly perspective. All I did was write personal essays inspired by old community cookbooks I found in secondhand stores. Strictly speaking, my food writing wasn't technically about food.

John T. said that didn't matter. He wanted me to explore "trash food," because, as he put it, "you write about class."

I sat without speaking, my food getting cold on my plate. Three thoughts ran through my mind as fast as flipping an egg. First, I couldn't see the connection between social class and garbage. Second, I didn't like having my thirty-year career reduced to a single subject. Third, I'd never heard of anything called trash food.

I write about my friends, my family, and my experiences, but never with a sociopolitical agenda such as class. My goal has always been art first, combined with an attempt at rigorous self-examination. Facing John T., I found myself in a professional and social pickle, not unusual for a country boy who's clawed his way out of the hills of eastern Kentucky, one of the steepest social climbs in America. I've never mastered the highborn art of concealing my emotions; my feelings are always readily apparent.

Recognizing my turmoil, John T. asked if I was pissed off. I nodded, and he apologized immediately. I told him I was overly sensitive to matters of social class. I explained that people from the hills of Appalachia have always had to fight to prove they were smart, diligent, and trustworthy. It's the same for people who grew up in the Mississippi Delta, the barrios of Los Angeles and Texas, or the black neighborhoods in Chicago, Memphis, and New York. His request reminded me that due to social class, I'd been refused dates, bank loans, and even jobs. I've been called hillbilly, stumpjumper, cracker, weedsucker, redneck, and white trash: mean-spirited terms designed to hurt me and make me feel bad about myself.

As a young man I used to laugh awkwardly at remarks about sex with my sister or the perceived novelty of my wearing shoes. As I got older, I quit laughing. When strangers thought I was stupid because of where I grew up, I saw it as them granting me the higher ground; I learned to patiently wait in ambush for the chance to utterly demolish them intellectually. Later I realized that this particular battle strategy was a waste of energy. It was easier to simply stop talking to that person—forever.

But I didn't want to do that with a guy whose name sounds like *jaunty*. A guy who'd inadvertently triggered an old emotional response. A guy who liked my work well enough to pay me for it.

By this time our lunch had a tension to it that draped over us both like a lead vest for an X-ray. We just looked at each other, neither of us knowing what to do. John T. suggested I think about it, and then graciously offered me a lift to meet my wife. But a funny thing had happened: our conversation had left me inexplicably ashamed of shopping at a thrift store. I wanted to walk, to hide my destination, but refusing a ride might make John T. think I was angry with him. I wasn't. I was upset, but not with him.

My solution was a verbal compromise, a term politicians use to mean a blatant lie. I told him to drop me at a restaurant where I was meeting my wife for cocktails. He did so, and I waited until his red Italian sports car sped away. As soon as he was out of sight I walked to the junk store. I sat out front like a man, with not a care in the world, ensconced in a battered patio chair staring at clouds above the parking lot. When I was a kid my mother bought baked goods at the day-old bread store and hoped no one would see her car. Now I was embarrassed for shopping secondhand.

My behavior was class-based twice over: buying used goods to save a buck and feeling ashamed of it. I'd behaved in strict accordance with my social station, and then evaluated myself in a negative fashion. Even my anger was classic self-oppression, a learned behavior of lower-class people. I was transforming outward shame into inner fury. Without a clear target, I aimed that rage at myself.

My thoughts and feelings were completely irrational. I knew they made no sense. Most of what I owned had belonged to someone else—cars, clothes, shoes, furniture, dishware, cookbooks. I liked old and battered things. They reminded me of myself, still capable and functioning despite the wear and tear. I enjoyed the idea that my belongings had a previous history before coming my way. It was very satisfying to repair a broken lamp made of popsicle sticks and transform it to a lovely source of illumination. A writer's livelihood is weak, at best, and I'd become adept at operating in a secondhand economy. I was comfortable with it.

Still, I sat in that chair getting madder and madder. After careful examination I concluded that the core of my anger was fear—in this case fear that John T. would judge me for shopping secondhand. I knew it was absurd, since he is not judgmental in the least. Anyone can see that he's an openhearted guy willing to embrace anything and everyone—even me.

Nevertheless, I'd felt compelled to mislead him based on class stigma. I was ashamed—of my fifteen-year-old Mazda, my income, and my rented home. I felt ashamed of the very clothes I was wearing, the shoes on my feet. Abruptly, with the force of being struck in the face, I understood it wasn't his judgment I feared. It was my own. I'd judged myself and found failure. I wanted a car like his; I wanted to dress like him and have a house like his; I wanted to be in a position to offer other people jobs.

The flip side of shame is pride. All I had was the pride of refusal: I could say no to his offer. I did not have to write about trash food and class. No, I decided, no, no, no. Later it occurred to me that my reluctance was evidence that maybe I should say yes. I resolved to do some research before refusing his offer.

John T. had been a little shaky on the label *trash food*, mentioning mullet and possum as examples. At one time this list included crawfish because Cajun people ate it, and catfish because it was favored by African Americans and poor Southern whites. As these cuisines gained popularity, the food itself became culturally upgraded. Crawfish and catfish stopped being trash food when the people eating it in restaurants were the same ones who felt superior to the lower classes. Elite white diners had to redefine the food to justify eating it. Otherwise they were voluntarily lowering their own social status— something nobody wants to do.

It should be noted that carp and gar still remain reputationally compromised. In other words, poor folks eat it and rich folks don't. I predict that one day wealthy white people will pay thirty-five dollars for a tiny portion of carp with a rich sauce—and congratulate themselves for doing so.

I ran a multitude of various searches on library databases and the Internet in general, typing in permutations of the words *trash* and *food*. Surprisingly, every single reference was to "white trash food." Within certain communities, it's become popular to host "white trash parties" where people are urged to bring Cheetos, pork rinds, Vienna sausages, Jell-O with marshmallows, fried baloney, corn dogs, RC cola, Slim Jims, Fritos, Twinkies, and cottage cheese with jelly—in short, the food I ate as a kid in the hills.

Participating in such a feast is considered proof of being very hip. But it's not. Implicit in the menu is a vicious ridicule of the people who eat such food on a regular basis. People who attend these "white trash parties" are cuisine slumming, temporarily visiting a place they never want to live. They are the worst sort of tourists—they want to see the Mississippi Delta and the hills of Appalachia but are afraid to get off the bus.

The term *white trash* is an epithet of bigotry that equates human worth with garbage. It implies a dismissal of a group as stupid, violent, lazy, and untrustworthy—the same negative descriptors used for racial minorities, for anyone outside the mainstream. At every stage of American history, various groups of people have endured such personal attacks. Language is used as a weapon: divisive, cruel, enciphered. Today is no different. For example, here in Mississippi, the term *Democrats* is code for "African Americans." Throughout the United States, *family values* is code for "no homosexuals." The term *trash food* is not about food, it's coded language for a social class. It's about poor people and what they can afford to eat.

In America, class lines run parallel to racial lines. At the very bottom are people of color. The white equivalent is me—an Appalachian. As a white man in America, I am supposed to have an inherent advantage in every possible way. It's true: I can pass more easily in society, and I have better access to education, health care, and employment. But if I insist on behaving like a poor white person—shopping at secondhand shops and eating mullet—I not only earn the epithet *trash* but somehow deserve it.

The term *white trash* is class disparagement due to economics. Polite society regards me as stupid, lazy, ignorant, violent and untrustworthy.

I am trash because of where I'm from.

I am trash because of where I shop.

I am trash because of what I eat.

But human beings are not trash. We are the civilizing force on the planet. We produce great art, great music, great food, and great technology. It's not the opposable thumb that separates us from the beasts, it's our facility with language. We are able to communicate with great precision. Nevertheless, history is fraught with the persistence of treating fellow humans as garbage, which means collection and transport for destruction. The most efficient management of humans as trash occurred when the Third Reich systematically murdered people by the millions. People they didn't like. People they were afraid of: Jews, Romanies, Catholics, gay men and lesbians, Jehovah's Witnesses, and the disabled.

In World War II my father-in-law was captured by the Nazis and placed on a train car so crammed with people that everyone had to stand for days. Arthur hadn't eaten in a week. He was close to starvation. A Romany man gave him half a turnip, which saved his life. That man later died, but Arthur survived the war. He had been raised to look down on Romany people as stupid, lazy, violent, and untrustworthy—the ubiquitous language of class discrimination. He subsequently revised his view of them. For Arthur, the stakes of starvation were high enough that he changed his view of a group of people. But the wealthy elite in this country are not starving. When they changed their eating habits, they didn't change their view of people. They just upgraded crawfish and catfish.

Economic status dictates class and diet. We arrange food in a hierarchy based on who originally ate it until we reach mullet, gar, possum, and squirrel—the diet of the poor. The food is called trash, and then so are the people who eat it.

When the white elite take an interest in the food poor people eat, the price goes up. The result is a cost that prohibits poor families from eating the very food they've been condemned for eating. It happened with salmon and tuna years ago. When I was a kid and money was tight, my mother mixed a can of tuna with pasta and vegetables. Our family of six ate it for two days. Gone are the days of subsisting on cheap fish patties at the end of the month. The status of the food rose, but not the people. They just had less to eat.

What is trash food? I say all food is trash unless there is human intervention. Cattle, sheep, hogs, and chickens would die unless slaughtered for the table. If humans didn't harvest vegetables, they would rot in the field. Food is a disposable commodity until we accumulate the raw material, blend ingredients, and apply heat, cold, and pressure. Then our bodies extract nutrients and convert it into waste, which must be disposed of. The act of eating produces trash.

In the hills of Kentucky we all looked alike—scruffy white people with squinty eyes and cowlicks. We shared the same economic class, the same religion, the same values and loyalties. Even our enemy was mutual: people who lived in town. Appalachians are suspicious of their neighbors, distrustful of strangers, and uncertain about third cousins. It's a culture that operates under a very simple principle: you leave me alone, and I'll leave you alone. After moving away from the hills I developed a different way of interacting with people. I still get cantankerous and defensive—ask John T.—but I'm better with human relations than I used to be. I've learned to observe and listen.

As an adult I have lived and worked in eleven different states—Arizona, California, Florida, Georgia, Iowa, Massachusetts, Montana, New Mexico, New York, Tennessee, and now Mississippi. These circumstances often placed me in contact with African Americans as neighbors, members of the same labor crew, coworkers in restaurants, and now university colleagues. The first interaction between a black man and a white man is one of mutual evaluation: Does the other guy hate my guts? The white guy—me—is worried that after generations of repression and mistreatment, this black guy will take his anger out on me because I'm white. And the black guy is wondering if I am one more racist asshole he can't turn his back on. This period of reconnaissance typically doesn't last long because both parties know the covert codes the other uses—the avoidance of touch, the averted eyes, a posture of hostility. Once each man is satisfied that the other guy is all right, connections begin to occur. Those connections are always based on class. And class translates to food.

Last year my mother and I were in the hardware store, buying parts to fix a toilet. The first thing we learned was that the apparatus inside commodes has gotten pretty fancy over the years: like breakfast cereal, there are dozens of types to choose from. Toilet parts are now made of plastic, copper, and cheap metal. Some are silent, and some save water, and some look as if they come from an alien spacecraft.

A store clerk, an African American man in his sixties, offered to help us. I told him I was overwhelmed, that plumbing had gotten too complicated. I tried to make a joke by saying it was a lot simpler when everyone used an outhouse. He gave me a quick, sharp look of suspicion. I recognized the expression; it's the same one John T. gave me when I mispronounced his name, the same look I gave John T. when he mentioned "trash food" and social class. The same one I unleashed on people who called me a hillbilly or a redneck.

I understood the clerk's concern. He wondered if I was making a veiled comment about race, economics, and the lack of plumbing. I told him that back in Kentucky when the hole filled up with waste, we dug a new hole and moved the outhouse to it. Then we'd plant a fruit tree where the old outhouse had been.

"Man," I said, "that tree would bear big old peaches."

He looked at me differently then, a serious expression. His earlier suspicion was gone.

"You know some things," he said. "Yes you do."

"I know one thing," I said. "When I was a kid I wouldn't eat those peaches."

The two of us began laughing. We stood there and laughed until the mirth trailed off, reignited, and brought forth another bout of laughter. Eventually we wound down to a final chuckle. We stood in the aisle and studied the toilet repair kits on the pegboard wall. They were like books in a foreign language.

"Well," I said to him. "What do you think?"

"What do I think?" he said.

I nodded.

"I think I won't eat those peaches."

We started laughing again, this time longer, slapping each other's arms. Pretty soon one of us just had to mutter "peaches" to start all over again. Race was no more important to us than plumbing parts or shopping at a secondhand store. We were two Southern men laughing together in an easy way, linked by class and food.

On the surface, John T. and I should have been able to laugh in a similar way last spring. We have more in common than the store clerk and I do. John T. and I share race, status, and regional origin. We are close to the same age. We are sons of the South. We're both writers, married with families. John T. and I have cooked for each other, gotten drunk together, and told each other stories. We live in the same town, have the same friends.

But none of that mattered in the face of social class, an invisible and permanent division. It's the boundary John T. had the courage to ask me to write about, the boundary that made me lie about the secondhand store last spring. And it's the boundary that still fills me with shame and anger—a boundary that only food can cross.

My Yankee Traitor Heart

Allen C. Shelton

By the time my father died, his wrecked Jaguar had been towed to the junk-yard, where it became just another inert hunk of metal—no longer the lumi-nous piece of speed my father imagined. The glove box was open and its contents askew. There was an ABBA CD on the seat; my father had become a fan after my mother died and he'd started dating. A fluorescent lime-green baseball cap lay on the passenger floorboard. Around the accident site the Judas trees were starting to bud.

At his house there was a stack of unopened bills, newspapers, and maga-zines sitting on the kitchen counter. The light on the answering machine blinked. His abandoned Seiko watch was in a drawer in his bedroom. The heat pump turned on regularly; the thermostat was set at sixty-five. My father was eighty-three. He had insomnia. But in the final two weeks of his life he was unconscious except for brief moments. He woke up at least once, mum-bling something. His eyes were wide; he was afraid. My sisters told him they loved him. He looked at them and slumped back into unconsciousness. Then he died.

I got a call from my brother with the tentative details of the wake and fu-neral; it was 10:17 A.M. I had no premonition that it was going to happen. I fully expected my father to recover and thought I would have more time to come to grips with our relationship. I didn't. I feel him pulling on me just as he did when I was a kid out past the waves in the ocean. Don't be a scaredy-cat. I dreamed he was in Buffalo, where I live. My dead mother's mastiffs ran up to me. My father was chasing them. The dogs smelled my hands and then ran off, with my father yelling their names. He brushed by me, intent on the dogs. They never listened to him. I ran after the dogs, caught them, and started back, but my father was gone. My father didn't abandon me. I'm sure my father loved me. He just wasn't there when I needed him, and when he was, I wished he wasn't.

I cashed in my frequent-flier miles and flew home. The wake was in a the-ater at the funeral home on Gadsden Highway outside Jacksonville, Alabama. The university coliseum hovered over the graveyard where my father's mother and father were buried. At the entrance there was a statue of Jesus taking a knee like a football coach posing for a photograph. My two brothers and I stood at the door of the theater, greeting visitors, as the line filed around the open casket. I never looked inside it. Few remembered me; I'd been gone from Alabama for twenty years. AC—that was my father's name—had another son, I explained. I'm AC III, the oldest. Really? Where do you live? I live in Buffalo, New York. Buffalo? From here the talk turned toward the awful snow and Yankees. How could I live there? Work; I teach there. There was a look that went with the talk about the snow. The mourners took a slight step back and measured the length and cut of my hair, the style of my suit and boots, my lack of a tie, and the absence of a Southern accent. I didn't look or sound like anyone else in this room. How could I be my father's son, and a Southerner? How could I calculate the betrayal I was guilty of? I was a Yankee traitor.

My ancestors have done it in diffuse ways. In the Civil War, E. P. Landers, my great-great-uncle wrote letters from the front in Virginia calculating how far he was from home. And then he died, twenty-something miles from his home outside Atlanta. My father's father, also named A. C. Shelton was a meticulous counter and record keeper; he recorded the lives of three hundred Black Angus cows like he was creating an actuarial table. He was still doing what he did as a young man: rounding up stray cows in the swamps.

My mother taught mathematics. I took algebra with her in junior high school. She gave me a D in the class. Was she grading me as a son, or on my ability to solve equations? Or were the two the same thing? I figured portions at the dinner table: how much each person would get to eat. When I was seven, I ate three foot-long chili dogs. My mother was very pleased. I had an abacus in my head, sliding the beads to match the bites. My father had given me a real abacus for Christmas when I was six years old and he was a marine stationed in Okinawa. I never learned how to use it to solve math problems, but I would hold it and smell it when I was anxious. The smell soothed me, even if it was an instrument I used to measure my aloneness. I often felt trapped in solitude, surrounded by my two brothers, two sisters, a bloodhound, and my mother, especially when we were all in our station wagon.

In the late 1950s my father wore a steel Rolex submariner watch. It was a straightforward steel watch and bracelet with a white face and a second hand. He would take it off and hold it up to my ear so I could hear it tick. He told me that inside it was a man with an ax chopping down a tree. I was mesmerized by the ticking and the thought of the ax and the forest inside the watch. I wanted to be that man with the ax.

I taught myself how to use an ax. I learned how to sharpen the blade with a bastard file and how to swing the ax so that a chunk of wood popped out and the cut resembled a grinning mouth. I thought of trees as whales; when I stepped into the woods, I was hunting whales. I bought a Wetterling, a hand-forged Swedish ax. I worked alone. I limbed the fallen trees and piled the brush in wigwam-like heaps in the understory. Tiny birds hid in the branches as I stood to the side, half hidden in the woods.

The wake was tiresome. Just after 6:30 P.M. I retreated to the back and watched the continuous slide show, a collection of photographs spanning my father's life. I was conspicuously rare in the show, as if an endangered species, though my ex-wife figured prominently. Also absent was my mother's father, Eli Landers—not that he should've had a prominent role, but I assumed he would show up in my parents' wedding photos. I'd never seen an image of Eli and my father together; now it was too late to ask Dad about this.

Eli had lived for a while in Yankee land, the only other member of my family to do so since their arrival in this country in the 1600s. He spent a year in New York City, finishing his degree at Columbia University in the late 1920s. But he didn't have a Yankee traitor heart: he returned to Jacksonville and became a professor at the college there. I regularly visited Eli's grave with my grandmother. He died six months after I was born, but I am told he called me Blue Eyes. Perhaps my eyes were tiny windows back to the sea he had seen in Yankee land.

Over the living room mantle in my grandmother's house there was a large painting of Eli sitting at his desk in his study. A photograph of the same scene sat on a bookshelf in the TV room. As a child, I saw Eli's handwriting on the inside covers of books, and I played with his fountain pens; I pretended they were submarines as I pushed them across the floor. I'm writing this with a transparent Pelikan fountain pen that looks like a submarine. As a young adult, I read Eli's books, which were stacked on shelves on both sides of the hallway through the center of the house. He had several copies of Xenophon's *Anabasis*, which chronicles the retreat of ten thousand Greek mercenaries from Mesopotamia back to Greece.

Eli was always a strong presence in my life; so much so that a girlfriend reported seeing his ghost. *Good*, I thought, *he's watching me.*

My grandmother Pearl told me stories about a relative who served in the Army of Northern Virginia during the Civil War. He had little to eat other than roasted sweet potatoes. He wore a ragged gray cotton uniform, and slept under a thin wool blanket. It was warmest if it snowed and he lay still under the snow, which acted as a heavy quilt. But if he moved, the snow would crack and the cold would pierce through. My ancestor moved. Maybe he was dreaming of home, a woman, or running with his dog in the woods. He froze to death. Above him the skeletal arms of the trees popped in the cold wind.

My grandmother's story of him ended here. He was probably buried in a shallow grave in the same woods, and the grave was likely marked only with a headstone. It was expensive to send a body south for a burial. My grandmother was born around 1895, which meant she'd heard the story thirty odd years after the event. She told the story to my mother, and then to me, and I have told it to my son. Perhaps at one time my grandmother knew this relative's name, knew where in Virginia he died; others in his regiment survived and had come home and could have told the account. But those details are gone; what's left are the trees hovering over his heart coming to a stop, like my father's watch, winding down, over and over again as the story is told.

After my grandmother died and I buried her, her ghost visited me. She didn't tell me any secrets about the other side; she directed me to take what books I wanted from my grandfather's library. I listened: the next day I went through his books. I was building something, and each book was a piece of the structure. For now, these books are in a storage shed in Alabama. Termites have eaten a few; the others are stacked on a large wooden table made from a nineteenth-century Methodist church pew and on my grandmother's kitchen table. The pew, and the scene, is very Protestant. Even her ghost is a Methodist. The books are eclectic: histories, Charlotte Brontë, Caesar, Charles Dickens, Herman Melville, Edgar Allan Poe, William Shakespeare, and Xenophon. I now own a complete set of the McGuffey Readers. Most of these books will never be read. They will eventually come to me in Buffalo and be placed in long dusty rows on a shelf—a stratum extracted from my family home in Alabama—and I will view them in the manner of a forensic geologist. Touching their spines, my own spine will shiver.

The books are part of a block of things I have inherited, all Southern: a mahogany, wicker-backed living room set; a pine table; an anvil and other tools; pictures; oak baskets; trunks; primitive wardrobes; straight-backed chairs; church pews; and a loveseat. They are mine for a short time. The question is, where will they go when I die? To my son, my girlfriend Molly, the dump, an auction? They will have left Alabama and be redistributed out of Buffalo. And me? I have no idea where I will be buried or where my ashes will be scattered. This is the fate of an exile.

Pearl's house was busting with books. My father's mother, Mary Pullen, was the city librarian, and she lived in an antebellum mansion that was sliding into decrepitude. Over my grandfather's desk was a large print of Robert E. Lee, Jefferson Davis, and Stonewall Jackson on horseback. He had no affection for these Confederate leaders, but they have formed part of my exterior shell. A grandfather clock ticked relentlessly in that house. I can still hear it. It is a landscape of time slid in between my muscles and fat. It's me. I recognize the movements with each tick from this ghost clock.

The houses in Jacksonville are haunted. Abraham Lincoln's ghost appeared to me one night in Mary Pullen's house, standing next to the closet in the upstairs bedroom. The closet was the size of a jail cell. He was a slender green mantis, poised on a spear-like branch in the dark world. His long arms were folded against his chest, clenching the lapels of his coat as if he were about to unfurl wings and fly into the Magnolia trees outside the room's windows. I waited for him to speak or move, but he didn't. I, too, was frozen. When I woke the next morning, there was no evidence that he had been there, other than a slight opening in the coats and dresses where a thin man could've slipped through. Shoes covered the floor, and against the back wall was a stack of paper boxes. There was no light in that closet; Lincoln's black coat and pants would've blended in with the coats hanging there.

The closet door must have led from this world to another; things could pass in either direction. There were other portals; if I spit on a grave, it could dribble on the dead man's face, or the dead could reach out and grab me. But on that night, Lincoln just stood there. He had on his stovepipe hat. He must've been going out, otherwise he would've removed it; he had manners.

There were three large bedrooms on the second floor. This happened in what was called the blue room. It was the scary one. Downstairs was a living room with a coal-burning fireplace; a shuttered dining room where I would fantasize about seeing Joan of Arc; a small bedroom; the sitting room, with its black-and-white TV, rocking chair, divan, and floor lamp; a large kitchen; and a closed-off room where my father had slept as a teenager; it had World War II fighter plane images stuck on the walls. In the basement there was a coal-fired furnace. It was where, as a child, I thought my grandfather hacked up baby hippos for meat.

In the town square was a colossal statue of a Confederate soldier. He looked through my bedroom window at me. By the time I was six years old he had shrunk to ten foot tall, but his shadow was etched on me. In 1969 my grandfather sold the house. It was torn down. He and my grandmother moved to a farm six miles over the mountain. The house he built couldn't accommodate Lincoln. There was no Confederate statue. There were gigantic longleaf pines standing alone on the edges of the pasture.

I calculated the costs of my relationship with my father. The last visit with him cost me $987.37. The airline ticket was close to $400. The hotel was another $175. The train was cheap, but its engine fell out outside of Atlanta. I had to buy lunch on the train; that was another twenty dollars. I bought three six-packs of beer and pizza for my family with a twenty-dollar tip for my son Tyree, who fetched it. There were other incidental costs that, when pieced together, took on a life of their own. I bought gas for Tyree's truck, cheese-burgers at Cecil's, and movie tickets. It was an unpleasant visit. My father ranted about me. He was unhappy with dinner even though it was one of his favorites. The family left quickly. Then Tyree and I left. This was early October. My father would be dead by February. He probably stayed up until after two in the morning. Day and night were blurring. Time and how he kept time were becoming more irrelevant to him. He no longer wore the Seiko watch, but a cheap digital one, which he pointed out kept better time; or he used his cell phone. He saw few people. One reason was his driveway. It was a one-lane concrete strip that went straight up the mountain for over a quarter of a mile through a tunnel of tree branches. It was monumental, and he never tired of talking about it. In the end, it had an unintended effect: it left him isolated on top of his mountain. Even friends were reluctant to drive up it. At night, with a full moon, the driveway looked like a cold tear sliding down the mountain. During the day it resembled a waterslide in Las Vegas.

The next day, when I came over to say good-bye, he was sitting in a big brown leather chair lit by a floor lamp. There were a stack of newspapers on the side table. He had on his reading glasses, and on his lap was an opened envelope. It was likely a bill. He was losing his eyesight, and his hearing was compro-mised. He never mentioned it, or that his vertigo was worse. My sister Mary informed me of his medical conditions. He was alone; his bevy of girlfriends had moved on once the illusion of his wealth melted away. There was a large supply of Viagra in his bureau. During my last visit he was quite concerned with getting his hot tub fixed for a visit that was about to happen. It was never fixed, and the visit never happened.

I don't remember what he said. I remember looking out the picture win-dow. You could see for miles down the length of the valley. On a clear night my father might have been able to see my plane coming into Atlanta. The Atlanta airport was 110 miles away, but he could glimpse jets coming out of the clouds on their final approach. Whether he ever imagined one of those lights in the sky was me coming home is doubtful. Now standing on the dark porch, looking east, I remembered what this valley looked like when I lived here. It felt like I was sliding down my father's driveway into an open grave. I looked at my watch. It was just after one.

On a job interview in Des Moines, Iowa, I lost my father's Rolex watch. He didn't care. He had quit wearing it when he left the marines and started working for Monsanto. By then he had bought himself the big Seiko quartz, and it didn't need to be wound like the Rolex. I asked my mother if I could have the Rolex. I needed a watch to keep track of my work on the farm. It had a flexible metal band that grabbed the hair on my wrist. It never quite fit; a link needed to be removed.

At the airport, just as I got off the tram, the band broke. I slipped the Rolex into my suit pocket. The watch protruded through the thin material. The flight was delayed. On the flight I took out my notebook and set the watch on it to monitor the time. I remember this. I never saw the Rolex again. I didn't realize it was gone until I was unpacking in my hotel room. I called the airline. No watch was found. "We aren't responsible for lost items." And that was that. I got the job and considered the loss a necessary sacrifice. I went to the jewelry store to buy a replacement. The cost was staggering. My wife bought me a quartz Hamilton. It wasn't sexy. The Rolex was gone.

I moved by myself to Des Moines. I lived in an early twentieth-century apartment building near downtown. It stayed below zero for what seemed like months. When it hit ten degrees it felt like spring. Around March 2, I glimpsed the Rolex. I had come out of the building. The snow cover had partially melted off. I looked up. There was a passenger jet outlined against the sky. I saw a watch in the grass. The Rolex had found me. I reached down and caught the steel watch in my hand like it was alive. Immediately it was clear, it wasn't the Rolex but a cheap steel watch from Hong Kong with jewel settings. I had loved the Rolex, but I didn't know it until this moment. I spent one more winter in Des Moines. The Hamilton didn't make a sound. There was no ax, tree, or man inside.

For years my watches were quiet. They made no sound. I wore the Hamilton, and then a Swatch with a blue face I got as a gift. Its second hand went silently around the dial. When my mother was ill, I spent the night of my birthday with her in the hospital. I sat in the chair next to her bed. The TV droned. Mom was in a delirium; she tossed and turned in the sheets, and her gown became entangled. I saw where I came from. I sat there trying to sleep but all I could manage was another kind of half sleep. I could hear the tick of the absent Rolex behind the TV. I was visited by the man with the ax. A week later she would die after waking up in the middle of the night with a headache. An aneurysm had burst in her head. She collapsed. I had heard the man with the ax.

On the day that began his death, my father had gotten up early to go into town for breakfast. He hadn't slept; the sleeping pills had proven ineffectual that night. He showered and dusted off with baby powder. He was a large man, and there was a white cloud of powder as he got dressed. He warmed up his Jaguar and slipped down the driveway at high speed through the oakleaf hydrangeas, oaks, sweet gums, and pines to White's Gap Road. He turned up the highway. He was going forty miles an hour, slow for him, when he fell asleep and slid off the road into a pine tree. He broke his hip, knee, and his back. The car was totaled. His favorite leather jacket had to be cut off by the EMTs.

Two weeks later he was dead. There were complications during the surgery and he never regained consciousness. I did not have a chance to say good-bye. The end was unexpected. We hadn't spoken over Christmas for the first time in my life, as if we were practicing for the future.

I think of his insomnia, when I'm wide awake in bed at two o'clock in the morning. Will I be like him? It makes my heart pound. He was a marine and a salesman. I'm a professor, but other similarities are overwhelming. I can't sleep unless I stretch into a particular configuration. My sciatica is a burr anchored above my hip that when my leg opens up soaks my thigh and calf with electricity. Why he couldn't sleep is irrelevant. He couldn't. He took sleeping pills. This was the announcement of a new phase in his life. I wonder if he examined every facet of his life to torture himself in those last years. I reevaluate everything I've done. It all might have turned out differently except I am me. That is the fate of character. At night in bed I recognize a mark in time waiting for me. In two years I will be sixty-two. My mother died when she arrived at that point; or I could go like my father and ease off the road into a tree on the edge of the woods. Their deaths are a spider's web strung from my memories to my imagining of the future. I remember my mother at the beach. We are collecting seashells and shark teeth at the water's edge. My father must be taking the picture. She's wearing a dark swimsuit. My dead ancestors have left open the door to the dominion of the dead; they've left memories for me. If I could solve my past by rearranging my memories of events into different conclusions, then maybe it all would be different. I would not be a Yankee traitor.

My father was six foot three. I was smaller, like my mother. He made and lost a lot of money. He could drink prodigiously. It was only toward the end of his life that he began to shrink in size. When I hugged him I could feel how soft his muscles were. He had quit exercising. At his death he weighed around 240 pounds. The coffin my brothers chose was oak. I stood off to the side and watched as my son and nephews maneuvered the coffin out of the hearse and shuffled through the grass to the grave. It was overcast and chilly. I remember the marine guard carefully folding the flag, pulling and smoothing the cloth. It was obedient. I felt the ground beneath the Astroturf carpet with my feet. Why hadn't the diggers smoothed the ground with a rake? The grave was poorly constructed: the walls were rough and jagged, and it was dug with no regard for aesthetics. For them it was just a four-foot-deep hole in the ground. Whether it went anywhere or not, I had to go through it. I would have to be folded with my hands crossed over my chest until I was small.

My father's house sat there, exactly as he had left it. There were dirty dishes in the sink. There were unpaid bills, and more arrived in the mail. The heat turned on and off. The property had to be equitably disbursed. Who would get what? There were his guns, the marine sword that lay inside a frame with a pair of dress gloves, the gigantic sofa, and art. But nothing could be done until a will was located. Dad owed a lot of money; not a penny had been paid on the principal for his house. He wanted people to think he was a millionaire. He wasn't. He couldn't afford to fix the leaks around the windows. He had two mortgages. Finally an old will was located, in which I was executor. That was impossible. My sister Mary stepped in. She and her husband lived on the mountaintop just down the paved lane from my father's house. They had the most to lose in the division of the property. But what if they bought my father's house? That seemed a plausible solution. At least a strand of history might be preserved. Our mother had been part of the planning of this house before her death, though it was always our father's mad project. An argument could be made that it was the last family home, though AC never considered it such or ever intended it to be that. I spent two nights in that house. It was his party house where he entertained various women and long-held fantasies.

Mary and Luis hired an inspector. How sound is the house? There are some small leaks. We know there are some problems. How much will it cost to repair? It was a reasonable precaution and very sensible. The answer surprised them: the inspector told them between $75,000 and $100,000. The house was coming unglued, just like a dollhouse left outside. Dad had cut costs and built the house on backfill, which was like building on sand. The house had moved. Whether AC knew how shoddily the house was built is debatable, even though he plainly saw the effects. This was consistent with his material legacy in other areas. He had no intention of leaving things, money, or unencumbered land behind.

That wasn't quite true. An insurance policy was located, and I got a check for $10,000. My airfare, rental car, and incidentals for the funeral totaled $917. At another moment in my life this money would've been a tidal wave. I could've paid off bills and been able to see my son more often. AC was never forthcoming with his money. When I was in desperate times he doled out increments of one or two hundred dollars, sometimes as much as five hundred; the same amounts he spent on dinners. What should I do with what was left? My dad had always criticized the way I dressed. *You look like a kid.* I decided to buy a bespoke suit from Brooklyn Tailors in New York. The process was overpowering. It was like the tailor was measuring me for a coffin. I might be buried in this suit. With the remainder, I put a down payment on an Omega diving watch. Inside my watch is a forest surrounded by the ocean. I'm already underwater when I wear it looking at the man with the ax and the tree being cut in the forest through a clear crystal glass. It ticks like a buried heart.

I hadn't seen my father as much alive as I do now that he's dead. He appeared in a dream Tuesday night. He was walking along the edges of the scene on a cattle trail strung like a thin dirt ribbon through the grass. I could see his footprints. His back was to me. His attention was fixed on something ahead. He resembled his own grandfather, whom I would watch when I was a child: plodding with a crook-handled walking stick stuck out in front of him like an antenna down the sidewalk between the statue of the Confederate soldier and my grandmother's house. He looked like a beetle. My father looked like a beetle. He was back on Sunday morning while I was reading the paper in the café: I had the clear sense of him sitting in his chair in the great room of his house doing the same thing. He said nothing to me, but looked over the top of his paper at me. My therapist tells me this is normal. *He was your father, even if you weren't close.* I would tell someone the same thing. My sciatica makes me walk bent over like a beetle. I am from a family of beetles.

My father hit a tree on the side of a lingering straightaway just off the top of the mountain. The Murray Mobile Home Park is down on the left. Above the crash site was where a man named Miller lived with his son. He was a lawyer. The son went to school with me. He was into drugs. He rode motorcycles. He didn't know who Herman Hesse was, though he listened to the band Steppenwolf. I look for the tree as I drive. There must be a gash on the trunk that matches the bumper. I haven't seen one. If there was one, it has closed like an eye. The tree dreams of me. When will I drive by? When will I slip off the road? If I had my ax I would cut it down and watch it fall like a man shot dead on a street.[1]

My father had scarcely died when I began to write about him. When Mary Pullen died I ate two Mexican steak sandwiches from a food truck sitting outside a laundry and started composing. At my mother's funeral, I collected vignettes. I don't know why. It could be that each written line was a rope lashed around their bodies, holding some part of them in this world. They were already gone when I began to write, but I might hold on to something. It's the acknowledgment of an emptiness that pushes me to write. I dug my grandmother Pearl's grave. I got paid two hundred dollars. She has no essay dedicated to her. The grave was my essay, and it was exquisitely constructed, with only one deficiency: the grave surface didn't settle in a flat plane with the surrounding turf. There is a slight indentation in the ground as if my grandmother was on her back and a mattress was holding her in an embrace. The page and the grave are similar surfaces for me, confused as I am about writing and bodies. How could I bury my father in a piece of paper except by falling asleep?

The legal dimensions for a grave in Alabama are four by four by eight feet. That is an awful lot of dirt. I am writing this on grid paper that measures seventeen by nineteen inches. The paper covers almost the entire surface of a café table. There is a 6,500-word limit on this essay. I'm near that boundary. Where am I in this essay? I'm in the list of contributors off on the edge of the book. This could be my epitaph if Tyree's and my girlfriend Molly's names were added.

Allen Shelton arrived in Buffalo in 1998 in a Toyota one-ton pickup with 233,000 miles on the engine. He owns a pair of R. M. Williams boots, a transparent Pelikan, Xenophon's *Anabasis*, cuffed Momotaro jeans purchased in Prague, Rhodia paper, a creek named Cottaquila in another life, a Wetterling ax, and an abacus. He wrote the *Dreamworlds of Alabama* and *Where the North Sea Touches Alabama*. He keeps time with an Omega mechanical inside his suit, which is made by Brooklyn Tailors.

It is midnight. There are no more words left to bury my father.

Note

1. It has been a cold winter in Buffalo. But today it's almost warm even without the sun. I carried Molly's suitcase to the car just before 11:00 in the morning. We kissed. Her lips were warm. I remembered the freckles on her back. The car is parked on the street in front of our building, which is anchored on the first floor by a café and what looks like an old bank covered in Masonic symbols. In 1917 the evangelist Billy Sunday preached here. It was a conversion theater, cramming as many as five hundred souls into its double-decker seating. Now it's storage space; the insides are gutted. There's no evidence of the Holy Ghost. The rumor is it's about to become a wine bar. I stood in the street like a pillar of salt as Molly drove off. A truck ran the light. On this day in 1757 a man named Damiens was drawn and quartered on the street in front of the Paris Cathedral and then his body parts thrown on a pyre and burned. The Italian courtier Casanova was in attendance, watching the event from a second story window. The execution took hours. It was after eleven at night when the last part of the condemned

man's disappearance occurred. By that time there were only stragglers left: a dog and a detachment of archers on a dark street. Casanova and his party had departed hours earlier. Damiens' ashes were scattered to the night breeze. The bone scraps were kicked to the edges to be carried off by animals. I have no connections to Damiens or the chronicler Michel Foucault, the French historian and philosopher. March 2 is another day in the year sandwiched between my father's death on February 13 and what would have been his birthday on March 17.

Foucault does not follow Damiens' descent into an uncanny Paris. He documents only one side of the transformation on the surface world. The other was taking place in the dominion of the dead in a spectral Paris. It, too, was transformed by an absorbed Damiens, albeit at different speeds and in different ways. Damiens joined what the Austrian émigré historian Elias Canetti identified as the invisible crowd, the dead who shadow the living. They were earnestly building a new city. What did this invisible city look like? The Paris the dead inhabited was exactly the same Paris but changed one moment to the next into other cities: Berlin, Rome, Jacksonville, or the forests in northern Virginia. Why? Because the world of the dead is the simultaneous strata of centuries existing in a single moment seen by God. The tree my father would hit had already witnessed the death of my ancestor who froze to death in the Civil War and the crucifixion of Jesus, had already been incorporated as a sill in my house in the valley, and stood over the people who constructed the winding graves in the shape of a snake swallowing an egg beneath my father's house in 57 AD. The same tree is being cut down inside the Rolex watch.

Dead, Damiens would've immediately recognized the site of his execution. Whether the cathedral was now on his left or right would be the first thing he would notice apart from the fact that his legs and arms were reattached and his hand, cut off, had returned. He was dressed more comfortably than in the shirt he had been wearing. It was certainly his outfit. The sun now appeared behind the cathedral; this was curious, but there it was. The cathedral was different from what Damiens recalled from the gallows and seemed to be supported on thousands of scrawny chicken legs. He waved his arms. They worked. The cathedral skittered across his field of vision into a thicket of what he could only suppose were magnolia trees from the American South. He'd seen these in the book on botanical species by an English naturalist. The trees were gigantic. Their color was gray, though he remembered them in the description as dark green. The trees were in bloom. He smelled the white flowers.

What my dead father saw I don't know. He was not a religious man. He was a marine. He wanted to be a millionaire. He believed in self-determination, which must've pained him as his debt mounted and his real estate plans fizzled out. Toward the end he started feeding birds on his porch. He collected Audubon prints. It was woods that surrounded him and his home on top of the mountain. He died like Damiens, in his Jaguar. I have his Audubon print of a Jaguar. My mother believed in reincarnation. Maybe my father will come back as a black bear to be with his birds and to roam the hills like he did as a marine when he could run twenty miles in a day. In Foucault's account there is a dog that keeps returning to the grave to sleep on the warm spot where Damiens' body was burned. I keep returning to this two-mile stretch of road in Alabama that has seen the passing of my elders, been the subject of two of my books, and was the last vestige of a home. I see this empire stuck inside me from a Yankee dream city from the late nineteenth century. Alabama won't let me go, even as my world gets smaller as people pass to the other side. My father was buried in the same cemetery I buried my grandmother in, and where I used to play freeze tag with my son. I stand here as still and cold as if I had been tagged. Is this Southern enough?

Southern Cinematic Slumming

The Rough South Turn in Post-South Film

Zackary Vernon

Scott Romine asserts that "once something is called 'authentic,' it already isn't."[1] The same could be said of "bohemian," a particularly provocative and yet elusive brand of cultural authenticity that people pursue doggedly the world over. Regardless of where in time or place, the very existence of bohemia necessitates a distinctiveness and novelty that contrasts starkly with either traditional or homogenized cultures. In order to find the bohemian South, one must first seek to find *the* South or at least *a* South. Quests to locate an authentic Southern culture have been mobilized for as long as notions of "the South" have existed and they have been drafted into all manner of ideological projects. During the mid-twentieth century, writers such as Allen Tate and C. Vann Woodward critiqued the idea that some sort of coherent Southern identity existed, and they highlighted the ways in which that identity is often performed in literature and culture. Since the 1980s and 1990s, debates about the status of Southern identity have become more eschatological, particularly after Lewis P. Simpson argued in 1980 that the South had entered a "postsouthern" era. Postsouthern studies has in recent years become a distinct subfield of Southern studies, with its own increasingly codified body of scholarship produced by leading academics, such as Martyn Bone, Michael Kreyling, and Scott Romine. Succinctly summing up this work in postsouthern criticism, Jay Watson writes, "A postsouthern South is thus one that appears to rest on no 'real' or reliable foundation of cultural, social, political, economic, or historical distinctiveness, only on an ever-proliferating series of representations and commodifications of 'southernness.'"[2] Contemporary postmodern/postsouthern Southerners are often so desperate to disavow cultural homogenization that they turn their gaze toward the cultures of the lower class because they seem to retain some sense of regional distinctiveness. To such culturally naked consumers,[3] lower-class Southerners appear to live at the fringes of society and thus they seem to inhabit a bohemian space free from restrictive bourgeois politics, aesthetics, and economics.

As regional diversity disappears and national and global homogenization continues apace, readers and moviegoers both in and outside the American South have been increasingly drawn to narratives about the "Rough South," because this marginal social and artistic space seems to have held on to both its Southern and bohemian qualities. Rough South narratives typically convey the stories of marginalized Southerners of the lower class from a perspective that appears tantalizingly "authentic" to target audiences primarily consisting of educated, middle- or upper-middle-class, urban or suburban consumers. In the introduction to *Grit Lit: A Rough South Reader* (2012), Brian Carpenter chronicles the "grit lit," "Rough South," "cracker realist," "trailer park gothic," "hick chic" turn in Southern literature.[4] A comparable study of Rough South film does not yet exist, and Carpenter does not interrogate the bohemian dimensions of Rough South culture or the wildly popular grit lit genre. In order to address these issues, we turn to three twenty-first-century films: *Big Bad Love* (2001), *Searching for the Wrong-Eyed Jesus* (2003), and *Beasts of the Southern Wild* (2012) to explore how some of the South's seemingly most bohemian films and filmmakers have engaged in the filmic aestheticization of the lower class.[5] Entering an era of acculturation, members of the middle and upper classes often ape the Rough South styles of the lower class and, in the process of appropriation, make them seem bohemian. In addition to fetishizing the Rough South, they also commodify it, turning a tidy profit on books and movies that are written by or about the actual inhabitants of the Rough South.

The Rough South Turn in an Age of Acculturation

In an analysis of Elia Kazan's *A Streetcar Named Desire* (1951), John Boorman's *Deliverance* (1972), the Coen brothers' *O Brother, Where Art Thou?* (2000), and John Hillcoat's *The Road* (2009), Daniel Cross Turner argues that "these famous films, whose characters labor under hard times, project the working classes as a source of cultural-economic fear and loathing. The blue-collar South is typically depicted as a disconcerting, unruly presence that needs to be contained. Indeed, members of the working class in these movies are less likely to be romanticized than primitivized."[6] Yet many other films, especially those from 2000 onward, portray neither the class conflicts of *Deliverance* nor the ironic postmodern wit of *O Brother, Where Art Thou?*[7] In their introduction to *American Cinema and the Southern Imaginary* (2011), Deborah E. Barker and Kathryn McKee note a range of recent developments in Southern cinema, including the rise of independent films about the region, and they suggest that these films provide "new cinematic ways to view the region, which undercut or complicate traditional iconic elements. Mirroring critical debates about postsouthernism and the global South, these movies unsettle the conviction that there is a 'real,' definitive South lodged somewhere just beyond our reach."[8] Present in Barker and McKee's collection is Jay Watson's "Mapping out a Postsouthern Cinema: Three Contemporary Films," which is to date the most sustained scholarly attention postsouthern cinema has received.[9] Watson examines two films from 1991—Richard Linklater's *Slacker*, which "gets at the postsouthern by way of the postmodern," and Mira Nair's *Mississippi Masala*, which "gets at the postsouthern by way of the postcolonial."[10] I would like to augment this critical conversation by suggesting that in addition to the cinematic class conflicts highlighted by Turner and the postsouthern turn highlighted by Watson, filmmakers have increasingly relied on "rougher" and "grittier" subject matter in an attempt to capture some special not-yet-beyond-our-reach quality for the South and a resulting bohemian quality for its cultural productions.[11]

The 2001 film *Big Bad Love*, starring and written and directed by Arliss Howard, is a particularly fitting place to start because it is an adaptation, albeit a very loose one, of Larry Brown's 1990 short story collection by the same name—particularly its final story, "92 Days." Brown is one of the progenitors of the Rough South literary genre, and the film, as an adaptation of one of his early books, can lead to a productive examination of how the Rough South moved from fiction to film as well as how to apply critical approaches to both Rough South and postsouthern literature, which are themselves still somewhat nascent, to analyses of Rough South and postsouthern cinema.

Big Bad Love tells the story of Leon Barlow (played by Howard), a house painter and Vietnam War veteran, who is struggling to write and publish fiction. On the one hand, *Big Bad Love* is a narrative about marriage, family, and the possibility of attaining a middle-class lifestyle; on the other, it is about the cultural conditions that best support the production of art. Everything about the film sets up these things to be in opposition to one another. Barlow, the film constantly insinuates, can have one or the other, but not both. His wife and kids, with whom he genuinely longs to be reconciled, get in the way of his writing and the "Rough South" life that facilitates the production of his fiction. Barlow's family, it is clear, is the answer to the alcoholism, loneliness, and depression from which he suffers; but, the logic of the film suggests that his family, while offering stability and even happiness, also prevents him from writing and writing well. This has long been a problem facing successful bohemian artists: as one increasingly acquires the trappings of the bourgeoisie, the quality of one's art suffers. Conversely, though, Barlow's craft improves as the quality of his life plummets. Drinking excessively, wallowing in misery over the departure of his wife and children, working pointless menial jobs: these are the endeavors that catalyze Barlow's fiction and lead to a significant publication that gets him "out of the slush pile." Moreover, these endeavors provide compelling subject matter for his fiction. Throughout the film, Barlow struggles to write a novel, the story growing from detached and rather unbelievable to deeply personal and moving. As the narrative progresses, the book begins to more closely resemble his own life until, ultimately, it becomes his story—autobiography thinly veiled as fiction.

Conveniently, the subject matter provided by Barlow's life (and perhaps also Larry Brown's) is similar to the list of Rough South attributes cataloged in the introduction to *Grit Lit*, where Carpenter notes that "we have defined 'Grit Lit' as typically blue collar or working class, mostly small town, sometimes rural, occasionally but not always violent, usually but not necessarily Southern."[12] Carpenter distinguishes grit lit from the Rough South by defining the latter as "mostly poor, white, rural, and unquestionably violent—Grit Lit's wilder kin or Grit Lit with its back against the wall and somebody's going to get hurt."[13] While writers' own lives (including Brown's) may have in part inspired this definition, such Rough South attributes, regardless of the extent to which they are anchored in reality, are also precisely what the consumers of Rough South literature and film long to see. *Big Bad Love*—first the book, and later the film—chronicles the moment in which the Rough South, or at least the latest iteration of it, rose to prominence.

In several scenes throughout the film, Barlow reads rejection letters that he receives from journals, magazines, and publishing houses. In one scene, Barlow obsesses over a letter from a "New York agent," who responds to his novel submission by saying, "Dear Mr. Barlow. We are returning the manuscript because the market at this time is not amenable to novels about drunk pulpwood haulers and rednecks in hunting accidents. Readers here at the agency found your work hilarious and touching, with terrific characters and great dialogue, and no typos. But we don't feel that this compelling novel can be placed with a publisher." If this response was representative of New York agents' attitudes several decades ago, that is certainly not the case now, as we have seen with the rise of popularity in Rough South fiction and the publication of books like *Grit Lit*. Such popularity, Carpenter points out, may be due to the fact "that Rough South writers '*do southern*' (to borrow Noel Polk's phrase), or what most people tend to think of as 'southern,' better than most."[14]

The ease with which publishers can now sell writers who "do southern" is a clear sign that Southern literature has incredible appeal in the regional, national, and global marketplace. Thus, it is important to remember Romine's assertion that "the long-heralded death of southern literature hasn't materialized, not least because the cultural marketplace has established a brand niche for southern literature, whatever its content."[15] At the end of *Big Bad Love*, Barlow gets an encouraging letter from an agent, saying that one of his stories and possibly his novel has been accepted for publication. Therefore, with Barlow and by extension Brown "out of the slush pile," we see the moment of transition: the Rough South has arrived.

If publishers—beginning in the 1970s and continuing to the present—have sought out Rough South texts to publish because they seem to represent a last vestige of Southern bohemianism, then such publishers could be regarded, to use David E. Whisnant's formulation, as cultural intervenors. Whisnant states that the intervenor, "by virtue of his or her status, power, and established credibility, is frequently able to define what the culture *is*, to normalize and legitimize that definition in the larger society, and even to feed it back into the culture itself, where it may be internalized as 'real' or 'traditional' or 'authentic.'"[16] Setting aside the question of whether or not writers like Larry Brown are "real" or "authentic" or even bohemian, we can say with some confidence that they are at least perceived to possess these traits. The danger, though, is that the culture "preserved" or "revived" by the intervenor tends not to be congruent or is only partially congruent with the culture of a given place or time. Therefore, the culture promoted by the intervenor "is a *selection*, an *arrangement*, an *accommodation* to preconceptions. . . . Thus the culture that is 'preserved' or 'revived' is a hybrid at best."[17] Larry Brown's culture, preserved initially by himself and then by the publisher-intervenor, is later selected, arranged, and accommodated a third time when it is adapted for the silver screen by Howard and his crew of filmmakers. At this point, we are witnessing a version of seemingly bohemian culture that is several times removed and was itself only one perception of that culture to begin with. Therefore, we are farther and farther from the "authentic" bohemian South, if such a thing ever existed, and we land, teetering, close to the realm of simulacra.

In 2003 director Andrew Douglas and writer Steve Haisman created a very different film, entitled *Searching for the Wrong-Eyed Jesus*, which attempts to document life at the fringes the American South. Before the opening scene, viewers see a list of production companies, including BBC Arena, Anonymous Content, the Andrew Douglas Company, and Lone Star, as well as three short epigraphic paragraphs:

> A simple enough beginning—a record received as a Christmas gift. A
> record with a highly unusual title, *The Mysterious Tale of How I Shouted
> Wrong-Eyed Jesus*. It was a record so full of strangeness you had to
> wonder, in a shrinking world, where this music comes from.
> This film sets out to look for that place.
> Jim White, the artist who made the record, agreed to come along as our
> guide.

That is all the information given to viewers before they enter the weird world
of *Searching for the Wrong-Eyed Jesus*, but this introductory material actually
conveys a lot about the documentary and the aims of the filmmakers. The film
was commissioned by the BBC and was made by British filmmakers. We then
get the inspiration for the documentary: the director, Andrew Douglas, received
Jim White's album *The Mysterious Tale of How I Shouted Wrong-Eyed Jesus* for
Christmas, and he was so intrigued by its "strangeness" that he went searching
for the place that produced it. Douglas and Haisman also state here that they
believe the world is "shrinking," and they imply that the place that inspires
White's avant-garde music—that is, the South—is somehow removed from
global homogenizing forces. Finally, we learn that White himself has agreed to
be a "guide" for Douglas and Haisman as they travel through the region.

On the official website for the film, as well as in the supplementary materials and audio commentary provided on the DVD, viewers get even more
information about the filmmakers' intentions in creating *Searching for the
Wrong-Eyed Jesus*. As the website explains, "The film is an attempt to answer
two simple questions—why does so much music and writing come out of this
place? What are the elements that come together to make it so stimulating for
artists?" These questions resonate with the objectives given in the opening of
the film: to find the strange place that gave life to Jim White's music. The website
goes on to state, "The film started with the grand ambition of presenting the
'Soul of the South' as a diagram, willfully omitting what may be the two largest
components (racial mix and the Civil War). This plan was of course completely
unfilmable, certainly by us, but we had a lot of fun trying."[18] Thus, from the
beginning, Douglas and Haisman's approach to the South is, as they acknowledge, incomplete because they bracket out the legacies of race and racism
within the region.

Yet they seem both aware and comfortable with their omissions and insist
that the documentary will be an attempt, and they admit an "unfilmable" one,
to present the "Soul of the South" and, in particular, how that soul has inspired
the region's perennial profusions of art. Although they do not use the term,

Douglas and Haisman's project is to discover the *bohemian* South—those spaces at the fringes of traditional Southern culture that have given birth to the region's most unique and innovative musicians and writers. In the DVD materials, Haisman underscores this point, saying, "We'd always been fascinated by the South, all those great artists—Robert Johnson, Hank Williams, Elvis and so on—and wondered what gave their art such authority. It wasn't any sociological or historical or even musical factors, but an otherworldly quality that was still thoroughly rooted in the real."[19] While Haisman mentions Robert Johnson in this quote, I should point out that the film deals exclusively with white musicians and writers, presumably because the filmmakers believed that dealing with racial issues in the South was beyond the scope of their documentary.

Instead the filmmakers seek out "Soul of the South," which they attempt to represent as a map that is included with the DVD. Haisman comments, "We decided that we didn't want a journalistic, balanced view of 'the South,' but something much more personal and open-ended. We knew we wanted something that combined opera and the road movie, and a map seemed the best way to organise a structure for our quixotic attempt to find what makes the poor white South so creatively fertile." At the center of the map are the words "The South." Surrounding this is a circular road that includes the things that ostensibly make up the region: "Backwaters," "Truck Stop," "Mountains," "Jail," "Church," "Honky Tonk," and a crudely drawn picture of a broken heart. The DVD materials also include stylized pictures of various Southern places and a handwritten recipe for moonshine.[20] This is the "Soul of the South" that the filmmakers are dealing with—one that relies upon a series of stereotypes about the region rather than one that exists in conjunction with the region's more organic bohemian elements.

In describing their presentation of the narrative of the documentary, Haisman says that it was the "Rough South" that they were specifically interested in capturing: "We realized that the story we were looking for lay all around us, in the peculiar alchemy and contradictions of the 'Rough South,' with its ever-present Hell and its medieval religion, and its yearning for the transcendental."[21] This quote is significant because it demonstrates not only that the filmmakers were aware of the "Rough South" genre (notice they put the phrase in quotations) but also that they may have had the genre in mind from the beginning of their journey, which may have determined what particular version of the South they sought out, witnessed, and depicted. In the DVD commentary, the filmmakers acknowledge that the film became about the "white underclass,"[22] but one may well wonder how much they sought out the underclass because of preconceived notions about the Rough South being a last refuge of the authentic and perhaps even bohemian South that inspired the music of the region.

Searching for the Wrong-Eyed Jesus ultimately fails to accomplish its central objective to understand how so much great art is inspired by the Rough South underclass. What ends up happening repeatedly throughout the film is that the underclass people inhabit different social and economic spaces than the musicians that are featured. While one may assume that the underclass is creating this new generation of musicians, this is generally not the case; instead these two groups remain largely separate. The filmmakers admit that critics have objected to the film because most of its musical contributors "aren't, strictly speaking, from the South. This became a big issue . . . Jim White is from California. Jim White chose the South as his environment. He needed it to create a voice, but he was born in California. The Handsome Family was born in the North. David Johansen . . . [is] a New Yorker." They go on to explain,

> One of the main reasons for [not featuring many Southern musicians] is quite honestly that we couldn't find anyone from the South that could actually say what we wanted to say, which was having that storytelling ability plus living in a modern world which we knew as well. They had to be people who had, in a sense, our eyes, an outsider's eyes. They had to be able to comment on their own world, on their own choices. That's what made Jim such an exemplary guide for us, because he in a sense had our eyes. He's somebody who could see what we were seeing, the way we were seeing it, as something not necessarily just grotesque.[23]

While one can understand the importance of possessing simultaneously the insider and outsider perspective, one becomes suspicious of Douglas and Haisman's ability to get at the "Soul of the South" and, more specifically, how that soul generates the South's music, if they were not interviewing many musicians who are actually from the region.

Instead Douglas and Haisman spend the majority of their time with Jim White and his hipster friends, most of whom are from outside the region. The audience is first introduced to White in the opening sequence of the film. As White's song "Still Waters" plays (a song from the album *The Mysterious Tale of How I Shouted Wrong-Eyed Jesus*, which inspired the film in the first place), we see beautiful shots of the sun flickering through Spanish moss–draped trees, with sun flares sparkling on screen, as the voice of a young boy asks, "Do you know what you're looking for? Do you think this place is on the map? Does it have roads you can walk down? Will you know it when you see it?" Following this introductory scene, White visits a man who lives on the edge of the river featured in the opening shots. White and the man seem to be acquaintances, and White tells him that he has "some buddies" in town who want to "ride around the South a little bit." These "buddies," it turns out, are the film crew. White says, "if you want to come and sort of infiltrate the South and learn about it, learn something important about it, you're gonna need the right car. You can't show up in some Land Rover or some Lexus or something and expect poor folks to talk to you and tell you about what's in their heart." White helps to broker a deal for a rust-covered 1970 Chevy, which the film's website states, "was totally inconspicuous among the pick-ups, and as authentic as grits and chicken gizzards for breakfast—but much more desirable."[24] In the contemporary world, with our ready access to a range of cultures, identities can be taken off and on and—in some cases, as we see here—purchased.

While White and the filmmakers drive around the South, White explains his personal history. He tells them that he was dragged to the South from California when he was five years old. He also says that when living in the South, he felt a kind of cultural suffocation—"like there's a blanket over the whole world." White was only able to come to appreciate the South after moving away and traveling the world. Then he began to see the "value" of the South, although he does not identify what exactly this value is. He does, however, indicate that the South provides material for songwriting and that his artistic persona necessitates a link to the region. He states, "I decided I'm gonna come back to the South and become a Southerner as best I can. I will never be a Southerner. I'll be this imitation of a Southerner." White suggests that the "real" South cannot be found along the interstate, which is dominated by chain restaurants and corporations: "You don't see the South when you're riding along on the interstate. You pull off and there's a Cracker Barrel or a Pier 1 Imports or a Dillard's or whatever. But you go five or ten miles off the interstate and you get the South as it was fifty years ago or one hundred years ago. And you can't do that in many places." Perhaps such easy access to the margins of Southern culture is what imbues White's music with its bohemian qualities; this is precisely why Douglas and Haisman say, "Jim White is from California. Jim White chose the South as his environment. He needed it to create a voice."

When White leads the filmmakers off the highway, they most often go to small towns inhabited by working-class criminals and religious fanatics, and White constantly romanticizes these people and the poverty-stricken conditions in which they live. Driving through one particularly depressed town, White says, "They've got some good garbage here. They've got some good stuff." After listing off some of the "good garbage," he claims, "This is my kind of road: a junkyard road." Later, while driving through a trailer park, he says, "The beauty of the people who have no wealth but still enrich their world with their stories and their songs and their language. You could go into any one of these places, walk into any one of these mobile homes, and you could hear the best story or the saddest story that you'd ever hear in your life." In another scene, White describes a house in Florida that was painted purple and had a tree outside of it covered in thousands of milk of magnesia bottles. He asserts that the owner of the house had "an aesthetic outburst. He just had to say something. He was desperate and the only tool he had was a thousand milk of magnesia bottles." While it may be true that poverty occasionally results in an "aesthetic outburst," one becomes weary of the tendency to bracket out poverty and its systemic causes in favor of waxing romantic about the storytelling and artistic profusion among the Rough South. This weariness is further compounded by the fact that White and the filmmakers have such difficulty finding Southern musicians to interview in the film, instead relying on White's friends who come from New York and California and who generally seem to have a culturally parasitic relationship to the American South.

White gets closer to the truth about class in the region when describing a typical Southern small town: "You come pulling into town and you see all the muffler shots and strip joints and cut-shoot bars. Then you work your way into the respectable realm of churches and main street businesses. It's kind of a crucible: the haves and the have-nots. The have-nots run to the edges, and they bury their powerlessness in sort of the ritual of sin." White assumes that the South contains authentic people and that they come from two polar opposite worlds; either they are religious fundamentalists or they while away their time drinking in bars. Visiting one such bar, he says, "What you got here is your basic Deep South cut and shoot bar, and to me I look at it as a thing of great beauty. It's a representation of the humanity for all its good and bad that lives there. It's real. It's a real place. To those people inside there, they don't know. They don't know it's a real place. That's just the place they go." Here White rather pretentiously suggests that working-class Southerners are "real" precisely because they are not aware of the authentic culture in which they dwell. He reinforces this idea in one of his final monologues: "You want to know the secret to the South, you got to get it in your blood, and you ain't going to get a transfusion from the blood bank for it." Thus, for White, authenticity is directly related to the Rough South—which is both a place and a class that one must be born into to ever fully comprehend. And yet White, like the

Handsome Family and David Johansen, can visit, slumming for a time in its roughest spaces. As a result, their art appears more "authentic" and bohemian when they return to places like New York and California.

Beasts of the Southern Wild (2012), directed by Benh Zeitlin and written by Zeitlin and Lucy Alibar, conveys yet another version of the Rough South. Like the creators of *Searching for the Wrong-Eyed Jesus*, Zeitlin is not from the American South—either its rough or more bourgeois factions. Rather, he is from New York City, and his parents were both academic writers and folklorists. Zeitlin developed the setting of *Beasts of the Southern Wild* after living in southern Louisiana to shoot a short film titled *Glory at Sea* (2008). *Beasts of the Southern Wild*, which builds on many elements of *Glory at Sea*, is focalized largely through a young girl named Hushpuppy (Quvenzhané Wallis) who lives with her alcoholic and seriously ill father, Wink (Dwight Henry). Hushpuppy and Wink, along with a host of other like-minded outsiders, live illegally on land, which they call the Bathtub, south of the levees in Louisiana. Because they are not protected by the levees, the inhabitants of the Bathtub are subjected to all types of inclement weather, particularly flooding, and, as a result, they dwell in makeshift shacks and houseboats. Having been abandoned by her mother and largely neglected by her father, Hushpuppy generally fends for herself, preparing her own food and gleaning emotional support from an imaginary version of her mother, to whom she regularly speaks. Early in the film we see Hushpuppy living alone while her father is in the hospital. When he comes back after several days, Wink and Hushpuppy have a fight, during which he ends up slapping her in the face. She retaliates by hitting him in the chest, which causes him to collapse. Hushpuppy fears that she has killed him, and her guilt leads her to imagine that her actions have resulted in the entire planet becoming unbalanced. In particular, she believes that the polar ice caps are breaking up, which frees enormous prehistoric boar-like beasts called Aurochs. Throughout the rest of the narrative, these beasts pursue Hushpuppy until she is forced to confront them, along with the childhood traumas they represent, in the final moments of the film.

Beasts of the Southern Wild depicts a community suffering from abject poverty, yet this poverty seems to be chosen and self-imposed; consequently, audiences are invited not to sympathize with but rather to celebrate the protagonists' down-and-out situation. This is a dangerous position because it enables us to consume and enjoy the Rough South without having to consider the fact that living a Rough South lifestyle (in this case, living in extreme poverty) is often detrimental to individuals and communities, and that it is not necessarily the beautiful, satisfying, bohemian existence portrayed in the film. For example, in the second scene of the film, we see Wink and Hushpuppy on a boat puttering along in front of the levee that cuts the Bathtub off from the rest of southern Louisiana. On the other side of the levee there is an oil refinery; the film is edited so that we see Hushpuppy's house, which is squalid and yet charming, juxtaposed to the industrial wasteland of the oil refinery. Wink takes Hushpuppy here in order to say, "Ain't that ugly over there? We got the prettiest place on earth." To further reinforce the juxtaposition of life on either side of the levee, Zeitlin follows the scene at the levee with a scene of various parties transpiring in the Bathtub. This scene begins with Hushpuppy articulating an antimodern fetishism that the entire community seems to possess:

> Daddy says, up above the levee, on the dry side, they're afraid of the water like a bunch of babies. They built the wall that cuts us off. They think we all gonna drown down here. But we ain't goin' nowhere. The Bathtub's got more holidays than the whole rest of the world. Daddy always saying that up in the dry world, they got none of what we got. They only got holidays once a year. They got fish stuck in plastic wrappers, they got their babies stuck in carriages, and chickens on sticks and all that kind of stuff. One day, the storm's gonna blow, the ground's gonna sink, and the water's gonna rise up so high, there ain't gonna be no Bathtub, just a whole bunch of water. But me and my Daddy, we stay right here. We's who the earth is for.[25]

Hushpuppy's prediction ends up coming true after a massive storm strikes southern Louisiana and the Bathtub is flooded. The people of the community soon realize, however, that they can blow up the levee and release the flood waters into the cultivated side of the levee, drying out the Bathtub and returning it to a habitable state; this is the opposite of what some believe occurred in New Orleans during Katrina—that is, the flooding of the poor areas intentionally in order to spare the wealthier parts of the city, such as the French Quarter, an argument that Spike Lee highlights in his documentary *When the Levees Broke* (2006).

After the community bombs the levee and drains the Bathtub, the landscape is worse off than before the flood. Mud and trash cover everything, and all the animals in the area have died. Health officials come and say that there is a mandatory evacuation and that people can no longer live in the Bathtub. When the officials come to take them away, viewers root for Hushpuppy and Wink, as the film leads us to empathize with them to the extent that we do not want them to be forced to leave even though they are living in such abject poverty. Herein lies the danger of the film. If the story parallels Hurricane Katrina and its aftermath, then the people of the Bathtub are the people of storm-ravaged New Orleans, especially in locations like the Ninth Ward. Thus, the film sets us up to think that these people actually enjoy living in poverty and that they would rather remain in squalor, albeit a rather bohemian one, rather than take government assistance. So enchanted have we become by the world Hushpuppy inhabits that the shelter she goes to appears utterly inhospitable. Although it is clean, it looks overly sanitized and artificial. Hushpuppy remarks, "It didn't look like a prison; it looked like a fish tank with no water." While in the shelter, Wink even warns Hushpuppy not to eat the food provided to them. This is, of course, ironic given that in the past, while under Wink's care, Hushpuppy has often had to go hungry. Wink soon attacks a doctor who is trying to help him, and he says, "I don't need nothin' from y'all!" Hushpuppy and Wink's story is so compelling that the film forces viewers to want the residents of the Bathtub to escape the shelter even though this is likely the worst thing possible for them.

The people of the Bathtub eventually do escape and return to the land beyond the levee. They seem to believe that life in the shelter, where they are well fed and clean, is not worth the sacrifice of leaving their native land and their fringe cultural enclave. Back in the Bathtub, the natives seem happy despite the deplorable conditions. Hushpuppy's concluding monologue confirms this idea: "I see that I'm a little piece of a big, big universe, and that makes things right." But the truth is that things are far from "right" in Hushpuppy's life; she is still mired in poverty and is, therefore, in need of precisely the kind of assistance that her father has led her to reject. The tragedy of *Beasts of the Southern Wild* is that it, like so many Rough South films, portrays members of the lower class as living aesthetically satisfying lives and as embodying a kind of bohemian cultural authenticity. Such authenticity is undoubtedly attractive not only to New York filmmakers longing to capture little-known bohemian backwaters but also to consumers desperate to find pockets of America, particularly those at the margins of mainstream culture, that appear to be not yet homogenized.

Rough South Cinema and the Problem of Social Justice

One of the most bohemian of impulses has always been to wander in search of diverse and unfamiliar people and places. The journey to the bohemian margins of the Rough South provides both subject matter and a sense of authenticity for writers and filmmakers who are from outside the region or who are from the center, rather than the fringes, of Southern culture. Yet this bohemian fetishism in the context of the contemporary South leads to faux bohemians who are essentially culture vampires devouring the hard-won attributes of the Rough South and commodifying them both for bohemian cultural cachet and economic gain.

If films unrealistically depict people in need as leading aesthetically satisfying lives, and if moviegoers constantly consume romanticized versions of the bohemian Rough South, then they may grow complacent when it comes to rectifying the social and economic pathologies facing the region; therefore, Rough South films may even detract from real-world social justice efforts. In the contemporary moment, when people desire an "authentic" experience of American South, they seem to believe that it is most readily available in lower-class cultures, among which they long to slum. But immersing oneself in lower-class cultures through the media of fiction or film is paramount to a cowardly brand of cultural slumming. From the safety of your living room or the movie theater, you can enter and even enjoy the narrative of someone living in abject poverty or suffering through menial labor, all the while never having to actually enter the physical space inhabited by the lower class. Such a cultural vacation enables the middle and upper classes to experience a seemingly exotic, othered culture and then return to the relative comfort and safety of their own separate worlds.[26]

In recent years, Rough South cinema has become more and more popular, and the genre has displayed no sign of waning in its appeal. Regardless of the extent to which these films can be said to be authentic, the fact remains that they are often perceived to be. As a result of their perceived authenticity, especially in a region that increasingly appears to be postsouthern, moviegoers will likely continue craving these types of films, and if the market is a predominant guide, then filmmakers will likely go on producing what consumers desire. Just as Wendy Griswold concisely argues that "the reading class tends to get what it wants,"[27] I would add that this is also true for the moviegoing class, which sees in Rough South cinema a brand of regional bohemian identity that appears not to have surrendered to the homogenizing forces of global capitalism. Furthermore, perhaps true Rough South films do not yet even exist in that they are generally not produced by the people they represent; films about the Rough South have, in the majority of cases, been made by filmmakers not living an existence at the margins. But these Rough South films may be on the horizon as new technologies make film production cheaper and easier. The Rough South story, told truthfully and from an insider's perspective, may yet be witnessed on the silver screen.

Notes

1. Romine, *The Real South*, 4.

2. Watson, "Mapping out a Postsouthern Cinema," 219.

3. For an analysis of "cultural nakedness" in the context of the American South, see Cobb, *Redefining Southern Culture*, 141.

4. Carpenter, "Introduction," xiii–xxxii.

5. There are many other recent films and TV series that could also be explored, such as *Deliverance* (1972), *The Rough South of Harry Crews* (1991), *Swing Blade* (1996), *O Brother, Where Art Thou?* (2000), *Monster's Ball* (2001), *The Rough South of Larry Brown* (2002), *Junebug* (2005), *The Hawk is Dying* (2006), *Black Snake Moan* (2006), *Shotgun Stories* (2007), *Crazy Heart* (2009), *The Road* (2009), *Justified* (2010–2015), *Swamp People* (2010–), *Winter's Bone* (2010), *Mountain Men* (2012–2015), *Mud* (2012), *Joe* (2013), *Rectify* (2013–), *The Mind of the Chef* (season 2, 2013), *The World Made Straight* (2015), *Outsiders* (2016), and various Southern Foodways Alliance documentaries.

6. Turner, "City Workers, Country Workers," 12.

7. For analyses of the history of working-class films, see Booker, "Introduction"; Turner, "City Workers, Country Workers," 116–33; and Barker and McKee, "Introduction," 7–13.

8. Barker and McKee, "Introduction," 12–13.

9. McPherson, in *Reconstructing Dixie*, also begins to read Southern cinema through the lens of postsouthern theory. She argues that Ross McElwee's poetic and deeply personal documentary *Sherman's March* (1986) is an example of a postsouthern film because it presents the region not as "a site of stultifying authenticity" but rather "a contested terrain mobilized for alternative histories" (129–31, 141).

10. Watson, "Mapping out a Postsouthern Cinema," 220.

11. The tendency to aestheticize the living conditions of the Southern poor has recently been a broader trend in national and international cinema. While in the United States this tendency often goes unnoticed, it has received considerable attention from critics of Indian cinema. For example, in an analysis of Karan Johar's *Kabhi Khushi Kabhi Gham* (2001) and Rajkumar Hirani's *3 Idiots* (2009), Anwer, "Cinematic Clearances," 107–8, argues that when a location of poverty, especially a slum, is shown in Bollywood films it is "spatially aestheticized in such a way as to altogether expunge the unsavory smell and ordure of 'scenes of poverty.'" This trend can also be seen in the 2008 film *Slumdog Millionaire*, which was made by British filmmaker Danny Boyle but draws heavily on Bollywood traditions. *Slumdog Millionaire* has been attacked by some critics who have said that the film is an example of "poverty porn."

12. Carpenter, "Introduction," xvii.

13. Ibid., xvii; for other definitions of grit lit, see Gingher, "Grit Lit."

14. Carpenter, "Introduction," xxvii; emphasis in the original.

15. Romine, *The Real South*, 232.

16. Whisnant, *All That Is Native and Fine*, 260.

17. Ibid., 260; emphasis in the original.

18. *Searching for the Wrong-Eyed Jesus* website, http://www.searchingforthewrong eyedjesus.com.

19. Douglas, *Searching for the Wrong-Eyed Jesus*, DVD audio commentary.

20. Ibid., DVD materials.

21. Ibid., DVD materials.

22. Ibid., DVD audio commentary.

23. Ibid., DVD audio commentary.

24. *Searching for the Wrong-Eyed Jesus* website.

25. Zeitlin, *Beasts of the Southern Wild*, DVD.

26. For further analyses of the literary commodification of the lower class and how such literature is consumed by the middle and upper classes, see Griswold, *Regionalism and the Reading Class*; and Satterwhite, *Dear Appalachia*.

27. Griswold, *Regionalism and the Reading Class*, 174.

References

Anwer, Megha. "Cinematic Clearances: Spaces of Poverty in Hindi Cinema's Big Budget Productions." *Global South* 8 (2014): 91–111.

Barker, Deborah E., and Kathryn McKee. "Introduction: The Southern Imaginary." In *American Cinema and the Southern Imaginary*, edited by Deborah E. Barker and Kathryn McKee, 1–23. Athens: University of Georgia Press, 2011.

Bone, Martyn. *The Postsouthern Sense of Place in Contemporary Fiction*. Baton Rouge: Louisiana State University Press, 2005.

———. "Postsouthernism and the New Southern Studies." Invited Lecture, Department of English, North Carolina State University, April 26, 2012.

Booker, M. Keith. "Introduction: Blue-Collar Culture Industry: Film, Music, Sport, and the American Working Class." In *Blue-Collar Pop Culture: From NASCAR to Jersey Shore*, vol. 1, *Film, Music, and Sports*, edited by M. Keith Booker, 1–13. Santa Barbara, CA: Praeger, 2012.

Brown, Larry. *Big Bad Love*. Chapel Hill, NC: Algonquin, 1990.

Carpenter, Brian. "Introduction: Blood and Bone." In *Grit Lit: A Rough South Reader*, edited by Brian Carpenter and Tom Franklin, xiii–xxxii. Columbia: University of South Carolina Press, 2012.

Cobb, James C. *Redefining Southern Culture: Mind and Identity in the Modern South*. Athens: University of Georgia Press, 1999.

Douglas, Douglas, dir. *Searching for the Wrong-Eyed Jesus*. London: Douglas, 2003. DVD.

Hawkins, Gary, dir. *The Rough South of Harry Crews*. Research Triangle Park, NC: North Carolina Public Television, 1991. DVD.

Howard, Arliss, dir. *Big Bad Love*. New York: IFC, 2002. DVD.

Gingher, Robert. "Grit Lit." In *The Companion to Southern Literature*, edited by Joseph M. Flora, Lucinda H. MacKethan, and Todd Taylor, 319–20. Baton Rouge: Louisiana State University Press, 2002.

Griswold, Wendy. *Regionalism and the Reading Class*. Chicago: University of Chicago Press, 2008.

Kreyling, Michael. "Fee Fie Faux Faulkner: Parody and Postmodernism in Southern Literature." *Southern Review* 29, no. 1 (1993): 1–15.

———. *Inventing Southern Literature.* Jackson: University Press of Mississippi, 1998.

McPherson, Tara. *Reconstructing Dixie: Race, Gender, and Nostalgia in the Imagined South.* Durham, NC: Duke University Press, 2003.

Romine, Scott. *The Real South: Southern Narrative in the Age of Cultural Reproduction.* Baton Rouge: Louisiana State University Press, 2008.

———. "Where Is Southern Literature?: The Practice of Place in a Postsouthern Age." In *South to a New Place: Region, Literature, Culture,* edited by Suzanne W. Jones and Sharon Monteith, 23–43. Baton Rouge: Louisiana State University Press, 2002.

Satterwhite, Emily. *Dear Appalachia: Readers, Identity, and Popular Fiction since 1878.* Lexington: University Press of Kentucky, 2011.

Simpson, Lewis P. "The Closure of History in A Postsouthern America." In *The Brazen Face of History: Studies in the Literary Consciousness in America,* 255–76. Baton Rouge: Louisiana State University Press, 1980.

Tate, Allen. *Collected Essays.* Denver: Swallow, 1959.

Turner, Daniel Cross. "City Workers, Country Workers: The Urban and Rural Working Class in Southern Film." In *Blue-Collar Pop Culture: From NASCAR to Jersey Shore,* vol. 1, *Film, Music, and Sports,* edited by M. Keith Booker, 116–33. Santa Barbara, CA: Praeger, 2012.

Watson, Jay. "Mapping out a Postsouthern Cinema: Three Contemporary Films." In *American Cinema and the Southern Imaginary,* edited by Deborah E. Barker and Kathryn McKee, 219–52. Athens: University of Georgia Press, 2011.

Whisnant, David E. *All That Is Native and Fine: The Politics of Culture in an American Region.* 1983. Chapel Hill: University of North Carolina Press, 2009.

Woodward, C. Vann. *The Burden of Southern History.* 1960. Baton Rouge: Louisiana State University Press, 1993.

Zeitlin, Benh, dir. *Beasts of the Southern Wild.* New Orleans: Court 13 Films, 2012. DVD.

Southern Expressions of the Blues Revival

Scott Barretta

On July 29, 1964, the New Orleans Police Department raided the Quorum coffeehouse on Esplanade Avenue during a performance by acoustic blues-man Jewell "Babe" Stovall. Seventy-three persons—including Stovall and his family members—were arrested for disturbing the peace through actions including "playing guitars out of tune" and "engaging in conversations that had no end or conclusion."[1] Vice squad chief Frederick Soule Sr., said the Quorum and an upstairs apartment "seemed a melting pot of everybody with a beef against society" and the scene of communist propaganda, homosexual parties, and integration agitation.[2] The result of a three-month investigation, the raid included two undercover African American policemen who had participated in impromptu poetry readings at the Quorum.

The local citizens council had long targeted the venue because it actively supported integration and was a regular meeting place for civil rights workers. During an era when many organizations resisted integration by becoming private clubs, the Quorum instituted a membership policy in order to maintain and protect its diverse audience. The coffeehouse was not primarily a folk or blues music venue, but the raid suggests the potential difficulties of presenting traditional African American music in a respectful setting in the South—by 1964 similar activities had become commonplace, and were addressed by authorities in a relatively benign manner, in places including Berkeley, California; Cambridge, Massachusetts; Chicago's Old Town; and New York City's Greenwich Village.

The "blues revival" was a musical movement in the late 1950s and 1960s oriented toward presenting older forms of blues music to a new audience in a manner intended to elevate the blues' relative cultural status. Closely associated with the broader folk revival, the blues revival is usually dated as beginning in 1959 with the publication of Samuel Charters's book *The Country Blues*. A romantic introduction to early blues traditions, the book inspired many others to search for and "rediscover" early recording artists (notably Son House, Mississippi John Hurt, and Skip James), uncover others through field trips to the South, arrange performances, and reissue long out-of-print recordings.

The notion of a "blues revival" is problematic because its activists and audience consisted largely of young, white, middle-class males who were far removed—temporally, geographically, and in lived experience—from the object of their interest. "Those of us who participated in the revival thought we had discovered an object called blues, which we set out to think about, document, analyze, and, in some cases, perform," recalled ethnomusicologist Jeff Todd Titon, a participant in the revival. "Instead, by our interpretive acts, we constructed the very thing we thought we had found." During the revival blues, he argued, became "a symbol of stylized revolt against conservative politics and middle-class propriety."[3]

In elevating blues, revivalists were also linked to earlier musical subcultures and bohemian scenes characterized by concerns of aesthetic purity, the authenticity of "the folk," and various romantic projections about African American culture. Most notably, the blues revival can be traced back to two musical movements that took off during the Popular Front era of the 1930s, when many leftist intellectuals and activists celebrated the works of "the people" through fields including music, literature (e.g., James Agee and John Steinbeck) and photography (e.g., the Farm Security Administration photographers Walker Evans, Dorothea Lange, and Gordon Parks).

The "trad jazz" revival was a template of sorts for the blues revival—the locus of its attention was on African American instrumental ensembles that recorded in the 1920s, and it involved cultural outsiders uncovering and reissuing long out-of-print discs, reviving the careers of veteran artists such as Bunk Johnson, and re-creating vintage sounds through retro-oriented combos. Its critics—largely leftists associated with the Popular Front[4]—posed the authenticity of "real" jazz against the currently popular and "commercial" swing.[5] While the trad jazz movement addressed blues as an important antecedent to jazz, relatively little attention was paid to the details of its development or to artists whose music was socially defined as "blues."[6] By the 1950s, though, younger generations of trad jazz enthusiasts began more serious assessments of blues recordings and artists, and subsequently became important players in the emergent blues revival as critics, festival organizers and in issuing recordings.

The political folk song movement that took off in the 1930s viewed "music as a weapon" in social struggles, and activists including Alan Lomax and Pete Seeger presented a wide array of traditional and newly composed songs as "people's music." Blues—viewed as reflecting the social condition of African Americans—was an important part of this movement, but was expressed through a token handful of artists originally from the South who were located in Chicago and New York: Big Bill Broonzy, Huddie "Lead Belly" Ledbetter, the duo of Sonny Terry and Brownie McGhee, and Josh White. Particularly prized among the folk audience were their protest songs, such as Broonzy's segregation themed "Black, Brown and White" and Lead Belly's "The Bourgeois Blues," which included the couplet, "White folks in Washington they know how / Throw a colored man a nickel to see him bow." In general, though, there was relatively little interest within this folk scene in the details of blues history and discography that would obsess many researchers during the later blues revival.

The trad jazz and political folk movements continued into the 1950s, albeit with considerably less force. The emergent popularity of watered-down Dixieland music dampened the underground character of trad jazz enthusiasm, while the folk scene was the target of aggressive efforts by anticommunist forces. Notably, Pete Seeger was subjected to decades of boycotts, while Alan Lomax went into European exile for a decade. Activity with both movements continued in bohemian strongholds including Berkeley, Cambridge, Greenwich Village, and Chicago's Hyde Park neighborhood—places that would all play a major role in the blues revival as the location of collectors and researchers, festivals, venues, and record companies.

Such activity, both during the 1950s and earlier, was rare in the South, though musicians from the region were the locus of much of folk and jazz enthusiasts' interest. Historically Southern whites were often both acutely aware of African American vernacular music, as evidenced by centuries of accounts of slave fiddlers, sharecropper moans, the raucous sounds of jug bands and, later, the ubiquitous R&B bands at Southern college fraternity parties. While blues was hardly exotic then, if recognized positively it was likely through the lens of entertainment or prevailing stereotypes that didn't challenge social and cultural stereotypes about African Americans. Both the audiences and musicians were keenly aware of the standard decorum associated with the de facto and de jure "color line," and enjoying the music was not necessarily associated with developing a higher regard for the people playing it. And as the example opening this chapter illustrates, challenging this decorum could have serious consequences.

Examples of blues revival activity from New Orleans, Memphis, and Houston illustrate how race issues shaped the trajectory of revival networks and scenes. Just as important, though, is how these scenes differed due to factors including the influence (or the lack thereof) of preexisting musical/bohemian networks and contact with activists from outside the region.

New Orleans

As New Orleans author James Nolan notes, "Three ingredients are essential for a bohemian community to take root and flourish: creative misfits, magic and cheap rent."[7] Add to these a libertine sexual climate and a lively musical street culture, and it's hardly surprising why the French Quarter historically stood, along with Greenwich Village and San Francisco's North Beach, as one of the pillars of American bohemia. For many decades the French Quarter served as a place of refuge for many artists, leftists, and gay people—particularly those raised elsewhere in the South.

While many white bohemians were attracted to the city's vibrant African American culture, engaging with the culture in a respectful manner often proved problematic. The ritual celebrations surrounding Mardi Gras provided opportunities to momentarily subvert the racial (and gender and class) order, but in many more significant ways the circumstances of its staging only reinforced the racial hierarchy.[8] And while African American culture was central to the work of the celebrated New Orleans bohemian artist circle known as the Famous Creoles in the 1920s, they had "serious vision problems when it came to seeing African American life that surrounded them."[9]

In the 1950s and 1960s more conscious efforts were taken to create alternative spaces that both actively challenged the racial hierarchy and provided relative respites from the continual revelry of the Quarter; it was here that we find expressions of blues revival activity, albeit not a full-fledged blues revival scene. The Quorum, founded in 1963 out of the ashes of the likewise integrated Ryder Coffee House, was one of several French Quarter area locales where an "important subtext" was voter registration and in which "many elements of the Beat milieu were borrowed from black culture, particularly from jazz musicians whose footloose travels, disdain for convention, and fondness for marijuana were eagerly embraced by young whites wanting to 'make the scene.'"[10]

The Quorum, whose decor included a table made from a coffin, was notable for the engaged dialogues of its regulars, and in the evening it hosted theater troupes, poetry readings, and singer-songwriters, including Jerry Jeff Walker. There's no evidence that blues was staged here regularly, and Babe Stovall's appearance here and at similar venues would appear to be related less to his representation of a particular art from than to how attendees regarded folk blues as having an elective affinity with other perceived "alternative cultures."

Acoustic blues singers were more important, if not necessary integral, to another subculture in New Orleans that was dedicated to the advancement of trad jazz. A pioneering organization in this area was the New Orleans Jazz Club (founded in 1948), which promoted performances by both black and white musicians, but it largely maintained segregation on the stage and in the audience.[11] A more equitable social situation for musicians and fans coalesced in 1954 when art dealer Lorenz "Larry" Borenstein opened the Associated Artists gallery in the French Quarter at 726 St. Peter Street and began holding informal sessions dubbed "rehearsals" to avoid trouble with the musicians union. Savvy as a businessman, Borenstein was also notable for the breadth of his ties to a wide variety of subcultural types. As William Carter notes, "An adversary of the establishment, [Borenstein] not only associated with bohemians, radicals, gypsies, uppity locals and outside agitators, but happily dealt with shady-looking businessmen rumored to have Mafia ties."[12]

The police regularly broke up the gatherings at the gallery, which was located next to the raucous tourist bar Pat O'Brien's, with charges of "disturbing the peace," though the racial undertones were sometimes made manifest. In 1957, for instance, a night court judge allegedly admonished a mixed group of musicians by noting, "We don't want Yankees coming to New Orleans mixing cream with our coffee," and pointed out that one black musician was a "good yard boy" who could be released if he'd promise to "remember his place" and not get "uppity."[13] In 1961 the venue changed ownership, soon operating as Preservation Hall, which gained international recognition.

The New Orleans trad jazz scene was unsurprisingly closely tied to broader networks of trad jazz enthusiasts, and in the 1950s witnessed new arrivals including William Russell, a contributor to *Jazzmen*, owner of leading trad jazz label American Music Records, and the proprietor of a New Orleans record store; Californian Sam Charters, who recorded five albums of traditional jazz for New York's Folkways Records during the 1950s; and Georgia native Richard "Dick" Allen, an oral historian and record store owner who in 1958 helped found (and later served as curator for) Tulane University's New Orleans Jazz Archive (later the Hogan Jazz Archive).

While trad jazz of the 1920s and earlier was the primary focus of attention, these enthusiasts also documented and occasionally staged performances of related forms of vernacular black music, including blues and gospel, and served as liaisons to others exploring the blues scene. Russell's American Music issued recordings of African American string bands and vaudeville blues singers, including New Orleans's Lizzie Miles; Charters began his mission of seeking out blues performers across the South while living in New Orleans; and Allen made recordings of Stovall (and other French Quarter street performers) as early as 1958.

Allen also assisted and advised the most prolific professional folklorist in the region, Harry Oster, who operated his own Folk Lyric label and documented a wide variety of vernacular music. Most notably, a tip from Allen resulted in Oster making extensive recordings of the most significant traditional blues performer in New Orleans, Snook Eaglin. The blind musician was also active as a performer of contemporary New Orleans R&B, but in his liner notes Oster framed him as an acoustic street performer, minimizing his more modernist musical excursions.[14]

During the 1960s New Orleans never became a popular stop on the blues revival touring circuit, but Allen would play a key role in the establishment of the most lasting institution dedicated to the promotion of the region's diverse musical tradition. When George Wein, founder of the Newport folk and jazz festivals, called for advice on starting up a new event in New Orleans, Allen suggested that he work with Jazz Archive employee Allison Miner and intern Quint Davis. The resulting New Orleans Jazz and Heritage Festival started in 1970, and the famously eclectic event debuted modestly in Congo Square (then Beauregard Square) featuring Clifton Chenier, Fats Domino, Snook Eaglin, Duke Ellington, the Meters, the Preservation Hall Jazz Band, and roaming Mardi Gras Indians and brass bands.[15] In essence, music that had been largely available to tourists, Mardi Gras attendees, and radio listeners was now being reframed as "folklore," particularly via interview stages and demonstration tents. Over the next decades the festival became one of the leading music events in the country, and would feature dozens of artists whose who were "rediscovered" during the blues revival.

Houston

Between 1920 and 1960 the population of Houston grew from about 140,000 to nearly a million, and many of the new migrants were African Americans from rural Texas. Among these was Sam "Lightnin'" Hopkins from Centerville, who became an R&B star in the late 1940s via electrified country blues—a retro sound also popularized at the time by John Lee Hooker and Muddy Waters, Mississippi natives now relocated to, Detroit and Clarksdale, Mississippi, respectively. Via its down-home themes and technological updating of early blues sounds, the style appealed to the life experiences of many African Americans who had likewise migrated from the country to the city.

A decade later Hopkins would, sans electric guitar, became one of the first major artists in the blues revival. His transition from "commercial" to a "folk blues" artist happened largely through the efforts of members of the Houston Folklore Group (later Society), which had close ties to national folk networks and interpretive frameworks. Notably, a founding member was John Avery Lomax Jr., son of the pioneering folklorist and the older brother of Alan Lomax.

A pioneer in the study of cowboy songs, John Avery Lomax Sr. had in 1909 cofounded the Texas Folklore Society, which published multiple articles on "Negro folklore,"[16] and he was later a pioneer in using recordings to illustrate the distinctive qualities of African American folk song. In 1933 he took his young son Alan on a recording trip whose highlight was the discovery at Louisiana's Angola penitentiary of Lead Belly, who possessed a remarkably broad repertoire of African American song traditions. An ideological rift between the culturally conservative father and liberal son soon became evident though, and Alan's subsequent public presentations of Lead Belly and other artists would be largely via the leftist folk song movement's conceptions of "the folk." In 1951 Alan left the country largely for political reasons, returning in 1959 at the dawn of the blues revival.

In 1932 John Avery Lomax Jr., had accompanied his father on an extensive folk song collecting and lecture tour, but ultimately chose music more as an avocation.[17] A visit to Houston in 1951 by Pete Seeger and his wife Toshi inspired John Lomax Jr. and others to found the Houston Folklore Group, whose mission was "to sing, collect, and perpetuate the folklore of the people."[18] The Houston Folklore Society's meetings, held at private homes, coffeehouses and the Jewish Community Center, were for many years "the only place to go" for folksingers, and their monthly meetings featured an informal "pass the guitar" structure. During the 1940s and 1950s it was common for middle-class participants to interpret "ethnic" material, often learned from books, and John Lomax Jr. was known—like his brother Alan—for performing African American work songs while chopping a log with an axe. In 1956 John Jr. recorded an album for Folkways, performing multiple songs by Lead Belly, cowboy songs, and prison laments.[19]

In the late 1950s and early 1960s a major turn in the world of folk music was an increased focus on "ethnic" performers, and in Houston there was no better example than Lightnin' Hopkins. His career as a "folk" artist began in early 1959 after Sam Charters tracked him down with the aid of Houston Folklore Society chairman Mack McCormick, an independent scholar also active in theater and jazz circles. Recordings made by Charters would soon appear on Folkways Records, a dominant force in the New York folk scene since the late

1940s. McCormick also recorded several albums by Hopkins for the New York–based folk label Tradition Records and the London-based label 77, operated out of a jazz/blues specialist store. The liner notes for all these records emphasized Hopkins's folk credentials.

Patrick Mullen argues that McCormick's liner notes followed a style set by John Avery Lomax Sr. in "constructing a pastoral ideal of the black folk singer" by minimizing their urbanity or commercial aspirations and instead emphasizing "rural and oral culture roots as the basis for his authenticity."[20] The trajectory of Hopkins's commercial career, for instance, was described by McCormick as "increasingly pursued by amplifiers, echo chambers and thudding drums" and a "near pathetic attempts to conform to the gimmick-oriented demands" of the industry. Underneath the commercial facade, though, the real Hopkins was a man "with a tribal sense of belonging to his culture" and "outside the modern dilemma."[21]

A trial run for Hopkins's career as a folk musician was a Houston Folklore Group–organized event at Houston's prestigious Alley Theater on July 20, 1959, called Hootenanny in the Alley. John Lomax Jr. was among the many folk song interpreters on the program, which featured a narrator. "I was apprehensive," McCormick later wrote about Hopkins's performance, "because I knew the audience had come to hear the familiar ballads and songs popularized by book-trained singers. Here, in this habitat, there has never been any interest in the blues."[22] Hopkins had never appeared before a white audience, and was taken aback when the audience remained silent. Used to the lively call-and-response rituals found in African American churches, nightclubs, and informal gatherings, Hopkins wryly commented to the audience, "Well, a preacher don't get no amen in this corner."[23]

The show was well received, written up in the *Houston Chronicle*, and the following year John Lomax Jr., who helped manage Hopkins along with Mack McCormick, negotiated with Irwin Silber, editor of the New York–based folk music magazine *Sing Out!*, to play at shows there, including a Carnegie Hall performance with artists that included Pete Seeger. It wasn't long before Hopkins became a leading performer in the blues revival and an icon of cool for the counterculture.[24]

Memphis

Long billed as the "home of the blues," Memphis seemed an obvious place for a resurgence of traditional blues in the 1960s, particularly as white Memphians were long well aware of blues.[25] Samuel Charters's 1959 book *The Country Blues* revealed the continuing vitality in Memphis of pioneers from the 1920s, including Gus Cannon and Furry Lewis, and over ensuing decades many out-of-state blues researchers would use the city as a base to explore the region. Unlike New Orleans or Houston, though, Memphis lacked any significant networks tied to traditional jazz or folk music prior to the 1960s. As a result, the emergent blues revival subculture was largely homegrown, although ultimately informed and partially guided by outsiders with experience in more established revival scenes.

The history of the Memphis blues revival is well illustrated in the experiences of Jim Dickinson, who later became a successful producer and session musician. Dickinson's musical outlook was shaped by homegrown rockabilly and the vibrant blues/R&B scene in wide-open West Memphis, but he first encountered blues at home via his family's domestic employee, Alec Teal. "Everybody learned it from the yardman," Dickinson said of his cohort of white, middle-class Memphis musicians, a statement that reveals both the physical proximity of working-class African Americans to whites and the prevailing racial hierarchy.[26]

In his late teens Dickinson discovered on his own milestones of the emergent blues revival, including the Alan Lomax–produced LP *Blues in the Mississippi Night*, which featured anonymous blues artists speaking candidly about racism,[27] and Charters's *The Country Blues*. A fascination with Texan Blind Lemon Jefferson, featured in the book, led Dickinson to attend Baylor University, where he studied drama. Dickinson became aware of the field of folklore via students at the University of Texas, where a folklore archive was established in 1957. "I became friends with these guys in the folklore class and saw that you could actually kind of study it, and I got interested in it in a different way," Dickinson remembers. "And when I came back to Memphis in late '62, there was a coffeehouse and it was just too easy not to do. You could do it without a band, play eclectic stuff that you were interested in. And through the coffeehouses, that's where I first met Furry Lewis."[28] Dickinson and friends, including Mississippian Sid Selvidge, also began staging hootenannies at the Market Theater at the downtown farmers market; the following year they hosted Memphis's first folk festival at the Overton Park Shell.

Older blues artists first entered the Memphis folk music scene in the early 1960s through bookings at the Oso coffeehouse near Memphis State University (now the University of Memphis), but the folk music and bohemian scene really coalesced in 1964 with the opening of the Bitter Lemon coffeehouse, where subcultural interests in art, folk music, poetry, and psychedelic drugs converged.[29] The founder was John McIntire, an Ohio native who arrived in Memphis in 1961 to teach at the Memphis Academy of Arts; his house, located near the Bitter Lemon, was known as Beatnik Manor and was as an extension of the coffeehouse scene.

Performers at the Bitter Lemon included locals who happened to be stars of the international blues revival scene, including Gus Cannon, Furry Lewis, Fred McDowell, and Booker White, as well as budding white performers including Dickinson and Selvidge. The scene extended to casual, often drunken, gatherings at the homes of many blues artists. It was easy for young participants to take the elders' presence for granted, as Dickinson came to realize when he traveled in 1964 to Cambridge, Massachusetts, a hub of the blues and folk revivals.

"The whole atmosphere in Cambridge was studied," remembers Dickinson. "But the real thing was here. The actual persons. We had Gus Cannon. Songs, styles were very associated with individuals, and a mimic was just that. It was something that most of us were consciously trying not to do."[30] Witnessing a performance by the popular revivalist Jim Kweskin Jug Band at Cambridge's Club 47 was also revealing. "Damn! I can do that!" recalls Dickinson of his reaction to seeing young whites playing vintage Memphis blues. "And I went home and did it—my first record was a jug band record, *You'll Do it All the Time* by the New Beale Street Sheiks."[31]

The do-it-yourself quality of the Memphis scene was altered in the mid-1960s by the arrival of 78-rpm collectors and accomplished blues guitarists Bill Barth, who had performed at coffeehouses in his native New York City, and John Fahey, from the Washington, DC, area, who had written his master's thesis in folklore at the University of California–Los Angeles on Mississippi blues pioneer Charley Patton. Fahey and Barth helped "rediscover" legendary recording artist Skip James in Tunica, Mississippi, and it was largely through their efforts that the Mississippi Country Blues Festival was established as an annual (and nationally noted) event at Memphis's Overton Shell. As was the case in other cities, interest in acoustic folk and blues music declined, relatively speaking, in the latter 1960s, as many musicians—Dickinson included—moved on to more electric and eclectic forms of music, albeit influenced by traditional blues. But the coffeehouse scene and early festivals in Memphis set a template for later appreciation of traditional music there. This would include the annual festivals put on by the Center for Southern Folklore since its establishment in 1972, as well as the significant investments in blues- and soul-related cultural tourism in recent decades, as reflected in the current face—for better or worse—of Beale Street.

IN JULY 1961, police in Clarksdale, Mississippi, detained two young white blues researchers from California, Donald Hill and Dave Mangurian, following reports that they had spent the night and attended church with local barber and bluesman Wade Walton. Investigator Tom Scarborough of the Mississippi Sovereignty Commission, a spy organization launched by the state in 1956, filed a four-page report, noting that the men had arrived in a Renault with California plates. Their purported mission was to locate older blues artists and, more specifically, to convince Walton to travel with them to New York City to record an album.

Scarborough questioned the men about their education, religious backgrounds, and views on the civil rights movement, and ultimately decided "they were doing what they claimed to be doing. I was impressed with them being crack-pots more than anything else." Walton, he suggested, was "an ignorant Negro who believes himself much smarter than he is," and surmised that Hill and Mangurian were possibly con men, as it was "an easy matter to make a Negro guitar strummer think he has real talent and get what money he can get hold of." The pair took the advice of the sheriff and district attorney to quickly leave town, and Scarborough noted, "to do otherwise might have been an invitation for other agitators to start coming to Clarksdale."[32]

Almost exactly fifty years later a marker for the Mississippi Blues Trail—a state-administered program to promote cultural tourism—was dedicated in Walton's honor at the site of his barbershop, acknowledging his music and long-standing efforts in assisting blues fans, including Hill and Mangurian. The marker was placed during Clarksdale's annual Juke Joint Festival, one of many blues-themed events now underwritten by the city, which actively celebrates its rich blues heritage; former residents include Sam Cooke, Ike Turner, and Muddy Waters.

Clarksdale also boasts the Ground Zero Blues Club, co-owned by actor Morgan Freeman and decorated in a faux juke joint style, and the Shack Up Inn, a blues-themed lodging facility where guests stay in restored sharecropper shacks—now outfitted with hot water, air-conditioning, and cable TV preset to the blues audio channel. The city's reinvention as a blues mecca is also expressed through multiple blues-themed businesses run by people who first came here as blues tourists, including Dutchman Theo Dasbach's

Rock & Blues Museum, Deak's Mississippi Saxophones & Blues Emporium, (known for its harmonicas), and Cat Head Delta Blues & Folk Art, a clearinghouse for information about, in the proprietor's catch phrase, "real deal" blues artists.

What's happened in Clarksdale in recent decades might be seen in terms of Richard Lloyd's concept of a neobohemia, usually employed to describe changes in the cultural economy of postindustrial cities rather than "posta-grarian" communities such as Clarksdale.[33] Like Lloyd's Wicker Park in Chicago, it's questionable whether the transformation in Clarksdale has resulted in a true "bohemia," but as Lloyd argues, these efforts might nevertheless be inspired by fantasies among the settlers of *la vie bohème*.[34] Cynical observers suggest that Clarksdale has become a blues Disneyland; that's hyperbolic, but it's certainly the case that outsiders pursuing the music is no longer a transgressive activity, as could be the case a half century ago. The rebranding of Clarksdale as a blues destination for tourists illustrates the broader trend of "heritage tourism" and signifies the dramatically changed cultural status of the blues. The proliferation of municipally sponsored blues festivals across the South and elsewhere reflects city planners' calculations that blues festivals draw an economically desirable demographic (notably white male baby boomers), with the additional political value of appearing to—at least theoretically—bridge racial divisions, as expressed by the naive, if frequently employed, slogan "No whites, no blacks, just blues."

The process of blues becoming culturally "legitimized" reflects generational change—notably via baby boomers' growing appreciation for blues due to its influence on rock 'n' roll—but it's also rooted in the specific activities of cultural entrepreneurs in discrete bohemian/subcultural circles. The "blues revival" encompassed a wide range of activities, and aside from a general orientation toward finding an alternative to mainstream cultural offerings, the impetus for engaging in revivalist activity varied widely. Active participants included 78 rpm collectors whose criteria were rarity and aesthetic purity, politically minded activists who saw blues as representing a voice of resistance from the working class, and those of a more existentialist bent who actively sought out what they perceived as a more authentic lifestyle, such as the subjects of Norman Mailer's conception of the "white negro."

As a new movement, the blues revival built upon preexisting social networks and interpretive frameworks, as is exemplified by the cases here. In Houston the folk scene largely followed a model established during the 1930s, with a catholic orientation towards folk music and an aesthetic that valued representation of "the people" over virtuosity. That said, its connections to established folk music institutions in the Northeast and beyond provided an opportunity to successfully reframe a commercial artist such as Hopkins as an established "folk blues" act.

In New Orleans the locus of subcultural activity associated with promoting blues was not associated with bacchanalia but instead via existing networks aimed at increasing the cultural status of another form of black music—jazz. Although oriented toward the classic sounds captured on vintage 78s, the trad jazz scene became increasingly interested in documenting associated musics, including traditional blues by artists such as Babe Stovall and Snooks Eaglin, and provided a framework for the later legitimization of more modern forms of local R&B.

In Memphis there was initially considerably less concern with conscious revivalism; instead, there was a more subtle reframing of the blues expressed though incorporation of veteran local musicians into the relatively informal music scene as revered, albeit eminently available, figures. The active presence of these musicians ultimately attracted outsiders with experience in more formal folk scenes, and the development of more formal means for recognizing artists on a national scale.

These three scenes were similar in the fact that they took place in the South at a time when de facto and de jure segregation were in full force, affecting the tenor of movements whose aim was to a large extent elevation of African American culture. While operating discretely, they were united in contributing artists and information to the new institutions of the emergent blues/folk revival—labels and LP series, festivals and venues, and publications.

The blues revival played an important role in creating more positive acknowledgment of blues, though like other successful subcultural movements its triumphs might be seen as contributing to its relative undoing. As blues became increasingly more mainstream, the bohemian impulses of wanting to be associated with and advancing a form of African American culture regarded as providing a more authentic alternative to middle-class "respectability" diminished. These same sorts of energies, unsurprisingly, would became associated with the movements dedicated to the advancement of other related vintage music—Southern soul, vintage gospel, funk, and the like.

While the framing of the music during the blues revival might now appear somewhat clichéd and serve as fodder for blues tourism promotions, the music itself still holds the potential as an alternative expression. In recent years, for instance, the Fat Possum label was able to successfully market "hill country" blues as having an affinity to contemporary alternative music by proclaiming it "not the same old blues crap,"[35] while younger fans' exposure to new music via sampling and streaming services provide multiple alternatives for reviving anew the blues.

Notes

1. "The Quorum."
2. "4 Plead Guilty in Quarter Raid."
3. Titon, "Reconstructing the Blues," 222–23.
4. Denning, *The Cultural Front*, 458.
5. Trad jazz enthusiasts were later attacked as socially conservative "moldy figs" by modernists who embraced bebop. See Gendron, "'Moldy Figs' and Modernists."
6. Oliver, "That Certain Feeling," 11–19.
7. Ellis, *Madame Vieux Carré*, 86.
8. See Mitchell, *All on a Mardi Gras Day*.
9. Reed, *Dixie Bohemia*, 65–66.
10. Ellis, *Madame Vieux Carré*, 86.
11. For a detailed discussion of the issue of race and the New Orleans trad jazz revival, see Raeburn, *New Orleans Style*, chap. 7.
12. Carter, *Preservation Hall*, 126.
13. Ibid., 116.
14. Wald, liner notes to *Snooks Eaglin*.
15. Branley, "NOLA History."
16. Abernethy, "African-American Folklore."
17. Lomax, "A Success in All He Did."
18. Govenar, *Lightnin' Hopkins*, 69.
19. Lomax, *John A. Lomax Sings American Folksongs*.
20. Mullen, *The Man Who Adores the Negro*, 120.
21. Ibid., 121.
22. Govenar, *Lightnin' Hopkins*, 79.
23. Ibid., 80.
24. Ibid., 104.
25. As Lee, *Beale Street*, 62, notes, "On Thursday nights the blues belong to the white people. They come in evening dress in high-powered cars, in overalls and Fords, to see scantily clad brown beauties dancing across the stage." In the post-war era whites ventured over to wide-open West Memphis, where African American bands at segregated venues, including the Plantation Inn, pioneered soul music. Many people have argued that white teenagers' appropriation and appreciation of R&B and rock 'n' roll in the 1950s was revolutionary, but I would argue that there was a qualitative difference between this and the conscious actions during the blues revival.
26. Gordon, *It Came from Memphis*, 44.
27. "In the 1950s if you were looking for any kind of alternative culture you had to fucking know where to look, 'cause certainly nobody had marketed it, thank God," Dickinson recalled. "There was like three places in town you could get an Evergreen book, literally [the *Evergreen Review*, first published in 1957]. And each one of those

places had a real small record section—that's where the Folkways [Records section] was. It was all clustered, the same kind of mind-set." Dickinson, interview.

28. Dickinson, interview.

29. According to Randall Lyon, a central figure in the emergent bohemian scene, "the Bitter Lemon was the place that drew us together. . . . If it wasn't for McIntire being in touch with artists, poets, musicians, there wouldn't have been a center for the situation, and he was it." Randall Lyon, quoted in Gordon, *It Came from Memphis*, 114.

30. Dickinson, interview.

31. Ibid.

32. Scarborough, report for Mississippi Sovereignty Commission.

33. See Lloyd, *Neo-Bohemia*.

34. Ibid., 236.

35. Evans, "Demythologizing the Blues," 8–9, argues that Fat Possum's approach reflects the contemporary popularity of the "myth of blues as chaos," and notes that "[one] can grant that the music and lives of these artists might appear chaotic in comparison to the more regulated middle-class experience that proponents of this myth are evidently fleeing, but the latter are confusing dissatisfaction, experimentation, and improvisation in the blues with chaos and anarchy."

References

Abernethy, Francis. "African-American Folklore in Texas and in the Texas Folklore Society." In *Juneteenth Texas: Essays in African-American Folklore*, edited by Francis B. Abernethy, Patrick B. Mullen, and Alan Govenar, 1–13. Denton: University of North Texas Press, 1996.

Branley, Edward. "NOLA History: The New Orleans Jazz and Heritage Festival." http://gonola.com/2013/04/22/nola-history-the-new-orleans-jazz-and-heritage -festival.html.

Carter, William. *Preservation Hall: Music from the Heart*. New York: Cassell, 1991.

Denning, Michael. *The Cultural Front: The Laboring of American Culture in the Twentieth Century*. New York: Verso, 1998.

Dickinson, Jim. Interview with author, November 6, 1997, Memphis, Tennessee.

Ellis, Scott S. *Madame Vieux Carré: The French Quarter in the Twentieth Century*. Jackson: University Press of Mississippi, 2009.

Evans, David. "Demythologizing the Blues." Paper presented at Annual Meeting of the American Folklore Society, October 22, 1999, Memphis, Tennessee. http:// www.crookedsaws.com/myths/.

"4 Plead Guilty in Quarter Raid," *Times Picayune*, July 31, 1964.

Gendron, Bernard. " 'Moldy Figs' and Modernists: Jazz at War (1942–1946)," In *Jazz among the Discourses*, edited by Krin Gabbard, 31–56. Durham, NC: Duke University Press, 1995.

Gordon, Robert. *It Came from Memphis*. Boston: Faber and Faber, 1995.

Govenar, Alan. *Lightnin' Hopkins: His Life, His Blues*. Chicago: Chicago Review Press, 2010.

Lee, George W. *Beale Street: Where the Blues Began*. New York: Ballou, 1969.

Lloyd, Richard. *Neo-Bohemia: Art and Commerce in the Postindustrial City*. New York: Routledge, 2006.

Lomax, John, III. "John A. Lomax, Jr. (1907–1974): A Success in All He Did." www .culturalequity.org/alanlomax/ce_alanlomax_profile_johnlomaxjr.php.

Lomax, John A., Jr. *John A. Lomax Sings American Folksongs*. New York: Folkways, 1956. LP.

Mitchell, Reid. *All on a Mardi Gras Day: Episodes of New Orleans Carnival*. Cambridge: Harvard University Press, 1999.

Mullen, Patrick B. *The Man Who Adores the Negro: Race and American Folklore*. Urbana: University of Illinois Press, 2008.

Oliver, Paul. "That Certain Feeling: Blues and Jazz . . . In 1890?" *Popular Music* 10 (1991): 11–19.

"The Quorum" (documentary film website). http://www.quorumthemovie.com.

Raeburn, Bruce Boyd. *New Orleans Style and the Writing of American Jazz History*. Ann Arbor: University of Michigan Press, 2009.

Reed, John Shelton. *Dixie Bohemia: A French Quarter Circle in the 1920s*. Baton Rouge: Louisiana State University Press, 2012.

Scarborough, Tom. Four-page report for Mississippi Sovereignty Commission investigation on Wade Walton, David Mangurian, and Donald Raymond Hill, July 17, 1961. Can be retrieved by entering "Donald Raymond Hill" in the search field at http://www.mdah.ms.gov/arrec/digital_archives/sovcom/#basicname.

Titon, Jeffrey. "Reconstructing the Blues: Reflections on the 1960s Blues Revival." In *Transforming Tradition*, edited by Neil Rosenberg, 222–23. Champaign, IL: University of Illinois Press, 1993.

Wald, Elijah. Liner notes. *Snooks Eaglin: New Orleans Street Singer*. Washington, DC: Smithsonian Folkways, 2005 (1959). CD.

Acting Out

The Athens, Georgia, Music Scene and the Emergence of a Bohemian Diaspora

Grace Elizabeth Hale

Before the late 1970s, American bohemians lived in big cities: in New York, especially, but also in San Francisco and elsewhere. Small towns and secondary cities might have had their eccentrics, but they did not have scenes. A scene was more than a few odd folks; it was a fusion of a physical place, a network of people, and self-consciously oppositional creative practice. When Teresa Randolph screamed, "I can't believe this is happening in Athens, Georgia!" at a 1977 Athens party as the B-52's played their second gig, "this" did not just mean this band making this music or these dancing people wearing their guess-who-I-am drag; it meant making a scene, people not just partying but creating an alternative culture in a particular, if unlikely, place.[1]

From the very beginning, this unlikeliness, a sense of surprise that a small Southern college town could nurture bohemia, drew journalists and music critics' attention. In the summer of 1980, the *New York Rocker* put it bluntly: "Something is happening in Athens, Georgia, and we don't know what it is." Reporting on the B-52's, who debuted in New York on December 12, 1977, at Max's Kansas City, set the tone. Few mentions of the band left out its Athens origins, as journalists repeated the quirky details the band provided to create an "up from the redneck wasteland" theme: Kate Pierson's tenant house outside town and her goats, Fred Schneider's jobs waiting tables at a hippie restaurant in an old building that had once housed a mortuary and where the band practiced in the "blood-letting" room, Ricky Wilson and Keith Strickland's work around the Greyhound Bus station managed by Strickland's parents, and the odd fact that everyone—even Schneider and Pierson, who were not from the South—spoke in a drawl.[2]

These stories set the tone for coverage of the bands that followed the B-52's. The *New York Rocker* took up the theme again in March 1981 in its cover story about another Athens band, Pylon: "Greil Marcus says bands are 'images of community.' There must be something about Athens, Georgia; it seems to breed eclectics. Maybe it's the fallout from the DuPont factory where the members of Pylon have worked? Maybe it's art studies at the University of Georgia; maybe it's the laetrile in the peach pits or the sweet summer sweat." The same issue included a piece by Athens musician Vic Varney, "'Nineteen Hours from New York': Small Town Makes Good," that provided an insider's view. Asked by an Atlanta journalist that same year about why the city his band Pylon was from had become as important as what they were playing, Athens scene maker Michael Lachowski answered "surprise": "They're freaked out, especially in the states, that bands with any measure of sophistication should come from a small Southern town." Two years later, *People* magazine still pushed the "unlikely" theme, describing the town as the key example of "regional rock, a flourishing grassroots movement characterized by strange compulsions to *not* move to New York or Los Angeles." In Athens in the late 1970s and early 1980s, the members of bands like the B-52's, Pylon, and R.E.M. and their friends and fans built a scene that became a major location of alternative culture and a key early site in an expanding bohemian diaspora.[3]

The new bohemians were different from earlier generations of self-conscious, mostly middle-class rebels against middle-class ideals and values. Older bohemians had grown up in small towns and urban ethnic neighborhoods characterized by local culture, knowing eyes, dense webs of family, and traditions imagined as deeply rooted. In contrast, the new rebels grew up in postwar suburbia—in instant communities with new traditions; interchangeable houses, shops, and streets; and culture made elsewhere and delivered through television or radio. As university attendance soared, young people raised in the suburbs collected in college towns and college neighborhoods in bigger cities where they experienced firsthand cultural landscapes quite different from the neighborhoods in which they had grown up. For them, quirky, particular, and old places where working-class and middle-class patrons mixed in restaurants and shops counted as alternative. Instead of running away from a distinctive place, these suburban-raised bohemians fled placelessness. Instead of looking for urban anonymity, they sought social connection. Inspired by punk's do-it-yourself ethic, the folk revival's celebration of local culture and participation, and pop art's transformation of old popular culture into avant-garde art, they made their own alternative cultures, in places as unexpected as Athens, Akron, Louisville, and Winston-Salem.[4]

In Athens, the low tuition and relatively easy admissions process at the University of Georgia (UGA), coupled with a low cost of living, drew thousands of young people to a town of about sixty thousand. These mostly white students came from the Sunbelt suburbs, where economic expansion in the 1970s ran counter to Rust Belt decline and softened the blow of the early 1980s recession. Too young to remember the civil rights victories of the mid-1960s, they attended integrated schools. As kids and teens, they watched the fighting in Vietnam and the scandal of Watergate on the television news. Older siblings and cousins, former student activists and hippies, had retreated into the woods or cut their hair and gone to work for the "man." It was hard in this context to believe any longer that organized politics could change the world. Making a self-consciously oppositional culture might not change the world, but it might change participants' lives. It might change their town.[5]

Athens, an hour and a half drive from Atlanta, was isolated. Local music there meant folk music revival events or Top 40 cover bands, and hippies and Greeks dominated campus. Yet key people and the media connected people to art and music being made elsewhere. The son of a UGA professor, Jerry Ayers grew up in Athens before moving to New York around 1970, where he remade himself as the Warhol superstar Silva Thin. When his younger friends and future members of the B-52's Keith Strickland and Ricky Wilson visited, they hung out with the drag queens at Warhol's Factory. After Ayers returned to Athens, he spent time with Wilson and Strickland as they created their band and wrote the lyrics to one of the first songs, "52 Girls." Later he mentored other androgynous young men, including R.E.M.'s Michael Stipe. The UGA art school inspired many students alienated from general campus life. Art professors Robert Croker and Judy McWillie, who played punk music in class; Art Rosenbaum, who performed folk music and taught a class on folk artists and musicians; and Jim Herbert, who treated talented young people like they were already working artists inspired students to make their own work. Publications like the *New York Rocker* and the *Village Voice* brought news of the New York art and music scenes. Nurtured by this small and inexpensive place, Athens scene makers experienced an ideal combination of education and isolation. What they did not know could not intimidate them. What they learned inspired them to make new music.[6]

In the crucial five years after the B-52's played their first party in 1977, that music transformed a small Southern college town into a new kind of bohemia, a nationally and internationally recognized site of alternative culture production in the 1980s and 1990s. As distinctions between rock subgenres, independent and major record labels, and commercial versus noncommercial culture grew increasingly murky, geography—the distinct location where people produced cultural artifacts—emerged as the most important marker of authenticity. Despite journalists' efforts to describe a common "Athens sound," bands in the first five years shared little sonically except a danceable beat. As former members of these bands recall, each group tried to carve out its own unique sound. Local status depended on this uniqueness. What bands like the B-52's, Pylon, and R.E.M. did share was an aesthetic that translated unlikeliness into musical form. Out of the disjuncture that characterized Athens bohemia from the start, they made music that was surprisingly out of place, out of time, and even out of tune.[7]

In Athens music, "out" meant "not in," not the Southern rock and hippie music that many young people in Athens liked in the mid-1970s. "Out" described the direction of participants' gaze, looking out from their emerging scene at other places and times, because their newly minted bohemia was not large enough to be self-referential. "Out" suggested their musical amateurism, the way they lost the beat or the note or the key, the way they played a little out of rhythm or out of tune, and they way they danced just slightly out of step. "Out" defined their mode of production, making new music and art out of old popular culture, from out-of-fashion clothes and used records to dated encyclopedias and decades-old magazines. And "out" referred to the practice of making public a lesbian, gay, bisexual, transgender or queer identity (not then named as such) and to the role of drag or dressing up as a style of performance and form of cultural and political commentary. Making a scene meant acting out and acting up, flaunting middle-class conventions, from playing with multiple partners of both sexes to adopting a self-consciously causal attitude about sex. As the music press reported on Athens and local bands toured, the "out" aesthetic developed there shaped the evolution and spread of new bohemias across the nation.[8]

Historically, drag or dressing up in ways that self-consciously play with gender has enabled practitioners to comment on gender and sexuality as well as culture and politics more broadly. In drag, pretending that an identity is real works, in the context of the performance, to remake the real and to question the relationship between the very meaning of concepts like reality and illusion, original and copy, and authenticity and artifice. Drag suggests a performer can make something real—a new gender identity or a new music or a new way of living that feels deeply right—out of something that is out-of-date, fake, temporary, or even trashy. In the early years of the Athens scene, musicians created meaning and affect out of disjuncture by playing with the gaps and highlighting the contradictions—by performing, as in a drag show, the fact that the act was an act. The collaged bits of past pop culture that musicians put on display, especially when performing live, worked because they were not only pieces of a past but also an art of the present and a vision for the future. Contradiction—authenticity made out of artifice, utopia made out of trash—was key.[9]

In performance, early Athens bands were out of place: from the small-town South and yet making "new" music. And they were out of time: performing in the present sounds and moves borrowed self-consciously from the past. They were also out of time in a musical sense: raw, off the beat, and out of tune. Live performance revealed the musical amateurism that could often be cleaned up in the recording process, and this rawness proved essential to any understanding of this music as avant-garde or oppositional. The slicker the act, the more it seemed like pop culture of the past rather than art making a comment about the relationship of the past to the pop culture present. Polished, the music lost its power to comment, to suggest that a collage of possible pasts could conjure a collage of possible futures. Live performance also foregrounded the layers of disjuncture and disconnection at work in the lyrics, sound, dance moves, and dress, a multilayered dissonance at once visual, aural, and symbolic.[10]

In the period between 1977 and the summer of 1983, at which time the University of Georgia radio station WUOG produced its first show on the history of music in Athens, around thirty bands formed including Art in the Dark, Limbo District, Love Tractor, the Method Actors, Oh OK, the Squalls, and the Tone Tones. Recordings of live performances by the three most important bands from this period—the B-52's, Pylon, and R.E.M.—illustrate the way different groups developed the "out" aesthetic that nurtured this new bohemia. Growing up placeless and immersed in mass-produced culture, Athens scene makers used old popular culture to create an alternative with a sense of place. By the mid-1980s, their success inspired a bohemian diaspora and paradoxically made it clear that bohemia, like suburbia, could exist almost anywhere.[11]

The B-52's: "Dance This Mess Around"

In March 1978, a little over a year after their 1977 Valentine's Day house party debut, the B-52's had played three Athens parties, one Athens folk club, three nights at Max's Kansas City and two at CBGBs in New York City, and one Atlanta gig at the great Southeast Music Hall's first (and seemingly last) Atlanta Punk Festival. The band had also recorded a single, "Rock Lobster," backed with "52 Girls." Buzz about the band had Atlanta fans of the music—which was increasingly called New Wave and postpunk—talking. "They were heroes to us," then Georgia State student Kelly Mills remembered. "We were all into the idea of the stripped-down sound and that anyone could be an artist." When Mills and his friends heard the band was playing Atlanta again at a club in Virginia Highlands called the Downtown Café, they took equipment from CCTV, the Georgia State closed circuit television station where they worked, to the show. Using two video cameras on tripods, they plugged into the soundboard and shot the show on black and white half-inch tape. With clear audio and visuals that flicker out but mostly into focus, the footage may not be a time machine, but it is the next best thing, an artifact that captures something of the sound, look, and feel of a live B-52's performance a little more than a year after the band debuted.[12]

In this video, the song "Dance This Mess Around" starts out urgently with guitar chords, drums and cymbals, and keyboards. As Kate Pierson pumps her finger, a beep rings out in rhythm with Keith Strickland's one-two drumbeat, insistent and piercing, fixing the audience's attention with its repetition. Ricky Wilson hits guitar notes that reverberate around this pumping foundation, and their distorted tones are less melodic than rhythmic, like he is playing bass on the wrong instrument. Vocalist Cindy Wilson then joins the rising swell of sound. The first word "Remember"—half spoken, half sung—suggests, like her thrift store dress, that the past will be on offer here, in a complicated conversation with the performance's present. As she sings the first line of the song, she and Fred Schneider raise their hands to their brows as if they are surveying the audience. Their moves are almost in unison, Schneider's gesture with his upturned palm, the fey echo of Wilson's more military salute. When she reaches the end of the line—"when you held my hand"—they continue their dance and thrust their upturned palms out toward the audience, their take on an Osmond Brothers' imitation of a Motown group. As Wilson repeats "Remember," and sings the second line "when you were my man," Schneider pounds out notes on a toy piano and Wilson adds a tambourine. The jerky movements of the band members and the one-two beat propel the song forward, as whatever melody exists emerges from the vocals. Rhythm, gestures, and the clichéd content of the lyrics cut across the yearning emotion of Wilson's voice. Schneider, wearing a wife-beater T-shirt, khakis, and the shadow of a beard, looks like a slightly off version of the husband too hungover to accompany a primly belted and buttoned Wilson to church.

In the second part of the song, Ricky Wilson's 1960s garage band guitar provides the melody, and the shift frees Cindy Wilson to scream, more than sing, her lines. Her raw, hurt voice—a mash-up of James Brown, Peggy Lee, and Patti Smith—expresses feelings that seem real enough as she asks, "Why don't you dance with me?" Yet the rest of the line, "I'm not no Limburger," uses absurdity to undercut its revelation of rage, vulnerability, and desire. If the man she is addressing thinks she is a piece of stinky cheese, she'll tell him she is *not*! And she will repeat it, her screaming voice drawing out the word *Lim-burger* three times, making it hold emotions that have no easy relation to its meaning. Schneider's rejoinder cuts against any expectation of a harmonizing backup vocal with its dissonant, flat sound: "Dance this mess around" and then the phrase again followed by "round round round round." This time the meaning of the word fits both the swirling feelings and the sound as the echo—human-made reverb—threads through Pierson's pan-flute-from-another-planet keyboard part. This and other hints of science fiction movie sound thrust past visions of the future into a present in which they are not the time to come but already the past. Underneath all the clanging, ringing, droning, and screaming, Strickland is speeding up the beat, adding to the sense of rising sound. Tone, rhythm, and lyrical meaning set up and yet disrupt pop music conventions and any sense of narrative that depends upon the orderly flow of time.

In a voice too close to Cindy Wilson's for a classic girl group sound, Pierson picks up the lead as the song shifts into its third part. "Everybody," she sings, the word stretched to emphasize the human figure in the word, "goes to parties, and they dance this mess around." Pierson and Schneider trade off the vocals now, naming the dances as Schneider demonstrates them in moves more jerky than fluid. The absurd dances—the Shugaloo, the Shy Turnip (or Turtle), the Camel Walk, and the Hypocrite—gesture at past pop dance fads to offer hints of a new future. These moves are not like stoned-hippie dancing, or punk slamming, or the swaying and bouncing that usually passed for dancing at Southern rock concerts. These dances require thought, they require timing, and they might even require thinking.[13]

Then the song shifts again. Cindy Wilson jumps back in with a rhetorical question, part snarl and part sexy come-on: "Hey! Now, doesn't that make you feel a whole lot better, now? Huh?" Schneider offers an instant answer in the form of another "Huh?" and Wilson asks again, and Schneider has to lay his answer, "Yeah," right over her sassy line, "What you say? I'm just askin.'" Schneider comes right back, his shouted vocal "Come on!" slightly off, not the harmony that listeners expect in pop songs. Then, Southern accent on over-drive, Wilson yells "Shake!" and they both sing, their voices rising and falling over the syllables "Oh oh oh oh oh." A measure behind where you would expect it, Schneider answers with "Bake!" Again, once is not enough, and the shake and bake chant repeats three more times, transforming the iconic meat coating, first introduced in 1965, into a dance. As the repetitions build, past and present again collide, and the mod cooking mix becomes, like the sugar in the coffee of old blues songs, a double entendre for sex. Wilson's fuzzy guitar lays out the only thing resembling a melody. After then Pierson and Schneider repeat their dance demonstration before Wilson returns with her bold questions. This time Schneider's answering "Uh" sounds both Southern in accent and noncommittal in affect. As Pierson's voice threads more rounds of "Dance this mess around" between the beats, Wilson and Schneider end the song scatting a series of yeah-yeah-yeahs that somehow evoke both jazz vocal styling and the repetitive flatness of machine-generated sound.

All this dancing and all this messing around suggest to listeners with a keen since of pop history one of Ray Charles's first hits, "Mess Around," released in 1957, in which "mess" means both dancing and loving. The B-52's song "Dance This Mess Around" is not a cover and not even any kind of straightforward homage, yet Schneider's call and response with first Wilson and then Pierson sounds like it should be with Ray Charles, as Schneider offers an almost echo of the older song's line, "Everybody is doing the mess around." In the context of Charles's song, "Dance this mess around" means "Dance this dance around" and, more pointedly, "Dance this sex around." Imagining Schneider—not really closeted and yet not in the context of his public performance really "out"— singing with Charles adds another layer of transgression.

In this 1978 live performance the B-52's use their sound, their costumes, and their moves to play with the pop culture past. The amateurism of the performance highlights the gaps: between expectation and execution, between an original, a copy, and a copy of a copy, and between the meaning of the words and the flow of the moves and the feeling of the sound. Early press reports often referred to the band's cartoonlike style. In the first published piece about the B-52's, Athens photographer John Taylor described how his friends "turn the dance floor into something out of a Saturday morning cartoon." A few months later, another local journalist described the band's shows as "cartoon sock hops." About a year later, the British music critic Jon Savage asked in a piece on the band in *Melody Maker*, "Why do all these new American groups come on like cartoons?" For kids of this generation, however, *The Flintstones*—and to a lesser degree *The Jetsons*—modeled how pop culture could remix conventional images, stories, and characters into a critique of contemporary America. *The Flintstones* mimicked and twisted the 1950s sitcom form (*The Honeymooners*, in particular) and gestures and jokes that ran back through radio and vaudeville to the minstrel show. Descriptions of the B-52's as "cartoonlike" suggested multiple layers of play-acting and reenactment at work and the band's connection to pop art.[14]

Cindy Wilson and Pierson's style also worked on multiple levels. In the late 1970s, some older working-class women in Athens still wore these hairstyles and these dresses. Yet the band's style also had drag origins. Ricky Wilson and Strickland took what they had learned hanging out with drag queens like Holly Woodlawn and Jackie Curtis at Warhol's Factory and perfected their look at parties and parading around downtown Athens. For the band, Ricky Wilson and Strickland hung their drag on Cindy Wilson and Pierson. Cindy Wilson and Pierson's dress was both a direct copy of working-class women's style and a copy of a copy of a copy, their version of Ricky Wilson and Strickland's version of professional drag queens' visions.[15]

As the first "punk" act from Athens, the B-52's profoundly shaped the emerging Athens scene even as band members moved to New York in the spring of 1979. Strickland, Schneider, Pierson, and the Wilsons were all eccentric and unconventional, given to self-conscious transgressions of middle-class American conventions. Within the context of the late 1970s small-town South, all the men in the band were relatively open about their sexuality and their attraction to other men. Writing and performing their own pop art inflected punk, the group was out of place in both their small Southern hometown and the larger landscape of American popular music. And the band was also out of time, as the songs played with 1950s and early 1960s references and styles in a punk comment on the way popular culture reworks the relationship of the past to the present. Rawness and amateurism were essential to the music's effects. In later years, as band members polished their performances, their music increasingly sounded and looked like a replay, like a copy of rather than a comment on the popular culture past. Then the B-52's lost the exquisite balance, the way early performances danced on the head of the pin at the intersection between silly and serious, nostalgia and a critique of nostalgia.

Pylon: "Danger"

The same month Pylon appeared on the cover of *New York Rocker*, critic Van Gosse wrote a piece for the *Village Voice* in which he noted, "My pal Danny voices the common hipster sentiment when he says, 'Pylon, they're like the 52's, but they mean it.'" Gosse applauded "the intrinsic value of a music that is kept blindingly simple, unsentimental, uncomfortable: that which embodies the particular contradictions of its historical epoch in three minutes of glorious noise." For Gosse, "'rock and roll' means nothing more or less than controlled rhythmsmack, an exquisite tension and release embodied in sound. Pylon exemplify [sic] this formal truth right now in a way that only the Rolling Stones ever have before." About two years after two UGA art students, Randy Bewley and Michael Lachowski, decided to start a band, some critics were pushing Pylon as nothing less than the future of rock 'n' roll.[16]

In early 1979, the B-52's made other people in Athens think that they too could make original, even avant-garde music that defied the local taste for Southern rock, hippie bands, and country music. Lachowski and Bewley, a little younger than the members of the B-52's and their friends, were inspired by the group and by what they were reading about via their subscription to *New York Rocker*. The UGA art school nurtured their sense of experimentation. As Lachowski remembered later, "We had an exuberant group of people, creativity was prized above all else, everybody was just putting out work. It led to us going out of the boundaries of our disciplines. . . . A lot of us in the art school were trying out different media with a punk rock message, which is just go in there and do it. You don't need training, or authority or legitimacy. Just figure it out." For Lachowski and Bewley, creating a band was another way of "making art." They bought secondhand instruments and started learning to play. Curtis Crowe joined on drums, and after a surprisingly serious "audition" process, they asked Vanessa Briscoe to sing.[17]

In April, Lachowski wrote to his former art professor Robert Croker, "Our only goal is to play in NYC at least once. . . . We are not musicians, we do not like to 'jam' or even practice, we only want to perform—we only care about the product, not the process." Still, "the experience of playing in public," he conceded, "is very intense, very pleasurable." Lachowski's comments make it clear that a kind of scene had already emerged: "In Athens, they receive us politely—they have to since 'we're all in this together.'" Right before they moved to New York, members of the B-52's heard Pylon play and liked the new band so much they offered to help secure a New York booking.[18]

As a performance art project that became a band, Pylon consciously worked the contradictions. The band name referred to "the kind in the road, not the architectural one or the ones that hold up electricity," and not the Faulkner novel. According to Lachowski, "we chose Pylon because it is severe, industrial, monolithic, functional. We subscribe to a modern techno-industrial aesthetic. Our message is 'Go for it!, but be careful.' Three of the 4 of us work @Du Pont [a local nylon factory] so we are safety conscious." Band members had even less musical experience than the members of the B-52's, and yet they became critical darlings, and guitar nerds shadowed Bewley, trying to figure out his alternate tunings. They also did not break up after they played their first New York show, an opening slot for the Gang of Four in August 1979 at Hurrah. How could they? After all, music critic Glenn O'Brien had, in Warhol's *Interview* magazine, described their performance in what they guessed was a compliment, even though they had to look up the meaning of the key term: "these kids sound like they eat dub for breakfast."[19]

For Pylon, "out" meant sexuality. Lachowski was gay, and although he did not announce it, he also did not hide it. In performance, Briscoe worked an aggressive, girlish femininity, thrusting her curvy body and alternately moaning, screaming, and chanting voice so far into the microphone that she seemed to be making love to it, her own form of drag reenactment of the classic male rocker move. Yet "out" also meant the odd fusion of genres understood as opposed to each other, like the band's mash-up of punk's emotional excess and industrial repetition and detachment with a four on the floor disco beat. Pylon worked the contrast between flat, machine-sounding minimalism and ragged, Southern-accented amateurism. They may have been "safety conscious," but their raw, pounding sound did not make anyone feel safe. Their music turned uneven development—the collision of Athens as a small Southern town with Athens as the home of a huge modern university and a peripheral industrial site—into a startlingly original sound, an audio portrait of postmodernity.

Like the B-52's, Pylon worked their "out" aesthetic best live. A video of a 1980 performance of their song "Danger" in New York conveys how much their art depended upon the physical presence of the performers. The song begins with a bass drum beat, and Briscoe quietly alternating between making a hissing sound and chanting words like "The sound of danger." Drum and voice hold the line as a bass note rings out and a scattering of guitar notes compete with a clanging cymbal. Someone thinks to turn up the stage light, and Briscoe's head and upper torso emerge from the dark. She stares straight ahead at the audience, her eyes barely visible under a thatch of brown bangs, hissing "Ssssss" sounds into the microphone. Lachowski's bass drum comes on strong, repeating a bouncing five-note phrase again and again, and the guitar and symbol clang repeatedly as Briscoe continues her impersonation of a snake or a machine valve letting off steam. Pylon's performance is the sound equivalent of the machine in the garden.[20]

The camera focuses mainly on Briscoe and Lachowski, and their bodies and clothes create a kind of visual dissonance. Briscoe wears a church dress gone wrong, its color a bit faded and its shape a little soft; as she shakes and twirls her head to the slowly building beat, a limp lace sleeve slips down her shoulder. Instead of a necklace, she wears a whistle. Her brown hair curves under at her eyes and neck, and her sweating skin shines in the light. The only sharp things here are Briscoe's cheekbones. Lachowski, on the other hand, is tall, hard, and thin, a pole of a man with slow, repressed gestures. He sticks out his tongue, and he turns his head a little, looking away from the crowd on one side and then the other. At times he seems a little scared. His T-shirt and jeans refuse attention. Against this bland background, his bass's blue body, with its overlay of white and red stripes suggests, that whatever the original meaning of the colors, any patriotic feelings that once went with them are gone; use value reigns. In Gosse's words, Lachowski and Bewley look "like bike mechanics or sculptors" who perform a kind of "abstract hopping around, cute yet unposed." Briscoe, in contrast, spins like a windup whirling dervish, slowing down and speeding up according to the tension in her spring. As she dances, her thrift store dress and dance moves accentuate her breasts and hips. Her accent is somehow flat and yet also sometimes lushly Southern. Like Cindy Wilson of the B-52's, Briscoe both conjures and contradicts drag queens, beauty queens, Patti Smith, and Yoko Ono, but she works a different angle on the intersection of white Southern conventions of femininity, drag's exaggerations, Smith's androgyny, and Ono's arty shock and awe.[21]

At about a minute into the song, Briscoe shakes her bangs from her brown eyes and half smiles, half grimaces at the audience as she increases the volume and the emotional intensity of her voice. "Dannnne . . . jarrrr," she sings, like a Southern girl struggling to speak a foreign tongue, "Be careful. Be caw . . . tious." Drawing out the "caw" until it mimics the sound of a crow, she over-enunciates and turns her head for emphasis, like a teacher trying to force the attention of her students. A heavy reverb sends the vocals echoing in all directions and conjures the large space of a factory or a church. With Briscoe's vocal shift, the song explodes. The drums are fat, big and bullying. The hooks are achingly simple—sprays of a few guitar and bass notes and shouted words. Sometimes, Briscoe blows a long blast on her whistle right into the microphone, and the sound of a safety alert at a factory or a foul in a gym rings out an elementary need—in outright contradiction to the very idea of a pop song. The serial riffs convey both the repetition of industrial machinery and a growing urgency as volume and tempo slowly build. At the end, the guitar and bass sound like they are unwinding. Briscoe begins to scream and moan, and the delay unravels her voice. Her dress has slipped all the way off one shoulder, caught only by her elbow, her creamy chest visible to just above her breast. Then she decreases the volume and cuts the speed, winding listeners out of the song on a wash of emotions that will not form.

The B-52's turned pop art into a form of punk music and proved a little bit of bohemia could flower even in as unlikely a location as a Georgia college town. Pylon, too, started with art and bohemians' usual opposition to middle-class culture and the disjuncture between a Southern small town and the usual urban grounds of the avant-garde before ratcheting up the intensity.

Pylon made performance art people could dance to, delivering a punk comment on the survival of individualism in the machine-made future in a Southern drawl more commonly associated with a handmade past. Live, the band's raw, intense music worked the contradictory meanings of repetition, how duplicated sounds and acts could evoke expansiveness or constriction, pleasure or boredom, play or work, and the body or the machine. Critics' darlings, repeatedly named the best band in Athens, Pylon carried its "out" aesthetic so far that in December 1983 the band broke up on the cusp of stardom. The members of Pylon might not have had a language for what people would by the end of the century be calling neoliberalism, but they had the sound.[22]

R.E.M.: "Wolves, Lower"

By the time two pairs of friends—Mike Mills and Bill Berry, Peter Buck and Michael Stipe—debuted as R.E.M. in April 1980, the Athens scene was thriving. Interlocking groups of friends and lovers came together around the art school, the house party circuit, record stores, coffee spots, and new music nights at the club Tyrone's OC. In May, the first venue dedicated solely to the new music, the 40-Watt Club, opened in an upstairs space right across from the college. The new bohemians were busy colonizing about two square miles of territory: downtown, the warehouse district to the west, the art school a few blocks south down Jackson Street into the campus, and deteriorating historical neighborhoods directly northwest of downtown.[23]

What R.E.M. did was take the scene on the road, but not yet to New York, where the B-52's and Pylon were already critical darlings and the postpunk equivalent of exotics—those wacky smalltown Southerners can make original music! R.E.M. held off on a New York debut until June 1981 (when like, Pylon, the band opened for the Gang of Four). In the meantime, they spent a year traveling (mainly the Southeast), visiting other college towns, small city discos with New Wave nights, and stray pizza parlors and bars that booked bands that did not play only covers. After New York, they expanded their gig playing all throughout the North and West of the United States R.E.M.'s early touring became legendary, spun by critics and band members into a story of dues paying and audience building, one can-we-sleep-on-your-sofa group of fans at a time. It also spread awareness of the Athens scene.[24]

R.E.M.'s members made their band out of the scene: they were inspired by the bands that formed before them, they met each other through connections among scene makers, and they launched their new band through the scene's party circuit and growing network of public venues. They also made music about the scene, communicating the experience of its emotional plea- sures and translating scene makers' yearnings—both sexual and otherwise— and the magical sense of possibility into sound. R.E.M.'s early music expressed what it felt like for Athens scene makers and other suburban kids—growing up after the political radicals and the hippies—to long for commitment, for something to believe in, even for something to love. And sometimes, for some of these kids, R.E.M. became the something fans could love—meaning the band but, more broadly, the Athens scene. They could even love these things enough to start their own band or make their own scene.[25]

R.E.M. also embodied the contradictions. Mills and Berry were experi- enced musicians—they met playing in a high school cover band. Stipe, too, had been in a band before R.E.M. Buck, on the other hand, came to Athens to work at a branch of the Atlanta-based Wuxtry Records and was still learning to play. Together, they embraced and expressed the do-it-yourself ethic of amateurism central to the scene—everyone could be an artist and, by exten- sion, a musician—and yet they had industry connections and professional ambitions from the start. In Macon, Berry worked at Capricorn Records' booking agency, Paragon. His boss there was Ian Copeland, brother of Miles Copeland, who founded I.R.S. Records, R.E.M.'s future label. Ian's other brother, Stewart Copeland, played drums in the Police, the band that gave R.E.M. its first big gig, an opening slot in December 1980 at Atlanta's Fox Theater. Telling journalists they played "for fun," they hired Jefferson Holt as their manager in their first year and Bertis Downs as their lawyer around 1981. By 1982, *Rolling Stone* quoted Stipe expressing exasperation with the way the Athens scene that had nurtured R.E.M. also seemed to be limiting the band: "We're not a party band from Athens, we don't play New Wave music, and musically, we don't have shit to do with the B-52's or any other band from this town. We just happened to live here. . . . It's ridiculous. You'd think anyone with an ear for music, anyone who was really listening, would be able to dis- tinguish between REM and the B-52's, or REM and Pylon."[26]

A video of the band playing October 10, 1982, at the Pier, a Raleigh club, reveals R.E.M. working its own not completely polished version of the "out" aesthetic that animated the music of the B-52's and Pylon. Stipe starts the first song "Wolves, Lower" speaking the words "mirror" and "flower" as Berry drums a pounding four-four beat, in an opening that owes something to Py- lon despite Stipe's protests. As the guitar and bass join in, Stipe softly says two words or sounds that are indecipherable before gasping out "Ehhhhhhh" into the microphone as the volume builds. He leaves the microphone and, unencumbered, bounces as he continues dancing, his body spinning in a circle horizontally as it also flows vertically as if some spark started at his head and worked its way rhythmically down to his feet. Low in his range, Stipe sings "Suspicion yourself / suspicion yourself / don't get caught." Then he almost repeats himself, "Suspicion yourself / suspicion yourself / let us out." He stays low, almost growling, as he continues, "while the lower wolves / here's a house to put / wolves at the door." As the song progresses, Berry increases the tempo. At the chorus, Stipe pushes his voice higher as Mills and Berry join in. Together, they sing, "House in order," and Stipe answers in a falling then rising series of syllables, "Ah-ah-ah-ah-ah." Through most of the song, Stipe leaves Mills and Berry to sing the chorus as a call while he waits, answering solo with the response.[27]

At the end of the first chorus ends, Buck plays his guitar close to Stipe who is holding the microphone, and Stipe pops his eyes wide and smirks in what can only be described as a leer. Buck looks down, smiles, and moves away. Stipe and Buck flirt like Mick Jagger and Keith Richards in the 1960s, a once radical and then tired gesture somehow revived by R.E.M.'s homage and Stipe's androgyny. On stage Stipe crafted a sexual identity as consciously in-decipherable as his lyrics. Unlike Fred Schneider, Ricky Wilson, and Keith Strickland of the B-52's, or Michael Lachowski of Pylon, Stipe did not claim a gay identity either publically or privately, though his friends knew he had sex with both men and women. He would not speak publically about his sexuality until 1994.[28]

Throughout the set at the Pier, Stipe is charismatic. His dancing is fluid and loose, his supple body speeding up and slowing down, in and out of synch with the rhythm, a flowing version of Vanessa Briscoe's snapping twirls. He wears eye makeup and a sorority shirt under a baggy suit jacket with a scarf hanging out of the pocket. Channeling Briscoe's take on male rock moves, Stipe mouths the microphone and makes love to the stand, moaning what could be words in an unknown tongue or sounds of pleasure. Buck wears a cut off black tee shirt, and by a few songs in his dark curly hair hangs in his eyes in wet tendrils. He looks and moves like Patti Smith playing Keith Richards. Mills, on the other hand, expresses little emotion. He wears a white long-sleeve, button-up shirt with French flapping sleeves and short, straight bangs that reveal a lot of forehead as he plays bass like a guitar. He comes across as a mash-up of nerdy New Waver and earnest folk revivalist, a 1980s version of the 1960s Pete Seeger.

In performance, the vocal harmonies of Stipe, Mills, and Berry come across as simultaneously sweet, transgressive, and sexy, male voices merging like the singing of a Motown girl group (a form also worked by the B-52's), men playing women and also perhaps playing too close, playing around. Channeled through the women of the B-52's and Pylon, R.E.M.'s drag makes rock masculinity seem real again. And the contradictions work in other registers as well. Throughout the set, Berry's melodic bass and Buck's jangling guitar produce a folk sound that in its contrast cuts through and redeems the rock 'n' roll moves and gestures that over time made intensity and detachment into inauthentic conventions. The band seems to have absorbed from 1960s folk rock not just a sound but, even more important, an affect: the folk music revival's belief that authenticity lies in getting the feelings right. R.E.M. here sounds like a fusion of folk sincerity and melody and punk rock simplicity and attitude: four yearning middle-class kids grabbing hold of the place they landed at by making folk revivalist punk music, the sound not of anger but of desire.

THE B-52's, Pylon, and R.E.M. nurtured and embodied an emerging Athens bohemia. Making an art of unlikeliness and disjuncture, they perfected and promoted the punk and pop art idea that anyone could be a musician and anywhere could be a scene. All that was necessary was to dip into the rich resources at hand everywhere, the leavings of pop culture past: old records, television reruns, thrift store clothes, and pawn shop instruments.

Together these and other Athens bands spread new sounds and ideas to old bohemias like New York and to the kinds of places that until around 1980 most would-be bohemians would have fled. That people in Athens could create a scene that received national and even international attention, in turn, suggested to the people who saw these bands, bought their records, and read about them in *New York Rocker*, the *Village Voice*, and *New Music Express* that they too could create these magical fusions of places and people and homemade culture in opposition to the middle-class suburban center.

An alternative culture created around an "out" aesthetic and a future built of bits of the pop culture past proved to be the perfect rebellion for the Reagan era. President Ronald Reagan's "morning in America," too, reused past popular culture, especially, as scholar Michael Rogin has argued, Reagan's own 1940s movie roles, to create a vision of a different future. Acting out—pretending to make it real—worked for Athens bohemians, but it also worked for Reagan. If his act was convincing enough, people might forget economic decline, stagflation, racial and class inequality, and the global challenges to American power. They might forget that the act was an act. The new Athens music was most radical in live and ragged performance, when the gap showed and when the audience could tell the act was an act: that Cindy Wilson and Pierson were women dressed up like men dressed up like women, that Briscoe and Lachowski were people acting like machines acting like people, and that Stipe was performing yearning, a deep desire for attachment, for a world in which the very idea was being lost. Reagan, on the other hand, never really performed "live," and he never consciously revealed the gap.[29]

Notes

1. Brown, *Party Out of Bounds*, 39; Gumprecht, *The American College Town*, 189–226; Shank, *Dissonant Identities*; Becker, *Art Worlds*; Bennett and Peterson, *Music Scenes*; Bennett, *Popular Music and Youth Culture*; Thornton, *Club Cultures*; Cruz, "Subcultural Identity in Alternative Music"; Gaines, "Local Economies."

2. O'Brien, "The B-52's"; Rockwell, "B-52's, Rock Band from Georgia"; Schwartz, "Update: The B-52's,"; Rockwell, "The Pop Life"; Rockwell, "How the B-52's Cope with the Success Trap"; Carson, "B-52's"; Rambali, "The B-52's"; Rambali, "*The B-52's* (Island)"; Savage, "Yesterday's Sound Tomorrow"; Holden, "The B-52's' American Graffiti"; Cohen, "The B-52's: Climate Control"; Van Gosse, "The B-52's Attack"; Goldman, "The Guide to Cult Status"; DeCurtis, "The B-52's Return Home"; Henke, "The B-52's"; Cateforis, *Are We Not New Wave?*.

3. McLean, "Something Is Happening in Athens, Georgia"; Moline, "Pylon: From Athens, GA," 15; Varney, "Nineteen Hours from New York"; King, "Athens"; "These Days Athens Is a Creative Center"; Harris, "O Little Town."

4. Hebdige, *Subculture*; Seigel, *Bohemian Paris*; Frith and Horne, *Art into Pop*. Throughout this chapter I draw on my interviews with about one hundred participants in the Athens scene, including David Barbe, Keith Bennett, Sean Bourne, Mark Cline, Robert Croker, Bertis Downs, Vanessa Briscoe Hay, Michael Lachowski, Judy McWillie, Art Rosenbaum, Sam Seawright, and Sally Speed.

5. Gumprecht, *The American College Town*, 189–226; Schulman, *The Seventies*; interviews with Keith Bennett, Mark Cline, Robert Croker, Vanessa Briscoe Hay, Michael Lachowski, Judy McWillie, Sam Seawright, Sally Speed, and Armistead Welford.

6. Bennett, Hay, Lachowski, McWillie, and Rosenbaum interviews; Michael Lachowski to Robert Croker (letter), Art Rocks Athens 2014, documents in the author's possession; Thin, "Interview with the Cockettes"; Bollen, "Michael Stipe"; "Closeup: Vanessa Briscoe."

7. McLean, "Something Is Happening in Athens, Georgia"; Moline, "Pylon: From Athens, GA"; Arnold, *Route 666*; Reynolds, *Rip It Up*; Azerrad, *Our Band Could Be Your Life*.

8. Rockwell, "B-52's"; DeCurtis, "The B-52's Return Home," 84; "These Days Athens Is a Creative Center"; Harris, "O Little Town." Coming out in the period covered by this study was more a process than a single event. Most participants in the scene did not hide their sexual orientation from friends, even as choosing a set sexual identity as

gay, bisexual, or transgender was less common than idealizing experimentation—having sex with all possible partners. Five members of the B-52's, Pylon, and REM, were out then and/or later came out as gay. See D'Emilio and Freedman, *Intimate Matters*; Garber, *Vice Versa*; Meyerowitz, *How Sex Changed*; Butler, *Gender Trouble*; Nyong'o, "Do You Want Queer Theory?"; and Cateforis, *Are We Not New Wave?*.

9. Benjamin, "The Work of Art"; Orvell, *The Real Thing*; Hall, "Notes on Deconstructing the Popular"; Hebdige, *Subculture*; Frith, *Sound Effects*; Garber, *Vested Interests*.

10. Live performances anchor sound and image in musicians' bodies, what scholars call embodiment. Audiences do not just hear and see the performers but experience the presence of the people making the music, the emotional and physical reactions of other audience members, and the visual and acoustic qualities of the performance space. They become part of the performance. See, for example, Phelan, *Unmarked*; Auslander, *Liveness*; Lepeck, *Of the Presence of the Body*; Jones and Heathfield, *Perform, Repeat, Record*; Small, *Musiking*; Byrne, *How Music Works*; Shank, *The Political Force*; and Kun, *Audiotopia*.

11. Deejay Susan Murphy broadcast this show, "Athens Music—The First Five Years," on July 4, 1983, on WUOG. See https://soundcloud.com/susan-v-murphy/athens-music-the-first-five-years-from-susan-murphy-wuog-july-4-1983-part-1 and https://soundcloud.com/susan-v-murphy/athens-music-the-first-five-years-from-susan-murphy-wuog-july-4-1983-part-2.

12. The video of the B-52's playing "Dance This Mess Around" at the Downtown Café is available at https://www.youtube.com/watch?v=VN8hV4AyNss&list=PLoAF6372F5B725846&index=6; for other videos from that show, see https://www.youtube.com/playlist?list=PLoAF6372F5B725846. See also "1978 B-52's Concert Kicks Off AthFest RockDocs," *Online Athens*, June 18, 2008. http://onlineathens.com/stories/061808/marquee_20080618021.shtml#.VWXtSof4Zw. Taylor, "The B-52's and Me"; Haines, "B-52's Dive into Last Resort"; Haines, "B-52's Are Taking Off"; Pierce, "The Next Wave"; David Barbe, Keith Bennett, Vanessa Briscoe Hay, and Sam Seawright interviews. On January 5, 1978, the Sex Pistols played their first U.S. gig at the Great Southeast Music Hall in Atlanta and sold out the venue. The Atlanta Punk festival, planned to build on that success, took place there a little more than a week later.

13. The notes posted on online lyrics sites suggest this lyric is "Shy Tuna," but the video does not confirm this. B-52's, "Dance This Mess Around" (lyrics). http://www.azlyrics.com/lyrics/b52s/dancethismessaround.html.

14. While pro-pleasure and certainly transgressive in the context of middle-class conservatism about sex, this kind of thinking sidestepped rather than addressed issues like sexism and homophobia. See Stipe's thoughtful discussions of his own "queerness" and his fears of AIDS in Bollen, "Michael Stipe"; Taylor, "New Wave Rock"; Haines, "B-52's Are Taking Off"; and Savage, "*The B-52's* (Island)."

15. Bennett and Bourne interviews.

16. Gosse, "Pylon Draws the Line," 61, notes that "compulsive-dance-bands out of Athens, Georgia, do not necessarily speak in the same tongues. The difference in this case is everything." See also Moline, "Pylon"; Palmer, "Critics' Choices"; Anderson,

"Pylontechnics"; "Closeup: Vanessa Briscoe"; Holden, "Music: Pylon at the Ritz"; and Carson, "Pylon up around the Bend."

17. Lachowski and Hay interviews; Bennett, "We Talked to Pylon's Michael Lachowski"; Gross, "Tribute to Randy Bewley; Gross, "Pylon Interview: Part 1"; Gross, "Pylon Interview: Part 2"; and Mills, "Everything is Cool."

18. Hay, *Vanessa's Pylon Blog*; Hay interview.

19. Michael Lachowski to Robert Croker (letter); Lachowski and Hay interviews; Reynolds, *Rip It Up*, 264; Frith and Horne, *Art into Pop*.

20. The video of Pylon playing "Danger" in New York is available at https://vimeo.com/50389377; Pat Ivers and Emily Armstrong worked as the resident video artists at Danceteria, where they made this video. See also O'Brien, "Beat."

21. Gosse, "Pylon Draws the Line," 3.

22. Ellison, "A Found Farewell."

23. Gumprecht, *The American College Town*, 189–226.

24. Varney, "'Nineteen Hours From New York'"; Barnes, "'Underdog' R.E.M. Upstages the Brains"; Slater, "R.E.M.: Not Just Another Athens, Georgia, Band"; Grabel, "Nightmare Town"; Puterbaugh, "R.E.M.'s Southern Rock Revival"; Considine, "R.E.M.: Subverting Small Town Boredom"; Gray, *It Crawled from the South*; Platt, *The R.E.M. Companion*; *The Rolling Stone Files*; Sullivan, *R.E.M.: Talk About the Passion*; Fletcher, *Remarks Remade*; Arnold, *On the Road to Nirvana*, 57–68.

25. "R.E.M. Timeline"; Arnold, *Route 666*.

26. Downs interview; Slater, "R.E.M.: Not Just Another Athens, Georgia, Band."

27. The video of R.E.M. playing "Wolves, Lower" at the Pier is available at https://www.youtube.com/watch?v=2fXdJ6syxLo.

28. As Stipe explains in DeCurtis, "Monster Madness," available online at http://www.rollingstone.com/music/features/monster-madness-19941020 "in terms of the whole queer-straight-bi thing, my feeling is that labels are for canned food. . . . I think sexuality is a much more slippery thing than that. . . . I've always been of questionable sexuality or dubious sexuality." See also Simon, "A Session with Michael Stipe"; Giles, "Everybody Hurts Sometime"; Goldberg, "The Mysterious Stipe-Man"; Heath, "Michael in the Middle"; Aron, "R.E.M. Comes Alive"; Pemberton, "Michael Stipe: Cash for Questions"; and Maus, "Intimacy and Distance: On Stipe's Queerness."

29. Berry, radio interview; Mills, television interview; Carson, "Sandbox Supermen"; Arnold, *Route 666*; and Rogin, *Ronald Reagan the Movie*.

References

Anderson, Steve. "Pylontechnics." *Village Voice*, November 9, 1982, 66.

Arnold, Gina. *Route 666: On the Road to Nirvana*. New York: St. Martin's, 1993.

Aron, Charles. "R.E.M. Comes Alive." *Spin*, August 1995, 34–45.

Auslander, Phillip. *Liveness: Performance in Mediatized Culture*. New York: Routledge, 1999.

Azerrad, Michael. *Our Band Could Be Your Life: Scenes from the American Indie Underground, 1981–1991*. New York: Little, Brown, 2001.

Barnes, William. "'Underdog' R.E.M. Upstages the Brains." *Red and Black*, May 7, 1980.

Becker, Howard. *Art Worlds*. Berkeley: University of California Press, 1982.

Benjamin, Walter. "The Work of Art in the Age of Mechanical Reproduction." In *Illuminations*, edited by Hannah Arendt, translated by Harry Zohn, 217–52. New York: Schocken, 1968.

Bennett, Andy. *Popular Music and Youth Culture: Music, Identity, Place*. London: Macmillan, 2000.

Bennett, Andy, and Richard A. Peterson. *Music Scenes: Local, Translocal and Virtual*. Nashville: Vanderbilt University Press, 2004.

Bennett, Kim Taylor. "We Talked to Pylon's Michael Lachowski Because He's a Legend." *Noisey*, August 7, 2014. http://noisey.vice.com/read/we-talked-to -michael-lachowski-from-pylon-because-hes-a-legend.

Berry, Bill. Radio interview, WRBN, 1985. https://www.youtube.com/watch?v =NOpVO4QPy1Y.

Bollen, Christopher. "Michael Stipe." *Interview*, May 4, 2011. http://www .interviewmagazine.com/music/michael-stipe/.

Brown, Rodger Lyle. *Party Out of Bounds*. New York: Plume, 1991.

Butler, Judith. *Gender Trouble: Feminism and the Subversion of Identity*. New York: Routledge, 1990.

Byrne, David. *How Music Works*. San Francisco: McSweeney's, 2012.

Carson, Tom. "B-52's." *New York Rocker*, June 1979, 4–5.

———. "Pylon up around the Bend." *Village Voice*, June 14, 1983, 84.

———. "Sandbox Supermen." *Village Voice*, September 2, 1986, 71–72.

Cateforis, Theo. *Are We Not New Wave? Modern Pop at the Turn of the 1980s*. Ann Arbor: University of Michigan Press, 2011.

"Closeup: Vanessa Briscoe." *Athens Observer*, January 20, 1983.

Cohen, Mitchell. "The B-52's: Climate Control in the Land of 16 Dances." *Cream*, December 1979, in *RocksBackPages*, http://www.rocksbackpages.com.proxy.its .virginia.edu/Library/Article/the-b-52s-climate-control-in-the-land-of-16 -dances.

Considine, J. M. "R.E.M.: Subverting Small Town Boredom." *Musician*, August 1983. Reprinted in John Platt, *The R.E.M. Companion*, 22–27. New York: Schirmer Books, 1988.

Cruz, Holly. "Subcultural Identity in Alternative Music." *Popular Music* 121 (1993): 31–42.

DeCurtis, Anthony. "The B-52's Return Home." *Rolling Stone*, November 27, 1980, 84.

———. "Monster Madness." *Rolling Stone*, October 20, 1994, 58–64, 161–63.

D'Emilio, John, and Estelle Freedman. *Intimate Matters: A History of Sexuality in America*. Chicago: University of Chicago Press, 2012.

Editors of Rolling Stone. *R.E.M.: The Rolling Stone Files*. London: Sidgwick and Jackson, 1995.

Ellison, J. Eddy. "A Found Farewell: Fans, Followers and Friends Sadly Try to Accept." *Athens Banner Herald–Athens Daily News*, December 2, 1983.

Fitzgerald, Helen. "Tales from the Black Mountain." *Melody Maker* 27 (1985). Reprinted in Platt, *R.E.M. Companion*, 29–35.

Fletcher, Tony. *Remarks Remade: The Story of R.E.M.* New York: Omnibus, 2002.

Frith, Simon. *Sound Effects: Youth, Leisure, and the Politics of Rock 'n' Roll.* New York: Pantheon, 1981.

Frith, Simon, and Howard Horne. *Art into Pop.* London: Methuen, 1987.

Gaines, Donna. "The Local Economies of Suburban Scenes." In *Adolescents and Their Music: If It's Too Loud, You're Too Old,* edited by Jonathon S. Epstein, 47–66. New York: Routledge, 2016.

Garber, Marjorie. *Vested Interests: Cross-Dressing and Cultural Anxiety.* New York: Routledge, 1997.

———. *Vice Versa: Bisexuality and the Eroticism of Everyday Life.* New York: Touchstone, 1995.

Giles, Jeff. "Everybody Hurts Sometime." *Newsweek,* September 26, 1994, 60–63.

Goldberg, Michael. "Cybersex, Sex, and the Mysterious Stipe-Man." *Addicted to Noise,* January 19, 1995.

Goldman, Vivien. "The Guide to Cult Status with those Wild! Wacky! B-52's!" *New Musical Express,* September 20, 1980, reprinted in *RocksBackPages,* http://www.rocksbackpages.com/Library/Article/the-guide-to-cult-status-with-those-wild-wacky-b-52s.

Gosse, Van. "The B-52's Attack." *Village Voice,* January 7, 1980, 95.

———. "Pylon Draws the Line." *Village Voice,* February 25–March 3, 1981, 61–62.

Grabel, Richard. "Nightmare Town." *New Musical Express,* December 11, 1982, 4–5.

Gray, Marcus. *It Crawled from the South: An R.E.M. Companion.* New York: Da Capo, 1997.

Gross, Jason. "Pylon Interview: Part 1." *Perfect Sound Forever,* May 1998. http://www.furious.com/perfect/pylon.html.

———. "Pylon Interview: Part 2." *Perfect Sound Forever,* May 1998. http://www.furious.com/perfect/pylon2.html.

———. "Tribute to Randy Bewley." *Perfect Sound Forever,* February 2010. www.furious.com/perfect/pylonrandy.html.

Gumprecht, Blake. *The American College Town.* Amherst: University of Massachusetts Press, 2008, 189–226.

Haines, William. "B-52's Are Taking off." *Athens Observer,* April 13, 1978.

———. "B-52's Dive Into Last Resort." *Red and Black,* January 31, 1978, 3.

Hall, Stuart. "Notes on Deconstructing the Popular." In *People's History and Socialist Theory,* edited by Raphael Samuel, 227–40. London: Routledge and Kegan Paul, 1981.

Harris, Art. "O Little Town of Rock 'n' Roll: Welcome to Liverpool South: Athens, Ga., Where the New Wave Thrives." *Washington Post,* August 29, 1984.

Hay, Vanessa Briscoe. *Vanessa's Pylon Blog.* http://www.netnik.com/jollybeggars/pylon.html.

Heath, Chris. "Michael in the Middle." *Details,* February 1995, 80.

Hebdige, Dick. *Subculture: The Meaning of Style.* New York: Routledge, 1979.

Henke, James. "The B-52's." *Rolling Stone*, December 11, 1980, 10.

Holden, Stephen. "The B-52s' American Graffiti." *Village Voice*, August 13, 1979, 60–61.

———. "Music: Pylon at the Ritz." *New York Times*, May 31, 1983.

Jones, Allan. "In the Heat of the Night." *Melody Maker* 15 (1985): 16.

Jones, Andrea, and Adrian Heathfield. *Perform, Repeat, Record: Live Art in History*. Chicago: University of Chicago Press, 2012.

King, Bill. "Athens: A City Attuned to New Wave-Length." *Atlanta Journal Constitution*, August 30, 1981.

Kun, Josh. *Audiotopia: Music, Race, and America*. Berkeley: University of California Press, 2005.

Lepeck, André. *Of the Presence of the Body: Essays on Dance and Performance Theory*. Middletown, CT: Wesleyan University Press, 2004.

McLean, Greg. "Something Is Happening in Athens, Georgia." *New York Rocker*, July–August 1980, 10.

Maus, Fred. "Intimacy and Distance: On Stipe's Queerness." *Journal of Popular Music Studies* 18 (2006): 191–214.

Meyerowitz, Joanne. *How Sex Changed: A History of Transsexuality in the United States*. Cambridge, MA: Harvard University Press, 2004.

Mills, Fred. "Everything Is Cool: Form Followed Function for Athens Postpunk Legends Pylon." *Harp*, December 2007. http://www.rocksbackpages.com/article .html?ArticleID=13437.

Mills, Mike. Television interview. KWHY, 1985. https://www.youtube.com/watch?v =BobUGIn6wZk.

Moline, Karen. "Pylon: From Athens, GA: New Sounds of the Old South." *New York Rocker*, March 1981, 15–17.

Nyong'o, Tavia. "Do You Want Queer Theory (or Do You Want the Truth)? Intersections of Punk and Queer in the 1970s." *Radical History Review* 2008, no. 100 (2008): 103–19.

O'Brien, Glenn. "Beat." *Interview*, September 1979, 74.

———. "The B-52's." *Interview*, July 1978, 34.

Orvell, Miles. *The Real Thing: Imitation and Authenticity in American Culture, 1880–1940*. Chapel Hill: University of North Carolina Press, 1989.

Palmer, Robert. "Critics' Choices." *New York Times*, April 4, 1982.

Pemberton, Andy. "Michael Stipe: Cash for Questions." *Q*, May 1999, 152.

Phelan, Peggy. *Unmarked: The Politics of Performance*. New York: Routledge, 1993.

Pierce, David Hannon. "The Next Wave." *Open City*, June–July 1986.

Platt, John, ed. *The R.E.M. Companion*. New York: Schirmer, 1998.

Puterbaugh, Parke. "R.E.M.'s Southern Rock Revival." *Rolling Stone*, June 1983, 42.

"Pylon/'Crazy.'" *New York Rocker*, June 1982, 43.

Rambali, Paul. "The B-52's: Hot Pants, Cold Sweat and a Brand New Beehive Hair Do." *New Musical Express*, June 9, 1979, reprinted in *RocksBackPages*. http://www .rocksbackpages.com/Library/Article/the-b-52s-hot-pants-cold-sweat-and-a -brand-new-beehive-hair-do.

————. "The B-52's: *The B-52's* (Island)." *New Musical Express*, June 30, 1979, reprinted in *RocksBackPages*. http://www.rocksbackpages.com/Library/Article /the-b-52s-the-b-52s-island.

R.E.M. "Interview." *Livewire*, Nickelodeon, October 30, 1983. https://www.youtube .com/watch?v=60WYma8jc9M.

"R.E.M. Timeline: The Complete R.E.M. Concert Chronology." http://www .remtimeline.com/.

Reynolds, Simon. *Rip It Up and Start Again: Postpunk 1978–1984*. New York: Penguin, 2006.

Rockwell, John. "B-52's, Rock Band from Georgia." *New York Times*, June 3, 1978, 11.

————. "The Pop Life" C15. *New York Times*, July 13, 1979.

————. "The Pop Life: How the B-52's Cope with the Success Trap." *New York Times*, August 31, 1979.

Rogin, Michael. *Ronald Reagan the Movie: And Other Episodes in Political Demonology*. Berkeley: University of California Press, 1988.

Rose, Cynthia. "The B-52's." *New Musical Express*, June 4, 1983, reprinted in *RocksBackPages*. http://www.rocksbackpages.com/Library/Article/the-b-52s.

Savage, Jon. "The B-52's: *B-52's* (Island): Yesterday's Sound Tomorrow." *Melody Maker*, June 30, 1979, reprinted in *RocksBackPages*. http://www.rocksbackpages .com/Library/Article/the-b-52s-ib-52si-island.

Schulman, Bruce. *The Seventies: The Great Shift in Culture, Society, and Politics*. New York: Free Press, 2001.

Schwartz, Andy. "Update: The B-52's." *New York Rocker*, April 1979, reprinted in *RocksBackPages*. http://www.rocksbackpages.com/Library/Article/update-the -b-52s.

Seigel, Jerrold. *Bohemian Paris: Culture, Politics, and the Boundaries of Bourgeoisie Life, 1830–1930*. New York: Viking, 1986.

Shank, Barry. *Dissonant Identities: The Rock 'n' Roll Scene in Austin, Texas*. Middleton, CT: Wesleyan University Press, 1994.

————. *The Political Force of Musical Beauty*. Durham, NC: Duke University Press, 2014.

Simon, Joshua. "A Session with Michael Stipe." *Life*, special issue, "40 Years of Rock and Roll," December 1, 1992, 102–4.

Slater, Andrew. "R.E.M.: Not Just Another Athens, Georgia, Band." *Rolling Stone*, October 28, 1982, 57.

Small, Christopher. *Musiking: The Meanings of Performance and Listening*. Middleton, CT: Wesleyan University Press, 1998.

Sullivan, Denise. *R.E.M.: Talk About the Passion: An Oral History*. New York: Da Capo, 1998.

Taylor, John. "New Wave Rock Comes to Town." *Athens Observer*, January 26, 1978.

Taylor, John Martin. "The B-52's and Me." *Hoppin' John's: John Martin Taylor's Personal Blog*. http://hoppinjohns.net/?p=263.

"These Days Athens (Ga.) Is a Creative Center." *People*, January 17, 1983.

Thin, Silva. "Interview with the Cockettes." *Interview*, February 1972, 47–49.

Thornton, Sara. *Club Cultures: Music, Media, and Subcultural Capital.* Cambridge: Polity, 1995.

Varney, Vic. " 'Nineteen Hours from New York': Small Town Makes Good." *New York Rocker*, March 1981, 20–21.

Reimagined Old-Time Music Cultures in the Trainhopping Punk Rock South

Daniel S. Margolies

Trainhopping punks began appearing in increasing numbers at Appalachian old-time music festivals in the early years of the twenty-first century. They were not hard to pick out from the crowds of locals and revivalist aficionados at places like the Mount Airy Fiddlers Convention in North Carolina, or the Appalachian String Band Contest in West Virginia. Trainhoppers looked different and were different. For one, the most hard-core of this group really did arrive by riding illicitly on trains and then, perhaps, hitchhiking the last few miles to the festivals. Even among the crowds of aging hippies and scruffy campers meeting in the woods and RV parks of the South to camp and jam, the trainhoppers stood out.

Like other subcultures, trainhoppers adopted a uniform that differentiated as much as defined. Their style presented a complex synthesis of old-time hillbilly mountaineer, mid-1930s bindlestiff, and postapocalyptic chic. A heavy emphasis was placed on tattered working-class clothing, beat-up caps, heavy boots, and sheathed knives at the belt. Trainhoppers were usually gloriously filthy, burnished by a combination of hard living and scrupulous nonbathing to a greasy, monochromatic, bronze-like shine. They sprawled across camping spaces that often seemed muddier, more chaotic, more unsettling, and more exciting than those of other festivalgoers. Yet trainhoppers also pushed beyond shallow trappings of self-display and idiosyncratic antifashion. They were passionate, even obsessed, musicians playing furiously paced and reverentially sourced old-time music, the traditional string band music of the South founded on fiddles and banjos. They foisted enthusiastic, all-night jams and impromptu square dances (some clothed, some not). This was partying with an undiluted and intense musical core. Nodding to street theater and Dadaist interventions, they also held riotous parades, sponsored "no talent" contests, and variously cavorted with a subversive flair. As a result of both a local emergence of kindred souls in the South and the chain migration of young people from across the country (and especially the West Coast), a sizable cadre of alternative-minded individuals have emerged or descended into the region to live in rural areas and hipster cities like Asheville and Richmond. In the past fifteen years, trainhoppers have built a vibrant and regionally situated subculture in the South. They are an innovative generation involved in the renewable quest for what Mike Seeger, the master vernacular musician, field recorder, and pioneering pied piper for old-time seekers, called the true vine of American music.[1]

These trainhoppers are young people seeking escape from cultural stultification and transcendence through old-time music. They are made mobile by riding trains and made coherent as a movement by a shared dedication of their lives to mastery of archaic old-time music styles and to alternative lifestyles rooted in idiosyncratic or fabricated variants of Appalachian culture. The trainhoppers fastened onto this world of tradition and depth in old-time music and have deftly remade it into an integral part of their own postmodern and postpunk existence, fostering fresh articulations of Southern music and identity by pushing backward to embrace old-time values as they define them.[2]

In this chapter we will meet three individuals, Michael Ismerio, Andrew Norcross, and Hannah Johnson, each of whom has found a musical and social home in old-time music, trainhopping, and a variant of homesteading that in turn has brought a wide breadth of spiritual impact and material results. These individuals also have become recognized as significant and talented within this small and self-referential scene, though each denies serving as a pioneer, or even being part of a defined movement.

The appearance of the trainhoppers is a tale of intersecting micromusical subcultures and a rising youth consciousness of personal transformation sideswiping the established alternative old-time music community. The countercultural embrace of traditional Southern music that came with the maturation of the folk revival in the 1960s and 1970s used old-time music as a means of rejecting the conformity and banality of postwar America. And as much affinity as this edgy counterculture claimed with "old-time," it also did not so much subsume itself in tradition as catalyze change, and even disruption, in it. St. Wish Wishnevsky wryly acknowledges this in his memoir of the era *How the Hippies Ruin't Hillbilly Music.*[3] Ethnomusicologist Thomas Turino, looking at the formation of subcultures in "a cultural cohort—a social group that forms around the activity itself" argues that the cohort is sometimes deeply valued precisely because it "provides an alternative to 'modern' capitalist lifeways." He places old-time music alongside punk, hip-hop, and the hippie counterculture as related formations "within the capitalist formation."[4] But nobody has yet taken seriously this strident underground group of punk-influenced youth as part of the old-time scene in the South. The subversive qualities of the trainhoppers—their challenges to both mainstream values and the now superannuated hippie counterculture, and especially its rejection of the logics and imperatives of the capitalist market—are not to be underestimated. Fresh as it felt to them, and radical as it can seem at times, the oppositional stance adopting Southern tradition bearers as inoculation against the ravages of capitalism and neoliberalism is in fact part of a well-established tradition of seeing oppositional utility in all that is considered "old-timey."

In trainhopping old-time culture, the Appalachian South serves as an ever-renewing imaginary for opposition to capitalist mass culture. The inoculation trainhopper sensibility situates "Appalachia" and "old-time" directly at the core of its unique spiritual and musicological firmament.[5] This mediated construct is grafted onto an embrace of the core punk-initiated do-it-yourself (DIY) culture,[6] which reifies the kinds of alternative communitarianism made possible in the spatial arenas and musicultural ecosystem of the old-time scene.[7] A central idea is that culture can *and must* be re-created by oneself, followed by community building. Sometimes it can become an almost messianic belief in the attainment of self-sufficiency, with subsequent disappointing outcomes. Ismerio, never short on self-reflection, muses that his own long experience has showed that it was a "false idea that community could be created [just] anywhere, or that I could create community anywhere"; he calls it an "almost ridiculous superhero mentality." The emphasis thus turns to community. As Ismerio explains, "What I see connecting, the bridge between the old-time and punk communities, is the desire for unmediated experience. So much of our world has become commodified and mediated, everything is given to you on a CD, or on television, or in print; everything is handed to you, this finished product you're supposed to consume. The old-time scene and the punk scene—and there are lots of places you can do this—are basically the idea that you can create culture yourself in your community for your community. It's the driving force for the punk scene and the old-time scene."[8] Trainhoppers present a radical challenge rooted in anarchist philosophical critiques of the cultures in which they exist. The back-to-the-land movement had related radical roots, as well as the significant performative characteristics that accompany such movements globally.[9]

The back-to-the-land movement was widespread, passionate, and sometimes nostalgic, and it had vigorous adherents from the time of its emergence in the nineteenth century. It was centered on a romantic belief in rural self-sufficiency as an antidote to urban problems and social distress, and was focused primarily on a dedicated search for simpler, sustainable living in rural and communal arrangements; Dona Brown notes that "dreaming was part of the back-to-the-land impulse from the beginning."[10] The movement had a period of enthusiastic growth in the 1970s, when it was intertwined with the broader countercultural challenge, environmentalism, feminism, the nascent DIY movement, and other efforts to reform, challenge, and sidestep dominant capitalist society. Trainhopper performativity is experientially based and ex-perientially expressed in similar ways, starting most obviously with a critique (or total rejection) of the mainstream culture and values of modern America—particularly the emphasis on work, ownership, consumption, and conformity. Trainhoppers conceptualize their actions as simply being and becoming, much as earlier back-to-the-land movements posited, and contrast this from what they consider to be mainstream objectification and commodification. The rejection of mainstream society also extends to the insufficiently hard-core countercultural elements. Hippies are held up for scorn generally, following the marked rejection of hippie culture by the punk movement.[11]

The assemblage that is trainhopping old-time culture developed within a fairly vast and complex nexus of subcultures across the South and the wider nation. This movement fuses punk, political and ecological anarchism, the straight edge movement, Dumpster diving, squatting, homesteading, the back-to the-land movement, and—most powerfully—expressions of a pro-nounced sense of DIY. It is not necessary, and may be impossible, to chart out which movement is dominant in influence since that varies widely among in-dividuals, but Ismerio, Norcross, and Johnson engage some or all of these subcultural worlds. Trainhopping and the old-time scene stand congruently together, but outside these movements. They might even be in opposition, especially in the ways the old-time scene simultaneously rejects many main-stream norms and reveres normative regional traditions. This is cultural rebellion as ideology and performance, rooted in a search for authentic expe-rience with a taste for the retrograde and vaguely reactionary sounds of old-time music.

Old-Time Music

My twenty-plus-year immersion in the community and culture of old-time music grew out of my immersion in the punk subculture of the 1980s. I was part of the small but meaningful movement of disaffected Midwestern 1980s punk rock adherents seeking something different but ill defined who were struck by the force, oddity, and powerful essence of Southern old-time music. Individuals instantly enamored of it have often articulated the feeling that old-time music opened an alternative path. It is a variant of what great guitarist John Fahey slyly noted in the title of his memoir, *How Bluegrass Music Destroyed My Life*. I only discovered that my own trajectory from the punk to the old-time scenes fell into a pattern followed by people across the country when I was interviewed as part of an ethnomusicology dissertation research project by Amy Wooley in 2003.[12] Half of a chapter is dedicated to my experience, while another interviewee in that project, and the subject of a whole chapter, was Michael Ismerio. We had not yet met at this time, but the two of us had congruent but quite different journeys through punk alienation and into old-time music (though I have never ridden a train without a ticket). I have known these trainhoppers, and others, for the past dozen years at least, played music with them in jams and contests, danced with them, and become quite close friends with several of them. Thus, my high level of familiarity and even some intimacy with this scene does not provide an especially objective view.

The punk rock sensibility might seem counter to the mores of the old-time scene as it has developed since the large, hippie-influenced revivalist boom of the 1970s.[13] But this revivalist music similarly incorporates a search for alternatives, authenticity, and identity.[14] Both old-time music and punk posit a talismanic meaning in the transformative power of musical form and musical expression. The 1970s archetype of old-time music, and the scene that both sustained and reflected it, was rooted in what John Bealle has called "the defiant looseness of the celebratory utopia to which audiences always felt they belonged," conjuring a "utopian anti-society" through the music.[15] Expertise, technical mastery of form and style, and exhaustive and encyclopedic understanding of regional variations in the music are key hallmarks of the mastery of the style.[16] And this mastery of arcana is one key to the deeper sensibility of what it means to be "old-time." Much of this sensibility remains ingrained in the genre today. Old-time musicians venerate tradition bearers and regionalism, and police the boundaries with the self-seriousness of the most committed guardian of punk authenticity against sellouts or poseurs. This veneration takes a unique form among the trainhoppers, who even inscribe "old-timeyness" onto themselves as a totem of authenticity. Many of them sport tattoos of fiddles, banjos, or other old-time imagery. Tattoos that look like old woodcuts or copperplate engravings are so common that some of the decorated young people look like walking nineteenth-century periodicals.

The Freighthoppers, a band that emerged as one of the most significant old-time groups in the contemporary era, catalyzed the newest wave of revival and popular bands of the 1990s within the subculture of old-time music; theirs was a wide-ranging influence comparable to the Highwoods String Band of the 1970s. Both bands emphasized and personified the social aspects of the music in their respective eras. David Bass, the powerful fiddler for the Freighthoppers, strongly influenced the initial generation of trainhopper fiddlers, who were drawn to his fluid, rhythmic, complex, extremely fast, and virtuosic playing. Bass presented a devil-may-care attitude as both a performer and a presence at festivals, carrying a beat-up fiddle case and wearing camouflage clothing that evoked the image of a Southern rounder and signaled a decidedly rakish approach to traditional old-time music cultures. Many trainhoppers have adopted his musical and sartorial style.[17]

It should be noted that the term *trainhoppers* is not one expressly employed by trainhoppers themselves. They might call themselves train riders, and it is not unusual in punk circles for people to call themselves "kids" or "punks." More commonly, they might not label themselves at all. As Hannah Johnson explains, "I would call anyone who rides a train a trainhopper or a train rider. But it is just something you do, you ride trains. It is not a subculture." This is part of the whole punk movement, of course—an allergy to the kind of categorizations that fuel both mainstream commodification and academic systemic analysis. Lauraine Leblanc notes that "few punk kids—and much less punk girls—would recognize themselves within these academic-jargon-laden interpretations of punk. . . . [P]unk was not only, nor even primarily, about punk music, or events, or obscure political and artistic affiliations—punk was, and is, about living out a rebellion against authority. In this sense, punk as a subculture is still alive, with kids all over North America spawning new scenes and constantly adding to its maintenance and development."[18]

The Square Dance Caller as Communitarian

Michael Ismerio is tall and lanky, with a beguilingly crooked grin and an almost comically split personality when it comes to old-time music. With a fiddle in his hand, he can be unsparing and quite fierce in a jam. Like many alpha fiddlers, he can be vaguely tyrannical in this role. Ismerio is drawn to tunes from eastern Kentucky, which are "notey, spooky, anything that is really crooked and weird and you have to memorize and really think about." This is the old-time music that can be inaccessible and obscure. "Music can be social and antisocial, and I am really drawn to the antisocial tunes," he says. "Those notey, crooked, intellectual tunes scratch a certain spot in your brain that I really like. It is why it comes down to why I don't have a band and am a caller. Michael the party guy square dance caller is what appeals to more people; that's what people want around, not the introverted intellectual fiddler. So I tend to do that on my own." As a square dance caller, however, Ismerio ex-

Michael Ismerio in front of his hand-built cabin, perched on the hillside of borrowed land on the outskirts of Asheville. Photo by Daniel S. Margolies.

udes positive and communal energy. Put a microphone in his hand at a square dance, and "there's no filter, whatever pops into my mind comes out. I'm having a great time. That's the side of me that is very opening and giving. Teaching fiddle, teaching dance, harmony singing. Getting people singing. Group singing. For some reason I can be a lot more lighthearted and open than when I have a fiddle in my hand. It just changes me. Like Dr. Jekyll and Mr. Hyde."

Ismerio speaks in long paragraphs. He is methodical in his thinking about his music and the cultures he moves in and has helped shape. He has had a lot of time to hone both his antisocial and social crafts. He was one of the first of the punk old-time musicians to appear, and subsequently he helped lay the cornerstone of what became an active old-time revival in the Pacific Northwest dominated by young people coming from punk origins. He was drawn to the South to fully realize his goals. After a disappointing stint in the old-time scene in Bloomington, Indiana, Ismerio eventually moved to Asheville, North Carolina because of "friends, music, mountains, and weather." He was also looking for *community*; it's a word that is never far from his lips. "I was lonely and wanting community and friends. Asheville had the biggest concentration of friends, the biggest community." It was quite different from what he was used to. "Old-time on the West Coast is very intellectual, and that was the scene I came up in; I thought about the music very intellectually." In Asheville, Ismerio believes the music is more a part of "the fabric of life," possibly more spiritually centered. In the South, he finds that people less often "geek out on tune origins, chord changes. In Asheville people really don't care about source recordings and all of that." He seeks out jams that are "a little rowdier and [where people] play fast."

Though he is not from the South, Ismerio does not feel isolated or like he is an intruder; he feels situated in the region. "I think what rubs people the wrong way about being from elsewhere is not owning up to it. There are some people who want it to just be handmade music, not recorded and packaged. And there are some people who want it to be just *Southern* music, not recorded and packaged by non-Southerners. I hear people rumble a bit, but it never comes up to me. Not to my face."

Despite his reputation as a pioneer of the West Coast trainhopping contingent that moved to the South, Ismerio believes the link was a brief, odd convergence. "Portland has a huge, overblown reputation from five young guys playing old-time music [during just] *one winter*. There is a huge punk scene in Portland, and a huge old-time scene, but there is almost no crossover. Most of the kids in the punk scene were not in it. And here in Asheville, I have noticed actual animosity in the punk scene for old-time musicians. Matty Semkovich [his friend and former bandmate] tells me stories about punk parties [in Asheville] where he is told not to even pull out his fiddle."

Ismerio taxonomically places trainhopping as a subculture within the punk and old-time subcultures. He started riding trains in April of 1995, and has noticed changes:

> I can't give you any statistics or anything, because I don't pay attention to that shit. When I first started riding trains, you run into people all the time, other people riding trains. There were basically three groupings of people. There are societal dropouts, you know—guys who just could not function in society, just riding the rails as a means of staying out of society. Migrant workers. And then there are people like myself, young adventure riders, middle-class, access to money, could function in society but

are choosing to ride freight trains for the adventure of it. By the mid-2000s, I saw very few dropouts and almost no migrants. All I'd see on trains were young dropouts, young punks. That's like all I saw. I just was running into punk kids on rails.

Nobody in the old days had instruments, he explains. "Nowadays you see kids everywhere with instruments."

Ismerio found a handful of other trainhopping punks who were enamored of old-time music—in particular, Semkovich and Andrew Norcross—and this was the beginning of the connection. "I met Andrew at a Food Not Bombs feeding in downtown Portland. He was sixteen or seventeen years old, playing banjo so fast I couldn't keep up with him, and he was already out riding trains at that point. We didn't know each other. Matty and Andrew were playing old-time music and riding freight trains, and so was I. We had always heard about each other, so by the time we met each other we already knew each other. I met Matty for the first time in 2000 on a Dickel Brothers tour, in Minneapolis."

The group all came together in 2003 when Ismerio, Norcross, Semkovich, and "this kid Scott and this guy Tiger were all living in Portland. So there was this convergence of punk kids in Portland that played old-time music and [we] put together a band called Blinkin' Freddie and the Lowbaggers. We toured via freight trains from Portland to Vermont, in the summer of 2003." *Lowbagger* is an affectionate name for a train tramp; it's "different than a dirt-bag," Ismerio explains, "and meant traveling around on the cheap."

Ismerio considers his turn as a lowbagger to be significant in some ways. "Hard to say what kind of impact we had," he mused, "but I think it definitely had an impact. After 2003, I noticed a distinct change. We played at punk houses all across the country." The new development was the kind of energy old-time musicians were bringing to the punk communities they traveled by train to. "I noticed a big impact on people," he remembers. "We didn't drink—at that time none of us drank. Matty was hard-core straight edge. Four really tall guys would roll into town with acoustic instruments and start making root beer floats and start playing old-time music. Just, like, to get people dancing. On streets, in houses. It really influenced people. We weren't just drunk punks. We were coming through town and doing really positive stuff." This was creating community through a trainhopping old-time liberation force.

It is this connection between community building and dance that animates Ismerio's interest in the transformative potential of square dance calling. He started calling in Portland by happenstance, and learned by listening to the well-regarded caller Bill Martin. "I didn't set out to be a caller, just got pushed into it. One, it's not that hard. Two, I'm good at it." There are many types of dancing, but Ismerio chose just one. "I do just one, Southern Appalachian traditional community square dances. I don't do New England squares. I don't do singing squares. I don't do modern Western squares. I don't do Quebecois squares. I only do one of them. Okay, so that's my role in society, a square dance caller."

Ismerio considers dance to be a tool more than a vocation. He turned to dance calling rather than music as a way to fulfill his vision of what old-time music should be in terms of community:

> I am not an old-time music missionary, like people like to paint me as. I am a community organizer who uses these things as a tool to bring people together. That's what I am doing. I am trying to get human beings to come together and engage each other in healthy and fun ways. Calling square dances and playing old-time music are the tools I use to do this. Not a political purpose, a social purpose. I see all these people disconnected from each other, from the earth. I don't separate these things. Music, dance, eating . . . you know, where you sleep at night. They're all connected. I'm not obsessed with square dancing to where I'm like, I need to learn about every kind of square dancing that's ever been done in America. It's like: I don't give a fuck about that! It is an incredibly powerful tool to bring people together. And so I have that tool with Southern squares. I already have that tool, and it's working just fine. I'm not a completist. It's all I need.

The Anarchist as Rounder

Slipping up the narrow muddy path on Andrew Norcross's mountainside, I wonder for a brief disorientating moment, does this place really exist? I have been at many back-to-the-land homesteads and plenty of ramshackle spots in the mountains, but there is something narrowly elusive about Norcross's kingdom. Perhaps it is his small, cluttered, solidly hand-built cabin perched on a ledge on a steep hillside. There are hardwood floors and walls covered with art, instruments, old fliers, and garlands of braided garlic he grew. The faucet is fed directly by a spring up the mountain, yet there is some fancy imported cheese on the table waiting to be eaten. Perhaps it is Norcross himself who is elusive.

Deep in Madison County, North Carolina, his place is situated in a region steeped in old-time music culture and lore. I had been told to turn at the partially dismantled house in Chandler Cove and to head up the hollow to

Andrew Norcross in his mountainside homestead/kingdom. Photo by Daniel S. Margolies.

Norcross's property; the Chandlers were some of the key informants for early field recorders and ethnomusicologists.[19] Norcross was dismantling this house to reuse the wood for his own timber-framed workshop. He was familiar with the history of the building and the details of its construction and use going back close to a century. "That house has more memory than anyone alive around here," he said, with obvious relish. Norcross has insinuated himself into this community with deliberate care, and he feels deeply engaged in it. "There are some people that are prejudiced" against outsiders, he says, but most are not. There is a wide community of his friends in the county "within ten to fifteen minutes, which is close around here. We all work together. They're doing the same thing that I do: growing food, building shacks, trying to get to know the ecosystem. Just enjoying the topography of where we live. It's really nice."

Norcross does not see his move to rural homesteading from his West Coast origins (after years traveling by train) as incongruous. Instead he sees his own position almost as an accident of birth.

It's a matter of perspective. You know, thirty to forty years back, in this county where I live now, if I happened to be born here and my name was

Chandler, I wouldn't have been a bohemian; I would have been like anyone else. Because I am here and what I like to do. Because I am a different
person, grew up in a different place, and it's a different time. I do the same
things for the same reasons as everyone else who lived around here
because it's a good place to be and it's a good community. You got your
family close by. My family is my friends. I don't really have a family, besides my mom. But the game has changed. The way to do it and not put
yourself in debt is to do it by any means necessary, you know? Get shit
done. Get grease for free. Dumpster dive. Work it however you can. The
game has changed, but from the historical perspective [I'm] still doing
the same thing people have been doing up here for a long time.

Norcross places himself not in an alternative movement but in the fulfillment
of a way of living that he simply has engaged. "The movement thing, that's a
vague thing," he dismisses. He does not consider what he is doing as going back
to the land because he and his family have no rural roots. "I don't feel back to
the land. I feel like an orphan of the world in a lot of ways. Not everybody does
have the lineage. I'm not from anywhere, don't have roots anywhere." There is
no doubt that Norcross stands in defiance to norms of behavior, and no question as to why: "There is a lot about this world I don't like."

If Norcross does have roots anywhere, it is in the punk trainhopping movement. He moved through anarchist and punk circles for years, beginning to
ride trains at the invitation of a potential girlfriend, and never stopped. He
continues to travel for two or more months each year on trains. Alternatively,
he drives his grease-powered car, using grease he procures for free in a variety of
creative [sometimes illicit] ways. He came to old-time music accidentally, out
of an interest in bluegrass coupled with a complete lack of understanding
of what it was. At the time, he was a sixteen-year-old anarchist punk activist
awaiting trial for his direct role in the 1999 anti–World Trade Organization
riots in Seattle:

We were breaking windows and burning buildings, just having fun, just
chaos, it was great! For a young punk who listed to bands like Aus Rotten
and all these bands that were all about the destruction of corporations and
stuff. Thousands of people all rioting, not really for anything, just *against*
things, you know? It was just against the corporations and the World Trade
Organization, which is a just a synonym for all the secret government
organizations in the world, the closed doors, controlling the world
around us and make it so sweatshops exist and all the evil things in the
world exist. We were all just there, rioting against that.

Waiting around for trial on three felony counts, Norcross was taught some licks on the banjo. He took the banjo on a train ride to Florida and back, and was hooked. "I didn't know anyone who could play it. Didn't even know it was 'old-time.' I could play very fast. Not well, but fast." He eventually made his way to Portland and to the Portland Old Time Music Gathering, which was founded by Ismerio. "Michael wasn't nice to me," laughs Norcross. That was fine with him, because old-time music simply clicked. "The inspiration really came from the old recordings. I think it floated in my head really well and really easily because it's fundamentally three chords and a four-quarter rhythm, which is punk music. And that is all I listened to up to that point. I had never really listened to anything else with passion, you know? It just made sense to me. Seemed so simple I could understand it and enjoy it." Norcross plays powerfully slippery old-time music with great grace and power. Yet he now thinks the music is boring unless played with the right group of friends at precisely the right moment. "Without the adrenaline rush, just sitting around playing tunes, it's boring." He would rather play drums in a metal band with his neighbors in the mountains; it is the local sound at the moment.

The Way I Live My Life

Hannah Johnson grew up on a farm in Keezletown, Virginia, a small rural community in the Shenandoah Valley. When I interview her she lives in an old house next door to her parent's farm, though later she will move to an organic farm in even more rural and remote West Virginia. She describes her Keezletown house as "antisolar," dark and not insulated by anything but the two separate beehives that live in the walls and throw out spring swarms, which she endeavors to catch and hive more formally. The house has no running water. It could, but the work required to get running water sounds to Johnson like a lot more hassle than it is worth. And anyway, she laughs with what is her characteristic good cheer, "I do live next door to my parents and can shower there and wash my clothes when necessary." She needs to do this because, unlike many other old-time trainhoppers, Johnson has a regular job and such regular cleanliness "is necessary if you make the crossover between living in that world and having a professional career."

Johnson is the youngest trainhopper of the three I interviewed, arriving on the scene as it was already being to flourish in the Southeast from its West Coast origins. She was partially inspired by meeting the new contingent of train-hoppers at the Mount Airy Fiddlers Convention in North Carolina. "I got into old-time music before I even knew you could ride trains," she said. "I didn't know it was a thing you could actually *do* nowadays." She took to it rather quickly.

Johnson started going to old-time festivals in Virginia in high school. At the time, she explains, "I just wanted to go somewhere where my parents were not." The music captivated her. "This is cool, this is what I wanted to do," she thought. She soon secured a fiddle from a teacher at Berea College, where she enrolled. Johnson then taught herself to play (and build) banjos, and in addition to these two principal instruments she soon became such an accomplished old-time pump organist that she was asked to accompany the winning fiddler at Clifftop, the most prominent contest in West Virginia. "That was kind of a shenanigan," she says with a laugh.

She had a fateful meeting with Norcross:

First or second time I was at Mt. Airy, I met Andrew and Matty; they were traveling together at that time. I was just walking around, listening to music; I didn't know any people except the ones I had come with. And these people, I liked their music, and they were dirty, and I was like, what's their deal? Sitting under a tarp and eating Dumpster food, what's going on here? You know, I grew up in Keezletown, you don't see shit like that in Keezletown! I started hanging out with them because I liked their music and they were friendly.

In short order, in 2005 Johnson and her close friend Bill Clemmer endeavored to ride a train themselves. "We are old pals, and we were like, okay, we're going to ride some trains, we are going to figure this shit out." Armed with a lot of enthusiasm and little information, they grabbed a southbound train in Shenandoah and rode it down to Roanoke. What followed were years of learning the ropes and the routes and riding trains around the United States and Canada. Johnson was in college at the time, and traveling on breaks, but "wishing I could do something else. I really wanted to play music and ride trains around." She dropped out and spent "three years being a bum, traveling around, just playing music." It was during this time that she met her musical partner Aviva Stiegmeyer (a kindred spirit who soon began a career in hand-made guitars). They busked their way across Canada and the United States and eventually settled back in Keezletown.

Like all trainhoppers, Johnson has a lot of captivating stories and related adventures. In 2008, in "maybe a lapse in my caution," she caught a train solo and "on the fly" (while it was moving) in Virginia with a fiddle, banjo, and bicycle in hand. She hooked the bike on the ladder of the train car, tossed her instruments on board, and climbed on. Johnson was on her way to join a trav-

Hannah Johnson playing her fiddle.
Photo by Daniel R. Easley.

eling, horse-drawn puppet and variety show in Vermont called the Old Reliable
Spectacular. The point of the experience she says, was "showing that Old
Reliable is where it's at, it never goes out of style."

Johnson does not claim to be constrained by external values, but she is a
hardworking person who became trained as a nurse to give herself maximum
flexibility to work anywhere, and to give her "a job in the community providing a service that is needed." She remains grounded in her hometown, but the
road still calls to her. While Ismerio has a structured and clear vision of his
purpose and intent, and Norcross has a sharp rejection of social structure,
Johnson has grounded her alternative life exactly where she was raised. "My
life is different," she explains; "not mainstream. Partly how I was raised, partly
my interests in life. Instead of being able to say it is a specific thing, it is just
the way I live my life, desiring to be self-sufficient, doing most things on my
own. I'm into growing my own food, making my own clothes, doing stuff for
myself. Providing my own amusement, not watching TV. Playing music."

Johnson most of all likes to spend her time outside. She grows most of the
food she eats, slaughters the animals she eats, and makes the instruments she
plays. Like other trainhoppers, she also rejects an easy categorization of her
approach. "I wouldn't call myself a punk. I have no history in the punk scene.

I have never liked or listened to punk music. Andrew's a punk; I'm not a punk. I don't know what people would call me. Ever see how mad Andrew gets if you call him a hippie? Some people might call me a hippie, but they would be wrong."

The Subculture of No Subculture

Michael Ismerio, Andrew Norcross, and Hannah Johnson have constructed lives linked to the land. Ismerio makes a living in old-time music, as a square dance caller and fiddle teacher. He has an elaborate website that presents his life as a nineteenth-century tome of adventure and vagabondage,[20] but this is merely a springboard to the gigs that allow him to sleep on an outdoor platform behind the tiny modular shack he built for himself perched on borrowed land on the outskirts of Asheville. He articulates a well-developed communitarian philosophy.

Johnson has a day job, but homesteads on a farm. "I like to spend my time outside doing stuff [like] planting," she explains. Norcross embodies a postmodern variant of life as hunter-gather and off-the-grid homesteader in the Appalachian Mountains. He speaks fearlessly of misadventures and irreverently of mores and responsibilities. This diversity around a core shared sensibility signals the philosophically anarchistic core of the trainhopper scene.

Trainhoppers synthesize at least four critical cultural strands. The first is the core punk alternative and sensibility, which combines a rejection of the mainstream with an equally enthusiastic embrace of the alternative. The second is the most recent iteration of the underground American romance of riding trains among a renewable, floating army of adventurers, hobos, Wobblies, and others. The third major strand is the enduring alternative allure of Appalachian singularity that is rooted in a recurrent sense that the region itself is one of the last frontiers of true difference. And finally, linking all of the strands is the well-honed search for authenticity that has tracked along with Southern music making and culture since the dawn of the commercial era and has equally served to define punk as a lifestyle.[21] While enacting the tropes of hoboing, trainhoppers do not seem especially interested in the intellectual antecedents stretching back to hobo Jack Black's 1926 book *You Can't Win*.[22] Trainhoppers largely eschew what and who came before in both the punk and old-time revival community except for a zealous embrace of regional vernacular old-time traditions, culture, and styles of music. Here they may even have surpassed the revivalist sensibility in vehemence and self-conscious purity.

Notes

1. On Seeger's lasting impact, see Malone, *Music from the True Vine*, 72–73, 96–97, 173–74.

2. This chapter is the first examination of the underground network of trainhoppers within the broader but still fairly obscure old-time music scene. There have been studies of punks in related vernacular traditions, such as Smithers, "Old Time Punk," but there is a decided difference between the trainhoppers and the connections described (or sought) between punk and the "alt-country" that Smithers discusses. Trainhoppers outside of the old-time scene have been documented in Cotton, *Hobo*, and George, *Catching Out*, among others. See also, more generally, Williams, *Subcultural Theory*.

3. Wishnevsky, *How the Hippies Ruin't Hillbilly Music*.

4. Turino, *Music as Social Life*, 187.

5. See Shapiro, *Appalachia on Our Mind*.

6. The literature on DIY culture is large and growing, with an emphasis on the cultural politics of the moment; see, for example, Chidgey, "Developing Communities of Resistance?," 103–14.

7. The term *musicultural ecosystem* comes from ethnomusicologist Jeff Todd Titon; see his *Sustainable Music* blog, http://sustainablemusic.blogspot.com/search/label/ecosystem.

8. Herein, quotations from Ismerio, Norcross, and Johnson are taken from the transcript of the formal interviews, though they are not individually cited. Other comments about the interviewees are from direct participant observation.

9. Wilbur, "Growing a Radical Ruralism," 149; Halfacree, "Back to the Land in the Twenty-First Century."

10. Brown, *Back to the Land*, 9. It should be noted that Brown does not see the back-to-the-land movement as "part of a large romantic impulse" (11).

11. As one participant in the Los Angeles punk scene has noted, "after the end of the Vietnam War, when the hippies decided to forget it and get high, I was extremely let down. After all, the sixties revolution was supposed to change the world, but where did it go? The punk movement was crazy and hectic and energetically full of life. I believe the statement punk made at that time was prophetic of where we are as a society today." Frank Gragani, quoted in Doe, *Under the Big Black Sun*, 89.

12. Wooley, "Conjuring Utopia."

13. On subcultural fusion and potentials for instabilities, see Hebdige, *Subculture*.

14. A good overview of old-time music and its popular revival is Ruchala, "Making Round Peak Music."

15. Bealle, *Old-Time Music and Dance*, 148.

16. Some of the contemporary old-time scene has been documented with characteristic self-referentially in a project titled The New Young Fogies. This name evokes the Young Fogies album originally released by Heritage Records in 1985 and later reissued by Rounder records, which captured the 1970s generation. See Hearth Music, "The New Young Fogies."

17. Bass's next band, the Forge Mountain Diggers, featured former punk rocker Allison Williams on banjo and described its old-time music as having "a background in the DIY punk scene"; see "The Forge Mountain Diggers." Williams, who went from punk roots to become one of the leaders of the Southern square dance revival in places like Knoxville, Tennessee, and Fayetteville, Arkansas, could easily have been a subject of this chapter as well; for more about Williams, see her website, http://www .allisonwilliamsmusic.com/.

18. Leblanc, *Pretty in Punk,* 34.

19. See, for example, the collected recordings on *High Atmosphere.*

20. See Ismerio's website, http://www.michealismerio.com.

21. This search is tracked in Peterson, *Creating Country Music,* among other works. On the many iterations of the floating army, see Mills, *In the Floating Army,* and McGuckin, *Memoirs of a Wobbly.*

22. Johnson described the very real possibility of being stranded for hours waiting for a ride as "waiting for nothing," yet she had never heard of Tom Kromer's classic 1935 account of Depression-era hoboing of the same name. See Kromer, *Waiting for Nothing.*

References

Bealle, John. *Old-Time Music and Dance: Community and Folk Revival.* Bloomington, IN: Quarry, 2005.

Brown, Dona. *Back to the Land: The Enduring Dream of Self-Sufficiency in Modern America.* Madison: University of Wisconsin Press, 2011.

Chidgey, Red. "Developing Communities of Resistance? Maker Pedagogies, Do-It-Yourself Feminism, and DIY Citizenship." In *DIY Citizenship: Critical Making and Social Media,* edited by Matt Ratto, Megan Boler, and Ronald Deibert, 103–14. Cambridge, MA: MIT Press, 2014.

Cotton, Eddy Joe. *Hobo: A Young Man's Thoughts on Trains and Tramping in America.* New York: Harmony, 2002.

Doe, John. *Under the Big Black Sun: A Personal History of L.A. Punk.* Boston: Da Capo, 2016.

"The Forge Mountain Diggers." http://www.indianafiddlersgathering.org/artists /forge-mountain-diggers#sthash.PXpUocvD.dpuf.

George, Sarah, dir. *Catching Out.* Los Angeles. Worthy Entertainment, 2003. DVD.

Halfacree, Keith. "Back to the Land in the Twenty-First Century—Making Connections with Rurality," *Tijdschrift voor Economische en Sociale Geografie* 98 (2007): 3–8.

Hearth Music, "The New Young Fogies: Documenting a New Generation of Old-Time." *No Depression,* November 25, 2012. http://nodepression.com/article /new-young-fogies-documenting-new-generation-old-time.

Hebdige, Dick. *Subculture: The Meaning of Style.* London: Routledge, 1979.

High Atmosphere: Ballads and Banjo Tunes from Virginia and North Carolina Collected by John Cohen in November of 1965. Nashville: Rounder, 1994. CD.

Kromer, Tom. *Waiting for Nothing and Other Writings.* Edited by Arthur D. Casciato and James L. W. West III. Athens: University of Georgia Press.

Leblanc, Lauraine. *Pretty in Punk: Girls' Gender Resistance in a Boys' Subculture.* New Brunswick, NJ: Rutgers University Press, 1999.

Malone, Bill C. *Music from the True Vine: Mike Seeger's Life and Musical Journey.* Chapel Hill: University of North Carolina Press, 2014.

McGuckin, Henry E. *Memoirs of a Wobbly.* Chicago: Kerr, 1987.

Mills, Frederick Cecil. *In the Floating Army: F. C. Mills on Itinerant life in California, 1914.* Urbana: University of Illinois Press, 1992.

Peterson, Richard A. *Creating Country Music: Fabricating Authenticity.* Chicago: University of Chicago Press, 1999.

Ruchala, James. "Making Round Peak Music: History, Revitalization, and Community." PhD diss., Brown University, 2011.

Shapiro, Henry D. *Appalachia on Our Mind: The Southern Mountains and Mountaineers in the American Consciousness, 1870–1920.* Chapel Hill: University of North Carolina Press, 1978.

Slobin, Mark. *Subcultural Sounds: Micromusics of the West.* Middletown, CT: Wesleyan University Press, 1993.

Smithers, Aaron. "Old Time Punk." In *Old Roots, New Routes: The Cultural Politics of Alt.Country Music,* edited by Pamela Fox and Barbara Ching, 175–91. Ann Arbor: University of Michigan Press, 2008.

Turino, Thomas. *Music as Social Life: The Politics of Participation.* Chicago: University of Chicago Press, 2008.

Wilbur, Andrew. "Growing a Radical Ruralism: Back-to-the-Land as Practice and Ideal." *Geography Compass* 7 (2013): 149–60.

Williams, J. Patrick. *Subcultural Theory: Traditions and Concepts.* Cambridge: Polity, 2011.

Wishnevsky, St. Wish, *How the Hippies Ruin't Hillbilly Music: A Historical Memoir 1960–2000.* Bloomington, IN: iUniverse, 2006.

Wooley, Amy. "Conjuring Utopia: The Appalachian String Band Revival." PhD diss., University of California–Los Angeles, 2003.

Formal Interviews

Michael Ismerio, December 27–28, 2014, Asheville, North Carolina.

Hannah Johnson, March 5, 2015, phone interview.

Andrew Norcross, December 28, 2014, Marshall, North Carolina.

Space, Time, and Race in Dirty South Bohemia

Zandria F. Robinson

On every third Sunday in Memphis, Tennessee, about a hundred black folks from the hip-hop and millennial generations gather for a different kind of evening worship service, one descended from the historically black and Southern creative spaces of the juke joint, the speakeasy, the chitlin circuit, and the club. Attendees are novelists, rappers, singers, poets, visual artists, thespians, artisans, nonprofit professionals, chefs, academics, photographers, schoolteachers, doulas, intellectuals, yoga instructors, bloggers, gardeners, and various combinations of the preceding. The Artistik Lounge, the brainchild of Memphis musical duo Artistik Approach, brings the city's black creatives and black creative consumers together to support a featured artist's performance, eat something good from a local black chef, buy some artisan jewelry or other handcrafted items by a local black artisan, and network across fields. Featured acts are neosoul artists, jazz-soul fusions, and soul-inspired hip-hop artists who are backed by reggae house band Chinese Connection Dub Embassy (CCDE). Between sets, CCDE may break into a Church of God in Christ–inspired run that compels attendees to offer some call and response, church dance, and ring shout. The night could end with a rap cipher, where local hip-hop artists lyrically converse with one another and with the audience about current goings-on, or with a second line, as the band's New Orleans–raised drummer breaks into the Crescent City's familiar cadence. It is worship service for the unchurched, a different kind of spiritual service for churchgoers, and a communal and gathering space for a variety of blacknesses on the margins.

Now located in the city's neobohemia,[1] the Artistik Lounge is one of several definitively and unapologetically black creative spaces in a landscape where artistic production runs along the same dividing tracks as Memphis's long-standing history of racial segregation. In these spaces, black creatives endeavor to reimagine historically black Southern spaces in the twenty-first century and develop resistive practices to protect and promote black art as a viable site for cultural entrepreneurship in the city. At the crossroads of the Old South and the New South, country and cosmopolitan, Memphis's Dirty South bohemians construct an alternative kind of Southern blackness that refashions tropes of the traditional black South into something that allows for difference that belongs.

In some ways Memphis, the urban center of a rural metropolitan area that consists of nearly a million people, seems an unlikely place for bohemian cultures, and black bohemian cultures in particular, to thrive and develop. A significant portion of its residents are still only two generations removed from "the country," and Memphis is still "the big city" for migrants from surrounding small towns and rural areas, which include places in the Arkansas and Mississippi Delta, rural places in west Tennessee, and counties east of Memphis. However contrarian, weird, or off-center it may be, the implicit pristineness of Southern bohemia is in direct contrast to the rural and working-class roots and sensibilities of the city. Memphis Grizzlies player Zach Randolph opined in one postgame interview that Memphis was a "blue-collar town" for which "nothing has come easy." In another postgame interview, fellow player Tony Allen characterized the team's play as "all heart; grit; grind," which the team and city took up as a branding tool to mark the city's distinctiveness as a Southern town.

These characterizations of Memphis as a city that grits and grinds are implicitly about reckoning with its large black population and the enduring racial inequality that undergirds everyday life in the city. Unlike other black Southern cities, Memphis was slow to elect an African American mayor, despite having a sizable demographic advantage. While black Southern bohemian capital Atlanta elected its first black mayor in 1974, Memphis did not elect its first black mayor until 1991, and did so by a small margin. Nearly half a century after Martin Luther King Jr.'s assassination in Memphis, black poverty, the issue that in part had brought King to the city, remains stubbornly high. It frequently has the highest percentage of black people living in poverty of all major metropolitan areas. In contrast, white poverty in the city actually declined in the first decades of the twenty-first century. Younger white migrants to the city are part of this change in economic fortune for whites, accelerating the blending of bohemian cultures and gentrification by transforming warehouses into breweries and art galleries. This cadre of young, relatively affluent white artists, arts patrons, and arts administrators unintentionally reifies the spatial and capital lines between a white Southern bohemia and a black one in Memphis.

Municipal support and cultivation of the arts is central to the success and proliferation of all bohemian scenes, but certainly black political power and presence are especially essential to the success of black bohemian scenes.

Southern cities in general are less segregated than their Northern counterparts, but Memphis's segregation index is often higher than that of other Southern cities. This signals two competing processes: a continuation of the separate city, a site of creative proliferation for black folks outside of the gaze and control of whites, and the marginalization of black bohemian cultures from access to arts resources and spaces that would sustain scenes and cultivate new generations of artists. Yet these contrasts between segregation and integration, city life and rural hinterland, art and grit, freedom and grind, are tensions at the heart of Memphis's black bohemian scene. Tending to these tensions allows us to move beyond shock headlines about Memphis's poverty and supposed backwardness to a more nuanced understanding of how histories of racial discrimination and segregation influence black bohemian scenes.

Dirty South bohemia is a real and lived space constitutive of multiple sites, like the Artistik Lounge, that move and shift into and out of locations and being. From a jazz club to a black repertory theater to a place for the spoken word, it is a safe space for cultural expression and entrepreneurship. These sites might operate as black-owned and -operated anchor institutions, like the black repertory Hattiloo Theatre or the nonprofit arts institution Memphis Black Arts Alliance, or may exist in a place at a given time, like the Madison Dance Studio at Minglewood Hall that hosts the Artistik Lounge. Thoroughly local and profoundly translocal, Dirty South bohemia can be found in various iterations in Southern towns and cities that are themselves connected to one another through the movement of people and social media. It is also a mediated site that occurs in film, sound, and cyberspace, discursively represented and reflected in several imagined black Southern spaces and places—the Church club in the film *Idlewild*, Big K.R.I.T.'s Cadillactica, and Outkast's Stankonia. Across these lived and imagined places, Dirty South bohemia traverses time and space to provide sanctuary for black cultural life on the margins.

Dirty South Bohemia developed vis-à-vis cities' recent push to attract (largely white) creative classes into urban centers. In this context, black cultural entrepreneurs endeavor to create a separate arts and intellectual space within the constraints of class and racial cultures in the city. Dirty South Bohemians combine features from black bohemian cultures concentrated in the urban Northeast, like the Afropunk movement, with regionally-inflected understandings of race and bohemianism to create a racially and regionally distinct articulation of bohemianism in racially segregated spaces.

Bohemian Cultures and New Urbanism

Since Richard Florida's introduction of the concept, cities have been preoc-cupied with cultivating the amenities that might attract the "creative class,"[2] a group that Florida characterized as sets of creative individuals and highly ed-ucated consumers of creative products who would drive economic develop-ment in postindustrial cities. In addition to coffee shops, yoga studios, and robust and diverse arts offerings, cities needed "talent, tolerance, and tech" to attract the creative class and its economy-boosting disposable income and job creation potential. However, Florida's work offered more of a description of existing places, like Austin, Silicon Valley, and North Carolina's Research Triangle, than a prescription for ailing cities. Thus, cities with a historically high percentage of residents in poverty, or with entrenched discriminatory policies, like those in the Rust Belt, or in Alabama, Louisiana, Mississippi, and Tennessee, were at a strategic disadvantage. Further, the prevailing assump-tion of whiteness and maleness that accompanied the notion of the creative class obscured race and gender disparities in creative labor, compensation, and consumption. It also made it difficult for cities to imagine what creative amenities would specifically attract communities of young professionals of color and African Americans in particular.

As supposed offshoots of the creative class, bohemian scenes—where art, culture, and intellectual exchange intersect with and support growing cul-tural economies—are increasingly central to how cities market themselves to young middle-class urbanites. Yet these scenes are largely tangential to how cities deploy the economics of art. Instead, municipalities still too often rely on a model of economic investment in which they seek to broaden the tax base and attract business investment and capital by supporting the kinds of businesses and experiences that young urban professionals will patronize. This is, at its core, a trickle-down approach to supporting the bohemian communities to which yuppies and buppies are to flock after a day at the office. The artists, cities estimate, will inherently benefit from the kinds of people who have the disposable income to patronize an IKEA store, an art gallery, and an organic gelato shop. While gritty neighborhoods dotted with abandoned warehouses still exist in some measures, they are now colliding with different uses of previously bohemian space.[3] Instead of being reinvented as artist workspaces and residences, abandoned warehouses now become breweries; run-down taverns are transformed into high-end cocktail and tapas bars; previously boarded-up spaces become exclusive art galleries. As with all processes of gentrification, the bohemian proletariat is often on the margins of these shifts. This is especially the case for black bohemians in Southern places with regionally specific spatial patterns of segregation and discrimination.

In the South, growing attention to bohemian capitals like Asheville, Athens, and Austin has highlighted some aspects of the regional distinctiveness of Southern instantiations of these scenes. In a region preoccupied with place, artists are always already reckoning with a past that is never past and the messiness of Southern race, gender, and sexuality repression and oppression. However, attention to these self-proclaimed weird places that pride themselves on novelty that is both Southern and playfully un-Southern obscures the longer, broader, and queerer histories of bohemianism in black Southern communities. In fact, the overwhelming whiteness of these college town boutique bohemian capitals reflects the inequalities of race and space that continue and exacerbate patterns of racial segregation in the region. In a postracial, postsouthern bohemian landscape, Jim Crow power and spatial organization continue to affect how and where bohemian culture is produced, consumed, and marketed.

While popularly curated and nostalgia-laden discourses about Southern scenes of cultural production erroneously imagine art as the great racial equalizer, black-white artistic collaboration has never fundamentally transformed the day-to-day realities of marginalization and repression experienced by black folks in the South. If, in fact, such collaboration carried this power, the evidence would be in new, progressive instantiations of power that support the creation of black wealth and tangible improvements in the quality of life for a range of African Americans. And though African Americans, Southern-born migrants, and migrants from other places have found tremendous opportunities in New South metropolises like Atlanta, Charlotte, and Dallas, African American poverty in the South has also increased in the past two decades. Moreover, even middle-class African Americans are struggling to hold onto hard-earned wealth invested in homes, battling cities to maintain and support public education, and resisting gentrification of historically black neighborhoods. These institutional battles occur in tandem with black folks' strivings to maintain Dirty South bohemia. That is, contention over such bread-and-butter urban issues as police brutality, neighborhood change, and access to quality city services is also about protecting black entrepreneurial art spaces in disappearing territory.

Dirty South Bohemian Genealogies

At the Word, the city's longest-running open microphone event, Juju Bushman, an acoustic guitar-playing singer with dreadlocks and black-painted finger-nails, is sitting on the edge of the stage. He has invited spoken-word artist and singer Michelle Antoinette Montgomery up on the stage to sing a duet with him, and the audience, on sofas, bar stools, and chairs placed about the down-town lounge are anticipating their collaboration. When Bushman croons the first words of Memphis soul singer Al Green's "Simply Beautiful," ecstatic shouts ring out across the dimness. Bushman's Afropunk aesthetic seemingly belies his Southern roots and penchant for quoting Southern gangsta rappers. Yet, conceptualized in the long view of the history of black bohemianism in Memphis, from Beale Street to soul to neosoul and hip-hop, Bushman is a reflection of the mash-up of sensibilities—black, Southern, indie, and unapologetic—that necessarily emerged when the black music industry col-lapsed after the bankrupting of Stax Records in the latter half of the 1970s.[4]

Bushman was one of many artists featured in the 2015 exhibition *Remote: A Photographic Journey*, a collection of photographs of young black creatives in Memphis by black bohemian scene photographer Darius B. Williams. The exhibition, accompanied by receptions and performances, documented art, fashion, race, and difference within the group of artists. Moreover, the exhibit and events reflected the scene's growing self-awareness and its desire to rec-ord, archive, and write itself into the record of the city's artistic production. It was also self-consciously Southern. Rather than setting the artists against an urban landscape, wooded pathways served as the backdrop for the photos, emphasizing the contrast between and coexistence of rural and urban that is characteristic of black Southern identities writ large and Dirty South bohemian identities in particular. Further, the exhibition's events, held at the Memphis Slim Collaboratory, a renovation of blues pianist John "Peter" Chatman's home by a community development organization, was a self-conscious reclamation of black Southern artistic space. For these artists, reclaiming the South in this moment means reclaiming and embracing difference, and creating space to live—and make a living on—difference.

Demographically, Memphis's Dirty South bohemians reflect the city's long-standing history as the big city in the Mid-South region, relatively cheap cost of living, and growing emphasis on arts administrators and marketers if not working artists. The scene is also the intersection of two, sometimes com-peting, generations—the hip-hop generation and black millennials. Some of the scene's participants, including artists and audiences, are college educated, with some having attended college outside of the region and returned home to work and/or care for relatives. Most are the kinds of self-trained, do-it-yourself artists with which bohemian scenes have come to be associated. And they, like the soul and blues musicians before them, are likely the epitome of hustle, grit, and grind. Disadvantaged by race, class, and artist status, they make space where there is none to continue the legacy they inherited.

If white Southerners are historically and satirically rendered incapable of bohemianism by virtue of race and region, black Southerners like Memphis's Dirty South bohemians are especially outside of popular imaginings of bohemian life. Although bohemianism has deep roots among black folks like all other American groups, black Southern migrants arriving in the cities of the Midwest, Mid-Atlantic, and Northeast during the Great Migration were quickly labeled green by the one-generation-more-sophisticated black cosmopolites they encountered in their new locations. Black Southerners, the narrative proceeds, were the backward and green country cousins being newly acquainted with the bohemian cultural possibilities of urban life via the Great Migration. Yet, many migrants from the rural South likely encountered the black bohemian cultures of Southern cities like Atlanta, Durham, Houston, Memphis, or New Orleans on their way north and west. The black bohemians in postslavery Southern cities had already created an alternative arts culture within a "separate city"—one outside of and also intersecting with the elite black arts societies and the respectability politics of black churches.[5] In this way, the blues culture of the late nineteenth and early twentieth centuries, which had been urbanized through its migration from the Mississippi Delta to Beale Street, juke joints, and black folks' front porches, is the historical antecedent to black Southern bohemianism. Describing the distinct circumstances that gave rise to the blues in plantation Mississippi and the blues epistemology that emerged from the contrasts between repression and self-determination, the geographer Clyde Woods notes,

> Born in a new era of censorship, suppression, and persecution, the blues conveyed the sorrow of the individual and the collective tragedy that had befallen African Americans. It also operated to instill pride in a people facing daily denigration, as well as channeling folk wisdom, descriptions of life and labor, travelogues, hoodoo, and critiques of individuals and institutions. It is often forgotten that the blues are also defined by those songs, music, stories, jokes, dances, and other visual and physical practices that raise the spirit of the audience to unimaginable heights. The men and women who performed the blues were sociologists, reporters,

counselors, advocates, and preservers of language and customs, and sum-
moners of life, love, laughter, and much, much more.[6]

These blues folks (and their audiences) who pushed the boundaries of art,
music, and sexuality in the early twentieth century urban South are the actual
and figurative great grandparents of today's Dirty South bohemianism.

Although there were real, nonnegligible divides between the folks of juke
joints, blues clubs, and brothels and the respectable middle-class church folks
for whom temperance and chasteness were central, there was also overlap
and productive tensions between these groups that served as the backdrop
for an early twentieth-century black bohemian space of blues musicians and
singers, artists, activists, and the working folks that patronized juke joints and
speakeasies. In Memphis, Beale Street—often called the Harlem of the South
or Black America's Main Street—was the site of cultures of black difference
and resistance. It was in these spaces, in fact, that the class, generational, and
epistemological differences in approaches to the civil rights movement would
emerge in cities across the South. Yet in the early twentieth century, intellectuals on the lyceum circuit where a young Ida B. Wells was radicalized were in
conversation with blues musicians, artists, and the working women of millionaire Robert R. Church's brothels. Alongside a powerful and secret site for
organized resistance, this segregated space of cultural expression inherently
fostered a bohemia where a range of ideas, sounds, and visual aesthetics were
tested, shared, and refined.

As Beale Street was systematically dismantled and eventually destroyed
through a set of targeted post–World War II urban renewal projects designed to
rid the space of crime, vice, and black people, black Memphians continued
creating resistive and expressive art. Now located in new sites made possible by
new technologies and a bourgeoning Southern music industry, the Dirty
South bohemia of the civil rights era emerged from the streets and porches
of South Memphis, itself a product of generations of black migration from the
surrounding rural areas to the big city. Hi Records, Royal Studios, and Stax
Records, though integrated compared to the norms of most of the rest of the
city, were decidedly black spaces that continued the tradition of blues musicians
in previous generations to author an alternative Southern blackness of Cadillacs
and capes. The soul music created by this iteration of Dirty South bohemia became the soundtrack of black resistance in and beyond the South, narrating both
working-class and middle-class existential struggles against white supremacy.

Despite the fact that a Southern brand of black bohemianism had spread
across the country and globe through Southern soul music, black bohemianism

was still discursively and popularly linked to the large metropolises of places outside of the South—in particular, New York City. The archetypal black boho emerged in popular American consciousness in Lisa Bonet's portrayal of Denise Huxtable on *The Cosby Show*. When Denise heads down south to the fictional and historically black Hillman College in Atlanta, her bohemianism is cast as an export from Brooklyn with no space in a debutante black South epitomized by Southern belle Whitley Gilbert. On *The Cosby Show*, just as on the spin-off *A Different World*, Denise was representative of a bourgeoning black boho movement whose capital was Brooklyn, and by extension, a specific kind of urban Northern blackness that was distinct from black Southern identities.

Indeed, Brooklyn is often situated as the capital of black bohemia. Brooklyn native and cultural critic Nelson George's *Buppies, B-Boys, Baps, and Bohos* traverses "postsoul" black culture with very little attention to the possibilities of a Dirty South bohemia. Diane Paragas and George's 2011 documentary *Brooklyn Boheme* catalogs a postsoul "Harlem Renaissance" in 1980s and 1990s Brooklyn that included a host of writers, artists, and filmmakers who were authoring contemporary blackness through words, visuals, and sound. When Ohio native and comic Dave Chappelle wanted to bring together black artists for a block party, Brooklyn was the gathering site. For nearly a decade, Afropunk, a festival for black and brown punks and bohos, has been held in Brooklyn; reflecting an increasingly cosmopolitan and global sense of blackness, the 2015 festival was held in Paris, France.

At the same time that Brooklyn emerged in American popular consciousness as a black bohemia in the late 1980s and early 1990s, Southern cities were increasingly hubs for arts and alternative expressions of black identity. In 1992, Atlanta-based hip-hop group Arrested Development introduced a country-inflected Afrocentric bohemianism that was firmly rooted in the South and traced its bohemianism to Africa. Although Arrested Development is often remembered for its distinctiveness from the East Coast and West Coast gangsta rap that was also popular in the early 1990s, the group is more notably reflective of alternative productions of black Southern identity that had long been percolating on local music scenes and at spoken-word events. The group's popular single "Tennessee" is a spiritual migration narrative of a dreamed journey through the rural parts of the state to gain existential solace from family and racial histories. Set largely on a Georgia porch in a wooded area, the video depicts a Dirty South bohemia that signifies via Holly Springs, Mississippi; New Orleans second-line dancing; the black power movement; and American enslavement. Arrested Development embodies a "country

cosmopolitan" bohemianism that blends rural and urban sensibilities to construct a best-of-both-worlds black identity for post-civil-rights black America.[7]

Like other Dirty South bohemians, Arrested Development drew on rural
signifiers to give purpose and shape to black difference, even as the rural South
is often imagined as a space of sameness. Country signifiers also created a racial
and regional history for Dirty South bohemianism, rooting black difference
in the original black bohemian culture, the blues. In this way Dirty South bohemianism linked itself to a specifically black set of socioeconomic struggles,
from enslavement to sharecropping to Jim Crow segregation to the prison
industrial complex. Where difference was both forbidden and dangerous in
the South, blues people, and their Dirty South bohemian descendants, carved
out spaces to achieve freedom through difference.

Imagined spaces are also central to Dirty South bohemia, particularly as
artists have worked to reclaim and assert a black regional identity since the
civil rights movement. These spaces are sites where alternative, marginalized
histories of race and region can play out. Southern musicians, key figures in
Dirty South bohemia, create these imagined spaces to reconcile pasts that are
not even past, carving out a place for themselves in the history of hip-hop and
a place for black folks in the history of the South and America more broadly.
Three sites in particular—the film *Idlewild*'s juke joint Church, Outkast's
Stankonia, and Big K.R.I.T.'s Cadillactica—serve as important temporal and
geographical sites in the Dirty South bohemia imaginary.

Bryan Barber's 2006 film *Idlewild* imagines a small-town interwar urban
precursor to Atlanta, complete with bootlegging, shoot-outs, fine women,
and an existential struggle between home and the past and migration and the
future. In telling the story of a Jim Crow–era black Southern bohemia, the
film authors an alternative history of hip-hop that situates the genre as emerging not from a corner in the Bronx but instead from a Georgia juke joint. It
also reaches back in time to explain Atlanta's ascendancy not only to the hip-
hop throne but moreover to the throne of urban black America. As Chris
Rock would quip three years later in his 2009 documentary *Good Hair*, to
answer questions about the politics of hair in African American communities, he had to begin by traveling to the "place where all black decisions are
made: Atlanta." Church, as the juke joint is appropriately called in the film, is
the gathering site of a plethora of blacknesses on the margins. There is piano
playing, singing, rapping, and bodies in motion at Church, and this collective
creative space—one in which whiteness is absent—is a site of religious resistance that prefigures today's Dirty South bohemian sites. Conscious of how
this blues people blackness traverses time and space, *Idlewild* features clocks

that turn backward and forward, sometimes at the same time; signifies via trains, migration, Chicago, and New York; and invites us to imagine a past that is not so different from the present and the future.

Before Church was born aesthetically and visually in *Idlewild*, Outkast had already described Stankonia, a place whence "all funky things come" and an erotic and protective space that celebrates black Southernness and the dirtiness, or stank, of black Southern life. The duo's 1999 album of the same name narrated a funky black South that was gangsta, melodic, experimental, erotic, and concerned with the structures of violence and inequality that plagued Southern black communities. Stankonia is both a time and a space in Outkast's rendering: the time is postsoul and the space is the black South writ large. Yet, like all ruminations on Dirty South bohemian spaces, Stankonia is for black folks on the margins—poor and working-class, quare,[8] blues people for whom the body is a site of movement and resistance rather than exclusively a site of shame. The album's title song articulates a black Southern erotic love, a "stanklove," that can only occur in this imagined resistive space beyond the strictures of whiteness and respectability politics.

Stankonia is both an imagined pan-black Southern bohemian space and a physical recording studio where the labor of creating takes place. Similarly, Cadillactica is a recurring spatial trope in Meridian, Mississippi, native Big K.R.I.T.'s work that allows him to imagine a space for the South in hip-hop and traverse the multiple Souths—past and present, Houston and Memphis, rural and urban—that constitute the Southern hip-hop landscape. His "old school whip with the big ass rims" is his time- and space-traveling machine, the vehicle in which he moves through Cadillactica. As a home space and a postsoul Southern worldview, Cadillactica captures a range of Southern senses and sensibilities: funk sounds and weed smoke, pimping and loving, gangsta bravado, and the varied tastes of the South, from biscuits to collard greens. Moreover, Cadillactica is the embodiment of twenty years of Southern hip-hop and a place where forgotten, buried, and obscured voices are resurrected. Further, it is a site where other Southern artists come to collaborate with K.R.I.T., and his discography reflects participation from both more nationally popular artists, like Rick Ross, as well as Southern hip-hop pioneers, like Memphis natives 8-Ball and MJG. Whereas Southern rappers' participation on non-Southern artists' projects provides the former with national exposure, it does so often at the cost of regional context. Conversely, K.R.I.T. hosts a Southern rapper family reunion of sorts, beckoning artists to a Cadillactica home space toward explicitly Southern—sonically and politically—ends. Notably, Cadillactica is also a destination site for a reverse migration of sorts, as rappers from other regions return "home" to Cadillactica to work with the Southern rap historiographer. Cadillactica is an archive that serves to make visible obscured artists, challenge the representation of Southern hip-hop in the mainstream, and speak back to an industry that constrains listenership.

While heterosexual men often dominate the landscape of black Southern bohemian life, their indebtedness to queer and/or women's sensibilities are evident in their insistence on producing work that is just outside of time, history, or space. Eatonville, Florida's Zora Neale Hurston is the progenitor of this particular black Southern sensibility, as her work took black Southern cultures and people on the margins seriously. In constant movement from place to place, gathering and archiving folk knowledge, Hurston both embodied bohemian sensibilities and collected other Southerners' articulations of them. Rather than conjuring a future and a place, like Stankonia or Cadillactica, through which to imagine a more equal and free life for black folks, Hurston dug into the present and the everyday, her work insisting that in the deep mining of the everyday, and of separate black spaces in particular, we might more readily find that freedom.

As Hurston mined everyday black life in the Jim Crow South and the global black South, singer Erykah Badu, the mother of contemporary black South bohemianism, excavates the everyday in the post-civil-rights South. Moving back and forth between a Jim Crow past and a post-civil-rights present, Badu, like Outkast and Big K.R.I.T., carves out a space for black Southerners in black popular culture and Southern culture. "On and On," the first single and music video from her 1999 album *Baduizm* features the singer's filmic mash-up of two Southern cultural standards, one white, one black: *Gone with the Wind* and *The Color Purple*. As the protagonist in the video who tends the children and the chickens in the shadows of other folks' contempt, Badu is the latter film's Celie, performing the reproductive labor of the Southern farmhouse. Yet, like Scarlet O'Hara, Badu dons an untraditional fabric of convenience—a tablecloth instead of curtains—and then transforms into *The Color Purple*'s Shug, transforming the farmhouse into a juke joint and singing for a gathered crowd. Badu's work reinserts black women, and implicitly queer black women, into a Jim Crow past and centers black people in a Southern past. Badu's work also ruminates on the future, but one that is more concretely concerned with what happens if equality is not achieved, and what this means for black people in general, but black women and their children specifically.

In the postsoul instantiation of Dirty South bohemia, neosoul and hip-hop artists revisit the sonic and visual aesthetics of the soul and blues eras to reflect on the past, think about the challenges of the present, and create new Southern black futures. The notion of the lounge, as marshaled by Artistik Approach for the Artistik Lounge, is a combination of previous juke joint and blues forms. Artistik Approach's fusion of jazz, bebop, scat, the spoken word, singing, and hip-hop reflects a commitment to erecting a transhistorical blues aesthetic for modern times. The call and response, black church signification, live reggae band, and rap ciphers are also mash-ups of black Southern cultures— American and global Souths—across time and space. This Dirty South bohemia, like its antecedents, exists between conservative black cultures and other descendants of the juke joint, like contemporary black clubs—including strip clubs. It also exists prominently in imagined spaces black Southerners create to produce alternative visions of the region, the nation, the future, and themselves.

Mapping Memphis's Dirty South Bohemia

There are four distinct but overlapping types of sites in Dirty South bohemia: (1) the historical juke joint, those clubs where "grown" black folks dance to blues and soul music and where working blues artists play; (2) black arts institutions, which are black-owned spaces for black-centered arts production; (3) temporary and/or recurring black spaces, locations that are traditionally white but transformed into black sites for a one-time or recurring event; and (4) virtual sites that chronicle the scene and also constitute an art location. As spaces for the production and promotion of art and culture, these sites make possible a black cultural economy that is largely separate from the dominant cultural economy.

There is no street, as it were, like Beale Street, that serves as the contemporary home for Dirty South bohemia. Urban renewal, desegregation, and black middle-class flight have shaped where black bohemian cultures can develop and survive in a still segregated city. Yet, Beale Street looms large as a historical black bohemia, and sites on the periphery of downtown and its adjacent neighborhoods have emerged as home spaces for a black neobohemia. In these venues black artists and black arts entrepreneurs have carved out spaces to host, work, create, and congregate. In the late 1990s, Precious Cargo, a café and artist space that was located just north of downtown in the Pinch District, became an institution that nurtured a host of black artists that later began their own arts enterprises. There were open microphone nights, hip-hop shows, Jamaican-style jerk chicken wings, black art, and an assortment of "alternative" black folks in and out of Precious Cargo's doors on any given night. After the shuttering of the original Stax Records and the comings and going of other black arts institutions,[9] for several years before it closed, Precious Cargo was the site of a renaissance of sorts for Dirty South bohemia in Memphis. It declared that physical, multipurpose black arts spaces were central to the maintenance of a black arts scene, and that such spaces should be the site of a black cultural economy that emphasized cooperation and artistic self-determination.

Just east of downtown lies the Edge District, home of Sun Studio and once lined with car dealerships from which the city's musicians, black and white, would purchase their customized rides. A buffer neighborhood between Downtown, Midtown, and the Medical District, the Edge District hosts a diverse set of black bohemian art cultures. Hip-hop shows are held in the Marshall Arts gallery, where breakdancers covered in body paint also come together in movement. The city's lesbian, gay, bisexual, and transgender club Spectrum attracts visitors across race. The city's black repertory theater, Hattiloo Theatre, got its start in a building in the Edge District. Today, Dizzy Bird Lounge, once the home of the Hattiloo's Children's Theatre, features soul, neosoul, and jazz acts in an intimate space.

East of the Edge District, inside the parkways that bisect the city from north to south and east to west, is Midtown, a collection of neighborhoods that serve as the city's metaphor for resistance to the traditional constraints and mores of Southern life. Traditional trappings of bohemia—coffee shops, art galleries, independent bookstores, antique and consignment haunts, historic homes, and walk-ups—coexist with the elements of gentrification, like organic gelato shops and olive oil stores, that have become fodder for jokes about millennial hipsterism. The Hattiloo Theatre, one of the city's longest-running black arts institutions, is now a part of Midtown's theater arts district, across the street from Playhouse on the Square and on the corner opposite the Circuit Playhouse. Midtown is also home to Madison Dance Studio at Minglewood Hall, where the Artistik Lounge is held; 1524, a black-owned event space that often hosts hip-hop and R&B shows; and Crosstown Arts, another event space in which visual artists, the city's all-black burlesque troupe, singers, and hip-hop artists are featured.

Midtown is flanked by Dirty South bohemian spaces. On its southwest edge is Soulsville, the historically black South Memphis neighborhood that singlehandedly produced some of the most influential artists of the twentieth century. Founded in 1982, four years after the original Stax Records closed, the Memphis Black Arts Alliance is the first full-time nonprofit cultural center of any kind in Tennessee. Located in a renovated fire station a few blocks from the original site of Stax, the alliance is the longest-running black arts institution in Memphis. South Memphis is also home to the Memphis Slim Collaboratory, or the Slim House, as artists call it. A collaboration space that supports professional musicians, the Slim House also hosts art exhibitions and hip-hop and R&B shows. South of Soulsville on Elvis Presley Boulevard is Java, Juice, and Jazz, the "Jewel of South Memphis," which hosts lectures, hip-hop and jazz performances, open microphone nights, and spoken-word artists.

On the northeast edge of Midtown, just outside of the parkways, is the Broad Avenue Arts District, a gentrifying neighborhood of warehouses bounded by an expressway on the south; Overton Park, which houses the Memphis Brooks Museum of Art and the Memphis College of Art, on the west; and a black neighborhood, Binghampton, on the north; and High Point Terrace, a white neighborhood, on the east. Among the galleries, boutiques, and makers' spaces in the Broad Avenue Arts District is Collage Dance Collective, a nonprofit that focuses on increasing marginalized groups access to classical ballet training and expanding diversity in classical ballet. There are also any number of private spaces in the Downtown and Midtown areas, and beyond the parkways on the periphery of Midtown where salons, collectives, and other collaborations and meetings of Dirty South bohemians frequently occur.

Beyond these physical places are the complementary virtual spaces in which Memphis's Dirty South bohemia unfolds. Neosoulville, a website founded by R&B singer Tonya Dyson, covers all aspects of the scene. Through the Neosoulville brand, Dyson hosts events like the annual Soulsville USA festival and the long-running weekly open mic event, the Word. Featuring a range of artistic expression from comedy to spoken word to hip-hop, the Word transforms its downtown space to the juke joint reimagined for a post-civil-rights moment, centering black Southern identities that were once squarely on the margins. Neosoulville, moreover, is an idea that attempts to capture the sentiments and experiences of a particular moment in black cultural production in Memphis, creating a definitive space that acknowledges a distinction between old and new, soul and postsoul.

These spaces—physical and virtual, in people's homes and in temporary places, concentrated in neighborhoods between Downtown, Midtown, and their respective peripheries—house Dirty South bohemia in Memphis. They make black cultural entrepreneurship possible as they facilitate black arts professionals and appreciation for creativity within black communities and beyond. Yet even as these spaces exist parallel with and sometimes next to and across the street from white spaces, the inequality between black arts communities and the dominant bohemia is evident in disparate access to funding, space, resources, and social capital. This continued inequality is particular evident in the music scenes, where hip-hop, the postsoul blues, is marginalized as generations of black youth it has come to reflect and symbolize.

Dirty South Bohemia and Neighborhood Change

Inequality across bohemian scenes is increasingly evident in the slippage between gentrification and bohemianism. Whereas cities with older bohemian scenes are more readily able to distinguish between artist gentrifiers and newer gentrifiers, gentrification occurs in tandem with the establishment of galleries, other arts spaces, and millennial recreation for the "creative class"— bars and adult play spaces like video game lounges. Two cases, one at the north end of Midtown and the other in South Memphis, exemplify how community development efforts, the expansion of the arts industry, and perceptions about arts consumers and young professionals shape and constrain Dirty South bohemia's access to sustaining resources.

At the north end of Midtown, renovations began in 2014 on the Sears Tower Crosstown, a behemoth building that was once the home of a Sears retail and distribution center that had been empty for nearly a quarter century. Its closure was correlated with the decline of several predominantly black North Memphis neighborhoods whose residents were employed by the distribution giant. Now, Crosstown has been reimagined as a mixed-used space that will house the Church Health Center, a health care facility that serves low-income populations, and studio and housing space for artists. While Dirty South bohemians have frequently used the Crosstown Arts space to host events, it is unclear how and if their vision for self-consciously Southern black art that is more permanently located will come to fruition as rents rise and the character of the neighborhood changes to reflect the sensibilities of young professionals.

In South Memphis, the Soulsville neighborhood is struggling to redefine itself as a destination art and living space for young artists and professionals. In 2015, Soulsville Town Center, a multiuse office building located across the street from the Stax Museum of American Soul Music that was supposed to help anchor the neighborhood, was sold at auction. In early conversations about the fate of the building, buyer and former filmmaker Tom Shadyac presented his ideas for the space: "a 'St. Jude–like' community center with space for counseling, classes, a rock-climbing wall and rental bikes, coffee shop with a sliding-pay scale restaurant, and—of course—a movie theater."[10] These conversations included few community members and none of the Dirty South bohemians who regularly use the Slim House across the street to work and thus might be among the new development's most frequent and long-standing patrons.

WHILE BLACK SOUTHERNERS have the remarkable capacity to imagine times, spaces, and places that fully incorporate their existence into histories of the region, and the region's art in particular, physically located space—especially in the long shadow of spatial segregation and racial inequality—is an increasing preoccupation of Dirty South bohemians looking to capture and ground a set of artistic moments. The shifting ownership, movement, and existence of black spaces and places, whether the closing of the original Stax Records or the coffee shop Precious Cargo, affects how and where black bohemians in Memphis can work and survive in the creative interstices of blackness and Southernness. Still, true to the legacy of the musicians, artists, and everyday people that protested mistreatment and advocated for their right to be and survive, Dirty South bohemians commit to the grit and grind.

Notes

1. Lloyd, *Neo-Bohemia*.
2. Florida, *The Rise of the Creative Class*.
3. Ocejo, *Upscaling Downtown*.
4. Stax's decline and closing was orchestrated by white elites intent on limiting African American economic mobility in post-civil rights Memphis. In December 1975, federal marshals seized the Stax Records building on McLemore and led label Executive Vice President Al Bell out by gunpoint. Financiers had called in a $100,000 loan, and Stax had been unable to pay. The label lost most of its masters, with the rights to the music now owned largely by California-based Concord Records.
5. Silver and Moeser, *The Separate City*.
6. Woods, *Development Arrested*, 17.
7. Robinson, *This Ain't Chicago*.
8. Oral historian E. Patrick Johnson uses the term "quare" to describe a distinctively black southern gay and lesbian experience, likening the difference between "quare" and "queer" to Alice Walker's distinction between "womanist" and "feminist."
9. These include the black bookstore Afrobooks, which was once housed in the Southland Mall in the middle-class black neighborhood of Whitehaven; the black repertory theater that preceded Hattiloo Theatre, the Memphis Black Repertory Theatre; and West African Artifacts, an import shop with furnishings and fabrics now reimagined as a restaurant and black arts space.
10. Faber, "ULI Panel Tackles Soulsville's Dilemma."

References

Faber, Madeline. "ULI Panel Tackles Soulsville's Dilemma as Shadyac Reveals Concept." *Memphis Daily News*, September 15, 2015. http://www.memphisdaily news.com/news/2015/sep/16/uli-panel-tackles-soulsvilles-dilemma-as-shadyac -reveals-concept/.

Florida, Richard. *The Rise of the Creative Class: And How Its Transforming Work, Leisure, Community and Everyday Life*. New York: Basic Books, 2002.

Lloyd, Richard. *Neo-Bohemia: Art and Commerce in the Post-Industrial City*. New York: Routledge, 2006.

Ocejo, Richard. *Upscaling Downtown: From Bowery Saloons to Cocktail Bars in New York City*. Princeton, NJ: Princeton University Press, 2014.

Johnson, E. Patrick. " 'Quare' Studies: Or, Almost Everything I Know About Queer Studies I Learned from My Grandmother." *Text and Performance Quarterly* 21 (1): 1–25, 2001.

Robinson, Zandria. *This Ain't Chicago: Race, Class, and Regional Identity in the Post-Soul South*. Chapel Hill: University of North Carolina Press, 2014.

Silver, Christopher, and John V. Moeser. *The Separate City: Black Communities in the Urban South, 1940–1968*. Lexington: University Press of Kentucky, 1995.

Woods, Clyde. *Development Arrested: The Blues and Plantation Power in the Mississippi Delta*. New York: Verso, 1998.

We Think a Lot

From Square to Hip in North Carolina's
Research Triangle

Alex Sayf Cummings

In 1961, a group of professors and businessmen met around a table for what was known as the Cultural Advancement Committee. Their task? To persuade top companies and scientists to come to Research Triangle Park (RTP), a high-tech district between Raleigh and Durham that was founded in 1959 as a center for scientific research. "Educated and cultured people are reluctant to leave large cities," North Carolina State University professor Howard G. Miller explained, "because of the great opportunities such cities offer for the theater and the arts, for education, and for the intellectual stimulation and excitement they provide." Universities in Raleigh, Durham, and Chapel Hill already attracted an inordinate number of smart people, he said, but North Carolina needed more: better facilities for the fine arts, ballet, chamber music, opera, and "all types of dramatic production."[1]

That was then. Today, the Research Triangle—the area bounded by the three cities, with RTP more or less at its center—is North Carolina's "Axis of Cool," as the *New York Times* put it in 2010.[2] While local leaders had once tried to lure scientists with highbrow cultural fare like ballet and opera, the area has since become better known for indie musicians like pop trio Ben Folds Five, country rockers Whiskeytown, and psychobilly veterans Southern Culture on the Skids. The Triangle gets good press for its coffee shops, food trucks, and craft breweries; *Forbes* and other publications frequently rank it among the best places in the United States for young professionals, and the economy in Raleigh and neighboring cities withstood recessions in the 1980s, 1990s, and early years of the new century with greater resilience than many other parts of the country. With a trendy image, respected universities, and big-name firms such as IBM and Quintiles, the Triangle has become a case study of what historian Margaret Pugh O'Mara has called a "city of knowledge"—a metropolitan economy devoted to science and technology, populated by highly educated workers.[3]

In fact, the promoters of RTP pioneered an approach to economic development that numerous communities around the world have copied since the

A sign in Durham, North Carolina. Photo by Alex Sayf Cummings.

research park's origin in the 1950s. By mobilizing the prestige and cultural capital of area universities, they lured jobs and investment from high-tech companies, painting a portrait of a metropolitan area with a climate of intellectual sophistication, abundant cultural opportunities, and a local population made up of smart workers and desirable neighbors.[4]

In recent years planners and scholars have championed the idea of the "creative city," arguing that urban areas can attract an educated, professional class of postindustrial workers by emphasizing local culture and an appealing quality of life. "There is a very strong track record of places that attract talent becoming places of long-term success," economist Edward Glaeser said in 2014. "The most successful economic development policy is to attract and retain smart people and then get out of their way."[5] Ann Markusen and Anne Gadwa have described this strategy as "creative placemaking," while urban theorist Richard Florida popularized the idea of a new category of knowledge workers in his 2002 study *The Rise of the Creative Class.*

Florida actually dismissed the Triangle in his influential book, saying that Raleigh-Durham lacked "the 'hip' urban lifestyle found in places like San Francisco, Seattle, New York, and Chicago."[6] Perhaps so; the Triangle has always been more suburban and car-centric than New York or San Francisco. But it's possible that Florida drew the lines of class and culture too narrowly. Whether bourgeois or bohemian, the appeal of culture remained at the center of the Research Triangle's development project from the late 1950s to the present day.

Its promoters realized they could attract better-paid and better-educated work-ers (and the firms that would employ them) by explicitly emphasizing the "creative" atmosphere of Raleigh, Durham, and Chapel Hill, and the value of living among university communities full of artists, intellectuals, and students.[7]

The Triangle, then, fits in an unusual place within the broader landscape of Southern intelligentsia. As a bastion of sprawling, postwar suburbia, it hardly aspired to become a bohemian grove, catering instead to the interests of cor-porate executives and chemists, computer scientists, and engineers—not the most left-leaning or subversive crowd. Yet much of RTP's sales pitch rested on the mystique of universities such as the University of North Carolina at Chapel Hill (UNC)—famously dubbed the "Capital of the Southern Mind" in the *New York Times*—which stood in sharp contrast to a South still broadly perceived as backward and provincial in the 1960s.[8] And in time the Triangle generated an arty, foodie, indie scene that ultimately helped it top the lists of places for young, "creative" types to live in the early twenty-first century.[9] Boosters may have originally sold RTP on the basis of opportunities for high culture, such as classical music and theater, but the area's regional identity in the twenty-first century was increasingly defined by the bohemian flair of its university communities.

Unlike Florida, *New York Times* pundit David Brooks never mentioned the Triangle in his seminal 2000 work *Bobos in Paradise,* but his idea of the "bour-geois bohemian" neatly captures the Triangle's combination of the square and the hip. In the 1970s, the sociologist Daniel Bell worried that a postindustrial society might falter if an emerging countercultural ethos clashed with the bourgeois values of hard work and self-restraint that had made capitalism successful, but Brooks recognized that the rebellious impulses of the artist could be reconciled with the instincts of high-achieving, middle-class profes-sionals.[10] Like the bobo, the Research Triangle itself symbolized an odd syn-thesis of bourgeois and bohemian, creative and corporate. And like other cities that have succeeded in attracting tech industries and educated workers, such as Austin and Denver, it relied on cultural amenities—whether high-brow or gutter punk—to sell itself to the world.[11]

A River in the Desert: Inventing the Triangle in the 1950s

The Research Triangle is, in essence, a slogan that became a city. Romeo Guest, an enterprising contractor from nearby Greensboro, coined the term in the early 1950s, tracing a line on the map from the University of North Car-olina at Chapel Hill to North Carolina State University in Raleigh and Duke

University in Durham.[12] Locals had not necessarily thought of the three cities as comprising a single metropolitan area, yet in the decades since Guest proposed using the universities as the anchors of a new high-tech economy, "the Triangle" became a place. There are Triangle breweries and Triangle pharmacies, Triangle yoga and cycling shops and even the modest GoTriangle transit system that runs bus lines between the area's cities and RTP.

Guest imagined RTP as "a challenge to the Charles River as the nation's research center," modeled on the cluster of scientific enterprises and universities that he had seen while studying at the Massachusetts Institute of Technology in Cambridge, Massachusetts.[13] His proposal ultimately led to the foundation of Research Triangle Park in 1959, a stretch of real estate between the three cities that was solely dedicated to laboratory research and eventually became the largest research park in the nation. But the venture would have gone nowhere without the unique intellectual heritage of the area's universities. (Other local institutions, such as North Carolina Central University, a historically black university in Durham, and Meredith College, a school for women in Raleigh, never really figured in the plans or sales pitches of RTP boosters, even if they did in fact add to the area's stock of students and faculty.)

The universities, especially UNC, had long contributed to North Carolina's reputation as an intellectual and cultural leader within the South—a place where criticism of the region's impoverished, racist social order was possible and nonconformists could flourish.[14] Frank Porter Graham led UNC as president in the 1930s and 1940s, attracting considerable scorn for his stances in favor of free speech and moderately integrationist views. He became a hero to liberals in the state during his tenure as university president, brief term as a U.S. senator, and historic loss to arch-segregationist Willis Smith in the 1950 Democratic Senate primary. Meanwhile, radical critics such as poet Langston Hughes, philosopher Bertrand Russell, and Socialist Party presidential candidate Norman Thomas visited Chapel Hill in the 1930s, incurring the wrath of conservatives throughout the Tar Heel State.[15] Industrialist and publisher David Clark notoriously inveighed against the university town's leftist streak in a 1940 address to the Charlotte Lions Club, decrying "a small group" of radical professors who were bent on indoctrinating young men into the twin evils of communism and atheism.[16]

This was the Chapel Hill of malcontents and rebels, an oasis of intellectual and political insurgency within an overwhelmingly conservative South. It was the home of the Intimate Bookshop, run by antimilitarist lefty Milton "Ab" Abernethy, where communist activist Junius Scales hung out before fleeing from the authorities and ultimately landing a six-year sentence for sedition in a federal penitentiary (for which he ultimately served fifteen months before the sentence was commuted by President John F. Kennedy). Not far away one found freethinkers such as Pan C. Athas, a Greek immigrant and entrepreneur who invited "stray professors" and other "curious townspeople" into his kitchen in neighboring Carrboro, regaling them with his views about John Dewey, Gottfried Wilhelm Leibniz, and donkeys during the Great Depression.[17]

UNC sociologist Howard Odum was the first to recommend taking advantage of the proximity of the universities in Raleigh and Chapel Hill. The professor proposed establishing "a research institute that would be in some ways apart from the university, and . . . a regional center of resource study and development at the consolidated level."[18] Some historians have treated Odum as the father of the Triangle, but his influence on the Research Triangle Park that would later come to be was indirect at best; Odum died in 1954, before the project took off.[19] The fruition of the RTP was made possible notably through the involvement of Odum's acolyte and former student, UNC sociologist George Simpson, who was picked to spearhead the Research Triangle Committee in 1956.[20]

In fact, the original impetus for RTP came from businessman Guest, whose firm built plants for industrial companies from the North. Guest realized in the early 1950s that North Carolina—at one point the leading manufacturing state in the South—was falling behind regional competitors such as Florida, Georgia, and Texas, which were attracting jobs and federal investment at the height of the Cold War.[21] He believed the Triangle's universities could serve as the basis for a more advanced economy in North Carolina, and he took his idea to Governor Luther Hodges, who had risen from humble origins in the textile mills to become an executive at Marshall Field and Company and, eventually, lieutenant governor. When Hodges took the reins of power in 1954, his signature issue was economic development. He embraced Guest's proposal with gusto the following year, gathering a coterie of leaders in business and academia to lay out a plan for bringing higher-wage jobs and scientific industry to North Carolina.[22]

George Simpson and his university colleagues began to travel the country trying to convince the likes of Pfizer, Texas Instruments, and Union Carbide to come to the Raleigh-Durham area, but they soon realized that prospective firms wanted more than the mere promise of proximity to the universities' libraries, equipment, and graduates. "There is great value in having something concrete, something that can be mapped and walked over, to place before people," Simpson noted in 1957. "Something tangible stimulates the imagination."[23] Henceforth, the idea of laying out a research park—a large tract of land strictly zoned so that only research, rather than industrial production, would be conducted there—took hold. Hodges turned to retired industrialist Karl Robbins, a Russian immigrant and New Yorker who had previously owned several North Carolina mills, to provide the funds to buy land for a for-profit venture, the Pinelands Company, that would lease lots to high-tech companies.[24]

The project seemed to be proceeding apace as planners quietly purchased land for the park between Raleigh and Durham in 1957, but they soon realized that tenants were not showing up in abundance. A 1958 pitch to potential investors in Charlotte fell flat, and a national recession dried up interest among businesses that might have relocated to the Triangle. A leading chemist at Union Carbide told Simpson that the Triangle's universities did not really impress outsiders that much, and the head of the American Textile Chemists and Colorists, a professional organization based in Lowell, Massachusetts, scoffed at the idea of moving to the backward South—even if most of the actual textile industry had already relocated there.[25]

Simpson began to ponder North Carolina's shortcomings when it came to recruiting advanced industries. "Our problem in North Carolina and in the South is not essentially technical," Simpson told a meeting of UNC faculty in February 1957. "Our problem is essentially cultural." He recalled visiting the nation's industrial heartland of the Northeast and Midwest, where people were surrounded by scientific research and technological advancement. "The young people of these regions are thus exposed, as they grow up, to this sort of environment," he said. "They see the values and uses of careers in science, in engineering; and so concentration in these areas begets concentration."[26] The South lacked the kind of intellectual milieu that gave rise to innovation—which is precisely what the Triangle had hoped to be.

Cultural Problem, Cultural Solution

Indeed, Simpson realized the need to focus attention squarely on the cultural and lifestyle advantages provided by the Triangle's universities in order to lure high-tech companies. Six months later, a visit from representatives from a major chemical firm gave a clue to this new direction: "The Cyanamid people have come and gone," he told a colleague. "They came for a general look. They were not interested in details but were anxious to get the general flavor and picture of the Triangle area. . . . On Friday we showed them around the Triangle, with emphasis on living conditions and that sort of thing."[27]

Boosters aimed to assure such visitors that the Triangle possessed a dynamic and inclusive cultural scene. The Research Triangle Committee had already taken an "inventory" of the cultural opportunities in Raleigh, Durham, and Chapel Hill, and subsequent literature heavily emphasized amenities such as the North Carolina Museum of Art, the North Carolina Symphony, and the National Grass Roots Opera Company in Raleigh. As one state pamphlet claimed, UNC was "an outstanding center of stagecraft and playwriting," thanks to its theater department and the Carolina Playmakers.[28]

Advertisements for RTP frequently boasted of the area's "research climate," though the desired target was almost always narrowly construed: white men in horn-rimmed glasses and starched collars.[29] "These are people who will be attracted to the area largely by the promise it offers of a life rich in intellectual and artistic pursuits and educational opportunities," Howard G. Miller told members of the Research Triangle Foundation's Cultural Advancement committee in 1961. He recommended highlighting the "free exchange of . . . ideas and people" in the Triangle, along with opportunities to attend concerts and lectures.[30]

The tastes and preferences of scientists were no minor consideration at the time. In the wake of the Soviet launch of *Sputnik* in 1957, the United States embarked on a major push into funding science, especially defense research, and corporate America soon found scientists and engineers in short supply. Companies considering a relocation or new laboratory had to think about whether they could successfully recruit qualified employees to a new site. "Research parks are notoriously slow starters," *Business Week* reflected a decade later. "Popular as they are with industry, some never get off the ground—partly because of poor location and lack of incentives to attract scientists."[31]

RTP's promoters argued that scientists and their families would be happy living in the Raleigh-Durham area, thanks in large part to the presence of a highly educated population. "The Research Triangle presents a most congenial environment in which scientists may live," Simpson told a conference of municipal leaders in 1957, "where they may associate with colleagues in the universities, where they may take part in activities of professional societies and where they may have the access to many cultural advantages."[32] The Triangle offered, according to one promotional piece, "a combination of the large, bustling metropolitan world and the quiet pools of life on the small scale—a locale eminently suited to the atmosphere of research." The universities made for a tolerant, open-minded community, which "for many years [had] accepted the scientist and the research worker on their own terms." The creative noncomformist, in other words, was welcome in the Triangle.[33]

When Chemstrand, a textile chemistry firm, decided to relocate from Decatur, Alabama in 1959, it extolled the same virtues to employees who were moving to the Triangle.[34] The company's relocation manual guaranteed that "colleges and universities in the Tar Heel State enrich cultural life by opening special exhibits, concerts, dramatic productions and forums to the public and by offering extension courses."[35] Chemstrand also supplied its employees with a pamphlet from the Raleigh Chamber of Commerce, which emphasized its Little Theatre, an "Art and Lecture series" at the city's various colleges, and the opportunity to hear opera and chamber music through local groups such as the Raleigh Civic Music Association.[36] Meanwhile, a brochure for Chapel Hill promised "liberal thinking and progress in a setting of Southern tradition and culture . . . small town living and cosmopolitan thinking."[37] The university community was "a town of individuals . . . of educated people where you can start school at kindergarten and finish with a Ph.D. without leaving the city limits."[38]

Corporate visitors seemed to accept the Triangle's self-presentation when they came to survey RTP as a potential site. "There is a well-developed cultural atmosphere with frequent musical performances, art exhibits, plays, originating from outside the community as well as from local groups," D. G. Crosby noted in his report to Union Carbide, which was considering opening a facility in the Triangle.[39] His colleague, J. Fellig, observed that "the cultural life of the area is very rich, probably in part because of the presence of the three universities."[40] Seven years later, when Tennessee-based textile firm Beaunit decided to build a research center in RTP, its president simply told reporters, "the colleges will help us attract scientists."[41]

In talking about the Triangle, boosters and outsiders alike were really talking about scientists. They spoke of a cultural climate, a "congenial atmosphere" where highly educated workers would be happy to live. Underlying such rhetoric was a whole set of assumptions about the arts, intellectuals, and science. For instance, scientists may not have been shaggy-haired subversives—like the politicians, businessmen, and university leaders who courted them, this was a buttoned-down group of white men—but the ambiance of being near a university still furnished cultural opportunities that affluent workers were thought to crave. And even if scientists favored typically white, bourgeois cultural forms such as opera and theater, Triangle planners thought of them as a slightly nonconformist lot for whom tolerance and individualism were key values.

Indeed, RTP sought to solve the state's "cultural problem" by using the arts and academia to allay the fears of businessmen, scientists, and their families about what they were getting into in North Carolina. Potential investors were concerned about matters of race and religion, as companies like IBM did not want to try to drag workers to a backward swamp of intolerance. Nearby academic institutions provided just enough cultural cover to make the Triangle look like a palatable destination for an educated, white-collar family. Such newcomers were most concerned about finding housing and good schools for their children. But, as W. B. Hamilton noted in 1966, the universities still played a critical role in selling the Triangle: "They [industrialists] inquire also about the availability of musical and dramatic performances and art galleries, and of professional company for their individualistic, well-paid scientists and other specialists. The state had obviously to encourage and support its universities—not harass them—and its other cultural assets."[42]

In the late 1950s and early 1960s, North Carolina leaders realized that the arts and education were assets. Scientists were not necessarily campus subversives, but they valued the currents of intellectual ferment that wafted through the redbrick buildings of Chapel Hill and the gothic facades of Duke. Hamilton even included a word of caution: the very rebellious tendencies on campus that sometimes upset the state's conservative leaders ought to be encouraged, not harassed—for the sake of economic development.

Still, RTP stumbled in its early days, never fully persuading outsiders that a tract of land between three modestly well-known universities in the South would be ripe for high-tech development. In the late 1950s and early 1960s, the park attracted only a few tenants, such as Chemstrand and the U.S. Forestry Service, while setting up its own Research Triangle Institute as a flagship project that would carry out contract research for government and industry.[43] But the events of 1964 and 1965 marked a watershed for both the park and the greater Triangle, as Governor Terry Sanford cashed in the political goodwill he won by endorsing John F. Kennedy for the Democratic nomination in 1960—a risky move in the conservative and still Catholic-phobic South— while Luther Hodges, who became secretary of commerce in the Kennedy administration, lobbied hard for the federal government to place an environmental health research laboratory in RTP.[44] When the new facility was announced, planning officer Lyle D. Prouse explained that the federal government valued access to labor in the form of graduates from the Triangle's universities, as well as opportunities for continuing education for employees. But "the critical criterion was the academic climate," Prouse told reporters.[45]

Soon after, IBM decided to place a large facility in RTP in 1965, moving away from its historic home base in the corridor between New York City and Poughkeepsie, New York. These moves gave RTP the imprimatur of approval from both the biggest of American corporations and the federal government, setting it on course to grow as a center of computing, pharmaceuticals, and biotechnology in the decades to come. Pharmaceutical giant Burroughs Well-come opted to move its headquarters from suburban Tuckahoe, New York, to RTP in 1969, and further successes mounted in the 1970s, as RTP won as the site for the American Academy of Arts and Sciences' new National Humanities Center, where scholars would scribble their thoughts in a gleaming, white, modernist structure amid the piney woods. Pharmaceutical company Glaxo followed in 1983.[46]

By the time of Glaxo's arrival, national and international media were heaping praise on RTP as the vanguard of a new economy. The Research Triangle was among America's "cities on the rise," combining the benefits of easy suburban living and warm Southern climes with the jobs of the future. "What could be more characteristic of today's 'information age' than a city whose basic industry is ideas?" the *Christian Science Monitor*'s Ruth Walker enthused in 1982. In her haste, Walker treated two intriguing assumptions as established fact: that the various municipalities of the Triangle did, in fact, make up a single city, and that "ideas" were actually an industry.[47]

The image of a progressive and successful metropolis full of smart people had been sealed. In 1962, Raleigh-Durham did not even rank nationally among the urban areas with the most holders of doctoral degrees per capita. Twenty years later, locals loved to brag that the Triangle had the greatest concentration of PhDs in the country, surpassing even brainy Boston—the university-heavy metro area that Guest and his allies had originally aspired to emulate.[48]

Becoming Bohemian

The 1983 sci-fi film *Brainstorm* offers a curious historical artifact of the Triangle's triumph as a postindustrial idyll. Shot in Raleigh and RTP, the film stars Christopher Walken as brilliant scientist Michael Brace, who works in the iconic, honeycomb-like building that Burroughs Wellcome built as its headquarters in 1972, based on a design by modernist architect Paul Rudolph. After work, Brace commutes by recumbent bike, riding through a leafy, green landscape of biotech companies to the eccentric, Frank Lloyd Wright–inspired home that he shares with his wife Karen (Natalie Wood).

In classic 1980s movie fashion, the scientists soon learn that the military-industrial complex wants to use their inventions for nefarious purposes, but the film is less interesting for its plot than for its portrayal of RTP as a high-tech workplace. Brace and his coworkers are a quirky bunch, including a chain-smoking, straight-talking scientist memorably played by screen veteran Louise Fletcher. They cut up at work and wear casual, even shabby clothes;

Fletcher's character is an older woman who seems to have eschewed marriage and kids—in short, they are the sort of unconventional, creative types who dream up great innovations in places like RTP. *Brainstorm's* depiction of a green, serene space for tech workers represented a fulfillment of RTP's original vision: a Southern paradise of the smart.

By the early 1980s that dream looked real enough. The Raleigh-Durham metro area's population grew by 23.4 percent between 1970 and 1980, and Governor Jim Hunt, a moderate Democrat who took office in 1977, committed the state to nurturing new industries with initiatives like the North Carolina Biotechnology Center, founded in RTP in 1984.[49] The Triangle promised "graceful living," according to the Research Triangle Foundation, combining "the cultural academic atmosphere with small town living and cosmopolitan thinking."[50] North Carolina's cultural bona fides were proven by the fact that it boasted "the first state university . . . the first state-supported symphony . . . the first state museum of art . . . [and was] the first state to establish, with public funds, a school for the performing arts."[51]

RTP may have succeeded in selling its image as a prime spot for high-tech firms, but not everyone was convinced. When historian Peter Coclanis, a postdoctoral fellow at Columbia University, was planning to visit UNC for a job talk in the early 1980s, a faculty member—a lifelong, inveterate New Yorker—joked about what he was getting himself into: "You could spend a night in Chapel Hill," the professor said. "Maybe a weekend, but you could never live there." (Coclanis, in fact, came to UNC to stay, becoming a distinguished professor of history and director of the Global Research Institute.)[52]

The Triangle's universities still sat somewhat uneasily in their conservative environs. As journalist Peter Range reported in 1972, Chapel Hill's more pious locals mostly "maintain[ed] a friendly respect for all of the hairy, booktoting atheists in their midst, and the intellectual community has less arrogant scorn for its non-academic, more fundamentalist neighbors than any assemblage of eggheads east of the Iowa Writers Workshop."[53] Novelist James Reston Jr., who taught creative writing at UNC, reinforced the Triangle's image as a hospitable place for artists and intellectuals: Chapel Hill offered "the right combination of things, if I'm going to write fiction. I have to have the country to walk. Yet I have to be involved with people intellectually." The village's literati could descend on the Carolina Coffee Shop for a beer, though North Carolina law still forbade the sale of liquor by the drink, making cocktails impossible—a legacy of the state's conservative heritage that many middle-class newcomers in the 1970s particularly loathed.[54]

Meanwhile, RTP began to attract a more diverse workforce in the 1970s and 1980s, but reminders of the state's less inclusive past lingered. Though Asian American scientists and engineers moved to work in RTP, the Triangle's demographics remained overwhelmingly black and white as late as the 1990s. (By 2000, Asian Americans still made up only 2 percent of the metro area's population—less than the national average at the time.)[55] The 1989 murder of Chinese immigrant Jim Loo outside a Raleigh bar sparked national attention, particularly since his assailants (who thought he was Vietnamese) heaped racist invective on the victim as they brutally attacked him. The incident underlined the dangers of racial exclusion in a South still not far removed from Jim Crow, although bigots lashed out with similar anti-Asian attacks around the same time in places such as Michigan and New Jersey.[56]

Newcomers also faced other, more prosaic problems. Smita Patel, for instance, moved to the Triangle with her husband, an engineer at Sperry Rand, in 1981, and found a local culinary landscape that was sorely lacking in ethnic cuisine. "You were lucky to find cilantro, you know," she recalled. The Triangle eventually developed several enclaves of South Asian culture, such as the affluent suburb of Cary's Chatham Square, but in the early 1980s such options were far more limited. Patel remembers having spices and other ingredients mailed to her by a brother-in-law who lived in New Jersey.[57]

Patel was not alone in feeling that the Triangle remained somewhat provincial despite its booming economy and oft-repeated claims to cosmopolitanism. When music writer Fred Mills came to Chapel Hill in 1973, he discovered that the local music scene was dominated by singer-songwriters and Southern rock. "If you rocked makeup or stack heels to prove your allegiance to a glam hard rock band you'd have a frat brother tie you up in duct tape and roll you around naked at the Saturday night kegger," Mills, editor of Raleigh-based *Blurt* magazine, remembers.[58] As late as the 1980s, when the musician Laura Ballance moved from Atlanta to Raleigh as a teen, she recalls being "hassled a lot more for the way I looked." "She looked like a goth superhero," high school friend and fellow musician Claire Ashby recalled. "She seemed very exotic, being from the big city of Atlanta, since Raleigh was akin to Mayberry at the time."[59] Ballance soon discovered the area's small but tight-knit music scenes: "Raleigh and Chapel Hill are just a short drive apart, but they had very different scenes. Raleigh was dark, angry, and punk—more leather jackets and houses with spray paint on the walls. Chapel Hill was collegiate and hip."[60] Ballance enrolled at UNC to study anthropology and, before long, attained notoriety by cofounding (with Mac McCaughan) the band Superchunk and the celebrated Chapel Hill indie label Merge Records.

Indeed, the Triangle gradually earned a reputation as a center of the arts and independent music. The Cat's Cradle launched as a destination for live music on Chapel Hill's Rosemary Street in 1969, and evolved to become one of North Carolina's premier destinations for independent music before moving to neighboring Carrboro in the 1990s. Punk acts such as Raleigh's th'Cigaretz emerged in the late 1970s, and the following decade saw a thriving music scene coalesce as such bands as Corrosion of Conformity and Southern Culture on the Skids attained a degree of national notoriety. (Th'Cigaretz, Corrosion of Conformity, Southern Culture on the Skids—each name implies a certain skewering of the state's dominant culture.) The subsequent mainstream success of piano-pop trio Ben Folds Five, neo-swing band Squirrel Nut Zippers, and other local artists in the 1990s brought renewed attention to the Triangle—and Chapel Hill in particular.[61]

Indeed, a mania for alternative music gripped the music industry during that decade, as A&R reps went hunting for the "next Seattle" in every nook and cranny from Omaha to Louisville. "We're seeing a minor renaissance of bohemianism," Grant Kornberg, proprietor of the Hardback Cafe and Bookstore in Chapel Hill told the *New York Times* in 1990. "We're selling a lot of poetry by guys who died before most of these kids were born.'"[62] Greg Feller, a Duke English major and member of the band Talking of Michelangelo, said at the time that "some people automatically hate campus culture and want the opposite of the mainstream. But the true bohemian really does not care what other people think and appreciates a little of everything." For Feller, being a bohemian meant art and music as well as environmentalism and bicycling—interests that continued to define hipster culture in the twenty-first century.[63]

As the media descended on the Triangle, Merge Records garnered considerable national coverage and soon became a major institution in Chapel Hill—despite never quite cashing in on the alternative buzz of the early 1990s. The "indie label that got big and stayed small" was home not just to local bands but also New York's Magnetic Fields and Montreal's Arcade Fire, one of the most popular and acclaimed rock acts of the early twenty-first century. Like his collaborator Ballance, cofounder Mac McCaughan had migrated to the area as a child when his father, a lawyer, came to work at Duke University.[64] McCaughan's and Ballance's families were part of a large-scale migration to the Triangle, as RTP and the universities attracted workers from around the United States and the world, eventually resulting in a local population that was more affluent, diverse, and educated than when RTP launched in 1959. Census numbers show that much migration was "internal," so to speak; many came to the Triangle from other North Carolina counties such as Mecklenburg (Charlotte), or, like Ballance, from elsewhere in the South. But many others hailed from the nation's largest urban areas, such as Chicago, Los Angeles, New York, and the suburbs of Washington, DC.[65]

In short, the Triangle started out bourgeois and became bohemian—at least, up to a point. In the 1960s boosters stressed the area's opportunities for high culture, such as fine art, theater, and classical music, in order to woo straitlaced scientists and corporate managers—an effort, no doubt, to dispel perceptions of the South's cultural backwardness. Gradually both the universities and RTP itself attracted new residents who contributed to the efflorescence of a hip, creative local culture by the end of the twentieth century. Durham, in particular, witnessed a considerable revival, reversing economic struggles that had plagued the city with the long-term decline of the tobacco industry and bitter conflicts over school desegregation in the 1970s. Under the stewardship of Mayor William "Bill" Bell—an engineer who had come to the Triangle in 1968 to work at IBM—Durham saw its downtown revitalize in the early years of the twenty-first century as tapas places and whiskey bars sprouted in formerly abandoned and derelict areas and the city was increasingly noted as a go-to destination for young professionals and hipsters. Meanwhile, Raleigh earned praise for its strong public school system and dynamic economy. Generous coverage of food trucks, restaurants, and breweries followed in the national media.[66]

The border between bourgeois and bohemian, it turns out, is more porous than often thought, as David Brooks reminded us in 2000. The scientist who spun Puccini on his hi-fi system in 1961 might favor thrash metal or dubstep today. Tastes change, but the importance of catering to the interests of affluent workers remains. If anything, it is more important than ever, as cities everywhere bid to attract jobs, investment, and the fickle members of the group now known as the "creative class." Raleigh and Durham succeeded in luring "young professionals back to the cities with redevelopment of old warehouses, mixed-use developments, and a revitalized arts, culture, and restaurant scene," David Kroll, a pharmacologist and medical writer in Durham, enthused in 2014. The Triangle offered up "tees, trees, and PhDs," thanks to its educated populace and excellent golfing weather.[67]

Golf may be far from bohemian, like much of the Triangle, but the key is Kroll's focus on appealing to an educated demographic, just as it had been for RTP from the beginning. Indeed, the Triangle's boosters perennially hyped arts and recreational opportunities that were at least implicitly coded as white—from "bohemian" cafés to classical music to indie rock—paying little attention to black arts, music, and cultural and educational institutions that had long thrived in Raleigh and Durham. Bohemianism was a lifestyle amenity that the privileged could sample à la carte. As Brian Holmes wrote in a critical essay about RTP in 2007, "What's striking is that here in the South, in cities like Durham or Raleigh with historically important black communities, everything that looks the slightest bit monumental tends toward an increasingly pure, clinical white . . . [gentrifying downtown Durham] conforms in every way to Richard Florida's descriptions of successful urban theme parks for the creative class, combining luxurious consumption environments with chic professional interiors, everywhere marked by the presence of art and design."[68] Holmes saw the Triangle for what it was: a highly effective strategy to appeal to a privileged (and, at least initially, white) workforce. Similarly, geographers David Havlick and Scott Kirsch described RTP in 2004 as a "production utopia" for knowledge workers, where the life of the mind reigned and traces of manual labor were either invisible or erased.[69]

Journalist Bill Bishop was among the first to notice the pattern of people clustering in such utopias, arguing in his 2004 book *The Big Sort* that Americans in recent decades have increasingly chosen to live near people like themselves, who share their cultural predilections—whether those run toward the conservative and traditionalist or the edgy and alternative. The promoters of the Research Triangle anticipated these very trends, explicitly arguing that scientists and their families would like living among other educated people.[70] By 2009 the *New York Times* reported adoringly of a land of biscuits and boutiques, "buzz-worthy bands," and "outdoor art," later raving about the area's "design collectives and rehabbed downtowns," where 150,000 college students attend school and a former vegan can be found roasting (presumably organic) hogs. The Triangle was much like Los Angeles's famous hipster enclave of Silver Lake, only "with a few more 'yes ma'ams.'"[71]

Are food trucks bourgeois or bohemian? What about indie bands and vegan biscuits? The Triangle offers a textbook study of the collapse of cultural distinctions and types in the late twentieth century—highbrow and lowbrow, mainstream and counterculture. A chemist who came to Durham in 1963 might not have dabbled much in things beatnik and bohemian, but he liked to think of himself as open-minded and tolerant. Meanwhile, the students and professors of nearby universities likely skewed more to the political left and counterculture than the man in horn-rimmed glasses and lab coat at Chemstrand. But the bohemian and the bourgeois always overlapped—a little at first, and more and more over time. Shifting attitudes toward high and low culture undoubtedly played a role, as critic Thomas Frank so trenchantly explained in 1997's *The Conquest of Cool*. By the 1990s, being sophisticated and upper-middle-class no longer necessarily required a nose for Berlioz, as boomers in corporate boardrooms across the country embraced the spirit and style, if not the substance, of rock music and countercultural rebellion. Meanwhile, commonalities of race and class made it easy for journalists and boosters to collapse all the Triangle's educated people—scientists, students, professors, even corporate managers—into one category, which Florida famously dubbed the creative class. They were (mostly) white, they were smart, and they liked the arts.[72]

By the early twentieth-first century, the line between bohemian and bourgeois hardly seemed to matter as much as it did in the age of Dobie Gillis and Maynard G. Krebs. Indeed, a wag with an offbeat sense of humor captured the Triangle's essence better than most other scholars and critics when he scrawled a message on a sign near the entrance to Research Triangle Park—WE THINK A LOT—a seeming nod to the 1985 hit "We Care a Lot" by alternative rock band Faith No More. Whether we call the denizens of the Triangle bourgeois or bohemian matters less than what they have in common: they all think a lot.

Notes

1. Miller, untitled manuscript, 1.

2. Goode, "36 Hours"; Heyman, "Raleigh-Durham."

3. Carlyle, "America's 15 Best Cities"; Gallagher, "Durham Named No. 2 Brainiest City"; O'Mara, *Cities of Knowledge*.

4. See Bowditch, "Leadership, Partnerships, and Networks."

5. Edward Glaeser, quoted in Miller, "Where Young College Graduates Are Choosing to Live."

6. Florida, *The Rise of the Creative Class*, 284–85.

7. See Landry and Bianchini, *The Creative City*; Markusen and Gadwa, *Creative Placemaking*; and Florida, *The Rise of the Creative Class*.

8. Range, "Capital of the Southern Mind."

9. Rohe, *The Research Triangle*, 97–98.

10. In his insightful study of Chicago's Wicker Park, sociologist Richard Lloyd linked this reconciliation to a new form of "flexible capitalism" that demands ever greater creativity and dynamism from professional workers. Lloyd, *Neo-Bohemia*, 71, 240. See also Brooks, *Bobos in Paradise*, 31–48; and Bell, *The Coming of Post-Industrial Society*, 478–80.

11. As self-described "social systems architect and entrepreneur" Tory Gattis puts it, cities like Austin, Denver, and Portland have succeeded in attracting residents and investment because "people today want the amenities, diverse culture, and career opportunities

of a big city with the heart of a smaller community." Gattis, "Houston Branding Identity Week."

12. Link, *A Generosity of Spirit*, 14–15.

13. Newell to Kramer (letter), 2.

14. As historian Hurewitz puts it in his study of artistic communities in Los Angeles, such bohemias were "thirdspaces . . . the place within the bourgeois social structure from which that new order could be critiqued." Hurewitz, *Bohemian Los Angeles*, 13.

15. Snider, *Light on the Hill*, 107.

16. Clark, "Speech, 'Communism and Socialism at Chapel Hill.'"

17. Scales and Nickson, *Cause at Heart*, 11–12.

18. Simpson, "The Research Triangle of North Carolina," 2.

19. Link, *A Generosity of Spirit*, 5.

20. Ibid., 31.

21. Deane, "Complex Factors"; "North Carolina: An Economic Profile," 2–4.

22. Rohe, *The Research Triangle*, 64–66.

23. George L. Simpson, quoted in Rohe, *The Research Triangle*, 67; see also Simpson to Hanes (letter), 1.

24. The project was converted into the Research Triangle Foundation when Simpson and others realized that it would fare better if it were not under pressure to turn a profit, and supporters raised donations from industrialists and other supporters throughout the state to buy out Robbins's stock. Rohe, *The Research Triangle*, 64–69.

25. Simpson to Luther Hodges (letter), 1; Clark, *Dyeing for a Living*, 110, 130.

26. Simpson, "The Research Triangle of North Carolina," 12; see also the discussion of this speech in Link, *A Generosity of Spirit*, 5.

27. Simpson to Brandon Hodges (letter), 1.

28. *Inventory of Selected Resources of the Research Triangle*, 3–13; North Carolina Department of Conservation and Development, *Living . . . North Carolina*, 11.

29. Campbell, "Modern Science Leads Industrial Development."

30. Miller, untitled manuscript, 1.

31. "Research Park Thrives in Academic Neighborhood," 1.

32. Simpson, "Research Development and Water Resources," 5.

33. *A Pervading Atmosphere of Inquiry and Research*, 1; *The Research Triangle Park of North Carolina*, 8.

34. "Real Estate Notes."

35. North Carolina Department of Conservation and Development, *Living . . . North Carolina*, 11.

36. Raleigh Chamber of Commerce, *Welcome to Raleigh*, 7.

37. Chapel Hill–Carrboro Merchants Association and Chamber of Commerce, Chapel Hill map and pamphlet. Research Triangle Foundation Papers, Southern Historical Collection, University of North Carolina at Chapel Hill, Box 9, Folder 93.

38. *Chapel Hill: The Place to LIVE*. Research Triangle Foundation Papers, Southern Historical Collection, University of North Carolina at Chapel Hill, Box 9, Folder 93.

39. D. G. Crosby, "The 'Research Triangle' of North Carolina," 3. Research Triangle Foundation Papers, Southern Historical Collection, University of North Carolina at Chapel Hill, Folder 4. July 21, 1958.

40. Fellig, "Research Department Trip Report," 2. Research Triangle Foundation Papers, Southern Historical Collection, University of North Carolina at Chapel Hill, Folder 4, Research Triangle Committee, Inc.: General, 1956–1958. July 25, 1958.

41. Hamilton, "The Research Triangle of North Carolina," 276.

42. Ibid., 278.

43. Freeman, "New Commerce Chief Pledges Research Step-Up."

44. Rohe, *The Research Triangle*, 72–73.

45. "Research Park Thrives in Academic Neighborhood," 2.

46. "Glaxo Subsidiary Gets New President."

47. Walker, "A North Carolina Renaissance Built on 'Idea' Industries," B8.

48. Cobb, *The Selling of the South*, 175; "Sites for Science," 16.

49. Rohe, *The Research Triangle*, 94, 146.

50. *A Dynamic Concept for Research*.

51. Ibid.

52. Peter Coclanis, e-mail correspondence with author, January 27, 2015.

53. Range, " 'Capital of the Southern Mind.' "

54. Ibid.; "Liquor by Drink Returns to N.C."; Crowell, *A History of Liquor-by-the-Drink Legislation*.

55. Rohe, *The Research Triangle*, 107.

56. U.S. Commission on Civil Rights, *Civil Rights Issues Facing Asian Americans in the 1990s*, 25–31.

57. Smita Patel, phone interview with the author, May 5, 2014, Durham, North Carolina; Brennin Cummings, "Chatham Square."

58. Fred Mills, e-mail correspondence with the author, February 6, 2014.

59. Cook, *Our Noise*, 1–2; Howe, "Superchunk Bassist."

60. Cook, *Our Noise*, 2.

61. Hicks, "How North Carolina Got Its Punk Attitude." For insight into the 1990s Triangle music scene, see Menconi, *Ryan Adams: Losering*.

62. Slade, "Campus Cafes."

63. Ibid.

64. Cook, *Our Noise*, 1.

65. Rohe, *The Research Triangle*, 106.

66. Grant, *Hope and Despair in the American City*, 91–108.

67. Kroll, "7 Reasons It's Finally Time to Live in Research Triangle Park."

68. Holmes, "Disconnecting the Dots."

69. Havlick and Kirsch, "A Production Utopia?," 269.

70. Bishop, *The Big Sort*.

71. Goode, "36 Hours"; Heyman, "Raleigh-Durham."

72. Frank, *The Conquest of Cool*; for a classic study of cultural hierarchies, see Gans, *High Culture and Popular Culture*.

References

Athas, Daphne. *Chapel Hill in Plain Sight: Notes from the Other Side of the Tracks*. Hillsborough, NC: Eno, 2010.

Bell, Daniel. *The Coming of Post-Industrial Society: A Venture in Social Forecasting*. New York: Basic Books, 1973.

Bishop, Bill. *The Big Sort: Why the Clustering of Like-Minded America Is Tearing Us Apart*. New York: Houghton-Mifflin, 2008.

Bowditch, Nathaniel. "Leadership, Partnerships, and Networks: Navigating 50 years of Dynamic Growth in the Research Triangle Park." Paper presented at the Twenty-Sixth International Association of Science Parks World Conference on Science and Technology Parks, June 1–4, 2009, Raleigh, North Carolina. https://www.rti.org/pubs/iaspo9_123-rti_bowditch.pdf.

Brooks, David. *Bobos in Paradise: The New Upper Class and How They Got There*. New York: Simon and Schuster, 2000.

Campbell, Robert F. "Modern Science Leads Industrial Development." *New York Times*, November 17, 1957.

Carlyle, Erin. "America's 15 Best Cities for Young Professionals." *Forbes*, August 18, 2014. http://www.forbes.com/sites/erincarlyle/2014/08/18/americas-15-best-cities-for-young-professionals/.

Clark, David. "Speech, 'Communism and Socialism at Chapel Hill,' delivered by David Clark before the Charlotte (N.C.) Lion's Club." University of North Carolina Libraries. http://exhibits.lib.unc.edu/items/show/163.

Clark, Mark. *Dyeing for a Living: A History of the American Association of Textile Chemists and Colorists: 1921–1996*. Research Triangle Park, NC: American Association of Textile Chemists and Colorists, 2001.

Cobb, James. *The Selling of the South: The Southern Crusade for Industrial Development, 1936–1990*. Urbana: University of Illinois Press, 1993.

Cook, John, with Mac McCaughan and Laura Ballance. *Our Noise: The Story of Merge Records, the Indie Label that Got Big and Stayed Small*. Chapel Hill, NC: Algonquin, 2009.

Crowell, Michael. *A History of Liquor-by-the-Drink Legislation in North Carolina*. Campbell Law Review 1, no. 1 (1979): 61–110.

Cummings, Brennin. "Chatham Square: Cary's Gateway to the World." *Cary Citizen*, May 31, 2011. http://carycitizen.com/2011/05/31/chatham-square-carys-gateway-to-the-world/.

Deane, C. B. "Complex Factors Enter into State's Low Wage Pattern; Lack of Education Is Sharply to Fore." *Greensboro Daily News*, August 14, 1955. Romeo Guest Papers, Duke University, Durham, NC, Box 10, Newspaper Clippings 1956, 2 of 2.

A Dynamic Concept for Research: The Research Triangle Park of North Carolina. 1981. Durham County Public Library, Research Triangle Park subject file.

Florida, Richard. *The Rise of the Creative Class: And How It's Transforming Work, Leisure, Community and Everyday Life*. New York: Basic Books, 2002.

Frank, Thomas. *The Conquest of Cool: Business Culture, Counterculture, and the Rise of Hip Consumerism*. Chicago: University of Chicago Press, 1997.

Freeman, William M. "New Commerce Chief Pledges Research Step-Up." *New York Times*, February 2, 1961.

Gallagher, James. "Durham Named No. 2 Brainiest City; Raleigh-Cary Ranked 12th." *Triangle Business Journal*, August 30, 2010. http://www.bizjournals.com/triangle /stories/2010/08/30/daily6.html.

Gans, Herbert. *High Culture and Popular Culture: An Analysis and Evaluation of Taste*. New York: Basic Books, 1974.

Gattis, Tory. "Houston Branding Identity Week: History and Strategy." *Houston Strategies*, July 25, 2006. http://houstonstrategies.blogspot.com/2006/07/houston -branding-identity-week-history.html.

"Glaxo Subsidiary Gets New President." *New York Times*, September 5, 1986.

Goode, J. J. "36 Hours: Research Triangle, N.C.," *New York Times*, July 14, 2009.

Grant, Gerald. *Hope and Despair in the American City: Why There Are No Bad Schools in Raleigh*. Cambridge: Harvard University Press, 2009.

Gregory, Raymond F. *Norman Thomas: The Great Dissenter*. New York: Algora, 2008.

Hamilton, W. B. "The Research Triangle of North Carolina: A Study in Leadership for the Common Weal." *South Atlantic Quarterly*, n.d. Durham County Public Library, Research Triangle Park subject file.

Havlick, David, and Scott Kirsch. "A Production Utopia? RTP and the North Carolina Research Triangle." *Southeastern Geographer* 44 (2004): 269.

Heyman, Stephen. "Raleigh-Durham: North Carolina's Axis of Cool." *New York Times*, November 19, 2010. http://www.nytimes.com/interactive/2010/11/19/t -magazine/21remix-scene.html?_r=0.

Hicks, Sam. "How North Carolina Got Its Punk Attitude, Part Two." *Perfect Sound Forever*, March 1998. http://www.furious.com/perfect/nc-punk2.html.

Holmes, Brian. "Disconnecting the Dots in the Research Triangle." *Deriva Continental*, February 26, 2007. https://brianholmes.wordpress.com/2007/02/26 /disconnecting-the-dots-of-the-research-triangle/.

Howe, Brian. "Superchunk Bassist and Merge Co-Founder Laura Ballance Bows Out of Touring, Not Out of the Music that Empowered Her." *Indy Week*, August 21, 2013. http://www.indyweek.com/indyweek/superchunk-bassist-and-merge-co -founder-laura-ballance-bows-out-of-touring-not-out-of-the-music-that -empowered-her/Content?oid=3700553.

Hurewitz, Daniel. *Bohemian Los Angeles and the Making of Modern Politics*. Berkeley: University of California Press, 2007.

Inventory of Selected Resources of the Research Triangle. Research Triangle Foundation Papers, Southern Historical Collection, University of North Carolina at Chapel

Hill, Folder 2, Research Triangle Development Council: Working Committee, 1955: December.

Kroll, David. "7 Reasons It's Finally Time to Live in Research Triangle Park." *Forbes*, February 4, 2014. http://www.forbes.com/sites/davidkroll/2014/02/04/7-reasons -its-finally-time-to-live-in-research-triangle-park/.

Landry, Charles, and Franco Bianchini. *The Creative City*. London: Demos, 1995.

Link, Albert N. *A Generosity of Spirit: The Early History of the Research Triangle Park*. Research Triangle Park, NC: Research Triangle Foundation, 1995.

"Liquor by Drink Returns to N.C. After 70-Year Ban." *Spartanburg Herald*, November 22, 1978.

Lloyd, Richard. *Neo-Bohemia: Art and Commerce in the Postindustrial City*. New York: Routledge, 2006.

Markusen, Ann, and Anne Gadwa. *Creative Placemaking*. Washington, DC: National Endowment for the Arts, 2010.

Menconi, David. *Ryan Adams: Losering, a Story of Whiskeytown*. Austin: University of Texas Press, 2012.

Newell, William A. to Kenneth Kramer, June 3, 1955. Letter. Romeo Guest Papers, Duke University, Durham, NC, Box 10, Research Triangle Correspondence 1955.

Miller, Claire Cain. "Where Young College Graduates Are Choosing to Live." *New York Times*, October 20, 2014.

Miller, Howard G. Untitled manuscript, ca. March 29, 1961. Research Triangle Foundation Papers, Southern Historical Collection, University of North Carolina at Chapel Hill, Box 25, Folder 375, Cultural Advancement, 1961.

"North Carolina: An Economic Profile." *Monthly Review of the Federal Reserve Bank of Richmond*, November 1962. https://fraser.stlouisfed.org/files/docs/publications /frbrichreview/rev_frbrich196211.pdf.

North Carolina Department of Conservation and Development. *Living . . . North Carolina*. Ca. 1959. Research Triangle Foundation Papers, Southern Historical Collection, University of North Carolina at Chapel Hill, Box 9, Folder 93, Chemstrand Research Center, Employee Relocation Manual, 1959.

O'Mara, Margaret Pugh. *Cities of Knowledge: Cold War Science and the Search for the Next Silicon Valley*. Princeton, NJ: Princeton University Press, 2004.

A Pervading Atmosphere of Inquiry and Research . . . N.d. Durham County Public Library, Research Triangle Park subject file.

Raleigh Chamber of Commerce. *Welcome to Raleigh, North Carolina: The Center of Activity in the South's No. 1 State*. Research Triangle Foundation Papers, Southern Historical Collection, University of North Carolina at Chapel Hill, Box 9, Folder 93.

Range, Peter. " 'Capital of the Southern Mind.' " *New York Times*, December 17, 1972.

"Real Estate Notes." *New York Times*, July 21, 1959.

"Research Park Thrives in Academic Neighborhood." *Business Week*, December 10, 1966. Durham County Public Library, Research Triangle Park subject file.

The Research Triangle Park of North Carolina. 1973. Durham County Public Library, Research Triangle Park subject file.

Rohe, William. *The Research Triangle: From Tobacco Road to Global Prominence.*
   Philadelphia: University of Pennsylvania Press, 2011.
Scales, Junius Irving, and Richard Nickson. *Cause at Heart: A Former Communist
   Remembers.* Athens: University of Georgia Press, 1987.
Simpson, George L. "Research Development and Water Resources: Speech before
   the Sixth Southern Municipal and Industrial Waste Conference." April 2, 1957.
   Research Triangle Foundation Papers, Southern Historical Collection, University
   of North Carolina at Chapel Hill, Folders 1–17.
———. "The Research Triangle of North Carolina." February 5, 1957. Research
   Triangle Foundation Papers, Southern Historical Collection, University of North
   Carolina at Chapel Hill, Folder 4, Research Triangle Committee, Inc.: General,
   1956–1958.
Simpson, George L., to Robert Hanes, February 26, 1957. Letter. Romeo Guest Papers,
   Duke University, Durham, NC, Box 11, Governor Hodges' Archival Papers 1955–1957.
Simpson, George L., to Brandon Hodges, August 26, 1957. Letter. Research Triangle
   Foundation Papers, Southern Historical Collection, University of North Carolina
   at Chapel Hill, Folder 4, Research Triangle Committee, Inc.: General, 1956–1958.
Simpson, George L., to Luther Hodges, November 6, 1956. Romeo Guest Papers, Duke
   University, Durham, NC, Box 11, Governor Hodges' Archival Papers 1955–1957.
"Sites for Science." *Industrial Development,* August 1962, 16.
Slade, Margot. "Campus Cafes Attract 'Neo-Beatniks.'" *New York Times,* September 16,
   1990.
Snider, William D. *Light on the Hill: A History of the University of North Carolina at Chapel
   Hill.* Chapel Hill: University of North Carolina Press, 1992.
U.S. Commission on Civil Rights. *Civil Rights Issues Facing Asian Americans in the 1990s.*
   Washington, DC: GPO, 1992.
Walker, Ruth. "A North Carolina Renaissance Built on 'Idea' Industries." *Christian
   Science Monitor,* June 15, 1982, B8. Durham County Public Library, Research
   Triangle subject file.

Bohemian Groves, Grooves, Gardens, and Guns

The Hybrid Worlds of Bohemian and Bourgeoisie Southern Magazines

Shawn Chandler Bingham

I'm in a Nashville record shop when the owner inquires if I am "interested in some *deal-in*." I'm unsure of whether he is offering me a bargain, or talking about Bob. Consider the mental clatter: his Tennessee drawl, *Blonde on Blonde* playing on the turntable, and a poster of the Akron, Ohio, based band The Black Keys, who now live in the same city as the very record shop in which I am standing. I'm embarrassed and stalling, unable to translate. Moving to distract or deter, I notice a half-sleeve tattoo that seems conversation-worthy; following the man's arm farther down, I see that he is thumbing a magazine with a rather peculiar title: *Garden and Gun*. Two hours later, we've plumbed the entire issue together (and listened to both vinyl discs of *Blonde on Blonde*). In this short period of time I learn that *Garden and Gun* designates a modest amount of space to both topics. It's a pretty mix of advertising for Land Rovers and articles on classic landscape architects coupled with stories about indie alt-county duo Shovels and Rope, slinky boho Mississippi blues group The Weeks, and a list of creative class innovators—artists, entrepreneurs, and artist-entrepreneurs—that are changing Southern cities. But the record shop owner was not reading the magazine for sardonic irony, nor with disdain. The magazine boasts a who's who of music, food, and literary contributors. Couple that with a circulation of subscribers with an average net worth of $1.4 million and you get a magazine whose detractors refer to it as *GAG*.

If *Garden and Gun* is a grown-up fraternity boy who likes to read about high-end gun engraving as nouveau art, its older and edgier English major brother who listens to B-side blues is the *Oxford American* magazine. Playing to a different crowd, the *OA*'s more edgy, literary approach delves further into the complexity of the American South, including race, foodways, and overlooked musicians and writers of the last fifty years; the Jackson, Mississippi, *Clarion-Ledger* has described it as the South's answer to the Atlantic. Yet within the *OA*'s quirk and complexity you can also find a few ads for a more bourgeois lifestyle: the fashions of Oscar de la Renta, economic development, and a luxury travel agency.

These are two very different magazines, aimed at different crowds, but if they have anything in common, it's a gritty kind of survival: both are alive at a time where print media is officially being declared dead. With the production costs of glossy and highly stylized magazines pushing aside content for advertising, the *OA* and *G&G* live another day by appealing to multiple identities, from financial adviser to fine artist. How do these magazines toss together the bohemian and the bourgeois, luxury and the literati? They are strikingly different, to be sure. But what kinds of bohemian and bourgeois aesthetics do they reflect?

Southern Magazines and Hybrid Worlds

Southern magazines that draw on bohemia are nothing new. They have long used bohemia in various ways, often merging it more directly with bourgeois elements; indeed, rather than use bohemia to direct their "slings and arrows" at the bourgeoisie, they sling them at the North.[1] As a buffer zone of sorts, these magazines provide a cultural space for new connections between bohemia and Southern identity—a space in which the bourgeoisie, in particular, might understand itself and its world. As Patricia Levin has pointed out, in past magazines "bohemian and the bourgeois existed in strict symbiosis, and were often one and the same."[2]

Perhaps the audiences for these magazines were predecessors for the newer generation that the cultural commentator David Brooks has written about in *Bobos in Paradise*: a generation of bourgeoisie reared on bohemian ideals.[3] According to Brooks, this group was party responsible for paving newer hybrid categories, a way of living where the old categories no longer make sense. Indeed, he sardonically argues that the two rival cultures have gone from clash to cash by co-opting each other.[4] Out came the "bobo," a hybrid reconciler of creativity and commerce, reality and ideals, inner virtues and worldly success. Bourgeoisie business leaders now embrace bohemian mainstays like "constant change, freedom, radical experimentation"[5] while bohemian types, once big city wanderers, now see small-town America as a "refreshing oasis from mass society" and potential "centers of community and local activism."[6] Bobos even take the "quintessential bourgeois activity, shopping, and turn it into quintessential bohemian activities: art, philosophy, social action."[7] And now businesspeople are talking like artists. Brooks even satirizes the tendency of this "third culture" to purchase and collect "artifacts of the less privileged"[8]—restaurants with exposed beams, distressed clothing, and furnishings, wares that are worn and earthy.[9] Bored with (regional) conflicts, and even the lifestyle of their parents' social class, bobos opt for different kinds of consumption.

Magazines provide an efficient venue for these kinds of hybrid worlds—particularly those that the merge the kind of authenticity and marketing that Brooks writes about. Certainly magazines have long had a subtext of consumerism insofar as they sell add space, subscriptions, or single issues to generate revenue. In this way they already integrate shopping or some forms of advertising into whatever special interests readers have, be it the arts or sports. But if Brooks thinks the bobo has mastered a hybrid approach to culture and commerce, the "reconciliation" of these two worlds unsettles. Something just feels wrong about closing some of the pages of *Garden and Gun* together after reading it. When you do, you are making alt-country Sturgill Simpson, deemed the "Country Philosopher" by author Matt Hendrickson, kiss an ad for Sperry topsiders.[10] Or worse, you might be slamming an ad for Elizabeth Locke Jewels (available at Neiman Marcus) into the face of civil rights pioneer and congressman John Lewis and the article that follows on his "campaign for hope and promise." If bohemia has often been "doomed by its very success,"[11] look no further than the allure of the "artifacts of the less privileged" packaged safely in a magazine that comes right to your door. *G&G*, for example, ran an ad for Auctionata, an auction firm, featuring the William Aiken Walker painting *Bringing Home the Cotton*,[12] which depicts a rural scene of slaves outside a run-down cabin, including a male figure balancing a basket of cotton on his head. The ad copy reads, "Beauty is in the details. And here, that detail is in the pig in the trough." The starting price for the auction: $10,000.

Other magazines take bohemian in a much different direction, more along the lines of the kind of neobohemia Richard Lloyd has defined.[13] Marc Smirnoff founded the *Oxford American* in 1989; the title was a nod to H. L. Mencken's *American Mercury*, and Smirnoff had his sights on other influential Northern magazines like the *New Yorker* and *Atlantic*, though in a different way from his predecessors. Forget that Smirnoff hails from just outside San Francisco, or that his jaunt into the world of Southern magazines was born when his BMW broke down in Oxford, Mississippi. The literati outside the South ate it up. The *San Francisco Chronicle* called it a "chicken-fried *New Yorker*" with work by big shots."[14] The *Boston Globe* deemed it "an eclectic mix" and a "welcome fix," presumably to what ailed the "Sahara" of culture.[15] Even the sterile and predigested *USA Today* weighed in: "Not only has Smirnoff found the Southern voice, but he's provided a wonderful platform to make it heard. . . . A sort of Southern version of *The New Yorker*."[16] The *OA*'s circulation strategy is "aimed at an audience of engaged and active 'cultural creatives'— connoisseurs of Southern writing, culture, and lifestyle."[17] This is flowery language for advertisers, but Smirnoff's vision for the magazine is that it ain't for the parlor crowd.

G&G, meanwhile, is squarely aimed at the high-spending Southerner (or consumers of things Southern). Demographically, its readers have a median household income of $171,000 and a median net worth of almost $1.5 million. As *G&G*'s media kit points out, these folks have the "means and motivation to live well."[18] Half own two or more residences, and they take more than one trip per month. Some could assume that with a name like *Garden and Gun*, the editors have no pretense nor pose about who they are and what they stand for. But, there's something more complex going on beyond the title; at times, this makes for a somewhat schizophrenic page-turner. In the thick of ads for such bourgeoisie mainstays as real estate and watches, you'll find print copy declaring that "Coffee Works Wonders," featuring a Rwandan farmer partner (whose product is available at Southern grocers like Bi-Lo, Kroger, and Winn Dixie).[19] In the same issue you'll also find a story about a former rock drummer collecting absinthe spoons as a way to "preserve his heritage," including a spoon from the Paris Exposition in 1889 that is shaped like the Eiffel Tower.[20] For as much as you see ads for the Silvercrest Asset Management Group, you'll also hear about the Southern Environmental Law Center or the Asian carp invasion and a proposal for what to do about it (filet them!).[21]

It's almost too easy to assume that all the packaging—the bohemian aesthetic wrapping with advertising on the inside—cheapens bohemia. After all, *G&G* boasts some thoughtful bohemian writers and does, at times, brings a sense of craft—some might even say "authenticity"—to the bourgeoisie nightstand. It gets even more complicated when you learn that non-Southerners have edited these magazines. It is true that bohemia becomes a way for the magazines to market authenticity, merging place, aesthetic, and consumption as a new form of Southern identity. And there is also a good share of the downward social class emulation that Brooks has written about. Despite their differences, though, the *OA* and *G&G* rattle and even blur a range of categories. Rather than feed into a homogeneous third culture, they provide a testing ground for experimentation of identities, which is partly why they are able to survive. They do make unique voices heard, but they also offer escapism from older myths of the South, partly through consumption of Southern identity. In doing so they depict irony and tension—sometimes in ways that bang up against each other, and sometimes in ways that work.

Garden and Gun: Consuming Southern Identities

Before his departure from the *Oxford American*, founding editor Marc Smirnoff fired a barrage of shots at *Garden and Gun* in his *OA* Editor's Box column titled "G&G Me with a Buccellati Silver Spoon!": "Add up all these gorgeous pictures of fox hunts, mint juleps, turkey hunts, polo matches, refurbished mansions, forest-sized gardens, pure-bred beagles, expensive fishing reels, silver flasks, artisanal knifes, engraved rifles, sexy riding crops, and what do you get but a near-replaying of The Old South Plantation Myth?"[22] It was a classic case of the more authentic Southern magazine's (non-Southern) editor calling out the competition as a poser—the Old South pervertedly packaged as a New South and sold to the bourgeoisie. Smirnoff was certainly not far off with a several of the gripes logged in his editorial, particularly with reference to the absence of discussions about race in such a "Southern" magazine. Even so, the complexities of *G&G* are worth exploring; the magazine wrangles together several worlds, cleverly moving beyond simply beagles and boxwood.

There is no doubt that the magazine basks in conspicuous consumption. It has its share of Land Rover and Mercedes advertisements. One poses the question "Are we there yet?" and then states emphatically, with the automobile centered as bourgeoisie symbols of success, "The question has been answered."[23] These ads fit squarely with the audience demographic listed in the magazine's media kit—high-income high spenders who plan to update their homes in the next year. Some ads draw on classic bourgeoisie values of save, prosper, and spend later, including one for Kiawah Island, a private resort community near Charleston: above a picture of an expansive sun setting on the back marshes of the Intercoastal Waterway, the print reads, "Invest in a truer gold, and get everything out of life you put in."[24] The island resort development near Charleston has "Pampering" (in its Sanctuary Spa), "Beauty" (private beaches), "Culinary Delights," "Retail Therapy" (in its Freshfields Village mall), and golf courses designed by the likes of Pete Dye, Tom Fazio, Jack Nicklaus, Gary Player, and Tom Watson.

Much of the rest of the advertising landscape inside *G&G* relates to investing, home decor, sporting life (guns, hunting, etc.), and real estate. Perhaps the most egregious version of this kind of conspicuous consumption was a separate mini-catalog called a "lookbook" inserted in the magazine for Sunbrella. Based in North Carolina, Sunbrella produces outdoor fabrics, shades, and awnings, with applications that range from marine to home furnishings. The insert features white wealthy folk doing such things as grilling, yachting (on what appears to be the West Coast!), drinking wine, and doing yoga. The print reads exactly like an advertiser's stilted attempt to frame freedom in slick ad copy: "These are the days we live for. Out on the water, feeling free, every moment full of possibilities. Go ahead, set sail with Sunbrella on board and leave your worries behind." The "lookbook" invites customers to "create a relaxing and rejuvenating sanctuary with worry free fabrics that will make you feel smart, stylish and right at home."

But make no mistake, *G&G* is also a magazine built on the assumption that the South, itself, can be consumed. Most issues highlight a particular city or town, including a guide section broken into all the ways one can consume the city: "Drink," "Sleep," "Eat," "Shop," and "See." You'll find must-experience bars, inns, restaurants, stores, and other places. If your consumption patterns are more seasonal, the "Summer in the South" issue tells readers "where to eat, drink and swim for the next ninety days."[25] *G&G* is also about consuming the South in very conspicuous ways—from entertaining to hunting. The special issue "Southern Secrets" teaches readers how to "make perfect deviled eggs, bet on a horse, throw a crawfish boil" and "tell a great story,"[26] while the headline of another issue could be right out of *Southern Living*: "Elevate Your Thanksgiving Spread."[27] Turn toward the back of any issue and you will find a range of *G&G* events that bring corporations, Southern pastimes, and locale together. The February–March 2012 issue includes a range of these: "Artisanal Pairing Party" (wines and small bites), the "Secret Society Supper Club" (in collaboration with the high-end but boho Blackberry Farm), and "Cast & Blast" (yes, that's fishing and shooting—in partnership with Audi). There's also a $150 per person "Members Only Shoot" and the "Hook, Slice and Drive" event—a collaboration between Porsche, the Ford Plantation, and *G&G* where attendees can enjoy an "action packed day of golfing and fishing fun, followed by a Porsche driving experience and a spirited oyster roast."[28]

There is no doubt that the magazine's roots in Charleston have shaped it from the beginning, at least on the surface. Some have found it too easy to satirize *G&G* for being too simplistic. (Smirnoff even mocks it by referring to it as "Gardening with Guns."[29]) The magazine actually took its name from a Charleston disco,[30] a progressive place where "everybody . . . movers, shakers, partyers, hipsters, social mavens . . . drank and danced from the late 1970s to the mid-1980s."[31] As one blogger remembers,

It was funky. . . . It was tacky. It was very sexual. . . . It wasn't all that clean.
Some of the drag queens were over the top, even by non-Charleston standards. But it was the wildest and craziest of all the Charleston-area discos
in the late '80s. It was mostly gay during the weekdays, but mixed gay &
straight on Friday and Saturday nights. Nobody hassled anybody. The
first smell that hit you when you walked in the door was dope. People
smoked fairly discreetly, but a lot. It was a great place to pick up or
take . . . well, anybody, of any persuasion. A number of M+F couples regularly went there to pick up bi girls for off-premises partying.[32]

Particularly for Southern standards in the 1970s and 1980s, it was a not only
ahead of its time but "progressive in that it was the first real gay bar where gay
people could feel comfortable in large numbers . . . the spot where everybody . . .
gay and straight . . . converged."[33] This scene is far afield from the magazine's
Thanksgiving tips or the highfalutin pictures of the polo crowd in leather
boots while eating charcuterie from the local farm-to-table restaurant and listening to a hip, up-and-coming bluegrass band. Do these origins illustrate
something more complex than the Southern bourgeoisie crowd happening
upon the record collection of an older brother? What does it mean that the
magazine is named after a now defunct gay bar that existed in Charleston?
Not too much, apparently. Factually, the magazine owner was not into gardening, guns, nor gay nightlife. She thought it was a "bold name," a "metaphor for
the sporting life" and "reminded her of working at GQ."[34]

Bobos in the Garden

If this is all enough to make you think *Garden and Gun* reads more like a
higher-class *Southern Living*, think again. The magazine definitely boasts a
rather thick lineup of serious writers, many of whom wrote for Smirnoff's *Oxford American* magazine before the editor penned his infamous critique of
G&G. Roy Blount Jr., Rick Bragg, John T. Edge, Clyde Edgerton, and Julia
Reed regularly contribute. Bragg, a native of Alabama, won a Pulitzer Prize
while writing for the *New York Times*, and his books cover such topics as the
lives of cotton mill workers, poverty in Alabama, and the Great Depression in
the South. Edge, founder of the Southern Foodways Alliance, writes exten-
sively on Southern food—his books include the *Truck Food Cookbook*, *Southern
Belly*, and the forthcoming *Potlikker Papers*, which looks at Southern history
through the lens of food from "lunch counter sit-ins of the 1960s forward."[35]
In other words, these authors' examinations of Southern life go far beyond

shallow consumption, delving into poverty, laborers, race, underappreciated writers, and landscape.

The magazine's aesthetic also bends it into more bohemian territory. Food articles often have botanical illustrations of lesser-eaten greenery like endive and watercress, drawn by artist John Burgoyne. Even an article on Virginia landscape architect Charles Stick, whose masterful classical symmetry tames nature at Georgian revival houses and large farms alike, visually draws on a more bohemian aesthetic: the photographs are muted, blurred around the edges, and play with earth tones—surreal at times, more than simple reportage. In one photograph the bearded Strick stands under a hornbeam arbor, on a bench imported from Paris, in an olive green sport coat, brown pants, olive boots, and contrasting scarf and vest.[36] On the opposite page, a silhouetted statue of Narcissus by a reflecting pool looks like an image from an Edgar Allen Poe story.[37] Even as his life's work dots the higher echelons of bourgeoisie landscapes, Strick himself speaks in more bohemian ways of shedding material possession in exchange for more spiritual pursuits, creating "layers of unfolding experience" and "expanding consciousness."[38]

Look beyond the "gaudy baubles"—to use Smirnoff's words—and even the "pretty photography,"[39] and you will find some interesting ways that *G&G* toys with bohemia, even if it does not succeed. You can read about important authors like Wendell Berry. More interested in photography? Read about physician-turned-photographer Shelby Lee Adams, whose images depict stark views of "poverty, deformity, bleakness" across Appalachia.[40] This is, at least, not intended as a way for wealthy folk to romanticize or gaze upon the poor. Adams, an Appalachian native, points out that "people are worthy of being seen and not as caricatures."[41] *G&G* also has the inside take on small-batch artisan whiskey. Into repurposing? Read about the restoration of antebellum cabins in Madison, Georgia: these are tiny houses with exposed beams and spare, worn wood; the insides are painted white, like French country houses, and include items bought from a Paris flea market.[42] This particular issue even has the section "Best Southern Bars," where the author points out that toward the "other ends of the socioeconomic spectrum from a bar catering to $600-a-day guides and the anglers who can afford them—there is a juke joint."[43] He goes on to write about such places as Snake and Jake's Christmas Club in New Orleans: a Frankenbuilding made from the parts of lesser buildings (and bulletin boards). Akin to writing about the boho saloons of New York City, the list includes "grungy or grand" places with names like Anvil Bar and Refuge, the Houndstooth, and the Cave (an underground bar with walls made of plastered chicken wire). Want the modern-day Ada Clare? There is a story of a prodigal daughter who went to New York as a marketing executive but then returned home to Hunstville, Alabama—to make artisanal goat cheese.

The quintessentially strange mishmash of bobodom in *G&G*, though, can be found in "Catfish Heaven—Soul Food at Taylor Grocery," in which author Curtis Wilkie writes about the popularity and importance of a hole-in-the-wall grocery store turned eatery. He recounts how he watched bluesman Taj Mahal play a free gig at Taylor's, concluding that "the cultural center of Mississippi did not lie in Oxford, eight miles away, but in the little village of Taylor. And that Taylor Grocery served as its anchor."[44] During the long wait to order, a hungry audience listens to musicians playing for tips (jug bands included). All of this seems like a glimmer of a more bohemian scene in the rural outskirts of Oxford until you read the description of the customer base: "Senators to sorority sisters to guys at a raucous bachelor party." It's easy to read *gentrification* or *commodification of authenticity*, especially knowing the ramshackle grocery store only became a catfish joint in 1998 when the inside was gutted and, later, successful sales brought an annex. Undeniably, though, Taylor's is a good indicator that even the tailgate crowd (which in the Oxford area often means those dressed in many of the gingham threads advertised in *G&G*) hungers for something more authentic.

Certainly the audience ranges beyond the description above. But, the reality is evident: bourgeois Southerners have come to the table. The neighborhood around Taylor's, according to Wilkie, has seen a "flowering of art galleries, pottery studios" and the Big Truck Theatre, "a poor man's Grand Ole Opry."[45] The town even won the governor's Excellence in Arts Award. The building remains, and, as Wilkie points out, it sits roughly where the fictional Varner's Store stood in William Faulkner's Yoknapatawpha County. More important, though, Wilkie's recounting of the changing nature of the building—from a dry goods market to a Model T repair shop to a grocery store to a fried fish shop (especially after catfish farming arrived in the area)—belies a very important fact: the building's survival can be linked to adaptation and evolution. Now a wide range of identities feast on its authenticity.

Critics like Marc Smirnoff, who see too much of the Old South in *Gardens and Guns*, playfully refer to it as *GAG*. But much like the evolution of Taylor's Grocery, or the "bobo," *G&G* occupies a strange hybrid world that deserves more than a simple thumbing of the nose and dismissal. For all its bourgeoisie bravado, craft remains important to the magazine; it routinely highlights independent Southern craft artisans—the purveyors of Cedar Mountain Banjos in Mills River, North Carolina; French Broad Boatworks in Asheville, North Carolina; and the small batch ice cream of Southern Craft

Creamery in Marianna, Florida. Yes, you will read about the House of Beretta (the purveyor of fine guns) in a small valley in Italy, but you'll also read about mobile boutiques run out of Airstream campers, retrofitted trucks, and trailers. The magazine's attention to heritage crops, handmade instruments, and museum exhibitions of regional artists tap into quintessential bohemian interests. This is a Ping-Pong of bohemianism and bourgeoisie, to be sure: less reconciled than David Brooks's bobo, more a conspicuous consumption of boho aesthetic. At its best it might be a soft entrée into some of these bohemian worlds, a testing ground for experimentation of other identities, a kernel of yearning for another world beyond the bourgeois realms. At its worst, though, it's a jarring mix of the boho and the bourgeoisie with a focus more on what's "trending" than the more muddy issues that a magazine like the *OA* relishes in tackling.

Bohemian Chops

Turn to the contributor section inside any issue of the *Oxford American* and you find a trail leading to the inner sanctum of the American literati: its authors are novelists, poets, professors, screenwriters, and even public radio contributors; they have written for heavies like the *New Yorker*, the *Village Voice*, and the *Atlantic*. The magazine's second editor, Roger D. Hodge, previously headed up *Harper's*. Just after Hodge took the helm, none other than the *New York Times* declared the *OA* to be the "best and most original new American magazine of the last 25 years. . . . It's worth pausing to revisit why this quarterly matters, and why so many people, not just in the South, will be paying attention."[46]

The magazine has a true bohemian heart: "The mission of the *Oxford American* magazine and the Oxford American Literary Project is twofold: cultural and educational. The *Oxford American* aspires to study, explore, and elucidate Southern culture via writing, music, food, photography, and art. The Oxford American Literary Project aims to promote the literary arts and encourage young and mature minds to pursue literature and literary journalism through fellowships, educational programs, and other unique projects."[47] If this is a most noble mission, it is also difficult to accomplish with the wallet of a bohemian. Thankfully, the *OA* has had such benefactors as novelist John Grisham.

The magazine has also had a number of starts and stops. In its early days, some pieces were actually donated by authors, credit cards funded some of the publication, and occasionally printing shut down completely (in 1994, 2001, and 2003). Later a secretary was found guilty of embezzling.[48] Over the course of this time the magazine would move from Oxford to Little Rock. In some ways, it's a history not all that different from that of bohemian literary magazines in the early scenes of New York City. But like many of those magazines, the *OA* has fostered a range of important Southern authors, musicians, and artists. It remains one of the only magazines to continue to press a CD for its yearly music issue—one that digs up long-lost and important Southern music, from juke joint to gospel. It is a magazine that in aesthetic, content, and (mostly) advertising continues to ride the bohemian rails. Yet it has made some concessions along the way.

In his 2007 essay "Oasis of the Bozart," *OA* publisher Ray Wittenberg writes, "In my mind, the *Oxford American* still rides the crest of the wave created by the Renaissance. We're still trying to help extend that brand, so to speak. Last year alone, The *OA* published over one hundred and twenty writers. As someone who loves good writing and the South, I'm convinced publishing the magazine is a really good thing to be doing."[49] Helping extend the brand it does, but by using a more bohemian approach, one that lives up to its cover tagline: "The Southern Magazine of Good Writing." From its deft contributors to the sheer amount of space it dedicates to the written word, the act of writing permeates the pages of the *OA*. Wittenburg's essay is a call for readers to support the magazine in various ways, and he pleads his case in a way that illustrates the magazine's mission: "My fellow Oxford Americans, please dive deeper into the *OA* community and become even more involved in this fantastic intellectual adventure."[50] Those last two words are keenly important, for the magazine wraps together bohemian tenets of the arts and writing with attention to tough social issues and a conscience about everyday life in the South. The writing is gritty, not sugar-coated; sometimes topics are mundane, but other times ugly, muddy, sticky, and even bloody.

A completely different beast from *G&G*, the *OA* includes fiction and poetry in every issue (and as many advertisements for presses and publishers as *G&G* has for high-end real estate). With such a singular focus on writing, the *OA* allows it writers much more space to delve into complexities. Many of the magazine's articles exceed eight pages—far greater than the one to two pages that might be found in other magazines about the South. The *OA*'s themed issues tackle various complexities as they play out in Southern life; its 2009 issue on race includes a forum with participants such as Morris Dees (Southern Poverty Law Center), Richard Thomas Ford (Stanford Law School), and Vanessa Siddle Walker (Emory University), among others.[51] Humorist Roy Blount Jr. takes a turn in the same issue, giving adjectives and nouns the business (including the "artificial concept" of being "colorblind").[52] Also included is a piece by outsider Jerald Walker—a non-Southerner—writing about his fear of the South.[53] The issue is creatively anchored by four short fiction pieces, poems, and a range of photographs and paintings—all of which address race in the South. Demonstrating a wide range, the issue even moves into the classroom, with essays on the relevance of historically black colleges and a teacher's experience in a poor school district.

The *OA* also dedicated a themed issue entirely to education itself. In it, John T. Edge tackles cafeteria food and its recipe of nationalism and "political machinations."[54] Over fifteen writers pen school memories, Ron Rash included. Other themed issues reflect the magazine's core boho aesthetic: fiction, winter reading, the visual South, art and architecture, the journalism of the New South, Southern movies, Southern food, and the very popular yearly music issues. Still others have taken on themes such as life after Hurricane Katrina in "3 Years After," and more surprising topics, such as the "Sports" and "Home Sweet Home" issues.[55] The sports issue includes an essay by John Updike and an article on an IQ test for college football coaches. The home issue is also probably not what you think—it includes a piece called "The Cult of House Worship" and an essay on kids living in motels. The cover could be ripped from a *Southern Living* model home foyer, save for the angry four-year-old in underwear and superhero cape, sulking on an antique bench that sits under a Queen Anne–style mirror.

The *OA*'s knack for gutting the elephant in the room is on display in pieces like David Payne's "Why Are Northern Writers 'National' and Southern Writers 'Regional'? On Economics, Media Bias and Literary Status,"[56] or in "Can You Blame Gus Cannon?,"[57] where Don Flemons gives readers a look at complexities of black involvement in minstrel music. Likewise, where *G&G*'s coverage of photographer Shelby Adams amounted to a one-page treatment (which essentially served as free advertising for Adams's black-and-white portrait show), *OA* writer Erik Reece sees gray nuances. His approach is evident even from the article's title, "Friend of the Underclass? The Controversial Appalachian Portraits of Shelby Lee Adams." The *OA* gives Reece the time (and space) to parse *photography as art* into both technique and portrayal: "There is no question that Adams is a talented photographer with a very sophisticated understanding of composition and light. . . . He is especially good at photographing children."[58] Reece points out that Adams has cast himself as a friend of the underclass; yet, in the show reviewed in the *OA*, he argues that Adams portrays his subjects as freaks and "does them no favors" since his images "transform actual people into pathetic clichés."[59] This level of criticism, known to regular readers of the *OA* (and of the present volume), certainly puts the magazine in a different genre from other Southern magazines that draw on a bohemian aesthetic but not necessarily a bohemian intellectual perspective.

And there is no shying away from Southern cultural mainstays like hunting culture, which has long been a theme of Southern writers. Lifestyle magazines like *G&G* and even *Southern Living* have favored the art of the hunt, as well as dressing (well) for the hunt. Indeed, hunting accouterments adorn the pages of both magazines. *G&G* pieces also regularly highlight specialty gun engraving that might depict a picturesque scene, or custom wooden gun handles forged by the hand of a craftsman. Similar to *G&G*'s approach to Adams's photography, the consumption of aesthetic takes precedence over the more grotesque elements of the hunt.

The *OA*'s foray into writing about hunting renders the act more real; it approaches hunting as the literati would war, death, and loss. In "Drowning Deer,"[60] Jim Minick writes as both a deer hunter and a vegan (most of the year). His hunting dogs are mutts, not the purebreds that grace the photographs of *G&G*. He writes about wounded deer mired in a river while making their escape from a rifle and dogs. He slings scientific evidence of how an overabundance of deer has dramatically changed the composition of the forests. Pointedly, he states "we are drowning in deer." Spoiler alert: the twist of fate is that the author, having wounded a deer during his own hunt, ended up having to put it down by drowning it when it got stuck trying to cross a river. Ernest Hemingway would smile, as it is a scene not made for the glossy gun porn printed in *G&G*: "The doe I shot, and rode, the fierce doe I needed to drown, did not want to die. . . . I gripped her neck, righted myself to stand and push her head under again. Watched her breathe in, imagined her lungs swelling and her throat burning. . . . When I sliced her open, I found her lungs exploded, her chest full of water."[61]

Later in the same issue, avid hunter Mark Lane begins his essay "Mr. Blue" by stating "When I was six years old, I shot a man."[62] He recounts the memories of hunting with his father, as well as the incident of Mr. Blue—a hunting accident that nearly left the man dead. By essay's end Lane is at a party, recounting the story of Mr. Blue in joke form, to which a longtime friend responds, "People were irate about it. Your dad basically got run out of the [gun] club." Lane's final paragraph unveils the harsher realities that emerge within a hunting culture: "For the rest of that night I nodded and smiled at people, pretending to be one of them. But I would never be one of them. I was six again, convinced that at some level, beyond language and the law, blood was on my hands. I would have to answer for that."[63]

A radically different funding structure is partly why the *OA*'s insides veer from the conventions of other Southern magazines. The *Oxford American* magazine is a nonprofit, part of the larger Oxford American Literary project, which is operated under the aegis of the University of Central Arkansas.[64] All of this content is brought to you (mostly) by a different kind of sponsor. Experiences are the things of consumption here: advertisers include graduate writing programs, book festivals, and museums. If it was possible to turn a bohemian candy store into ad copy, the *OA* has: the History Museum of Mobile showcasing Alabama artists in India; the Southern Foodways Alliance exploring "Counter Culture" (of diners) through inclusion and exclusion at the Southern table; the University of Texas Press publicizing books on alt-country singer and novelist Ryan Adams, Merle Haggard, and Lightning Hopkins. The magazine even includes an independent listing section for its advertisers, which the magazine describes as follows: "Like a classified section but bigger and in full color, this section is for independent record labels, publishers, university presses, and cultural experiences who want to reach our dedicated readers for less money."[65] Less than 20 percent of the magazine's content is made up of advertising. (By comparison, more than 50 percent of the pages in *G&G* include ad print.) This translates into a different reading experience. In the winter 2013 issue, readers can actually go eighteen pages without seeing any advertisements.

With such different approaches, it seems rational to view the *G&G* crowd as more bourgie and the *OA* crowd as more boho. But the demographics of *OA* readers complicate this dichotomous thinking: more than half of *them* have spent or are planning to spend "$3,000 or more on travel/vacations in the last/next 12 months."[66] Some of their other reading meets expectations: *Art in America*, the *Atlantic*, *Harper's*, the *New Yorker*, *National Geographic*, *Smithsonian*, *Vanity Fair*, and the *Virginia Quarterly Review*. But they also indulge in *Better Homes and Gardens*, *Country Living*, *Golf Digest*, *Newsweek*, *Reader's Digest*, *Southern Living*, and—yes—even *Garden & Gun*. A little less than half plan on purchasing a home in the next year, while more than three quarters plan some form of remodeling or home improvement. Ninety-two percent have an income above $50,000 and more than a quarter of the entire audience makes more than $100,000 per year.[67] Education levels of *OA* readers area also very high: 93 percent have attended some college, 75 percent have obtained bachelors' degrees, and 32 percent have a postgraduate degree or higher;

43 percent classify their career as "professional/managerial/administrative," and 88 percent own a home. Certainly the magazine's claim in its media kit demonstrates truth in advertising: the *Oxford American* reader is "an affluent and educated consumer."[68]

What this suggests is that while some of the people depicted in the magazine—writers, artists, and musicians—may very well be leading a bohemian lifestyle, its audience members, per the *OA*'s own market research, are more akin to the hybrid bobo lifestyle that David Brooks sardonically describes in his book. The magazine's audience is consuming an array of goods that come from both the bohemian and bourgeois worlds. The *OA*'s 2015 media kit lists readers' leisure activities as "antique shopping, art shopping, cooking, dancing, dining out, movies, photography, sporting events, reading, & weekend travel/getaways," and it uses this lifestyle and the word "affluent" to appeal to advertisers—to sell advertising space.[69] To be sure, the *OA* does provide a more authentic bohemian outlet than a magazine like *G&G*, but it also, from time to time, violates the a sacred rule of authenticity: don't let your marketing show.[70] Indeed, there are clear cases when even the *OA* goes mainstream. Consider an ad for restaurant One Eleven at the Capital Hotel in Little Rock, which brings a tinge of the upscale to the gritty magazine. The print copy claims "A pinch of Southern hospitality, a dash of global influence and an entirely new dining experience,"[71] and the bottom of the ad promotes the hotel as part of the *Southern Living* (magazine) Hotel Collection. The same issue also promotes a 2014 in-car concert series sponsored by Landers Fiat and the *Oxford American*;[72] the copy reads, "Get inspired! By our weekly concert series—an audiovisual experience brought to you from inside a FIAT and featuring some of the best artists in the region." On the back cover, readers find an advertisement for the Alabama resort towns of Gulf Shores and Orange Beach in which a yuppie couple is barefoot on the shore; and the copy reads, "Suddenly, you are in a whole different state of 'kids? what kids? Who cares what time it is? Hey, is that a dolphin out there?'"

There are other places where the bourgeois lifestyle leaks out, too. The winter 2013 issue of the *OA* includes an advertisement for the Tennessee Department of Economic and Community Development, whose industries include manufacturing, aerospace and defense, auto, chemical, plastics, rubber, films, food, health care, and transportation—worlds far from bohemia.[73] The ad depicts a middle-aged pudgy golfer on a course, with one hand pointed up at the sky, striking a classic Elvis pose, and the other hand holding a golf club as if a microphone; the copy reads, "Where life is a sound investment. . . . The stage is set for you in Tennessee. This is the place where work feels more like a vacation." In a rare back cover advertisement for something other than books, a woman is kicking up her high heels, surrounded by shopping bags. The ad, ironically for Poe Travel, offers an "exclusive by-invitation-only network of luxury travel agents . . . from privileged access and upgrades to complimentary spa treatments and gourmet meals."[74] Perhaps this has gotten the magazine on better financial footing, though. Besides, it's easy to forgive these cracks when the writing is so damn good. The 2014 issue featuring the hotel and Fiat ads also includes pieces on the politics of suing big oil in Louisiana and a journalist's memory of interviewing the man who organized the murders of civil rights workers in Philadelphia, Mississippi.[75] Those stories are not being published in other Southern magazines, many of which are more squarely aimed at polishing the South's image.

Remaking Southern Myths

The boundaries between bohemia and bourgeoisie have never been as clearly defined in America as myth suggests. We have seen evidence of this throughout the present volume: Ada Clare reinvented herself and funded her bohemian lifestyle with the help of her inheritance; Henry Clapp's *Saturday Press* was built with the proceeds of his rare book collection. The funky subcultures that have arisen around North Carolina's Research Triangle emerged with the help of well-educated academics and industry researchers. In the same way that early bohemian Southern magazines would "embrace the bourgeois ethos of the local Board of Trade,"[76] lifestyle magazines like *G&G* and *South* (published out of Savannah) have been incorporating bohemia into their aesthetic since they started. They are illustrations of Roland Barthes important argument about the bourgeois tendency to remain unnamed and even to pull in elements of the revolutionary:

> [O]ur society is still a bourgeois society. . . . As a political fact, the bourgeoisie has some difficulty in acknowledging itself. . . . As an ideological fact, it completely disappears: the bourgeoisie has obliterated its name in passing from reality to representation, from economic man to mental man. . . . [I]t makes its status undergo a real *ex-nominating* operation: the bourgeoisie is defined as *the social class which does not want to be named.*[77]

The *OA*, on the other hand, might be somewhat shielded as a nonprofit, but it is not immune to the economic realities of a capitalist economy. It has needed to adjust accordingly. Many of its own writers understand that they need to peddle their words and wares in order to eat good food, travel, and hear good music (even if that means these same authors are peddling to *G&G* at times). Alas, even bohemians must face the economic music. Despite their differences, though, *G&G* and the *OA* tinker with some of the same myths of a one-dimensional South: that it is the land of boring gentry and uneducated folk lacking any creativity. If these myths work as a form of "open-work meaning," as Roland Barthes has argued,[78] both magazines rework and reimagine these ossified myths and meanings in important ways.

There is no doubt that, as more of a traditional lifestyle magazine, *G&G* more often signifies "Southern" through the consumption of products, a focus that makes it more about the individual. But the magazine's structure makes more in-depth inquiry on the South far more difficult. Probably one of the best illustrations of this is its feature on "The Hidden Bahamas," which gives readers "30 Reasons to Head South, Way South."[79] This is a case where you *can* judge an issue by its cover, and this one depicts clear aqua beach water and a large green sea turtle being held, white belly up, toward the camera. The white of the turtle deeply contrasts with the dark-skinned hands holding it out of the water (and the large turtle actually obscures the identity of whomever is holding it). The "Hidden Bahamas" feature highlights the "game fish, the marine life, the waves, and the easygoing attitude."[80] The Bahamas become "unhidden" through coverage of bonefishing (Andros), snorkeling (Harbour Island), bumming around (Eleuthera), and surfing (the Abaco Islands); the "hidden" aspect is really mostly about finding the untouched parts of the Bahamas—and then consuming those, too. This issue of *G&G* questionably avoids seriously addressing definitions of the South, its relationship with the Caribbean, and issues of race and exploitation.

Yet the magazine does provide a (small) window into bohemia in ways that move myths created by magazines like *Southern Living* beyond a highly starched and stiff bourgeoisie with no appreciation for anything outside its own class (even if the venture outside that social class is often consumed as a packaged product). The newer myths that emerge out of *G&G* show that Southern bourgeois life does not have to be stuffy, and certainly that Southern identity has appeal beyond the South. (A whopping 45 percent of *G&G* readers live outside the region.) Indeed, *Southern Living* even took some design and content cues from *G&G* (presumably as a way to become more hip to a newer generation of readers); its new aesthetic bears a striking resemblance to that of *G&G*. This is a point worth considering because *G&G* itself owes some of its success to *Southern Living*, the iconic magazine that paved the way for a new brand of Southern lifestyle magazines:

Born in Birmingham, Alabama, amid race riots and social turmoil in February 1966, *Southern Living* was envisioned, developed, and implemented by the Progressive Farmer Company (now Southern Progress Corporation, a division of AOL–Time Warner) as a solution to remedy declining readership of the *Progressive Farmer* magazine and to ensure company growth. . . . Growing suburbs in the region were the heart of the magazine's target market, and the flourishing consumer interest in products for home and leisure provided a strong advertising base for the new magazine . . . that celebrated the positive aspects of the South by focusing articles on the people, places, and pursuits that represented the regional personality as well as promoting a New-South vision of progress and promise. One of the most successful magazine launches in history, *Southern Living* soon became the lifestyle guide to the seventeen-state region.[81]

Generations of Southerners have memories of this "lifestyle guide," which was often stacked primly on the coffee tables of an aunt whose carpet remained perpetually vacuumed. (Even libraries in rural New England still stock the magazine.) That *Southern Living* adapted its own style to look more like that of its upstart follower, *G&G*, makes it all the more worth wondering what newer Southern myths *G&G* will generate by drawing even loosely on bohemia. And what happens when a generation raised by the Southern bourgeois (who grew up on *Southern Living*) take in these different myths?

The *OA* plays hard with the "desert" mythology of noncreativity in the South. The magazine not only showcases a wide array of Southern creatives but also redefines the lifestyle magazine beyond the hyperconsumerism of the traditional magazine structure—here creativity *is* the lifestyle. In a difficult and shifting market, the *OA* remains the only magazine so vehemently dedicated to in-depth Southern writing, art, music, food, and telling the quirky and gritty stories of Southern life.[82] It still runs full pages of art, from Clyde Butcher's silver gelatin photographs of clouds rising up over a Florida key to William Eggleston's early 1970s photograph of a half-empty Nehi bottle on the hood of a car.[83] And it might even be busting myths about bohemian survival, including those put forth by the scholar of mythologies, Roland Barthes: "True, there are revolts against bourgeois ideology. This is what one generally calls the avant-garde. But these revolts are socially limited, they remain open to salvage. First, because they come from a small section of the bourgeoisie itself, from a minority group of artists and intellectuals, without public other than the class which they contest, and who remain dependent on its money in order to express themselves."[84] There is some dependency here—the *OA* has taken out loans and appealed to mainstream writers like John Grisham—but the magazine lives on, and it has not sold it soul in order to survive.

The *OA*'s bohemian blood flows best when the arts cannot fully be distinguished from explorations of the civic, the public, the local, or the community. Its "Southern Art and Architecture" issue includes an article by Tom Vanderbilt, "Power for the People: The Herculean Relics of the Tennessee Valley Authority," in which he explores the role of public architecture, public works, electricity, economics, and flood control.[85] The 2007 music issue includes an excellent piece on Little Rock's Lee Hays ("The People's Singer"),[86] who cowrote "If I had a Hammer," played with Pete Seeger in the Weavers, and directed theater programs at Commonwealth College, a labor organizing school in Mena, Arkansas. This brings us to the crown jewel, if bohemians have such a thing: the *OA*'s most popular issue each year, by far, is the annual music issue, which typically tells lesser-known stories of over twenty-five artists, some of whom are themselves lesser known. The music issue manages to blend history, economics, politics, sex, and religion through stories of song. It is great writing on great music, featuring cuts from artists who popularized Southern music beyond the South. Included with each music issue have been eclectic CDs that, over the last decade, have covered nearly every genre and time period of recorded music done in the South. Staying true to the magazine's nonprofit mission, the CD documents and celebrates Southern music in ways that bypass the consumption machine of most magazines.

You find two very different bohemias (and even two different Souths) in these two magazines. Should it then be a surprise that some of the same authors write for *both* magazines, or that their audiences overlap? Or that a magazine like *G&G* surfaces in a record shop where gingham is taboo? Not if history is any guide. Bohemia has always been a place to merge identities and lifestyles. It has, as Joanna Levin has pointed out, been "portable and shape-shifting," both a connector and disconnector of "the regional and the national, the national and the cosmopolitan, the modern and the traditional."[87] It is a place to play with cultural options. The capitalist marketplace has always subsumed these kinds of alternative subcultures for profit. If Davis Brooks's "bobo" has found a way to have the best of both worlds, *G&G* applies this difficult task to Southern identity, merging culture and commerce in the process. It uses bohemia both as a marketing tool and a (brief) novel escape from bourgie life. In a different way, bohemia provides the *OA* with a place to question the ugliness of Southern myths about things like creativity and race; it provides a space for the magazine's writers to question other sacred elements of Southern life: sports, hospitality and home, and even guns.

Despite their differences, the survival of the two magazines demonstrates desire, within and outside the South, to consume its creativity as both product and as authentic experience. Both magazines, in Richard Lloyd's neobohemian sense, provide benefits to local economies through features and advertisements. In effect, their use of bohemia sells *place*. Bohemia sells both legitimacy of a place (based on perceived creativity and authenticity) as well as the products that help to create these images. In this way, *Gardens and Guns* and the *Oxford American* function like other media that "simultaneously reflects and drives the development of neo-bohemia."[88] The magazines also help keep Southern writers writing about the South, rather than exporting *themselves*. What does get exported, though, are newer myths of the South, along with Southern art, writing, commerce and culture. Through these newer myths the magazines are reshaping the ways that others portray and interpret the South, from the *New York Times* to *Southern Living*, in record shops and on Ethan Allen nightstands. And, it is through bohemia, the great "shapeshifter," that these multiple identities of the South converge and collide—the packaged, the poetic, the subversive and the suburban.

Notes

1. Parry, *Garrets and Pretenders*, xv.
2. Levin, *Bohemia in America*, 262.
3. Brooks, *Bobos in Paradise*, 2000.
4. Ibid., 112.
5. Ibid.
6. Ibid., 105.
7. Ibid., 102.
8. Ibid., 96.
9. Ibid., 58–59.
10. See *Garden and Gun*, April–May 2014, 32–33.
11. Grana and Grana, "Preface," xviii.
12. See *Garden and Gun*, January 2015, 83.
13. Lloyd, *Neo-Bohemia*.
14. Benson, "Tam High's Oxford Man."
15. As cited in *Oxford American* Music Issue Press Release, Winter 2014.
16. Minzesheimer, "Grisham's New Book."
17. *Oxford American Media Kit*, 3.
18. Ibid., 6.
19. See *Garden and Gun*, February–March 2015, 54.
20. Johnson, "Collections," 55.
21. Greenberg, "The Trouble with Asian Carp," 32.
22. Smirnoff, "G&G Me with a Buccellati Silver Spoon!," 10.

23. See *Garden and Gun*, October–November 2012, 22.

24. See *Garden and Gun*, February–March 2012, 12.

25. See *Garden and Gun*, June–July 2011, front cover.

26. See *Garden and Gun*, February–March 2013, front cover.

27. See *Garden and Gun*, October–November 2013, front cover.

28. See *Garden and Gun*, February–March 2012, 100, 102–3.

29. Smirnoff, "G&G Me with a Buccellati Silver Spoon!," 8.

30. Miller, "Garden & Gun Magazine Has an Awkward Debut."

31. Katchkie's Daughter [pseud.], "Garden and Gun Club," *Sweet Moments in Charleston* (blog), http://sweetmomentsincharleston.blogspot.com/2007/05/garden-and-gun -club.html.

32. Ibid.

33. Ibid.

34. Haughney, "Garden and Gun Claws Its Way Back."

35. See the website of John T. Edge, http://www.johntedge.com.

36. Ward, "Charles Stick," 82.

37. Ibid., 83.

38. Ibid., 83, 80.

39. Smirnoff, "G&G Me with a Buccellati Silver Spoon!," 10.

40. King, "Seeing Appalachia," 24.

41. Ibid.

42. Kessler, "A Southern Restoration," 38.

43. Martin, "The Perfect Bar," 54.

44. Wilkie, "Catfish Heaven," 120.

45. Ibid., 120.

46. Garner, "It Was the New Yorker with Hot Sauce."

47. *Oxford American Media Kit*, 3.

48. Fell, "Former Oxford American Staffer Pleads Guilty."

49. Wittenberg, "Oasis of the Bozart," 21.

50. Ibid., 28.

51. "Publisher's Forum: A Great Debate."

52. Blount, "Gone Off Up North."

53. Walker, "My Fear of the South."

54. Edge, "Missing Grandma's Kitchen."

55. "3 Years After: New Orleans and the Gulf Coast," *Oxford American* 62 (2008); "The Sports Issue," *Oxford American* 59 (2007); "The Home Sweet Home Issue," *Oxford American* 60 (2008).

56. Payne, "Why Are Northern Writers 'National' and Southern Writers 'Regional'?"

57. Flemons, "Can You Blame Gus Cannon?"

58. Reece, "Friend of the Underclass?," 146.

59. Ibid., 147.

60. Minick, "Drowning Deer."

61. Ibid., 11.

62. Lane, "Mr. Blue," 28.

63. Ibid., 31.

64. Following the embezzlement scandal and unpaid taxes, the university and an anonymous donor bailed out the magazine.

65. *Oxford American Media Kit*, 8.

66. Ibid., 10.

67. Ibid.

68. Ibid.

69. Ibid.

70. I have borrowed a line here from Douglas Rushkoff, Rachel Dretzin, and Barak Goodman's documentary *The Merchants of Cool*.

71. See *Oxford American* 86 (2014): 19.

72. Ibid., 109.

73. See *Oxford American* 83 (2014): 29.

74. See *Oxford American* 51 (2005): 177.

75. Giseleson, "Flood Protection"; Sim, "No Twang of Conscience Whatever."

76. Levin, *Bohemia in America*, 262.

77. Barthes, Mythologies, 137.

78. Ibid., 132.

79. See *Garden and Gun*, December 2008–January 2009, front cover.

80. Ibid., 59.

81. Lauder, "Southern Identity," 27.

82. Brodie, "Riding Dirty Face"; Hudgins, "Unmentionable"; Reyes, "Secondhand Sublime."

83. See *Oxford American* 51 (2005): 33.

84. Barthes, *Mythologies*, 137.

85. Vanderbilt, "Power for the People," 42.

86. Sharlet, "The People's Singer."

87. Levin, *Bohemia in America*, 5.

88. Lloyd, *Neo-Bohemia*, 164.

References

Barthes, Roland. *Mythologies*. Translated by Jonathan Cape. New York: Noonday Press, 1972.

Benson, Heidi. "Tam High's Oxford Man." *San Francisco Chronicle*, February 2, 2003. http://www.sfgate.com/books/article/Tam-High-s-Oxford-man-2637009.php.

Blount, Roy, Jr. "Gone Off Up North: Preposterous Links." *Oxford American* 64 (2009): 22–25.

Brodie, Mike. "Riding Dirty Face." *Oxford American* 73 (2011): 74–78.

Brooks, David. *Bobos in Paradise: The New Upper Class and How They Got There*. New York: Simon and Schuster, 2000.

Edge, John T. "Missing Grandma's Kitchen." *Oxford American* 74 (2011): 18–21.

Fell, Jason. "Former Oxford American Staffer Pleads Guilty, Sentenced to Prison for Embezzlement." *Folio*, May 13, 2009. http://www.foliomag.com/2009/former -oxford-american-staffer-pleads-guilty-sentenced-prison-embezzlement/.

Flemons, Don. "Can You Blame Gus Cannon?" *Oxford American* 83 (2013): 128–37.

Garner, Dwight. "It was the New Yorker with Hot Sauce." *New York Times*, December 3, 2012. http://www.nytimes.com/2012/12/04/books/oxford-american -hail-to-literary-magazines-past-and-future.html.

Garden and Gun Media Kit. Charleston, SC: Garden and Gun, 2015.

Giseleson, Anne. "Flood Protection: John Barry Goes Coastal on Big Oil." *Oxford American* 86 (2014): 56–61.

Grana, Cesar, and Marigay Grana. "Preface." In *On Bohemia: The Code of the Exiled*, edited by Cesar Grana and Marigay Grana, xv–xviii. New Brunswick, NJ: Transaction, 1990.

Greenberg, Paul. "The Trouble with Asian Carp." *Garden and Gun*, February– March 2015, 32.

Haughney, Christine. "Garden and Gun Claws Its Way Back from the Brink." *New York Times*, September 2, 2012. http://www.nytimes.com/2012/09/03/business /media/garden-gun-magazine-survives-in-an-ailing-industry.html.

Hudgins, Andrew. "Unmentionable: The Secret Life of Skimpies, Scanties, Teddies, and Panties." *Oxford American* 52 (2006): 36–39.

Johnson, Pableaux. "Collections: Cocktail Curiosities." *Garden and Gun*, February– March 2015, 54.

Katchkie's Daughter [pseud.]. *Sweet Moments in Charleston* (blog). http://sweet momentsincharleston.blogspot.com.

Kessler, John. "A Southern Restoration: Cabin Fever." *Garden and Gun*, February– March 2012, 38–41.

King, Dean. "Seeing Appalachia: Photographer Shelby Adams' Portraits." *Garden and Gun*, February–March 2012, 24.

Lane, Mark. "Mr. Blue." *Oxford American* 84 (2014): 28.

Lauder, Tracy. "Southern Identity in *Southern Living* Magazine." *Journal of Geography* 111 (2007): 27–38.

Levin, Joanna. *Bohemia in America: 1858–1920*. Stanford, CA: Stanford University Press, 2009.

Lloyd, Richard. *Neo-Bohemia: Art and Commerce in the Postindustrial City*. New York: Routledge, 2006.

Martin, Guy. "The Perfect Bar." *Garden and Gun*, February–March 2012, 54–59.

Miller, Lia. "Garden & Gun Magazine Has an Awkward Debut." *New York Times*, April 30, 2007. http://www.nytimes.com/2007/04/30/business/media/30garden.html.

Minick, Jim. "Drowning Deer." *Oxford American* 84 (2014): 8–11.

Minzesheimer, Robert. "Grisham's New Book Takes Literary Turn." *USA Today*, February 22, 2001. http://usatoday30.usatoday.com/life/2001-02-06-grisham.htm.

Oxford American Media Kit. 2015. http://www.oxfordamerican.org/images/PDFs/OA _MediaKit_2015_website.pdf.

Parry, Albert. *Garrets and Pretenders: A History of Bohemianism*. Mineola, NY: Dover, 1960.

Payne, David. "Why Are Northern Writers 'National' and Southern Writers 'Regional'? On Economics, Media Bias, and Literary Status." *Oxford American* 59 (2007): 118–23.

"Publisher's Forum: A Great Debate." *Oxford American* 64 (2009): 14–21.

Reece, Eric. "Friend of the Underclass? The Controversial Appalachian Portraits of Shelby Lee Adams." *Oxford American* 51 (2005): 146–50.

Reyes, Paul. "Secondhand Sublime: Junking with the Weirdest Landscape Painter in America." *Oxford American* 52 (2006): 106–15.

Rushkoff, Douglas, Barak Goodman, David Fanning, Kimberly Tabor, and Lisel Banker. *Frontline: The Merchants of Cool*. PBS, 2001.

Sharlet, Jeff. "The People's Singer." *Oxford American* 58 (2007): 30–36.

Sim, Patsy. "No Twang of Conscience Whatever." *Oxford American* 86 (2014): 35–48.

Smirnoff, Marc. "G&G Me with a Buccellati Silver Spoon!" *Oxford American*, 76 (2012): 8–11.

Vanderbilt, Tom. "Power for the People: The Herculean Relics of the Tennessee Valley Authority." *Oxford American* 81 (2007): 42–47.

Walker, Jerald. "My Fear of the South." *Oxford American* 64 (2009): 30–32.

Ward, Logan. "Charles Stick: The Path Less Taken." *Garden and Gun*, February–March 2012, 78–83.

Wilkie, Curtis. "Catfish Heaven." *Garden and Gun*, December 2008–January 2009, 120.

Wittenberg, Ray. "Oasis of the Bozart." *Oxford American* 58 (2007): 21.

Liminality and the Search
for the New Austin Bohemianism

Joshua Long

The old metal Quonset hut on Barton Springs Road was ugly, drafty, and had poor acoustics. It had been built as a National Guard armory, not a concert hall. But the blankets on the floor, the smoke in the air, and the beer in the bloodstream seemed to incubate the motley congregation of Texans who had traveled from every corner of the state to hear the new gospel of cosmic country in this spacious metal shack. The building was named after an armadillo: a dirty, paranoid little beast that keeps its nose in the grass and doesn't seem to mind cohabitation in the most humble of conditions. That description, once offered up by local author Bud Shrake, resonated well with the folks in the audience. They wore beads and cowboy hats and listened intently as their double-braided leader joined the hippies and the rednecks in musical matrimony. Police officers and out-of-session legislators sat with them, sedated by secondhand pot smoke and public nudity. The building's owner, Eddie Wilson, was acutely aware of the ephemerality of it all. He would stand behind the stage and wonder which would come first: a sting operation or bankruptcy. While they lasted, these moments would become legendary in Austin, infusing the social landscapes with a sense of bohemianism, tolerance, and creativity still promoted by city leaders and citizens today as part of the "Austin vibe." But like all liminal spaces, the Armadillo World Headquarters was a symbol of cultural transition that was itself experiencing a metamorphosis.

Many in Austin refer to the 1970s as the city's golden era. Others refer to it deliberately as the "Decade of the 'Dillo," a romantic nod to the nucleus of Austin hippie culture that sheltered acts like Jerry Garcia, Willie Nelson, and Ravi Shankar. Today, there is no Armadillo World Headquarters. It was razed to make way for a high-rise office tower whose shadow now looms over a small plaque that provides a brief historical note and ends with the phrase "Remember the Armadillo." Across the street, the former co-owner of the Armadillo manages the famous Threadgill's Restaurant. From the porch of Threadgill's, even the most casual observer can see that the little college town is gone. As Wilson tells it, "Austin was gonna get discovered eventually. We had all the music and all the dancing girls and we'd been living it up here for a while. But I guess all of that was gonna catch up with us. It was bound to eventually."[1]

A narrative of loss permeates the story of Austin bohemianism. Many of the once sacred liminal spaces of Austin's bohemian past have vanished. The psychedelic Vulcan Gas Company and the Armadillo World Headquarters are now eulogized in song and on historical plaques. The intimate music venues of slacker culture—Club Foot, Fingerhut, Liberty Lunch, and Raul's— were demolished, bought out or, in the case of the Black Cat Lounge, burned down. The explosive growth of the past four decades has shown little mercy for Austin's historic sites of counterculture, many of which have been replaced with shiny landscapes of wealth, industry, and consumerism. A towering block of boutique shops now looms where Liberty Lunch once stood; Vulcan Gas Company is a posh outdoor clothing store.

Admittedly, it is easier to reflect on past glories than acknowledge the unwieldy landscapes of the new Austin cool. Old hippies eulogize the city's golden age and aging slackers blame hipsters for corrupting their look as the nouveau boho flock to Austin in search of the social capital so readily available in America's trendiest creative city. Hidden in their midst, a dedicated cadre of iconoclasts, artists, and social justice advocates write, speak, create, and protest. Like their bohemian predecessors who migrated to Austin for the music and the solidarity, they work as bartenders, servers, and couriers, finding time in between their mostly part-time service sector schedules to exchange ideas and pronounce the new rhetoric of social transgression. But unlike the bohemians of Austin's past, who found cheap housing in the mostly white, undervalued neighborhoods of a once sleepy college town, the new bohemians are relegated to the recently integrated, gentrifying neighborhoods of Austin's poorest minority districts. Here they must weigh the ethical and idealistic contradictions of their "privileged marginality."[2] Their presence urges us beyond the issue of whether or not Austin bohemianism is dead—a question so frequently murmured by old hippies and new hipsters alike. Rather, members of the recent wave of Austin bohemianism must ask themselves whether or not their actions will abet the political and socioeconomic forces that exacerbate inequality or serve as a positive force for social change in a city struggling to support the weight of its own success.

The Liminality of Bohemia

Bohemianism is a story most often located in liminal space. Whether at the margins of societal norms, the physical space that buffers neighborhoods, or the temporal space between oppression and revolution, bohemianism is liminal. The concept of liminality has been interpreted broadly by scholars across multiple disciplines, and many of the current applications draw from Victor Turner,[3] who describes liminality as a state "betwixt and between" situations or moments that allow people to experience a detachment from socioeconomic structures, usually resulting from a rite of passage, a pilgrimage, or societal marginalization. "Liminal entities" he writes, "are neither here nor there; they are betwixt and between the positions assigned and arrayed by law, custom, convention, and ceremonial."[4] Liminal space offers a sense of comradeship outside of normal social structures, an area of common living (Turner's "communitas") between secular and sacred, politics and religion.

In nineteenth-century Paris, for instance, bohemia was identifiable but not so easily defined. To trace the frontiers of bohemia "was to cross constantly back and forth between reality and fantasy."[5] As Jerrold Seigel points out, the interstitial spaces of Bohemia were located where the contradictions of nineteenth-century bourgeois society could be acted out and resolved. Just as they would later in London's Chelsea or New York's Greenwich Village, bohemian spaces emerged where bourgeois society—and later, mainstream consumerism—was defining its borders. "It was a space in which newly liberated energies were continually thrown up against the barriers being erected to contain them, where social margins and frontiers were probed and tested,"[6] notes Seigel. Turner's and Seigel's works complement each other in portraying liminality as a space of marginalization and resistance, transgression and creativity, but they also remind us that liminality is both vulnerable and ephemeral.

The fleeting nature of liminality and the longing or nostalgia for its previous moments are important components of its existence. Nostalgia and bohemia have always been close partners;[7] whether we write of the sincerity and idealism of artists past or romanticize a bygone moment of authenticity, "true" bohemianism is rarely spoken of in the present tense. There is always a past era to romanticize—a bygone society whose morals were free and whose ideals were uncorrupted. Bohemians frequently call upon an age untainted by commercialism and tourists; they "always believed that they were the last of the *real* bohemians."[8] The nostalgia for a romanticized earlier time complements their existence. Theirs, too, is a moment that is passing.

The avant-garde resides within liminal space, but the tensions associated with liminality also serve as a precondition for its existence. The genesis of bohemianism's creative resistance lies outside the security and homogeneity of the mainstream while its transgressive attraction remains an object of consumerism and imitation. Its residents inhabit peripheral spaces only until the popular allure of bohemian chic appropriates. Elizabeth Wilson points to the commercialization of bohemian dress, art, and lifestyle in general in mainstream culture: "We have reached the point at which virtually the whole of metropolitan mass culture is bohemianized."[9] Such actions quickly puncture the credibility of social protest. But it isn't just the message and the lifestyle that are being appropriated; the physical space of bohemianism is envied by those in search of *la vie bohème*. Sharon Zukin explores how the glamorization of bohemianism led to the gentrification of artists' living space in New York City, particularly the loft spaces of SoHo.[10] During the 1960s, popular magazines such as *Life* and *New York* featured the avante garde lifestyles of SoHo artists, which drove demand for real estate in the district as a second wave of upper middle class gentrifiers sought to acquire social capital by living in lofts near the artists whose lifestyles they wished to emulate. And, as Kristen Forkert notes, in early popularizations of bohemian living, the "loft itself played a central role as the setting for creative work and home and as a site of self-expression through display."[11] The popular search for loft living spaces has well served savvy developers throughout the United States and abroad who recognize the appeal to young creatives and knowledge workers. Today the appropriation and production of neighborhoods with lofts is a well understood mode of gentrification,[12] a way for nonartists to acquire social capital,[13] and a strategy for economic development, place branding, and the attraction of the "creative class."[14] As Richard Lloyd notes, in the new creative economy, "the concentration of artistic subcultures is crucial for the new accumulation strategies enacted in the neighborhood space."[15]

Certainly the dual process of commercializing the artist's aesthetic while also colonizing their living space adds another layer of complexity to bohemian life, but it has significant consequences for others. The residents of gentrifying neighborhoods know this all too well. This is particularly acute in Austin, where the new liminal spaces of bohemianism occupy a position "betwixt and between" the marginal and the powerful. After four decades of subversive integration and creative resistance, the legacy of Austin bohemianism is now a threat to itself.

Background: Four Decades of Austin Bohemianism

The demographic and cultural changes of the 1960s and 1970s provide a logical starting point for the story of Austin bohemianism. In many ways, the city served as an ideological antithesis to the rest of conservative Texas. In Austin, the young and idealistic found solidarity, not to mention easy access to music, drugs, and—for men—a college deferment from the draft.[16] The population of the University of Texas alone doubled in size from twenty thousand to forty thousand during the 1960s, and the wave of new clubs and music festivals served as important loci for the nascent local counterculture. The occupants of these spaces often embraced a particularly Texan bohemian aesthetic. Ragged troubadours and gypsy cowboys with braids and beads flowing from their ten-gallon hats wandered amid the usual droves of flower-adorned Zen children. There wasn't much talk of revolution, but there was more than enough rebellion in the lyrics of the country rock that rose to prominence with the likes of Waylon Jennings, Janis Joplin, Doug Sahm, and others.

Historians, writers, and folklorists speak of the influence that this era had on subsequent generations of Austinites and the culture of the city they loved.[17] Many hippies who wandered into Austin never left; they opened up record stores, bookstores, and cafés and sunk deep roots into the central Texas limestone. Austin was cheap, laid back, and fairly tolerant of tasteful artistic expressions like daytime drinking, impromptu outdoor concerts, and occasional public nudity. As new waves of college students arrived in town in the late 1980s and early 1990s, they blended well with the locally grown, lost Generation Xers, many of whose earliest memories were of sitting on mats next to their parents at the Old Armadillo World Headquarters or on the grassy knolls of Zilker Park. This new generation of bohemians weren't hippies, but they also stood in stark contrast to the yuppie workers who had begun to migrate to the city in search of jobs at IBM, Motorola, Texas Instruments, 3M, and other tech companies. This was a new breed of Austin bohemian: the slacker.

When Richard Linklater wrote and directed his 1991 independent film *Slacker*, he was stitching together seemingly disparate vignettes of a generation of twenty-somethings reacting with lethargic cynicism to the commercialism of artistic pursuits and the failure of utopian dreams. The film was an inspiring portrait of a new wave of bohemianism emerging in cities like Baltimore, Portland, and Seattle. Its wandering artists, pseudophilosophers, and conspiracy theorists characterize a cultural intermezzo in Austin's history— the generational bridge between Austin's hippie roots and its hipster present. The film was set against the backdrop of 1980s Austin, a time when the city "had not yet become the self-conscious nexus of music and media—and money and fame and power—that's now epitomized by the spectacle of the annual festival South by Southwest."[18]

In the mid-1980s, Texas was experiencing one of its worst economic recessions in recent memory, and the effects were evident in the Austin landscape—

especially downtown, where vacancy rates soared. But the recession also allowed a brief respite to housing costs. The counterculture scene thrived in areas around West Campus and South Austin, where housing was cheap and budding iconoclasts could live comfortably with a part-time job and a few roommates to help cover the rent. These slackers ambled about the city performing Dadaesque installations in front yards, coffee shops, and along city sidewalks by transforming the banal (toilet seats, beer cans, and scrap metal) into the eccentric. Building upon the sense of nonconformity and tolerance of their hippie predecessors, they added an artistic layer to the cultural landscape that was simultaneously critical and insouciant.

The slacker heyday was short-lived. By the mid-1990s a new Austin was emerging. The recession years also witnessed increased environmental activism and grassroots politics, tech industry boosterism, and a growing music/festival scene. As the local economy grew again, the city embarked on a new smart-growth planning strategy that directed growth away from sensitive watersheds and instead concentrated mixed-use development in the downtown and low-income neighborhoods east of Interstate 35. Austin was entering the twenty-first century with a reputation for progressive politics, a tolerance for "alternative" lifestyles, and an educated workforce with tendencies toward creative entrepreneurialism. But it was also struggling with newfound problems of gentrification, accelerating cost of living, and threats to many of its cherished counterculture landscapes.[19] It was about this time that a grassroots expression of Austin identity began to take hold, one that seemed to capture the latent expressions of nonconformity and bohemianism that had been overshadowed by recent growth.

In recent years, the legend of "Keep Austin Weird" has become both an inspiring and cautionary tale of creative protest and the power of commercialization. In the spring of 2000, local librarian Red Wassenich, a veteran of the Austin counterculture scene, was calling in to pledge his donation to an all-volunteer community radio station. When the deejay asked Wassenich why he wanted to pledge his donation, he replied that this was the kind of show that *kept Austin weird*. Soon thereafter, Wassenich and his partner ordered a thousand blue-and-white bumper stickers and started handing them out to friends. They read, simply, KEEP AUSTIN WEIRD.

The reasoning was simple. Austin was booming, and with a jarring influx of new citizens and new money, things were starting to seem a bit commercialized. Affordability was on the decline, and the pace of the city now felt rushed. Wassenich felt that this was the right time to remind his fellow Austinites that theirs was a laid-back kind of place, a bohemian city with artistic inclinations and a tolerant embrace of the eccentric. A movement began to emerge around the slogan, one that celebrated conspicuously peculiar art displays, unique and bizarre local landscapes, and Austin's most valuable artistic asset: its weirdos. From Lizardman to the Thong Cyclist to its perennial cross-dressing electoral candidates, Austinites were finding solidarity and a sense of identity in the fact that its eccentric people, places, and practices were to be celebrated rather than reviled.

There were no financial considerations to the "Weird" movement, which has since spread to other cities, such as Asheville, Boulder, Portland, Santa Cruz.[20] Red Wassenich purposely never copyrighted the phrase or trademarked the logo, and as the slogan gained popularity, he was content to see the idea spread freely by environmentalists, advocates for local businesses, and supporters for various community initiatives. The slogan was visually present at events like Eeyore's birthday party (a yearly recognition of Winnie the Pooh's melancholy friend) and Spamarama (a festival dedicated to America's favorite potted meat). Similar messages began emerging around the city: "Homogenize Milk, Not Austin," and "Keep Austin Austin."

Slackers and old hippies alike found assurance in the idea that Austin had gained recognition for its weird ways. For many there was a sense that the city might be able to maintain its bohemian vibe despite the growth. Then, just a couple of years after its inception, a local design company trademarked the slogan. Wassenich did not have the time or the financial means to challenge the company in court; it was an ironically painful moment for him and all the other weirdos who had been using the slogan to protest the commercialization and corporatization of their city.[21] Today, "Keep Austin Weird" has become—for many—a kitschy symbol of the Austin tourist scene, appearing on anything that can be sold for profit: T-shirts, shot glasses, and postcards. Locals said it was the canary in the coal mine, a sign that no display of nonconformity and artistic creativity was free from commercialization. Others argue that "Keep Austin Weird" is a successful story of boosterism, a great brand for a creative city with a reputation for eccentricity.

This latter message seemed straight out of the pages of Florida's *Rise of the Creative Class*, a national best seller published just after "Keep Austin Weird" became popularized. Florida wrote of a class of creative workers who were now dominating the American labor force and clustering in cities with reputations for technological innovation, bohemian inclinations, and a cosmopolitan sense of tolerance. Using measures such as the "Bohemian Index" and the "Gay Index," Florida observed a pattern among creative, high-tech cities and began to outline those economic, cultural, and environmental factors that fostered their economic development. He praised the abilities of bohemian artists and other counterculture types to revitalize blighted neighborhoods, something he encouraged city leaders to promote. Austin was Florida's poster child.

Securing the top spot on Florida's "Creativity Index" (a list of America's most creative cities) was both a blessing and a curse for Austin. It reaffirmed a growth model that the Greater Austin Chamber of Commerce had championed since the 1980s and simultaneously galvanized an image of the city that had been popularized by the likes of the long-running PBS concert series *Austin City Limits* and the SXSW festival. Drawn by Austin's cool reputation and the promise of creative sector employment, tech workers, entrepreneurs, musicians, artists, and recent college graduates inundated the city. As they did, many began to adopt a look that blended an authentic Austin slacker aesthetic with a boho fashion sense that was trending among the Hollywood beau monde. They were also looking for affordable housing options in neighborhoods that were seen as trendy, artistic, and "up and coming."

Back When It Was Cool

Unlike many of the counterculture scenes of the past, this one seemed, at least at first glance, to be motivated more by an aesthetic claim to cool than a pursuit of art, protest, or revolution; the scene was characterized by easily identifiable pseudoartist types who were moving into the minority neighborhoods of East and South Austin. Of course, it is misplaced to blame hipsters for gentrification, just as it is a mistake to say that hipsters are the reason that Austin bohemianism is dead. But the stigma persists. There are few kind words spoken about hipsters in Austin—or seemingly anywhere, for that matter. The vitriol reserved for a group so readily identified and yet never claimed is palpable. Phrases like HIPSTERS RUIN ALL; MORE HIPPIES, LESS HIPSTERS; and DIE HIPSTER DIE! can be seen spray-painted on cement barricades and scrawled upon bathroom stalls. Hipsters are blamed for everything these days, but the bar owners, baristas, and food truck operators that service this crowd suggest that their customers aren't the problem; *it's the posers that are ruining everything.* Unfortunately, these days it has become very difficult to separate the authentic from the effete in Austin.

Cultural critic Douglas Haddow describes hipsters as a universally loathed "class of individuals that seek to escape their own wealth and privilege by immersing themselves in the aesthetic of the working class."[22] And while the counterculture zeitgeists of the past typically evolved as reactionary movements,

Haddow suggests that hipsterdom is a commercialized "amalgamation of its own history . . . left with consuming cool rather that creating it." Hipsters feel compelled to react ironically to everything. But as Christy Wampole points out in the *New York Times*, ironic living is a privileged stance, and the "hipster can frivolously invest in sham social capital without ever paying back one sincere dime."[23] These characterizations are certainly abrasive, but other critiques are worse. Pointing to several examples of "ironic" hipster jokes aimed at racism and sexism (as historical rather than contemporary social problems), Meghan Murphy notes, "Irony functions as a disguise that protects hipsters from critique. It's the 'Don't you get the joke?' defense against offensiveness."[24] Murphy argues that the proliferation of racist jokes and the conspicuous performance of sexist language and pornography normalizes these acts behind a veil of ironic humor that suggests "we live in a post-sexist and post-racist society now and that these issues are safe to joke about."[25]

As the backlash to hipsterdom grows, notable patterns begin to emerge. The hipsters perform a modern incarnation of counterculture that—while admittedly enveloped by a dose of vogue consumerism—still represents a departure from the mainstream. At least they represent the longing for departure, something that is challenging in a world where trends spread and markets appropriate at the speed of a mouse click. Still, they are widely castigated. The disdain underscores an ongoing identity crisis in a city that is growing and changing faster than any resident can recall. It is reminiscent of the hate directed toward Austin hippies, who in their day represented for many the breakdown of family values and the decline of patriotism. Slackers, too, spent time on the receiving end of public backlash; they are now glamorized in popular media, but they were once reviled as grungy, minimally employed potheads. These homologizing terms (*bohemian, hippie, slacker, hipster*) oversimplify the generational challenges, quests for identity, and artistic expressions of an entire cohort into "movements" that were much more disparate than are written about in popular books and documentaries. The scapegoating also allows an overshadowing of more significant and complex problems.

Like all histories, the narrative of Austin bohemianism is one that obfuscates as much as it reveals. The city's landscape has never been a tabula rasa for the evolution of weird and the birth of creative resistance. In celebrating the birth of a creative movement, it is easy to overshadow the plight of its neighboring liminal entities—those whose protest is not as visible or artistic product as bankable. As Austin's young dissidents struggle to find their voice in a competitive and ideologically complex landscape, their situation and status still allow greater access to opportunity than many of the populations they are replacing. Of course, this isn't the first time this sort of thing has happened in the Texas capital, but never before has it been so visible or pronounced.

Conflict, Marginalization, and the Future of Creative Resistance

The story of the golden age of Austin bohemianism is well known. It is gilded in nostalgia—a time when young people from all over the state flocked to Austin for the music, cheap housing, educational opportunities, and easy employment. But that world was only accessible to some. The early Austin bohemians were certainly liminal entities in their own right, but theirs was still a privileged position in comparison to other groups in the margins. While hippies were finding cheap housing options in West Campus and South Austin, urban renewal projects in black East Austin raised housing costs for 70 percent of the residents affected by the project, displacing nearly 20 percent of the preproject homeowners and denying homes for one-third of families in the "renewal area."[26] On the other side of town, the only other predominantly black residential neighborhood, Clarksville, saw 33 families forcibly removed for the construction of a new highway, the MoPac Expressway; this despite organized and peaceful protests from neighborhood residents and allies. The University of Texas opened its doors to minorities during the 1960s, but the campus and surrounding businesses remained officially segregated until the passing of the Civil Rights Act of 1964, and unofficially segregated in the years that followed.[27] While unemployment remained low and wages stable for whites, minorities were experiencing unemployment rates that were triple the average of their white counterparts and were often paid substandard wages. During the late 1960s, businesses such as IBM and Texas Instruments were bringing high-paying jobs to West Austin at the same time that Mexican American workers in East Austin were organizing a labor strike at the largest furniture manufacturing warehouse in the American Southwest, where many of the workers were paid $1.75 an hour even after fifteen years of service.

These are just a few examples that highlight the difference of experience in Austin during its golden era. The liminal spaces of Austin bohemianism, while inclusive to some, remained inaccessible to many who struggled for basic rights. The history of Austin bohemianism and the history of other marginalized groups (racial and ethnic minorities; the homeless; and lesbian, gay, bisexual, transgender and queer people, among others) only rarely intersected throughout the 1980s and 1990s. Today tales of Austin's counterculture music scene, environmental activism, bohemian "weirdness," and outspoken eccentricity continue to be the more popular story of marginalization and protest, overshadowing other struggles. Yet the histories are no longer severable.

For several disparate reasons—including historic Jim Crow planning policies, boom-and-bust cycles of economic development, and city council politics—Austin had witnessed successive waves of counterculture flourish without seeing a great deal of competition over housing and social space. But that has changed. Drawn by comparatively cheap housing, proximity to the downtown area, and the promise of work in the creative industries, both starving artists/musicians and the nouveau boho have flocked to East Austin neighborhoods. A slew of art studios, boutique bistros, dive bars, coffee shops, tattoo parlors, and yoga studios have sprouted amid the newly repaired sidewalks and increasingly policed streets of Rosewood, East Cesar Chavez, and East Sixth. Older residents, once overlooked or actively ignored, now see their rents rising and their property taxes increasing. Since the 1990s gentrification and minority displacement in East Austin has become a significant issue of concern.[28] Central East Austin (specifically the 78702 area code) has been identified as one of the fastest-changing neighborhoods in the United States based upon ethnic makeup.[29] The percentage of white residents nearly doubled between 2000 and 2010, while the percentage of African American residents and Hispanic residents shrank by 40 percent and 9.3 percent, respectively, during that same period.[30] And despite seeing a more than 20 percent population growth rate between 2000 and 2010, Austin witnessed a 5.4 percent decrease in its African American population, making it the only major U.S. city to see such a decline.[31] For the families that have stayed, property taxes are rising, the cost of living is increasing, and the surrounding housing in the community is soon to be out of reach for many.[32] For those residents East Austin bears little resemblance to the home of their youth. Many are faced with a difficult decision: hold fast to the spaces in the cracks of the newly evolving landscape or find another place to live. Either way, they must keep moving, occupying a state of liminality that is not as easily romanticized as that of their bohemian counterparts, most of whom are at least buoyed by social capital and receipts of higher education.

Creativity, Consumption, and the New Liminal Spaces of Austin

To walk around East Austin on a Saturday night is a surreal experience for me. I am walking south from East Eleventh Street toward East Fifth, zigzagging along streets like Lydia and Comal. I probably would not have done this when I was younger; when I was in high school, this was an area of town that was to be avoided. It once consisted of empty lots, run-down houses with bars on the windows, a liquor store, and a couple of churches. There were few people walking the streets at night back then, but tonight I pass by someone wearing a bow tie. I have just left a dinner date with friends at Hillside Farmacy, a chic new bistro where a mustachioed waiter in black-rimmed glasses suggested a jalapeño margarita to "libate your charcuterie plate." He emphasized the rhyme.

I walk south and move through a neighborhood that was once a transition zone between predominately black Central East Austin and Latino East Austin. Today the streetscape is a patchwork of modern, industrial style homes and condos; occasionally a small deteriorating cottage with folding chairs in its front yard breaks up the pattern. If I were here during the day, as I occasionally am, I would be counting the number of young moms in yoga garb jogging along with their sport utility strollers. But tonight I move casually toward East Fifth, passing dive bars, a barbershop, a trailer park eatery, and a yoga studio. As I walk by the East Side Show Room—a steampunk-vaudeville themed restaurant on East Sixth—I notice a woman in her twenties asking her friends to wait up. She is wearing suspenders and a top hat and trying to reaffix her fake imperial mustache. During the day I count yoga moms. At night I count mustaches.

I'm already a little dizzy with irony by the time I've reached my destination, the Yellow Jacket Social Club, and look down to see the words HIPSTERS RUIN ALL written inconspicuously across an outer wall. Like so many new bars in Austin, the Yellow Jacket is a combination of beer garden, bistro, and decidedly polished dive bar carved from the remains of a seedy motel. The menu is full of gourmet small plates and craft cocktails. A Townes Van Zandt song is coming through the speakers, and I realize that I've likely arrived in between sets of a band.

This was my first night doing research "in the field" for this chapter, and the whole experience felt like a circus, complete with top hats, handlebar mustache, animals, body art, and the smell of sawdust . . . or maybe it was dry rot. I was feeling nostalgic for an Austin that I'd never truly experienced, one that had disappeared just before I was born. This seemed more like a site of conspicuous consumption than the revolutionary and transgressive liminal spaces of Austin's golden era. It was the first of several nights I sat and spoke to patrons in one of Austin's many quirky watering holes. I also visited urban farms, artists' co-ops, new cocktail and faux dive bars while trying to solve the riddle of Austin's disappearing weirdness. There is no doubt that many of my

informal interviews and impromptu conversations galvanized a tired stereotype that has been forged by new Austinites in recent years. I listened as mostly
recent migrants spoke in pretentious tones of their screenwriter friends, the
musicians next door, the web design business they were kick-starting, or their
new guerilla gardening group. They were on a lazy and self-important pilgrimage, it seemed, in search of the Austin myth they had read about in *Vice*
magazine or had witnessed during SXSW. Theirs was a movable feast of
social capital, of the musical, weird, artistic, and pseudoaltruistic. They were
quick to deny culpability for gentrification. They hated hipsters.

Yet despite the seemingly formulaic responses I received from so many
during my research, other comments were insightful. It was clear that some of
those I interviewed were avid followers of, or at least participants in, the East
Austin art scene. They were servers, artists, students, urban farmers, gallery
part-timers, and musicians. Many of the responses were impassioned, sincere,
and sharply divergent from the hipster stereotypes. These folks were also vocal
about the changes in the neighborhood.

I sympathized with the people I interviewed. I also noticed the complexity
of their contradictions. They bemoaned gentrification, but would not see
themselves as complicit—not if they participated as "part of the community"
(which essentially amounted to frequenting local businesses). Theirs was a
situation that embodies the new liminality of bohemianism in the age of
neoliberalism. It is a situation with few easy scapegoats. To blame gentrification, or capitalism, or revitalization is to speak abstractly of a distant, unseen
force. Unfortunately, those forces touch down and occupy the landscapes and
neighborhoods we share.

Those who study the contradictions of bohemianism are quick to point
out that amid neighborhood change and commercialized consumption there
is room for reflexivity, solidarity, and empowerment—although the contradictions and potential legacies of contemporary bohemia remain unresolved.[33]
They may very well intensify growing economic inequality, but may also provide opportunities for solidarity and collective resistance. Richard Lloyd
hints that while artists sometimes abet the forces of neoliberal gentrification,
they also imbue the neighborhood with a sense of creativity and empowerment and may actively lend voice and awareness to a situation previously
ignored.[34] There is some evidence for this in East Austin: art education programs, workshops on gentrification and property tax protests, an emerging
cadre of vocal minority artists, and the like. There are plenty of murals of
empowerment and resistance, and there is a dedicated group of community

activists eager to preach a sermon of positive change. But at the same time, the evidence of social injustice is pronounced.

So whither the Austin artistic activism for which the city is so well known? On the surface, Austin bohemianism is alive and well. Its artistic products punctuate cultural landscapes (new and old), and its explicitly quirky vibe personifies a city with a strong reputation for eccentricity and nonconformity. But it remains haunted by the ghosts of Austin past, the economic complexities of urban growth, and the future of social justice. Any nostalgia for the departed landscapes of bohemianism must recall the contentious space and time in which they emerged, recognizing that it was the liminality of circumstance that allowed protest and the emergence of counterculture icons.

Bohemianism is now too easily viewed as a popular lifestyle or occupation instead of a political or social position. Despite current arguments by economists, social commentators, and consultants, creativity is not a commodity. Activism is not an occupation. Protest is not a product. When they are viewed as such, the results of transgression become mediums for complicity. If Austin is to maintain its true bohemian ethic rather than just its marketable counterculture veneer, its citizens must interrogate the pervasive remnants of racism, classism, sexism, and environmental injustice. Rather than throwing up their hands and denying culpability, they must recognize these issues not as distant unseen forces but as tangible, local processes in which they are unwillingly, yet unmistakably, complicit. It seems likely, or at least possible, that both awareness and salience for such issues is rising in the cities of the bohemian South, where rapid growth and the stained legacy of heritage politics has created a landscape ripe for change. In Austin and elsewhere, the latent energy of the liminal is positioned against the cultural, spatial, and economic barriers that restrict its movement. Historically such situations serve as catalysts for social change. They are the liminal spaces that inspire the next moments of bohemian activism.

Notes

1. Eddie Wilson, interview with the author, July 14, 2007, Austin, Texas.
2. Lloyd, "Neo-Bohemia," 526.
3. Turner, "Betwixt and Between."
4. Turner, "Liminality and Communitas," 359.
5. Seigel, *Bohemian Paris*, 3.
6. Ibid., 11.
7. Ibid; Wilson, "I Am the Prince of Pain."
8. Wilson, *Bohemianization of Mass Culture*, 9.

9. Ibid., 20.

10. Zukin, *Loft Living*.

11. Forkert, "The Persistence of Bohemia," 51.

12. Lees, "Super-Gentrification."

13. Podmore, "(Re)Reading the Loft Living Habitus."

14. Florida, *Rise of the Creative Class*.

15. Lloyd, "Neo-Bohemia," 526.

16. Long, *Weird City*; Reid, *The Improbable Rise*; Shank, *Dissident Identities*.

17. Olsson, *Waterloo*; Reid, *The Improbable Rise*; Shank, *Dissident Identities*.

18. Ramirez, "I Watch *Slacker*."

19. Long, *Weird City*.

20. Long, "Sense of Place."

21. Long, *Weird City*.

22. Haddow, "Hipster."

23. Wampole, "How to Live without Irony."

24. Murphy, "The Rise of Hipster Sexism."

25. Ibid.

26. Barr, *Black Texans*, 222.

27. Burr, "History of Student Activism at the University of Texas."

28. Mueller and Dooling, "Sustainability and Vulnerability"; Tretter, "Contesting Sustainability."

29. Petrilli, "The Fastest-Gentrifying Neighborhoods in the United States."

30. Ibid.; Castillo, "Census Data Depict Sweeping Change in East Austin."

31. Tang and Ren, *Outlier*.

32. Lyndon B. Johnson School of Public Affairs, *Community Change in East Austin*.

33. See, for example, Forkert, "The Persistence of Bohemia."

34. Lloyd, *Neo-Bohemia*.

References

Barr, Alwyn. *Black Texans: A History of African Americans in Texas, 1528–1995*. Norman: University of Oklahoma Press, 1996.

Brooks, David. *Bobos in Paradise: The New Upper Class and How they Got There*. New York: Simon and Schuster, 2000.

Burr, Beverly. "History of Student Activism at the University of Texas at Austin: 1960–1988." M.A. thesis, University of Texas, 1988.

Castillo, J. "Census Data Depict Sweeping Change in East Austin: White Newcomers Transformed Longtime Minority Enclaves." *Austin American Statesman*, April 18, 2011.

Florida, Richard. *Cities and the Creative Class*. New York: Routledge, 2005.

———. *The Rise of the Creative Class: And How It's Transforming Work, Leisure, Community and Everyday Life*. New York: Basic Books, 2002.

Forkert, Kristen. "The Persistence of Bohemia." *City: Analysis of Urban Trends, Culture, Theory, Policy, Action* 17 (2013): 149–63.

Haddow, Douglas. "Hipster: The Dead End of Western Civilization." *Adbusters*, July 29, 2008. http://www.adbusters.org/article/hipster-the-dead-end-of-western -civilization/.

Lambeck, Michael. ed. *A Reader in the Anthropology of Religion*. Oxford: Blackwell, 2002.

Lees, Loretta. "Super-Gentrification: The Case of Brooklyn Heights, New York City." *Urban Studies* 40 (2003): 2487–509.

Long, Joshua. "Sense of Place and Place-Based Activism in the Neoliberal City: The Case of 'Weird' Resistance." *City: Analysis of Urban Trends, Culture, Theory, Policy, Action* 17 (2013): 52–67.

———. *Weird City: Sense of Place and Creative Resistance in Austin, Texas*. Austin: University of Texas Press, 2010.

Lloyd, Richard. *Neo-Bohemia: Art and Commerce in the Postindustrial City*. 2nd ed. New York: Routledge, 2000.

———. "Neo-Bohemia: Art and Neighborhood Redevelopment in Chicago." *Journal of Urban Affairs* 24 (2002): 517–32.

Lyndon B. Johnson School of Public Affairs. *Community Change in East Austin*. Policy Research Project Report no. 160. Austin: Lyndon B. Johnson School of Public Affairs, University of Texas at Austin, 2007.

Mueller, Elizabeth, and Sara Dooling. "Sustainability and Vulnerability: Integrating Equity into Plans for Central City Redevelopment." *Journal of Urbanism* 4 (2011): 201–22.

Murphy, Meghan. "The Rise of Hipster Sexism." *Herizons*, summer 2013. http://www .herizons.ca/node/541.

Olsson, Karen. *Waterloo: A Novel*. New York: Farrar, Straus and Giroux, 2005.

Petrilli, Michael. "The Fastest-Gentrifying Neighborhoods in the United States." http: //www.edexcellence.net/commentary/education-gadfly-daily/flypaper/2012/the -fastest-gentrifying-neighborhoods-in-the-united-states.html. Accessed June 2013.

Podmore, Julie. "(Re)Reading the 'Loft Living' Habitus in Montréal's Inner City." *International Journal of Urban and Regional Research* 22 (1998): 283–302.

Ramirez, Enrique. "I Watch *Slacker* to Read Austin in the Original." *Places*, October 2011. https://placesjournal.org/article/i-watch-slacker-to-read-austin-in -the-original/.

Reid, Jan. *The Improbable Rise of Redneck Rock*. Austin: University of Texas Press, 2004.

Seigel, Jerrold. *Bohemian Paris: Culture, Politics, and the Boundaries of Bourgeois Life, 1830–1930*. Baltimore: Johns Hopkins University Press, 1999.

Shank, Barry. *Dissonant Identities: The Rock 'n' Roll Scene in Austin, Texas*. Hanover, NH: Wesleyan University Press, 1994.

Tang, Eric, and Chunhui Ren. *Outlier: The Case of Austin's Declining African American Population*. Austin: Institute for Urban Policy Research and Analysis, University of Texas at Austin, 2014. http://www.utexas.edu/cola/insts/iupra/_files/pdf /Austin%20AA%20pop%20policy%20brief_FINAL.pdf.

Tretter, Eliot. "Contesting Sustainability: 'SMART Growth' and the Redevelopment of Austin's Eastside." *International Journal of Urban and Regional Research* 37 (2013): 297–31.

Turner, Victor. "Betwixt and Between: The Liminal Period in *Rites de Passage*." In *The Forest of Symbols*. Ithaca, NY: Cornell University Press, 1967.

———. "Liminality and Communitas." In *A Reader in the Anthropology of Religion*, edited by Michael Lambek, 358–74. Oxford: Blackwell, 2002.

———. "Variations on a Theme of Liminality." In *Secular Ritual*, edited by Sally Moore and Barbara Myerhoff, 36–52. Assen, Netherlands: Van Gorcum, 1977.

Wampole, Christy. "How to Live without Irony." *New York Times*, November 17, 2012. http://opinionator.blogs.nytimes.com/2012/11/17/how-to-live-without-irony/?_php=true&_type=blogs&_r=0.

Wilson, Elizabeth. "The Bohemianization of Mass Culture." *International Journal of Cultural Studies* 2 (1999): 11–32.

Wilson, Mandy. " 'I Am the Prince of Pain, for I Am a Princess in the Brain': Liminal Transgender Identities, Narratives, and the Elimination of Ambiguities." *Sexualities* 5 (2002): 425–48.

Zukin, Sharon. *Loft Living: Culture and Capital in Urban Change*. New Brunswick, NJ: Rutgers University Press, 1989.

Afterword

Lindsey A. Freeman

The bohemian South cannot be captured in a collection of sixteen essays. The bohemian South does not come in a Mason jar. The bohemian South cannot ride on a slab of Benton's bacon straight to your mouth. The bohemian South cannot be laid out on a yard of gingham. The bohemian South cannot be tamed through your Willie Nelson box set or your collection of Elephant 6 seven inches, though that's a start.

The bohemian South can be found in literature, from Edgar Allan Poe to William Faulkner to James Agee, and in the circles those writers traveled; it can be glimpsed through the peregrinations of the *hippikat* poets, Southern superrealism, and the Afro-futurism of Sun Ra, Janelle Monáe, and Outkast's Andre 3000 and Big Boi. The bohemian South is locatable in the punk train-hoppers playing old-time music in Virginia and North Carolina, and in the new microgenres of metal that are being created in the sylvan environs of the Blue Ridge mountains, where young bohemians live in houses they've made with their own hands. The bohemian South is alive in the postsoul Southerners in Memphis making community alongside the ghost grooves and musical memories of Stax Records. And the bohemian South is with Big Freedia, down in New Orleans, as she continues developing the gender-bending party genre known as Sissy Bounce.

The bohemian South is comprised of communities rooted in landscape, both contemporary and historical, but it is also a constellation of ideas, memories, and imagined worlds. The bohemian South can be found in tangible places like cities, bookstores, and restaurants, but it can also be experienced through texts, sounds, and images—in literature, music, and film. The bohemian South is a cultural force. The influence of its music and arts can be experienced all over the world. As culture moves, it changes—it is absorbed, altered, and reflected back. In an interview with *Guernica*, Valerie June, who defines her own sound as "organic moonshine roots music," describes this surreal experience. Reflecting on hearing Southern music co-opted by musicians in Europe and farther afield, she notes, "They learn it so well and they do their version of it."[1] Alternative versions of Southern music proliferate across the world, from zydeco subcultures in Japan to the blues phenomenon in

Russia to bluegrass clubs in Brazil. Some of the best jazz music I've ever heard was in a barn in the tiny town of Oberschlierbach, Austria (population: 462); inside a rustic Alpine structure, an atmosphere of the bohemian South was created, if only for a short time. Inspired by the set, my friend, a South Carolina native, took up the trumpet upon returning home.

Bohemian

When we set out to do this project—to explore and to think seriously and critically about the American South and its pockets of artists, musicians, writers, and cultural producers of all stripes—we knew we needed a new concept, distinct from the contemporary catchall term *hipster*. Hipster culture did not capture the scenes and creators we wanted to think with. We needed another way of looking. What we ended up with was an old term with a deep history and varied traditions—a flexible frame that could be reworked and rethought. Thinking with *bohemia* helped us to think historically, which also allowed for an opening up in the present.

The term *hipster*'s etymology dates to the 1940s, drawing from cultures around jazz and the literatures and lifestyles that music-saturated world inspired.[2] While some of the authors in this volume wrestle with the term (and we are glad that they do), we wanted to avoid it as our guiding concept.[3] It is not quite right to refer to the actor, writer, and Pfaff's bar regular who begins our book—Ada Clare, born in 1834 in Charleston, South Carolina—as a hipster, but she was a bohemian, certainly. You wouldn't think of the poet, feminist, and self-described working-class storyteller Dorothy Allison as riding a fixie bike in skinny Japanese denim to grab a cold brew at the newest coffee shop; she's not who you would think of as a hipster, even if she studied anthropology at the New School for Social Research. But bohemian, yes: the concept works. And the writer Chris Offutt, who takes on the generalized notion of "trash food" in this collection and has most recently written about his father's career as a prolific writer of pornographic novels, might not be mistaken for a hipster, but he fits squarely within a bohemian worldview.[4]

Hipster has become the go-to term for describing a kind of alternative-leaning yuppie or, perhaps worse, a culture tourist. A hipster is a detested social type, often seen as a cool-hunter, obsessed with consumption. The hipster social identity is one to which few people claim membership. Bohemian, by contrast, is a large enough and stretchy enough concept to contain the disparate subcultures and countercultures we cover in this book, even though many folks do not self-identify as bohemians. To be called a hipster in this day and age is to be hit with a verbal slap. To be called a bohemian is often done with goodwill, an expression directed toward someone who is freethinking and not given to conventional modes of life, someone living for art and ideas. At the core of the identity of the bohemian is the drive to make culture, to produce art, and remake the world.

South

Bohemians need bohemias: geographies where they can live and create. While the bohemian lifestyle often implies a kind of mobility, it is a searching mobility that aims to find if not likeminded individuals, then compatible ones. Place is important for bohemian communities. Cities and sections of cities— neighborhoods, music venues, bookstores, cafes, and bars—play important roles in the creation of communities, from the Left Bank of Paris to Manhattan's West Village to Pirate Alley in New Orleans to Austin's Armadillo World Headquarters, where cosmic/outlaw country was first nurtured and celebrated.

The peculiarities and contradictions of the South influence the kinds of bohemian communities that crop up there. The translation of the New York art world to students in the arts department at the University of Georgia gave them something outside to borrow from, twist, and combine with styles and genres of their own making and drawn from their own lives in Athens to produce something entirely new. The deep history of the blues in Memphis has provided fertile ground for a series of revivalisms of that form. The blues is dead; long live the blues! And the clash of the industrial and the pastoral, the modern and the traditional, in and around Knoxville, Tennessee, and rural Alabama influenced the Southern superrealism of James Agee's prose, while the mnemonic cartography of a lost Alabama infuses the Southern sociologist in exile Allen Shelton's fictocritical writing. And elsewhere, Southern cartographies of the imagination appear, such as in the hip-hop dreamworlds of Cadillactica, Idlewild, and Stankonia, giving us alternative visions of the South.[5]

The South is a slippery topic; one reason is that it travels. Those of us from its bays, bayous, hills, hollers, swamps, and shores take it with us when and where we go. We sometimes take it up north with us to get PhDs, or encounter it for the first time in pursuit of MFAs; we carry the South across the country and to other continents for love and adventure. Sometimes we meet others who have carried the customs and cultures far beyond Southern boundaries, like the excellent Southern restaurant I ate in last summer on the shores of Lake Michigan. We hear it in a North Carolina accent on top of a mountain outside of Vancouver; taste it in a perfect biscuit in Brooklyn, and feel it in handcrafted, selvedge denim from Richmond, Virginia's Shockoe Atelier encountered in Paris. The South catches up to us when and where we least expect it. The South moves. Even those of us who have stayed put in the South all our lives, or those who have left and returned, feel its shifts and altered trajectories. The South is not static, but that has been its reputation.

Any attempt to set down and define the American South must wrestle with its contradictions. One of the most difficult of these puzzles is to draw the exact boundaries of the place. A Google image search of the term *American South* shows so many variations that an accurate understanding of the region is hard to grasp: Oklahoma is sometimes included, mostly not; ditto Maryland; in some versions, Florida is mysteriously excised; and in others Missouri squeezes in. Typically, the states that make up the South include Alabama, Arkansas, Florida, Georgia, Kentucky, Louisiana, Mississippi, North Carolina, South Carolina, Tennessee, Texas, Virginia, and West Virginia, but even Southern folks who are reading this right now will likely not wholly agree on these boundaries.

Another challenge in writing about any regionalism, and the American South in particular can easily lean toward the past and the nostalgic. The authors in this book do not entirely escape this tendency, but when we do look back, we try to do so with a critical nostalgia, and not with lost-cause longing.[6] We look back with an understanding of the moral injustices and social ills the region has produced and participated in. These include the horrific legacies of the attempted destruction and forced migration of indigenous nations, the institution of chattel slavery, and the Jim Crow laws that followed. These histories shape the space of the South and resonate in contemporary struggles. With this volume we also hope to show that the contemporary South is an area of rapid change and creativity, even as it battles contemporary conservative legislative moves against intellectual freedom in some of its finest state universities, anti-immigrant sentiments, and draconian legal measures pointed at lesbian, gay, bisexual, transgender, and queer communities.

We look toward the American South with an eye for the rich cultural traditions and delightful eccentricities found in the region's literature, culinary genres, musical virtuosity, flourishes of fabulous queerness, and dandy style. In the creation of this book we felt it was important to show that the South has always had bohemian pockets, and always will, but the rhythms of these places change over time; sometimes the old beats are sampled and rapped over, and sometimes whole new genres are created. Younger queers now prowl Durham, North Carolina, once home to a place I considered a mecca, the now defunct Mr. Lady Records, which was formed in 1996 by Kaia Wilson of the queercore bands The Butchies and Team Dresch and Tammy Rae Carland, an artist and photography professor at the University of North Carolina. For all of us Southern queers spinning Le Tigre's "Hot Topic," a song that is really a laundry list of awesome queer and feminist poets, musicians, and writers, recited over a catchy beat, knowing that it came out of North Carolina gave us an added pleasure when we shouted "Dorothy Allison!" and drawled "Hazel Dickens." We could feel the pink triangle inside the Research Triangle, and that really meant something to us.

Just as there are dangers in romanticizing the past, thinking about the Southern bohemian present is also not without its traps. The contemporary moment has placed heritage brands and heirloom produce as components making up the good life, favoring living closer to nature, eating local, and honoring craftsmanship over mass production, but often the sweet stories riding on the labels of these products cloud over the unpleasant or even violent histories behind them; sometimes these brands have roots in plantation culture or in other exploitative labor practices, while their ad copy makes nods toward multiculturalism and cultural exchange.[7] The contemporary appeal of the South (both inside and outside the region) also puts the culture at risk of doubling down on old stereotypes, even as it aims for new kinds of Southernness. Existing and emerging bohemian sectors of the South will have to continue thinking about these issues, while scholars of the region will continue to try to make sense of the structures of feeling at play. The present collection of essays is merely a fraction of the work that needs to be done.

To the Neglected

In the hunk of land that extends from West Virginia to the Florida Keys and as far west as Texas, there are countless Souths and Southern regions; here we have not done all these places justice. Nashville, we know we've neglected you. Ditto Louisville. Same goes for you Houston: we know you're not just rockets anymore, and that you never have been only that. And Marfa—what can we say?—we know you're out there, weird and wild and in the middle of the open Texas landscape with your faux Prada store and your bookshop full of poetry and critical theory. There are others we couldn't include, too many to even mention here.

The essays in this volume are the reflection of the interests and eccentricities of its authors and scholars. We know we have not even come close to exhausting the space of Southern bohemia. Our aim was to give a sense of Southern bohemian landscapes through time; we did so by skipping enormous terrains and temporal expanses. We do not pretend to offer a complete accounting; we hope only to spark some new conversations and to add to the thinking and writing about the American South and its bohemian enclaves. We hope others will pick up where we've left off and continue to write about the wonderfully off-kilter, sometimes queer, often radical, and always contradictory Southern bohemian spaces.

Notes

1. June, "Sound Medicine."
2. For an introduction to the history and present of the hipster, see Broyard, "A Portrait of the Hipster"; Cowen, "Hipster Urbanism"; Cummings and Reft, "Behind the Mustache"; Greif, "What Was the Hipster?"; and Mailer, "The White Negro."
3. For a critique of hipster hating as sociopolitical action, see Long, "Hipster Hate and the Sabotage of Real Social Commentary."
4. Offutt, *My Father, The Pornographer.*
5. See Hale and Robinson in this volume.
6. I first wrote about critical nostalgia in Freeman *Longing for the Bomb,* 7–9.
7. See Hartman, "Garden and Gut."

References

Broyard, Anatole. "A Portrait of the Hipster." *Partisan Review,* June 1948, 721–28.

Cowen, Deborah. "Hipster Urbanism." *Relay,* September–October 2006, 22–23.

Cummings, Alex Sayf, and Ryan Reft. "Behind the Mustache: The Cultural, Racial, and Class Implications of the Hipster Identity," November 11, 2010, *Tropics of Meta* (blog). https://tropicsofmeta.wordpress.com/2010/11/16/behind-the-mustache-the-cultural-racial-and-class-implications-of-the-hipster-identity/.

Freeman, Lindsey. *Longing for the Bomb: Oak Ridge and Atomic Nostalgia.* Chapel Hill: University of North Carolina Press, 2015.

Greif, Mark. "What Was the Hipster?" *New York,* October 24, 2010. http://nymag.com/news/features/69129/index1.html#.

Hartman, Matt. "Garden and Gut." *Awl,* March 9, 2016. https://theawl.com/garden-and-gut-e2bdce1b0fc8#.8281ln44d.

June, Valerie. "Sound Medicine." Interview with Henry Peck. *Guernica,* March 17, 2014. https://www.guernicamag.com/interviews/sound-medicine/.

Long, Joshua. "Hipster Hate and the Sabotage of Real Social Commentary." *The End of Austin,* May 24, 2016. https://endofaustin.com/2016/05/24/hipster-hate-and-the-sabotage-of-real-social-commentary/.

Mailer, Norman. "The White Negro." *Dissent,* Fall 1957. Reprinted 2007. https://www.dissentmagazine.org/online_articles/the-white-negro-fall-1957.

Offutt, Chris. *My Father, The Pornographer: A Memoir.* New York: Simon and Schuster, 2016.

Contributors

SCOTT BARRETTA is an instructor of sociology at the University of Mississippi and a writer/researcher for the Mississippi Blues Trail. He is the editor of *Conscience of the Folk Revival: The Writings of Israel "Izzy" Young* (Scarecrow, 2013), and formerly edited the magazines *Living Blues* and *Jefferson*.

SHAWN CHANDLER BINGHAM is an assistant professor of sociology at the University of South Florida and assistant dean of the USF Honors College. He is the author of *Thoreau and the Sociological Imagination: The Wilds of Society* (Rowman and Littlefield, 2008), editor of *The Art of Social Critique: Painting Mirrors of Social Life* (Lexington Books, 2012), and coauthor (with Sara Green) of *Seriously Funny: Disability and the Paradoxical Power of Humor* (Lynne Rienner, 2016). He dreamed up this book while driving south on Interstate 95 to convince himself that moving back to his native Florida was a good idea. He later thought better of writing it alone.

JAIME CANTRELL is a visiting assistant professor of English and faculty affiliate at the Sarah Isom Center for Women's and Gender Studies at the University of Mississippi, where she teaches courses in sexuality studies, Southern studies, and twentieth-century American literature. She is the coeditor (with Amy Stone) of *Out of the Closet, into the Archive: Researching Sexual Histories* (State University of New York Press, 2015), a Lambda Literary Award finalist for LGBT Anthology. Cantrell she has published essays and reviews in the *Journal of Lesbian Studies*, the *Journal of Homosexuality*, *Study the South*, and *Feminist Formations*. She is presently at work on a book project titled "Southern Sapphisms: Sexuality and Sociality in Literary Productions, 1969–1997."

JON HORNE CARTER is cultural anthropologist interested in twentieth-century avant-garde movements and anthropological modernism. His forthcoming monograph on crime and politics in Central America considers how practices of ethnographic surrealism, emerging during the interwar period in Paris, might contribute to the writing of the contemporary neoliberal cityscape where criminal underworlds, technological surveillance, and mass mediation recast the contours of urban life.

ALEX SAYF CUMMINGS is an associate professor of history at Georgia State University. His work examines how the transition to an "information society" reshaped American political culture and economic policy as well as the built environment. He received his BA from the University of North Carolina at Charlotte and PhD from Columbia University. His first book is *Democracy of Sound: Music Piracy and the Remaking of American Copyright* (Oxford University Press, 2013), and his essays have appeared in the *Journal of American History*, *Southern Cultures*, and the *Journal of Urban History*.

Since 2010 he has been coeditor (with Ryan Reft) of the academic blog Tropics of Meta.

LINDSEY A. FREEMAN is a sociologist who teaches, writes, and thinks about cities, memory, art, and sometimes James Agee. She is the author of *Longing for the Bomb: Oak Ridge and Atomic Nostalgia* (University of North Carolina Press, 2015) and coeditor (with Rachel Daniell and Benjamin Nienass) of *Silence, Screen, and Spectacle: Rethinking Memory in the Age of Information* (Berghahn, 2014). Her work has also appeared in *Space and Culture, Memory Studies,* and the *International Journal of Politics, Culture, and Society.* Freeman is an assistant professor in the Sociology and Anthropology department at Simon Fraser University.

GRACE ELIZABETH HALE is the Commonwealth Professor of American Studies and History at the University of Virginia, where she teaches courses in U.S. cultural history, the history of the U.S. South, visual culture, documentary studies, and sound studies. She is a cofounder of the UVA American Studies Program and has served as its director. Hale is the author of *Making Whiteness: The Culture of Segregation in the South, 1890–1940* (Vintage, 1999) and *The Romance of the Outsider: How Middle Class Whites Fell in Love with Rebellion in Postwar America* (Oxford University Press, 2011). She is currently working on two book projects. *Cool Town: Athens, Georgia and the Promise of Alternative Culture in Reagan's America* (forthcoming, 2016) is a history of the Athens, Georgia scene in the 1970s and 1980s. "'The History We Make': Documentary Work in the South from the Civil Rights Movement to Katrina" examines documentary audio recordings, photographs, and films made in and about the rural U.S. South and the relationship between documentary practices, aesthetics, and political and social movements.

JOANNA LEVIN is an associate professor and chair of the English Department at Chapman University. She is the author of *Bohemia in America, 1858–1920* (Stanford University Press, 2010) and coeditor (with Edward Whitley) of *Whitman among the Bohemians* (University of Iowa Press, 2014).

JOSHUA LONG is an assistant professor of environmental studies at Southwestern University in Georgetown, Texas. He has an interdisciplinary background in urban and human geography, and is perhaps best known for his 2010 book *Weird City: Sense of Place and Creative Resistance in Austin, Texas.* Much of Long's scholarship focuses on Austin, where he explores issues related to urban sustainability, city politics, sense of place, and social and environmental justice.

DANIEL S. MARGOLIES is a professor of history at Virginia Wesleyan College. His historical research examines legal spatiality in U.S. foreign relations, and his ethnomusicology work focuses on cultural sustainability in the *conjunto* music of South Texas. His latest monograph is *Spaces of Law in American Foreign Relations: Extradition and Extraterritoriality in the Borderlands and Beyond, 1877–1898* (University of Georgia Press, 2011). Margolies has been a visiting scholar at the Center for the Study of Law and Society at the University of California–Berkeley, a Fulbright Senior Scholar at Sogang University in Korea, and a faculty fellow at the American Center for Mongolian Studies in Ulaanbaatar. He is currently completing a study of jurisdiction in U.S. trade and resource regimes, and a memoir with *conjunto* accordion legend Santiago Jiménez Jr. titled "El Chief de San Antonio."

CHRIS OFFUTT is the author of six books set in Kentucky. He wrote and produced 10 screenplays for *True Blood, Weeds,* and *Treme.* His work has appeared in many anthologies, including *The Pushcart Prize, Best American Short Stories,* and *Best American Essays.*

ZANDRIA F. ROBINSON is a black feminist writer whose work covers African American experiences at the intersection of identity, inequality, and culture in the post–civil rights South. She earned her BA and MA at the University of Memphis, and a PhD in Sociology from Northwestern University. She is author of *This Ain't Chicago: Race, Class, and Regional Identity in the Post-Soul South* (University of North Carolina Press, 2014), which won the 2015 Eduardo Bonilla-Silva Outstanding Book Award from the Division of Racial and Ethnic Minorities of the Society for the Study of Social Problems. Robinson is coeditor (with Sandra L. Barnes and Earl Wright II) of *Re-Positioning Race: Prophetic Research in a Post-Racial Obama Age* (State University of New York Press, 2014). Her work has appeared in *Issues in Race and Society, The New Encyclopedia of Southern Culture,* the *Annual Review of Sociology* (with Marcus Anthony Hunter), and *Rolling Stone.* Robinson blogs at New South Negress and tweets at @zfelice.

ALLEN C. SHELTON was born in Alabama, and ended up a professor of sociology at a small school in Buffalo. He arrived there like Johnny Yuma in a Toyota one-ton pickup with 233,000 miles on its engine. The truck was stolen. He was left with a pair of R. M. Williams boots, a transparent Pelikan, a ten-foot chain, Xenophon's *Anabasis,* a creek named Cottaquila, a Wetterling ax, an Ikaria disk, and a flower shirt that has never been washed. He keeps time with an Omega mechanical. Shelton is the author of *The Dreamworlds of Alabama* (University of Minnesota Press, 2007) and *Where the North Sea Touches Alabama* (University of Chicago Press, 2013). His new project is based on an ancestor's letters written during the Civil War; he got as far north as Gettysburg.

DANIEL CROSS TURNER is author of *Southern Crossings: Poetry, Memory, and the Transcultural South* (University of Tennessee Press, 2012), and coeditor (with Taylor Hagood) of the collection *Undead Souths: The Gothic and Beyond in Southern Literature and Culture* (Louisiana State University Press, 2015), and coeditor (with William Wright) of the poetry anthology *Hard Lines: Rough South Poetry* (University of South Carolina Press, 2016). His essays have appeared in numerous journals, including *Five Points, Genre, Mosaic, Mississippi Quarterly, Southern Literary Journal,* and *Southern Quarterly,* and in edited collections from Cambridge University Press, Oxford University Press, and Continuum, among other publishers. Turner is an associate professor of English at Coastal Carolina University.

ZACKARY VERNON is an assistant professor of English at Appalachian State University. In both his teaching and writing, he focuses on American literature, film, and environmental studies. Vernon's research has appeared in a range of scholarly books and journals, and he is a coeditor (with Randall Wilhelm) and contributor to *Summoning the Dead: Critical Essays on Ron Rash* (University of South Carolina Press, forthcoming).

EDWARD WHITLEY teaches American literature at Lehigh University. He is the author of *American Bards: Walt Whitman and Other Unlikely Candidates for National Poet* (University of North Carolina Press, 2010) and coeditor (with Joanna Levin) of both *Whitman among the Bohemians* (University of Iowa Press, 2014) and *Walt Whitman in Context* (Cambridge University Press, forthcoming). He is currently writing a book tentatively titled "The Literary Culture of Bohemian New York, 1855–1865."

Index

Note: *Italic* page numbers indicate illustrations.